CHASIN

'Ndrangheta,

Anna Sergi

With a Foreword by
John Dickie

BRISTOL
UNIVERSITY
PRESS

First published in Great Britain in 2022 by

Bristol University Press
University of Bristol
1–9 Old Park Hill
Bristol
BS2 8BB
UK
t: +44 (0)117 374 6645
e: bup-info@bristol.ac.uk

Details of international sales and distribution partners are available at bristoluniversitypress.co.uk

© Bristol University Press 2022

British Library Cataloguing in Publication Data
A catalogue record for this book is available from the British Library

ISBN 978-1-5292-2243-2 hardcover
ISBN 978-1-5292-2244-9 paperback
ISBN 978-1-5292-2245-6 ePub
ISBN 978-1-5292-2246-3 ePdf

Cover design: Liam Roberts
Front cover image: Anna Sergi

To Nonna Mimma

Forever in My Mountain

Contents

Foreword

John Dickie

Anna Sergi is Professor in Criminology at the University of Essex, but she is no ordinary criminologist. As a result, these pages contain something far, far more than criminological analysis.

The first thing that distinguishes her is that she was born and brought up in Calabria, the Italian region (the 'toe of the boot') which has been afflicted by its own mafia organization, the 'ndrangheta, since the 1880s and possibly even earlier. Moreover, Anna's father, Pantaleone Sergi, is one of the *grandi firme*, the 'great signatures' of Calabrian and Italian journalism; he is also a man who (as I can personally attest) is a mine of information and anecdotes about the 'ndrangheta, whose bloody history he has charted since the 1970s.

For Anna, therefore, Europe's most powerful underworld network could never be just an object of analysis. It has been there from the earliest years her memory can reach, when it was something that surrounded her, something from which she could never be completely sheltered, something she sensed more than saw, something that has left her with questions to which she still seeks answers today.

For all its deep Calabrian roots, the 'ndrangheta is the most global of criminal networks. Anna has followed it to its furthest outposts: Australia, Canada, the United States. At the same time, she has also explored its subtly varying manifestations in different parts of Calabria – that most centreless of Italian regions. The experience, as she candidly lays out in this book, could only be a test of emotion as well as of intellectual method and interpretation.

Herein lies the great fascination of this highly unusual, ambitious and honest volume. It blends analytical reflection and travelogue, autobiography and exposition. Anna is never afraid to air doubts and uncertainties, to leave questions open when there is no definitive answer to be found, to think things through, to make an ally of doubt. Her writing is by turns scientific and poetic, denunciatory and meditative. Everywhere she travels, she finds distorting mirrors of her own Calabrian identity. The 'ndrangheta makes home seem strange and makes the foreign seem strangely familiar. At each stage of her journey, to be the criminologist she aspires to be, she has to become something different: a migrant, a journalist, a police officer, a genealogist, an anthropologist, a historian, a memorialist, a tourist, a target of threats … And, of course, both a Calabrian, and an outsider.

The result, in *Chasing the Mafia: 'Ndrangheta, Memories and Journeys*, is a portrait of a fine mind engaging with one of the most complex problems in her field: *what is the 'ndrangheta?*

Prologue

From within, it's where I have met this mountain. I was simply born to know it, between the blackberries and the bushes, the nettle and the little water springs. And the narrow creeks, the cross, the silence.

Dinner was always at 7.30 pm; did I even have a watch? I wonder how I knew when the clock was striking 7.30 pm. I wonder if I even cared. I should have cared, though, because Grandma expected me to be there on time, with or without the two bags full of blackberries I picked every day. There she was, Grandma, without even saying a word, standing 50 metres from me, from us, cousins, friends, cousins' friends, and friends' cousins, people you knew only during summer, and you forgot during winter. She was standing there watching us and that was our clock.

'Anna is such an introspective little girl', people said back then. I was a loner; I could spend entire days without talking to anyone if they let me. The mountain was my favourite make-believe, just wandering there, getting lost, or pretending to, was so easy. *What on earth did I do there for hours and hours, before cell phones, without watches? I used to write stories about fairies and parallel worlds.*

It was right up the road, then right up the hill, a five-minute walk, maybe ten minutes if you wanted to get in deeper. Deeper into those scars cut into nature; too close for me to understand properly back then. It was gigantic, the mountain, and yet it was not scary. It was electrifying, the green all around, the dark caves, the rocks beneath when you stared down from the very precarious guardrails. It was dense, wrapped in itself, thick and impenetrable. *It was marvellous.* That kind of nature that will always win over men.

So many things have gone wrong in those caves. So much blood and terror and despair, of children, women, men, families, spilled and spread by those who, cruelly, make fear their business. So much pain in those years, the very same years I spent there, with my t-shirts spotted with chocolate ice cream, my books, my imagination, my melancholic solitude and my made-up stories. So much pain, absorbed by all that grass, softened, maybe silenced, or muffled. It shielded me, the mountain, swallowing the screams, soaked and dirty with blood, spitting out only silence. *The eyes of the mountain getting fiercer and more bruised, year after year.*

You could have walked for miles without meeting anyone, and that was forbidden, actually; Mum and Dad would not have approved. And Grandma asked me every day – *aundi jisti?* – where did you go?

And I did write back then. With a notebook from school, I wrote all the time. Because the mountain was my first muse. From within, indeed, it was pouring out. I might have been seven or eight or ten or 15 years old, God knows, but I always had something to write when I was there. It was almost always summer. And it was always silent. People were always resting. *Grandma said, sssssshhh, people are resting.* All the time! So many tired people, I thought. And it was always a bit difficult to recognize the thrill from the calm, the suspense from the silence, for me, always imagining make-believe adventures.

What stories I could make up, about doors to another world, while I climbed up across the slim creeks, up where there was a place called Calivi, where you couldn't go too far, or it would be difficult to come back, in between the water and the rocks. I was already stubborn back then, always looking for something new, a new cave, a different rock; I imagined that old and wrinkly trees could just turn up to talk to me, like in *Pocahontas*. If only I moved farther, there was something magic behind that rock. I have always believed in magic; I still do.

I had the silence inside, at that time, at that age, from within me; it was natural. It did not bring me negative thoughts, it did not crush me down, like it often does today. How I loved that silence in the mountain village. Buried deep in the dust of its ruins, in the blood of years and decades and centuries of secrets, in the roots of the trees, old and eternal, in the rocks, sharp, that always scratched my bare legs.

Without an open mouth, the pain remained unspoken, it was muted. The rocks and the emerald trees, so grave, so thick, every once in a while, surely trembled, as they still do. For me, Aspromonte was fullness, surrounded by the apparent nothingness. *A very full nothingness.* With my eyes that every summer wrestled to readjust to all that green, I grew up almost used to constant natural struggles, to the decay and the rebirth, to what was there one year and had disappeared or changed the year after; a little bit destroyed, a little bit wounded.

And there was Grandma, Nonna, in Aspromonte, before we said goodbye to her in 2013. Her charisma and her warm heart. The internal jokes, her language, the local dialect that I spoke only with her, her way of speaking, witty, sincere, simple. Her primitive love, without any justification or explanation, her most personalized gestures. Her rules and her exceptions to the rules. *Wake up early, lunch as the church tower strikes 12, make up your bed, do some chores, go to the market, stand by me, bella mia, I'll teach you how to cook the pumpkin fritters. And I'll slip you some money when Grandpa doesn't see us!*

Living with the silence of the mountain was natural for Grandma, who was born there; there she lived and there she died. Embraced by, and trapped in, that place, in the heat of the summer days and the silence of winter of a semi-deserted, heavily depopulated village, at the foot of the mountain. I felt with her how solitude could be both welcome and necessary. I had a distinct feeling, as a child, of not needing anything else when I was with her. *I was happy as long as Mum and Dad called every night and Grandma was cooking fritters and I was eating corncobs.* And as long as every year, in the evenings from the 24th of August to the 2nd of September, we were going up the road, in front of the statue of the Madonna della Montagna, the Madonna from Polsi, to do the *novena*, the nine days of prayer. I wasn't Catholic nor baptized, but that was never an issue; it was not about religion as much as it was about tradition. And I was so proud when they asked me to read the prayers or lead the chanting!

And today I study those scars and the blood and the cruelty of those places, I try to explain them to others, without condemning, maybe rationalizing them. I write about men who have destroyed and exploited that precious silence. I remember those people who have lost hope, or maybe they never had hope. Those who fear my wonderful mountain. And I struggle to put into words how much it meant to me to learn about all that history, and to reconcile the blood with the silence.

Aspromonte taught me how to be alone, in a timeless zone that was mine alone; the mountain taught me how to recognize useless and unusual noises, how to trust my mind and its images, how to consider solitude natural and how to love it, how to recognize genuine and primitive love. *From within.* How could I forget all of this, in the very moment when, as an adult, as a researcher, I went back to those places, with open, aware eyes?

Mafia, Memories and Journeys

It

It did hit me one day – but I instantly forgot about it – that I did know what mafia meant. What *it* was.

Do you know that feeling you get when you have been around ugliness for so long that it appears almost beautiful at some point? Or the feeling you get when you realize you have been underwater long enough that drowning feels like breathing hard and you could barely tell the difference? *That* awareness.

I wish I could remember the first time that I heard the word 'mafia'. I would probably be able to shake off the feeling I had been born around *it*, in *it*, in close proximity to *it*. In some way breathing ugliness, I guess, and turning it into some twisted form of *normalized* beauty. Because a child needs to believe in beauty. I certainly did.

I do remember, and I do see today, the beauty of where I grew up. Calabria is stunning, I always say to anyone who asks or who has never been. But is that true? Is that *always* true? Has it always been true? I had to open my eyes eventually and see what was what. And – spoiler alert – no, it wasn't, it isn't always true. Not always beautiful. And yet, one can create some sort of relationship with what is ugly.

I wish I could remember the first time I realized that 'ndrangheta meant mafia and that the two words were interchangeable. I don't remember anyone explaining any of this to me, but surely my father played a role in my child-self learning about those difficult things. All I remember, in fact, is the feeling of uneasiness that pervaded me, still too young to make any sense of things on my own, when hearing certain words around him, from him. 'What is the 'ndrangheta, Dad? It's the mafia.' For years, those words, some sort of unformed *it* in my head, meant that he was going away for work. Not that far away, mind you, only a couple hundred kilometres south of the region, and yet it often lasted for days. *It* – mafia or 'ndrangheta, whichever – was not a good thing – surprise! – *it* was something that appeared on TV often, for some gruesome murder maybe, and kept my father driving in the car to report macabre things happening somewhere in Calabria, often close to Grandma's village, in the mountains, near the city of Reggio (Calabria).

But what was *it*? How did I learn what *it* was? How did I even realize it? And why does it matter now?

Self

There are moments when what we are, or part of what we are, becomes clear, undressed. They are not necessarily the most important moments of our lives, or even those moments you are supposed to remember. Not like a first kiss or the first time you skipped school, for example. No, these are moments that by mistake lead you to stumble on a reflection of yourself, as if, until that moment, you struggled to recognize yourself and suddenly, and by sheer coincidence, you can. These moments you tend to forget, as they are too private to be shared or too short or fragile to be fully remembered.

One of my favourite writers, Milan Kundera, wrote that 'the imagination is unable to help our memory along and reconstruct what has been forgotten'.[1] We, as humans, cannot hold on to any present moment in our memory nor reconstruct it through imagination. We are left with a sense, an abstraction, a feeling of a moment, and that is what we preserve, a *sense* of a moment. The meaning of that sense, if any, comes later.

It did hit me one day – and I instantly forgot about it – that I knew what mafia meant. What *it* was.

The sense of that moment came much later. For a long time, I was utterly unable to speak any word about what I thought I knew.

It was 2008, it must have been November, in London. I was sitting in a seminar room at King's College Law School, attending a class on transnational organized crime. The lecturer, a young American woman, was not exactly what I had expected a lecturer on organized crime to be. I could not single out what was wrong with the whole experience back then; later I realized what was missing: her passion. There was no passion. She talked about organized crime as if it was just another topic, one among many topics in criminology or criminal justice. *Shouldn't it be, though?* For some reason, that bothered me.

Anyway, there I was, sitting in a circle, much as in an AA meeting, just more cultural, preparing for a debate on the mafia. Actually no, back then, in that class and in the Anglo-Saxon terminology used there, it was 'The Mafia' – article 'the' and capital letter, Italian–American *thing*, very Tony Soprano and Vito Corleone. One of the readings for the week was an extract from *Cose di Cosa Nostra*, by Giovanni Falcone. Yes, I did read *Cose di Cosa Nostra*, for the first time, in 2008 and in English. Very late, one might think, for a future scholar on organized crime. Bizarre that it was in English, thinking of it. That day, I had read the whole book and not just the extract selected and, at first, I thought that was where my *hubris*, my arrogance, was coming from. When the class discussion started, someone probably said something about *it*, this Mafia *thing*, some comment surely linked to the readings or perfectly justifiable in a Master of Law class. And yet I remember a mounting sense of *urgency* inside. I had to say something, but what? I knew better than them, I knew about *it*. But did I? Where was that arrogance coming from? Then I said, 'I am from the South of Italy'. *How is that relevant?* Next I said, 'we do talk a lot about the mafia in Italy and in the South, you know'. *Again, so what?* If I truly try to recollect that moment, I admit that I was somehow trying to justify some sort of superior understanding. To explain why I thought they did not get it and I did. *What sort of drive was that?* I wondered for many years about that episode. It was probably part of the reason why I started my dissertation on *it* and eventually started researching *it*. It was one of the triggers for really wanting to understand what a part of me already recognized intuitively.

The more I look back, the more I can only give one name to that emotion: *belonging*. And it was horrifying to learn that I felt a sense of belonging in relation to something, *it*, which by then I knew was a despicable thing. I would later call this a form of 'negative pride'.[2] While interviewing prosecutors, law enforcement agents and experts on mafia in Southern Italy and in New York City in 2013–2014, I found that feeling I was trying to pin down from the past in others: some of them were proud to be able to explain what mafia meant, what *it* was. Some of them were indeed almost *too* proud. Was that pride for the fact that *their* mafias – Italian–American mafias – are considered the most dangerous, most powerful, around the world? Or maybe pride that they knew how to fight mafias better? The difference between positive and negative pride about mafia (and, positively, for anti-mafia) was slim. It still is; mafias still provoke that enticing 'emotional kick'[3] that characterizes many representations of organized crime.

American sociologist Charles H. Cooley wrote in 1922 that the self has three main elements: 1) the imagination of our appearance to another person; 2) the imagination of others' judgement of that appearance; and 3) some sort of self-feeling, such as pride or shame.[4] Obviously, this self-feeling could manifest in relation to many different experiences and aspects of life, as social relationships form the self. Cooley was referring to the idea of the looking-glass self that reacts to what is around it and is defined by shame or pride. This feeling of pride seemed to me more the product of shame – in line with some literature on the subject.[5] Probably it was the result of a chaotic looking glass. Communities are entangled webs of social interactions and social meanings. The good and the bad, the virtuous and the wicked, are nothing but binary constructions. They are difficult to separate, especially in a hypothetical looking glass.[6] After all, as we are reminded by Nietzsche, '[t]here is no such thing as moral phenomena, but only a moral

3

interpretation of phenomena'.[7] Family values, school predicaments, church norms, books and songs, social interactions and social reprimands make up the complexity of communities, their morals, their compass; they enable formal and informal control systems, everyone's sense of morals, everyone's compass.[8] It all reflects on the self, eventually, on the looking glass. That negative/false pride I witnessed – still witness – towards mafias as *special* social phenomena of a country or of the Italian South, and that feeling of *belonging* I experienced, are products of my/our forming selves in the looking glass. That looking glass, and my own reflection, maybe needed to be broken down even further.

What 'it' means

Mafia is a strange concept. It's a bit like the concept of love. *Yeah, I know it's a strange comparison, but bear with me.* Many seem to think that it refers to something special, original, difficult to comprehend or recognizable only when experienced directly. Instead, much like love, it is something that many experience without realizing it, or they just refer to it in other ways; a set of behaviours that can be a choice as much as a burden, that can happen everywhere, and it is usually less original and glamorous than people might think.

Every country can experience mafia-type behaviours, as every country has manifestations of organized crime. But not every country qualifies or criminalizes certain behaviours as mafia or organized crime. This is quite normal, if we think that even in the same country mafia-type behaviours are not interpreted in the same way. For example, people from Palermo, Sicily, might feel that the mafia *they* know is different than the mafia their friends from the Northern city of Trieste know. I witnessed debates in which Sicilians ended up raising their voices because they thought another speaker was not doing justice to the gravity and the importance of the mafia, the 'real' mafia, *their* mafia. Indeed, in between taking offence and negative pride, it would be naïve to deny that there is, in some Southerners – myself included – a mix of a heavy burden and a sense of responsibility. Sharing what some of us have experienced on our skin, or on our streets, can stir up some sort of moral duty. The 'you-don't-know-what-you-are-talking-about' feeling that some people might direct towards those who approach the topic from a different angle. I do know this feeling pretty well myself, even if I eventually realized that interacting with those with a different perspective was actually extremely enriching, as it helps to rationalize notions into a research field and not reduce them to an idea or an opinion or – dramatically – just a feeling.

But on some things, I remain inflexible. For example, as I tell my students when I teach a master module on organized crime, mafia should not take the capital letter, ever. That is, to me, non-negotiable. Even if Microsoft Word corrects it every single time, my students know that using the capital letter when writing mafia or 'ndrangheta or camorra is part of a glorification of this phenomenon into a *thing* that has agency and boundaries and, as such, demands recognition. No, mafias cannot have the capital letter; they are not 'things' nor 'persons' nor 'institutions' (and yes, I know some might disagree with me on this).

But what, then, makes mafia *special*; what justifies the emotionality *it* causes? And what about Italian mafias especially? The answers given in literature, academic literature most of all, speak differently to different people, so anyone can instinctively choose what resonates with them the most as they read different interpretations and debates.

Mafias have been described as forms of organized crime – prototypical or archetypical forms of organized crime – that share characteristics, or overlap, with other social phenomena, such as secret societies, narco-trafficking, terrorism, group violence and white-collar and corporate criminality.[9] There are early studies on the relationship between the state and mafia clans in Sicily that look at mafias as suppliers of protection,[10] at their interactions with their territories,[11] and at the changing relationships among mafias, industries, businesses, money and power.[12] There are studies on the role of mafia groups in drug trafficking and importation in Italy and abroad,[13] and studies on the changing role of women in mafia families.[14] There are studies on the economic and social effects of mafias on communities,[15] and studies on mafia infiltration in the legal economy and politics.[16] There are studies on mafia mobility in the United States and related investigations on the relationships between Cosa nostra in Sicily and so-called La Cosa Nostra (LCN) in the US.[17] Recent studies have looked at the mobility[18] of the 'ndrangheta in Canada,[19] Australia[20] and Germany.[21] Over a hundred years of research, debate and discussion of mafias in Italy have seen contributions from a wide array of disciplines, including criminology, sociology, economics, history, psychology, political science and anthropology.

One might wonder whether this abundance of studies is the effect or the cause that makes mafia special. And this is only the academic side of the story. The journalistic production is probably even vaster and sees contributions aimed at exposing scandals, explaining history, showing the true nature of the economy and the real origins of power. Often, when mafia is evoked in journalistic writing, the judgement precedes any court of law: suspicion becomes proof, allegations become facts.[22] Such is the special character of the mafia word.

Is the interest in mafia justified by its special character? After all, if one thinks about it with a criminological mind, one might argue that there are other activities, other crimes, more gruesome, more pervasive, or even more harmful in the long term than most mafia crimes. Indeed, as prosecutors in Italy often claim, when mafias are not violent – when they don't kill – they often fall off the radar of the police, especially outside Italy. And yet the myth doesn't fade. Curiosity doesn't falter. Indignation doesn't vacillate.

To answer a question about how special mafias are, another question – way more perplexing – needs to be asked first. What is *wrong* with mafia? This question is problematic on many levels. Of course, mafias are *bad*. Of course, they are *wrong*. And anyone who has ever said otherwise is just part of it or too close to it. If someone argues that, after all, mafias have at times offered jobs, protection or support to communities when local governments and authorities were somehow failing, they would be telling a half-truth. Prima facie, of course, if someone needs a job and cannot find it for lack of opportunities or lack of transparency in hiring processes, having a *mafioso* as a friend could help them find a job. But that would come with a price to pay, whether a mere debt of gratitude or something more substantial than that.

The history of the Mezzogiorno, the South of Italy, is a history of broken promises, false positives and initiatives gone bad. To say that mafias have historically changed their skins, that they kill less as they grow in sophistication and they behave more as entrepreneurs now, is also a half-truth. Next to the increasing sophistication of mafias, the gradual abandonment of violence and the embracing of an entrepreneurial modus operandi remains the blindness of people; a condescending acceptance that everything ought to remain the way it has always been; the difficult recognition that our legal tools might not be enough to tackle social problems. 'If we want things to stay as they are, things will have to change', writes Tomasi di Lampedusa in *The Leopard*.[23]

I have written elsewhere that to ask what is wrong with mafias is a matter for legal philosophy and, in particular, the thorny issue of morality in criminal law.[24] Should we punish what we don't *like*? Should we criminalize what we consider to be *immoral*, or should the law never get mixed up with a morality that is bound to change and can rarely claim to apply equally? This is not the place to have such a debate, which has engaged some of the most brilliant minds of legal doctrine.[25] To answer a question on what is wrong with mafias, therefore, the first step is to admit that mafias are, of course, legal constructs – either on their own (the offence of mafia association, article 416-bis of the Italian penal code) or as a package of activities linked to organized crime(s) and corruption. Apart from any moral judgements on conducts that mafias carry out and that might be harmful to the many or the few, what is wrong with mafias is partially what the law constructs mafias to be: mafias involve crimes against public order, against national security, against democracy, against financial wealth, against competition – depending on the jurisdiction and on the moment and the circumstances in which the phenomenon made it to the process of criminalization.[26]

However, for the law to construct a criminal typology, the behaviour, or set of behaviours, that gets criminalized needs to break the rules and *harm* the social contract, threatening the values society stands for. Criminal law is – should be – a last resort, which is the reason why it can touch very sensitive highs and lows, and it is subjected to moral judgements, or attempts to avoid moral judgements, all the time.[27] It's in the disappointment in a too lenient sentence. It's in the outrage of an innocent person convicted or a guilty person who walks free. Criminal law – which was my first academic passion – can be the realm of tears of joy and despair. And this is why, when we ask what is wrong with mafias – and we don't just want the arid, and lucid, answer about legal constructionism – we hit profound chords. Mafias are wrong because they have killed people, not even sparing children. They have kidnapped for ransom. They have impoverished lands and stolen possibilities for growth. Mafias have intimidated and extorted and corrupted to gain unfair advantages. Mafias are about behaviours of arrogance and privilege for the few and not the many. They trade in drugs and sustain addictions. They are in the eyes of entrepreneurs who cannot pay nor submit to extortion or loan sharking anymore. Mafias are in the villages, towns and cities where they bend the rules of fair competition. They are the twisted version of family honour and affection – twisted because they elevate family to some sort of shield to the disadvantage and, at times, even the damage of others. Ultimately, what is wrong with *it*, with mafia, is the feeling of loneliness it builds and the fear it nourishes. It's the feeling that there are powers and interests that will always overrun individual wellbeing. It's the feeling of being alone against something that has no rules and is selfish, that is bigger than any individual alone. *Hit first if you don't want to be hit*. In certain places, mafias will chew up every residue of hope and mix it up with fear.

Where mafia power is strong, the place takes on its look: sharp-cornered, distrusting, deprived. Mafia changes places; it can change architecture and urban landscapes even as it seems to change the air people breathe. *Mafias don't like beauty*.[28]

The special character of mafias could perhaps be in the capacity this phenomenon has had to stir up emotional responses and civic actions. But mafias are naturally conservative drives that hinder change and wish to maintain the status quo; they seek acquiescence. Mafias are in the culture of places and communities, they originate in it, they stick to it, they mould culture to their needs, they distort it, adapt to it.

In *it*

When I was little and lived in Calabria, I knew that in certain places – mostly my dad's village – I was not supposed to accept any '*caffè pagato*' (literally, paid coffee). The '*caffè pagato*' is a typical gesture of respect in many parts of the South of Italy and certainly in Calabria. Sometimes you are having something at the bar – not just coffee, by the way, anything from drinks to ice creams to pastries – and someone you know is there, too; they usually say hello but at times they might choose not to disturb you if you are in conversation. When it's time to pay for what you had, the cashier will inform you that your coffee was *paid for*. The interesting thing about the '*caffè pagato*' is that normally you know who paid for you – you spotted them, too, in the bar, maybe, they usually approach you to shake hands and enjoy the natural 'respect' that follows their gesture. The problem might arise when you don't know where the *paid for* came from and you are afraid it comes from someone you don't 'respect'. The cashier usually tells you who paid. And to refuse is impolite; it will be considered as a statement. More importantly, it will be noticed. A strident statement. *Why would you refuse kindness – especially as it is usually about a couple of euros?* For the child I was, this was always a bit difficult to understand. I never really knew the people in the bar, so if they paid for me – as a sign of respect to my parents – I couldn't really tell whether I should refuse or not. If you don't know who paid for you, as a child, you can't really thank, refuse or complain. The only option was to pay for myself beforehand to avoid any issue. *When they let me.* The key to this social norm is precisely the concept of respect – or lack of it – that this tiny gesture carries, not universally, but in certain places and for certain people. It has meaning *situationally*. It is indeed cultural. If you make the same gesture in a bar in Trieste, no one will really dwell on it too much and probably they will just find it either really nice or a bit quirky.

There was a man in my father's village who used to sit at the bar when I was little. Everyone went to kiss him and greet him and I was never, ever, supposed to even look at him, let alone accept anything paid for by him or from people around him.

This is one of many behaviours that – normally done with good intent – can be twisted and used in mafia culture. It only works where these behaviours are interpreted with their original meanings. But sometimes these meanings travel very far.

It was the end of July 2017 in Melbourne. Who knew, Melbourne in winter gets freezing cold. I couldn't actually register that July there is winter. I had plenty of clothes on but, in my head, it was still too cold for July. While walking on Lygon Street, after the cemetery, I decide to stop to get a cup of tea in a café. My phone rings, my mum. I answer, obviously in Italian, and hang up very quickly, telling her I will call back. A man in his seventies smiles at me and asks me, in Italian, whether I am from the South. His accent is from the South. I say yes; he smiles and says 'me too, from Calabria'. I smile back, and I say 'Calabria as well'. We don't say another word; the coffee place is busy, and I take a stool at the counter. Half an hour later, a bit less cold, I try to pay, and I find my '*caffè pagato*'. *Calabrian recognizes Calabrian and pays his respects. And for the coffee.* And that made me smile.

We did not smile when my father, my friend Petr and I, in November 2011, drove to the village of San Luca, in the heart of Aspromonte. San Luca is sadly known as a mafia stronghold – the '*mammasantissima*' of San Luca being among the most respected and powerful '*ndranghetisti*. San Luca is a nice little village, tucked into the mountains – one way in and one way out – too bad for the blinders all shut down, the ghost town feeling in winter, and the neglect that the place suffers. In San Luca, a couple of young men, or children actually, might circle you with their Vespas if they don't know who you are – they keep their eyes open, they report back to someone; they are *sentinels*. We go to say hello to the priest; Dad decides it is safer – that is, we attract less attention if we are seen with the priest. We then go to the house of Corrado Alvaro, a famous Italian journalist and writer from San Luca, as tourists would do. We come back and get a coffee. With Petr I must speak in English, and that's an oddity there, of course. At the bar, only a couple of people lazily raise their eyes to look at us. Everyone says hello to the priest, the bar owner recognizes my dad – *weren't you that journalist from* La Repubblica*? Does he really remember who he is? Or someone already checked on our car ...?* We chat a bit, I try to speak a little less than normal in English, we just nod. We try to pay, ready to leave. *Caffè pagato*, by whom? Not sure. And there it is, the kick inside like when I was a child and that gesture wasn't acceptable, for reasons that I couldn't quite understand then and now just sound like paranoia. Coffee accepted; there is the priest with us and to refuse would be too weird. *Thank you very much, bye.* Explain *this* – explain how this behaviour can change depending on the circumstances – to people who don't have this behaviour coded in them.

The willingness to explain the meaning of the '*caffè pagato*' led me eventually to dig deeper into cultural studies. Indeed, mafia, as a complex and multifaceted phenomenon, in its linguistic and symbolic dimensions is probably best described as a *cultureme*:[29] a mix of cultural information and behaviours that bears allegorical values and meaning for a group of people, but not necessarily for others. In translation studies, Katan defines culturemes as 'formalised, socially and juridically embedded phenomena that exist in a particular form or function in only one of the two cultures being compared'.[30] The components of the mafia word and concept as cultureme are multiple and difficult to disentangle.

A cultureme concentrates a universe of information and interpretations in a word. A cultureme activates shared cultural norms and conveys a set of responses, interpretations and information about a given phenomenon. A cultureme encapsulates certain aspects of a culture, or subculture, such as the one of mafias.

In Italy, for example, the word mafia is used interchangeably with organized crime in both institutional and public knowledge.[31] Speaking of mafias, in Italy, is often a way to refer to dishonesty more generally. Discourses on legality, anti-corruption, ethics and integrity are often intertwined with anti-mafia campaigns. Indeed, civil society in Italy tends to see sleaze, greedy economy and the general lack of respect for legality as behaviours that contribute to the spread of mafia behaviours.

Even though mafias are criminalized in Italy as unlawful associations, it is their methods that are felt the most. Mafias are made of the intimidation of communities, the backwardness of certain areas of Italy, the challenges to development and the perceived mistrust towards institutions. Mafias infiltrate politics and business; they are seen as exploitative and greedy for money and power. Mafias are about getting power to get more money without earning it lawfully. At least in certain parts of Italy, mafia can become synonymous with everything that goes wrong in public administration and social life. This is the cultureme of the word mafia at play.

When we cross Italian borders, the identity of mafias changes drastically. Indeed, many people abroad are curious about 'the Mafia'. However, their conceptualizations are often tied to the Hollywood imagery of the family-based clan engaging in honour violence, gambling and drug trafficking. Who, as an Italian abroad, has not heard someone make puzzling statements such as: 'Oh, you are from Italy – mafia, pasta, pizza!' I swear this sentence has been pronounced in my presence! And I am sure I am not the only one. Among the things people abroad associate with Italy there is mafia, but their perception of *it* is very different from that of Italians. The cultureme of reference is extremely different. If we think of mafia as a cultureme, then translating the Italian mafia cultureme into the American(ized) one and vice versa is the real struggle. Culturemes are difficult to translate not only linguistically, but also socially and culturally.

As I said earlier, in Italy mafia means a much wider phenomenon beyond the unlawful associations. The cultureme absorbs it all and condenses a dynamic and constantly changing phenomenon that feeds off corruption and widespread illegality more generally. The crystallization of the US-based conceptualization instead has become a cultureme in its own right.[32] It encapsulates references to the 'Mob' and the five families of New York, a static and fixed historical legacy constructed by different institutions through the years. Its main components are *ethnicity* (Italian) and *vice*, from gambling to sex work, from night-time economy to drugs. In the process of sedimentation and internalization of this cultureme, the concept of 'the Mafia' has become synonymous with Italian criminality, at times in a deterministic way, as if every Italian, or Southerner, who committed a criminal act could be suspected to belong to 'the Mafia' by default. This process is probably even more insidious than direct stereotyping. In fact, it is collateral damage caused by the crystallization of history into a myth.[33]

The clash of these two culturemes and their overlapping has been detrimental in the way the 'ndrangheta is currently perceived and narrated abroad. Very simply, for now, what used to be a stereotype about Sicilians (or Italians altogether in certain cases)[34] has now migrated onto Calabrians as well. If a Calabrian commits crimes of a loosely organized nature abroad, it is very likely that they will be associated by default with the 'ndrangheta, especially in Canada, Australia, parts of Europe and the United States.

'Ndrangheta

When, aged 19, I moved to Bologna, in the North of Italy, to study law at university, I realized that not only did people not know Calabria much, but they certainly did not know the 'ndrangheta. The people I met, students like me, in 2004, did not know about the Calabrian mafia, its clans, its ruthlessness, the blood, the killings, the violence, the money or the drugs. The idea of mafias in the northern region of Emilia Romagna was the crystallized and at times fictional collection of narratives on Sicily mixed with Hollywood, closer to the US cultureme. Those more interested in the topic quoted murdered judges Falcone and Borsellino and read about the stories of Corleone or Palermo in the anti-mafia documents. Those interested in politics in those years shouted with indignation about the (then alleged) links between Prime Minister Silvio Berlusconi and Sicilian Cosa nostra. Those not interested in social or political affairs simply associated mafia to Sicily, Sicilian life and perhaps the Italian diaspora in America. *How things have changed in ten years or so.* With the trials for Operation Aemilia ongoing since 2015,[35] the region of Emilia Romagna has learned that some Calabrian clans mostly from the area of Crotone have not only settled their businesses there but also made *friends* with various locals, businessmen, politicians and professionals.

That the 'ndrangheta was for decades the forgotten sister of its more famous Sicilian neighbour is a well-recognized fact.[36] This is not the case anymore. *What changed that brought the Calabrian mafia out of its shadow?*

Prosecutors and anti-mafia investigators agree in pointing out that two events have changed the course of history for the visibility of the 'ndrangheta. During my first weeks in the Erasmus programme in England in October 2005, I remember waking up and reading in the news that individuals on a speeding motorbike had killed the vice president of the Calabrian regional council, Francesco Fortugno, during an election day in Locri, in plain sight. The media cried out the name 'ndrangheta and Calabrian politics became national news.[37] This is indicated as the first *mistake* of an otherwise extremely secretive and careful criminal organization. The second mistake was earlier, in August 2007, when a feud from the core of Aspromonte spilled over to Germany, with the so-called Duisburg massacre,[38] in which six people were shot near the train station of Duisburg in front of a mafia-owned pizzeria. The whole world talked about the 'ndrangheta then, *the mafia no one knows.*

Slowly, national and international media became interested in Calabria. *What had gone wrong in one of the poorest regions of Italy, to underestimate the Calabrian mafia for so long, to the point that they had been crossing borders and dared to kill in Germany?*

The answer, as is often the case, is in the *memory* – the memory of Calabria, its culture, migration history and collective norms and traditions, its villages, its populations and its mafia.

Only in 2010 did Italian law include the 'ndrangheta in the mafia organizations recognized in article 416-bis of the Criminal Code (offence of mafia-type unlawful association). But the Calabrian mafia is as old as the Sicilian mafia, its roots dating back to before the unification of Italy, its tradition rich, its organization resilient.[39]

More than other mafia groups, the 'ndrangheta is characterized by the extraordinary ability to adapt archaic and traditional values to the necessities of the present day, handling changes and opportunities with flexibility. The clans – the *'ndrine* – have been able to use technological innovations as well as exploiting political and economic changes. The dangerousness of the 'ndrangheta is linked to a reputation constructed on the fierce violence of the 1970s and 1980s, as well as a great capability to pursue both profit and power with determination in different territories, by diversifying inputs and investments, depending on the area.

It might have been 2007 or 2008; I was living in Milan back then, after finishing my degree, wishing I was in London instead. On my way back from the Easter vacation in Calabria, I had finally done something that I was supposed to have done years before: pick up a copy of *La 'Santa Violenta*, my father's book on the 'ndrangheta and the kidnappings, published in 1991.[40] One of the first books on the subject, *La Santa Violenta* had a powerful title already. It translates directly as *The Violent Saint*, where *la Santa*, the Saint, refers to an overarching structure of the 'ndrangheta, a reserved faction in it, accessible only to a few elected individuals whose role was (arguably still is) to be a bridge between the underworld of the clans and the upperworld of institutions. I will specifically focus on the role of the *Santa* when I move to talk about the city of Reggio Calabria in this book. For now, it suffices to say that investigations of the 'ndrangheta since the 1970s have consistently revealed that there exists within this organization another 'superior' organization, called 'the *Santa*' from early on, where political, economic and social powers are held. One of the most recent trials in Reggio Calabria, the trial 'Gotha', still pending in 2022, notices:

The society of the Santa [...] is a precursor to today's invisible or occult structure of the 'ndrangheta. [...] It is characterised for the double level of secrecy: on the one hand it's a secret structure whose existence is only known to its own affiliates (santisti); on the other hand, the Santa is not – and should not – be known by other 'ndrangheta affiliates.[41]

The birth of the society of the Santa was an evolution of the organisation dictated by necessity. It was strongly wanted by the progressive wing of the association to exploit new occasions to profit illegally, primarily the infiltration in public works and construction. This was done precisely through the creation of an elite of 'ndranghetisti, placed above the rest of the organisation.[42]

My father's book was written at the sunset of the twentieth century, just after the first investigations into the functioning of the 'ndrangheta and the *Santa* in the city and province of Reggio Calabria. It should be very clear that the existence of the *Santa* confirms the evolution of the 'ndrangheta as much as its violent roots. The *Santa*, and all the intentions to step into the world of industries, business and institutions, secretly but steadily, is indeed built on blood.

The year 1991 is the year of the so-called *pax mafiosa*, a gentlemen's agreement (with the involvement of Cosa nostra from Sicily)[43] to end the mafia feuds in Calabria. The so-called second mafia war in Calabria (following the first mafia war in the 1960s and 1970s) counted over 700 victims between 1985 and 1991, killed sometimes in spectacular ways, with cars blown up in the air, bazookas and showers of bullets on targets.[44] But by 1991, some 'ndrangheta clans were also heading towards the end of the kidnapping season. Between the 1960s and the 1990s, with a peak from the mid-1970s to the late 1980s, some of the main clans from Aspromonte carried out an unknown number of kidnappings for ransom, in the region of around 300 (ascertained or suspected).[45] The kidnapping season can be read as a phase of capital accumulation,[46] whereby the money paid for the ransoms became investments into drug trafficking, especially cocaine, or into construction and other businesses.

The years of the kidnappings are well ingrained in my brain, the brain of a child whose father was reporting on it. However much he wanted to shield us from it, some things still made their way through the corridors of our home. Once, my father got a call at the dinner table; he stood up and went to talk in the other room, to a colleague, I think. Our voices were covering most of the conversation – just a moment of silence though, enough to hear him say: 'What ... you don't remember? It was that little girl, she was nine, her whole body was blown up into pieces.' I remember it as clear as day. I was also nine.

Do you know that feeling of knowing something on the surface, some facts and figures, enough to tell a bit of a story and compose a timeline? And do you know that feeling when you realize that you had not seen all of that through the right set of emotions?

When I read *La Santa Violenta* for the first time from front to back, I cried. In the middle of a waiting area at the airport, I cried for those stories I thought I knew and yet really didn't. The stories of children kept hostage in the caves of the mountains, *my mountain*, and stories of violence, of a Calabria that seemed so far away from my Calabria, the one I thought I knew.

Without that kind of compassion for the human lives and the landscape that have been caught up in the 'ndrangheta's web of power, what is left is a sterile knowledge of an unlawful association and its organized crime activities.

Not that there is a problem with focusing on the criminal activities, of course. Indeed, the 'ndrangheta clans have been diversifying their portfolio of criminal activities since the 1990s, following the accumulation of capital from kidnappings and drugs. But that was never my approach; it couldn't have been.

The Italian National Antimafia Prosecutors Directorate – Direzione Nazionale Antimafia (DNA) said in 2017:[47]

> We are facing, more than in the past, a complex system of emergencies linked to the 'ndrangheta. The 'ndrangheta is present in all the neuralgic sectors of politics, public administration, and economy; this creates the conditions for profit, not only through traditional criminal activities such as extortion and international drug trafficking, but also through the possibility of accessing entrepreneurs (thanks to front men or directly) and therefore important economic flows, also public contracts at every level – local, regional, national and European.

And also:[48]

> Investigations confirm the widespread presence of the 'ndrangheta in almost all Italian regions, and in different states, not only in Europe, but also in America – the United States and Canada – and in Australia. Also confirmed are the relationships with criminal organisations in Central and South America, for the management of the drug trade, especially cocaine, the business where the 'ndrangheta maintains absolute supremacy in Europe.

The power of such statements and the alarm they provoke have inspired books from investigative journalists, further reports from anti-mafia authorities, and civil society's responses and indignation. Files from investigations for over two decades now have painted a picture of power-hungry and profit-driven clans that engage in a variety of activities depending on their 'expertise', networks and resources. Of course, we are talking about drugs, murder, corruption, money laundering and a series of other satellite crimes.

But not all 'ndrangheta clans are the same. *How could they be?*

They share a modus operandi – intimidation, trafficking of favours, violence if needed – and the ability to bend and adapt to the challenges of the time and of increasing interest from law enforcement. The one thing that everyone should understand about the mafia, any mafia, but specifically the 'ndrangheta clans, is that their link with the territory is like an umbilical cord – it defines them as much as the relationship with one's parents defines a child. That doesn't mean that every *'ndranghetista* loves Calabria, no more than every child loves their parents. It means, however, that the territory nurtures and protects; it provides resources and it seldom judges. Calabria is home. As Calabrians are obviously not all *'ndranghetisti* but *'ndranghetisti* are Calabrians (if we don't count occasional associates) or of Calabrian-descent, they are recognizable to each other. At times one's relationship with *home* can be difficult. From Calabria, some clans and their affiliates have travelled the globe and engaged in different illicit activities across borders. The allure is money, risk-taking, the prestige that crime brings, especially back at home.

But, as I said, not every clan is the same.

In the 'ndrangheta there is no strict hierarchy among clans; at times, hierarchy emerges to coordinate responses for conflict and crisis management. Hierarchy exists *inside* the clan, which is a very different thing.

As money brings power, a large portion of clans' revenue remains illegal. In particular, the two main sources are international drug trafficking and local extortion. Each drug importation job is an independent business, essentially ruled by the survival of the fittest. It's a fragmented market. The 'ndrangheta *name* acts as a brand, but how well the clans do is eventually up to them and their ability to network, solve problems, take risks and avoid police detection. This is why observers might have the impression that, notwithstanding the continuous arrests and trials, 'ndrangheta power still appears solid and intact.

Because it's true that arresting people in one clan might affect others only marginally.

That each clan is autonomous doesn't mean that there is no structure or no glue. The 'ndrangheta is a collective name that identifies some shared behaviours, characteristics and connections existing across the clans. As a mafia subculture – and I am not using this term lightly – the 'ndrangheta is a conservative force. And it is upheld by almost religious rituals that are the glue and the *raison d'être* of the organization.

'There are 100 years of history, here, and you can't ruin that!' says a senior 'ndrangheta man in Operation Cento Anni di Storia (One Hundred Years of History), run by the anti-mafia prosecutors of Reggio Calabria. 'History counts for something, sacrifices, prison and all the rest, it counts … we respect the past and we respect history … and we won't be wrong.'[49]

Between rituals and symbols, the 'ndrangheta clans share history, and they share values, norms and culture underpinning that history: they share Calabria.

The internal structure that the 'ndrangheta presents, not only in Calabria but at times also exported to the North of Italy or, in similar versions, abroad, is a stage of imagery and allegory.

Question: 'Young man, what are you looking for?' Answer: 'Honour and blood'.

> 'Good Evening,
> At your leisure
> To form the "Società di Santa"
> In the name of Giuseppe Garibaldi
> Giuseppe Mazzini
> And Ferdinando la Marmora
> And of Saint Elizabeth who
> Takes the place of Saint Annunziata
> The "Società di Santa" is formed.'

The formula, contained in Operation Minotauro,[50] in Piemonte – but repeated in similar forms in other operations since the 1980s – is a formula to start a ceremony for the award of an upper ranking, the '*dote*' (gift) or '*fiore*' (flower) of the *Santa*. It shows the recurring numerology of *three* of the 'ndrangheta rituals, the appeal to female figures – the 'ndrangheta name is indeed feminine – and echoes Masonic rituals, with which many 'ndrangheta rituals overlap.

'The ritual is noble in all its things ... what it does to you ... it gives moral comfort ... no, rituals are needed, all of it, it needs to be prepared', says a high-profile *'ndranghetista* in the region of Liguria in Operation Maglio 3.[51]

The rituals give meaning to all the rest. Whether it is drug trafficking, money laundering through online gambling, political corruption, bid rigging, match-fixing, investing in construction, green economy or the food sector, the rituals unite the clans and make them recognizable with a collective identity.

In fact, there is a question that has been haunting investigators, magistrates and reporters for decades when it comes to the Calabrian mafia, which is the question of unity. I said there is no real hierarchy among clans. *Does that mean that this is not a unified mafia? Or that it is not homogeneous? Is the level of organization enough to qualify a structure beyond the family clan?* The answer is yes: you don't need hierarchy to have an organization, as you can build networks on reputation, common ground and coordination structures.[52] With sentence No. 830/2016 (30 December 2016), the Italian Supreme Court confirmed the structure of the 'ndrangheta as described in Operation Crimine in 2008. The 'ndrangheta, in the trial for 'Crimine', appears as a vertical organization, with a coordinating structure at the top, named Provincia or Crimine, and divided up into three territorial junctures (*mandamenti*) across the province of Reggio Calabria. Two societies, minor and major – depending on the *doti* of the affiliates – form the territorial articulations named *locale* in different municipalities. Anyone who has read about the 'ndrangheta has heard about the 'locale di Africo', 'locale di Platì', 'locale di Oppido Mamertina' and many others. Societies make up the *locali*, which unify the *'ndrine* in the territory; the importance of the *locale* depends on the *doti* of the *capi-bastone* – the heads of each *'ndrina* – in the *locale*. Crucial to note: a 'ndrina can belong to different locali depending on where it moves or settles. For example, the 'ndrina Barbaro can exist both in the locale of Platì (Calabria) and in the locale of Volpiano (Piemonte) and in the locale (or whatever it is called) of Griffith (New South Wales). Very rarely are there more *locali* in a given territory (such as in Reggio Calabria, for example), a sign of multifaceted criminal power. Operation Crimine and the trials that followed made it possible to fix something in jurisprudence that was known by investigators for over 30 years: the existence of coordination within a criminal structure that seemed random and unorganized instead: not a top-bottom approach, but a bottom–up one, across clans.

The structure of the 'ndrangheta, as an organization, is complex, and names and functions overlap – it's a form of secret society, after all, which tries to hide its internal mechanisms. There is, however, not a complete overlapping between the organizational structure and the way the system of power is perceived, internally and externally. And this is probably where a lot of people get confused in studying the 'ndrangheta. Internally, the *capo-bastone* or the *capo-società* will control the activities on their territory, and they will have a certain *dote* (level/ranking) recognized by others in the hierarchy of the area. Notwithstanding the *reality* – the concreteness – of their power over others, these men usually lead simple lives, work real jobs and often have their social recognition limited to within their own village/territory. Externally, the system of power of the 'ndrangheta is made of *capi-bastone* or *capi-società* (heads, bosses) who elect the *capo crimine* – the person who, in the area, holds the presidency in the 'ndrangheta meetings; their role is oversight and conflict resolution. Even though the organization of the 'ndrangheta entails multiple leadership roles, the power system remains in the hands of a few who, either for historical reasons or due to their ability to 'marry well' and 'rule well', do retain primary roles and reputation.

In between the symbolism of rituals, the complex structure and the power dynamics of the 'ndrangheta, *how can we explain 'ndrangheta methods?*

Already in 1984, the then Chief Prosecutor of Vibo Valentia said it all, for a good start of any analysis:

> The 'ndrangheta clans are based on omertà, on terror, on violence, as means to approach any form of competition during work or commerce

activities or criminal feuds. These tools are the bases to impose their own power and are used to gain, through easier and quicker ways, wealth and entrepreneurial opportunities. They will end up suppressing their own followers and their own bosses, just as Kronos was known to eat his children.[53]

Memories and journeys

T.S. Eliot writes in the last poem of the *Four Quartets*:[54]

> We shall not cease from exploration
> And the end of all our exploring
> Will be to arrive where we started
> And to know the place for the first time.

This phrase started resonating with me in early 2011 and has stayed with me as a mantra to follow throughout my research.

I cannot be sure when I first heard the word mafia, or the word 'ndrangheta. My father swears he never had 'a talk' with me, that I just grew up and learned it by observing, listening, asking questions.

I am not sure when it was specifically that I started collecting memories and organizing them as one would do with a very busy and messy set of drawers. I know, however, that I have started to try to make sense of the mass of knotted fabrics in my head since I began my research on the 'ndrangheta, especially abroad. I have discovered that some of my childhood memories were more than just memories. They were partial *testimonies*, if only I were able to place them accurately on a timeline and contextualize them.

This is the start of the methodology for this book: the intention to put some order in a childhood wardrobe of memories. A bit like the wardrobe of Narnia, I have entered and started digging my way into the past in order to fully understand my own biases, my own starting points and, more importantly, my own so-called − so-perceived − *intuition*, when it comes to Calabria and its mafia. So this is not a book about the 'ndrangheta, the history of the 'ndrangheta's history or a map of the 'ndrangheta's mobility. This is not even a book about the 'ndrangheta as a mafia organization. It's about all of this; it's about the elusiveness of the 'ndrangheta as an object of social research. This is a book about the complexity of the 'ndrangheta as a social artefact.

It did hit me one day − but I instantly forgot about it − that I did know what mafia meant. What *it* was.

And how has that happened? Through what mysterious process, at some point, did I simply know certain things? And how did this, or could this, affect my research?

The following chapters will focus on recollections, historical narratives, fieldwork explorations and tribulations. In brief, there will be memories and there will be journeys, journeys that have stirred up memories, and memories that have called for further journeys. All of these make up my contemporary understanding of the Calabrian mafia, but mostly of the 'ndrangheta within its own territory. An attentive contemporary observation of the 'ndrangheta, I believe, requires distinctive skills of memory of its original places and history.

The main objective of this book is to use memories and journeys that I have experienced during both my personal life and my professional life inside and outside Italy. Not just my memories, but collective memories of Calabria and other places as well. Not just my journey, but the journeys of other Calabrians – some of whom are alleged or proved *'ndranghetisti* as well. The final goal is to enhance an analytical comprehension of the 'ndrangheta phenomenon, to go deeper. I am combining different qualitative research methods: self-ethnography to build a quasi-memoir; ethnography to describe the journeys; archival research to make sense of the past and the 'ndrangheta from an external point of view; judicial research; and analysis of public debates.

Every effort has been made to be faithful to both my childhood memories and history. Indeed, one of the most problematic aspects of writing this sort of quasi-memoir, even in the form of a self-ethnography, is the arrogance of memory. You think, you are convinced, you remember something, but that something might not have happened how, when or where you remember it. Redefining my past experiences and the impact they have had on my future actions and understanding is obviously a revision – an *awakening* narrative.[55] Rather than proposing a new truth about any portion of the social world I have been revisiting, my intent is to accept all the truths together: my own – probably biased and incorrect – memory, cross-checked with the memories of those around me when necessary or possible; my own observations during fieldwork, also subjected to different degrees of researcher's bias; judicial and official narratives, clearly subjected to legal requirements; and media accounts and other public-oriented sources, also responding to information agendas.

We can combine all the different interpretations, admit all the bias, and allow all mistaken and incorrect formulas that our brains are letting us remember and reproduce. In so doing, maybe we can start to see – just start – parts of reality, in all their messy, complex, incorrect and irrational *being*. And this is probably a good starting point for an analysis that aims, at the very least, to move consciences and ask difficult questions.

2

Wine, Cannabis and Ancestors: Rural Australia

Viva la Madonna!

Object Name: Lady of Loreto statue.
Collection: Griffith Italian Museum – Pioneer Park Museum, Griffith, Australia.

'Calabrian painted plaster statue of the Lady of Loreto mounted on a carved wooden stand with concealed wheels, topped with an arch of electric light bulbs, decorated with plastic flowers. Holy card depicting the original statue in Platì Catholic community.'[1]

'Where is this statue again?', I asked my friend Marie, with whom I was sharing the trip from Sydney to Griffith. 'The Italian Museum, we'll get there tomorrow, right after you finish your meeting.'

One of my first times driving in Australia, and I am not a confident driver.

'This is going to be interesting', I had told myself that morning; it was 6 August 2017. I was nervous, I recall. I don't know how to easily do some things many people do, like rent a car and drive. I always feel slightly anxious. I had to take lessons back in London because I hadn't driven for a long time and the idea of going cross-country down under for a good six- or seven-hour drive was not a comfortable thought. We had taken Marie's car; we were going to split the driving time. And we had booked a room for two nights, which had not been an easy thing, either.

'Your surname, you know, your surname here in Australia ... you know, right?'

I had been asked that question by an agent of the Australian Federal Police (AFP), in Melbourne, in 2015, my first trip down under.

'It might be better if you don't book under your own name, and even better if you book somewhere at the edge of the city, a chain hotel, maybe, the Quest?' – had been the comment of another AFP agent prior to my trip in 2017. We booked under Marie's name.

'Why don't you take the plane to Griffith?' was another question/suggestion. No, I had to get there by driving. And with my surname concealed.

The drive to Griffith became pretty two hours in, after getting out of Sydney and many miles of cars and clouds.

Marie was driving for the first part, getting out of the city and the crowded roads so I didn't have to. We had been chatting all along, as we do, so tight as I had only experienced a few other times in my life. The kind of talk that makes your head pound with the effort of keeping up, as interesting, deep and intense as it gets. We were talking about her work in Italy and in Calabria, her impressions, her observations, so very punctual and so very challenging for me. We were also talking about my research up to then and my trip to Griffith. Meeting with agents of the local police and other institutions the next day, then the Italian Museum, then the cemetery. Don't forget the cemetery. I love cemeteries.

Driving in the countryside in Australia is an experience, truly. Miles and miles of nothingness, with blue skies and fluffy clouds ahead, narrower and narrower roads, hills and valleys, counting dead kangaroos on the edges. Seventeen, I counted on our way to Griffith. More than once, I felt I was losing control of the wheels as I was looking at those corpses on the roadside.

The arrival in Griffith was perfect. The sun had gone down, the sky was purple-pink. A neon sign welcomed us to the Riverina Valley; a sense of intrigue was in the air. The preparation for that trip clearly was getting to me. The meaning of that first trip to Griffith was somehow linked to something very deep inside; I was not yet aware of what that was.

Local historian Kevin Pesman reports that, upon arrival in New South Wales (NSW), especially Griffith, the Calabrian community did not attend churches as frequently as other regional communities from Italy.[2] The uninventive practices of Australia probably needed more colours to appeal to Calabrian communities. In the 1950s, a plaster copy of the Lady of Loreto statue was imported from the small town of Platì in Calabria, in the mountain of Aspromonte, home to many migrants in the area.[3] The Madonna, full of gold and colours, was placed on an altar and its presence sparked union and cohesion across the Calabrian community of Griffith.

'Viva la Madonna!' someone shouts.
'Viva! Viva!' responds the congregation.

Bagpipes (le ciaramelle!) would play, with drums, singing and dancing, through the kilometre-long procession. After the procession, with the Madonna on the altar outside the church entrance, people would approach and pin cash donations to the statue.

I couldn't be there when the *festa* was celebrated because this official celebration in Griffith stopped in 2003, after decades in which it wasn't always organized anyway. But that Madonna was a symbol of unity and it was a symbol of cohesion for a community of migrants who needed a piece of home so far away from home.

Marie and I wanted to see *that* Madonna. She is quite fascinated by anthropological, religious and historical artefacts. I needed to see something that was so clearly connected to Aspromonte, to my mountain.

The Italian Museum is a circular, yellowish building with a red brick roof within Griffith Pioneer Park. We obviously visited the whole park, as, seriously, *how can you not?* The place is full of historical buildings from the settlement period, from a post office to the doctor's and nurses' quarters, from the machinery shed to various little cottages, from the saddlery to the blacksmith, the irrigation house, the fire station. It resembles some sort of Western movie set.

It was touching for me to see the exhibition about wine-making traditions in Griffith. A lot of Calabria there. A lot of Calabria – not just Italy – *everywhere* in Griffith.

Calabria Family Wines, a family-owned company, established by Francesco and Elisabetta Calabria in 1945. Lillypilly Estate, established between the 1970s and the 1980s by Pasquale Fiumara, who migrated from San Ferdinando in Calabria before the Second World War, and his family, who joined him right after the war. And then, finally, Warburn Estate, founded by none other than the Sergi family. Father Giuseppe, mother Maria and son Antonio (Tony) migrated from Platì in 1952. Known first, since 1968, as the House of Sergi, then the Warburn label in 1994, becoming one of the most important wineries in NSW and a major Australian wine producer, in the top ten of the national market.

Seeing my surname, on a giant billboard, there was a ping inside. Not that I didn't know about the various Sergi families there already. But still.

According to the website of the Pioneer Park, the Italian Museum recognizes the 'contribution of the Italian community to the social, cultural and physical development of Griffith and the Murrumbidgee Irrigation Area'. Vintage clothes, needlework, household items, sewing and knitting machines. And old bicycles, the same kind my grandma had pictures of back at home in Calabria, *those with the giant front wheel, remember?* The towns and regions of origin of the Italian community of Griffith are all represented in the museum. From Abruzzo to Veneto, from Calabria to Sicily, each region has its own showcase. It's like entering some sort of shrine to the preservation of memory and the defence of the past.

The Italian Museum and Cultural Centre remains a project funded and sustained by the Italian community. The names and surnames of patrons are on a massive wooden board at the entrance. I recognized many surnames as

Calabrian: Agresta, Catanzariti, Colla, Aquino, Piromalli, Sergi, Zappacosta, Zirilli, among other Italian and a few Anglo-Saxon ones.

'Hello there, might I ask you where I can find the statue of Our Lady of Loreto?'
'Excuse me …?'
'This Madonna here, look, on the webpage … it says it's in the Griffith Italian Museum …?'
'Ahem … I am sorry … I have never seen that?'
'Have you worked here long?'
'About ten years …?'

Marie stood there speechless, unsure how exactly to respond to that. She most certainly did not expect *not* to find the statue.

We started a statue hunt because, when Marie gets something in her head, she must follow through. Asking a local police agent seemed the obvious next step. Needless to say, the police agent had no idea where the statue was. She was born and raised in Griffith, and she had never seen it. 'Maybe ask the priest?' 'Of course, the Italian church!' There are actually two churches that are routinely attended by the Italian community. Maybe someone moved it to one of the churches; of course, that makes sense.

Church number one, not there. The priest was curious, of course, but he had not seen the statue either. He came with us to church number two.

Church number two, not there either; the church was shut when we arrived. Then we called out for the priest, who, again, had no idea where this statue was.

We were a group of people, Marie and I, the policewoman, the priest, another police agent. Looking for a lost statue. *It looked bizarre, yes.*

'You cannot lose a statue …', commented the police agent. Clearly. And yet we could not find it, this replica of Our Lady of Loreto, a gift to the Calabrian community of Griffith from Platì, symbol of the *fil rouge* between the motherland and the new home.

'Maybe someone took it', said Marie.
'You mean, theft? Wouldn't someone report it?' replied the agent.
'Maybe … it was in someone's custody?' I advanced.
'What do you mean?' they both inquired.
'I don't know, just thinking aloud here. It would be honourable to give it to the most respected family to keep.' Not sure where I was going with this.
'Some Orient Express murder mystery, where everybody knows and everyone is on board with the crime!' laughed the agent.

Okay. Sure.

I still wonder where the statue is. Its preciousness is not just in the materials, of course, but also in the symbolic meaning it carries. Maybe it was melted down, or it was sold, or it has, indeed, been stolen.

Viva la Madonna! Indeed.

As we drove around Griffith and the roads opened up wider and wider through the farmland, the agents talked about their children. Someone's son was dating a Calabrian girl, but then they had to break up because her family did not quite approve. 'Well, she wasn't Calabrian – from Calabria, you know? Her parents were. Her sister had married aged 18, she didn't want to and was dating my son, but her family, no they were not happy, they had to break up eventually.' 'Now, my son went away, for a while, came back, they got back together, as she never married! Still, her family doesn't approve. Her father is one of those who still goes to meet his childhood friends, all from Calabria, at the bar every Sunday at midday for the aperitivo.' They talked about how it was to grow up and now work in Griffith, the Italian town of Australia they called it. 'They all went to the same school, you know, they still tend to stick together, that's my impression.' *The Calabrians, they meant.*

'Look, this is a quail farm, quails are big business here! It's another Sergi business too!'

And then, as they were turning around to bring us back to our hotel, one murmured: 'There are good Sergis and bad Sergis here, you know?'

Hell, yeah, I know. *Look at me!*

I followed my research instincts, but my personal intuition and interest – in what was closer to me, my name, my places of origin – clearly guided investigations and enquiries in that visit and afterwards.

Promised land

'Are you from Platì?'

That was one of the first questions a very nice woman, working for the Australian Federal Police, asked me when we met in Glenelg, the suburban area by the sea of Adelaide, in October 2015. I smiled and replied that no, I was not, but some family members of mine – my mum's side – did have relatives in Platì. 'You know', I said, 'it's literally on the other side of the mountain from where my mum is from, if only they repaired the road.'

It was my first time down under, and I thought I knew a thing or two, enough, about the 'ndrangheta in Australia. I had already published a paper with some historical analysis, mostly from secondary data. *And, oh boy, I was quite wrong.*

My surname, of course. What one would call a 'mafia surname'. Linked to mafia clans from the little village of Platì, in Aspromonte, a mafia *stronghold*, some would say. It's something of an old story, one that you find on Wikipedia, for example, that the Sergi clan is one of the oldest and strongest clans of Aspromonte, particularly active in the Milan area and in various other parts of the North of Italy, in Germany and Switzerland, and in Australia, of course.

I would come to realize that, in the minds of many Australians who were professionally countering so-called Italian Organised Crime, the whole of Aspromonte – at times the whole of Calabria – was Platì, or near Platì. Because Platì was in Adelaide, in Melbourne, in Canberra – a million *fils rouges* that kept people from Platì all connected and seemingly homogeneous in their cultural background. Fairfield, a populous suburban area of Sydney, is still Platì's twin town. And then, of course, Griffith, the town that more than others represented the multi-ethnic experiment of Australia. Indeed, there was a disproportionate amount of interest, I found, in the little town of Platì.

Have you ever been to Platì? Have you seen it? In pictures, photos, news articles? Videos? Google it. It looks like something hit that place and it never really recovered.

It's one of the places I go back to, not that often, but sometimes, to make soap bubbles. My own personal way to remind myself of beauty, even when it is fragile.

Severe flooding hit Platì in 1951, causing 17 or 18 deaths. 'When the river Ciancio came, furious out of water, from the throat of Aspromonte, [and] took away two-thirds of the poor households',[4] wrote my father in the newspaper some decades later.

A monument, by the riverside of Platì, still commemorates those events. The village seems to have never gotten over that disaster.

Early reports talked about almost 5,000 people (of the 7,200 inhabitants of the village) who gradually left after that flood – many of whom reached Australia.[5] Chain migration brought emigrants to move closer to one another and form neighbourhoods around families.[6]

Imagine if you had to move to the other side of the world, to a country where you didn't speak the language and from where you probably couldn't leave for a while. Of course, you would be looking to connect with someone who had gone there before you and ask for help or just support with the language, if nothing more.

Calabria was – and still is – afflicted by poverty and natural plagues. Platì is one of the obvious examples of these afflictions. Peasants, workers, skilled craftsmen and enterprising merchants, migrating to Australia, settled mainly across New South Wales, Victoria, South Australia. Those who had stayed back in Platì often thought of the life and their families in Australia. They called it Nuova Platì (New Platì) – at times Fairfield, at times Griffith – an indistinct reference in the minds of those who had remained in the village. The Promised Land of New South Wales, so far away and yet still accessible, benefitted greatly from the will to succeed that my co-regionals brought with them across the oceans.

When I first presented a reconstruction of the 'ndrangheta to a team of law enforcement agents in Adelaide, one of them couldn't help but comment: 'Is that all? Wow, I thought of Plati (without the Italian accent on the final i) as more or less a small Rio de Janeiro!' He was looking at my maps of Calabria and Aspromonte, the tiny, tiny dot that was Platì, together with the many other villages, and the pictures from Platì.

As I said, there was a time, in the Riverina Valley of New South Wales, when the town of Griffith was essentially *Platitown*. And understanding the relationship, real or imagined, between Platì, Italo-Australian migration and the 'ndrangheta, eventually, is indeed step one of anyone's journey down under, chasing mafia ghosts.

> Plati is a small village in Calabria, in Southern Italy. It is not in a rich area. Families have emigrated from Plati to Australia and they have preserved, in their new country, the closely-knit relationships that were formed in Plati. Several of these families played a part in the events described by the evidence in these proceedings.[7]

Curiously, in 1979 an Administrative Appeals Tribunal in Australia decided to start its judgement with such an opening statement. This was an appeal to a deportation order, and it was successful; the appellant was not deported in the end. Platì's family life and norms somehow protected him.

Luigi Pochi was a Calabrian from Platì (always Plati – without the accented 'i' – in early Australian writing). He had left Platì with his family to move to Australia and, after living for some time in Canberra, he had married Rosa Mary Sergi, whose family was also from Platì and owned a winery in Griffith, once known as the House of Sergi (*remember Warburn Estate?*). The deportation order was based upon a conviction of 17 March 1977 before the District Court at Griffith. Pochi was convicted of the supply of Indian hemp and sentenced to imprisonment for two years. The minister ordered his deportation on 7 August 1978, considering that Pochi was still an alien because his citizenship request had not gone through. He could, and did, appeal.

Other Calabrian men are mentioned in his sentence: two brothers, Pasquale and Giuseppe Agresta, for starters. Luigi Pochi was found in proximity to marijuana that belonged to them, as he was working as a temporary farm labourer. The tribunal heard evidence that Pochi and other persons, all immigrants from Platì or towns nearby, were involved in the growing of marijuana in large quantities: 30 acres at Coleambally, four acres at Leppington, 15 acres at Euston, five acres at Taree and significant quantities at Loxton and Port Pirie in South Australia. But, more than that, Pochi's in-laws, a Sergi family, became of interest.

Between June and August 1975, Luigi Pochi and Rosa Mary Sergi contributed approximately $117,000 to the capital of a partnership known as Vignali Wines, a contribution that was used to meet nearly half the cost of the partnership's premises at Fyshwick. Too bad, said the Minister of Ethnic and Immigration Affairs who heard this evidence, that Pochi and his wife did not have this money at their disposal, notwithstanding the claims that the money was coming from the donations of family or friends or rather obscure bets they claimed they had won. Antonio Stalteri, Rocco Musitano, Francesco Perri and the Zappia family were all said to have lent Pochi money. All of them Calabrian, all of them from Aspromonte, to be specific.

'These families exhibited the strengths of family allegiance and mutual support which enrich the lives of many who come from Southern Italy', noted the tribunal.

Even though the minister was suggesting that those funds could perhaps be the proceeds of Pochi's involvement in the commerce of marijuana, nothing more came of it.

No one apparently considered that the money might have come from Calabria directly and had been clothed to look as if it originated somewhere else. That it could have been the proceeds of the kidnappings in Calabria, as alleged by investigators in Italy, instead. An anti-mafia prosecutor in Italy, who in the 1980s was working in Calabria and following the Australian routes, has no doubt: money from Calabria did go to Australia; it was used to buy land, it was invested in farms; it was meant as a partial transfer of power – at least economic power – from Calabria to Australia – 'because Australia was seen as a clean slate, you could hide in Australia, yourself, your family, your money, maybe even start over'.

In 1979, the Administrative Tribunal that had to judge upon the totality of circumstances around Pochi's immigration and deportation saga kept referring to Platì.

Pochi's family and his friends who come from Plati are clearly bound to a close and trusting relationship. That relationship has an ambiguous significance: it may explain the seemingly extraordinary generosity of the lenders, or it may explain their willingness to assist the applicant to clothe the funds which he intended to use with a false appearance. In some cases, the former explanation appears the more likely, in others the latter. It is not necessary to decide which explanation fits each transaction, for the question is whether, in all the circumstances, one may infer that the applicant had funds which represented the proceeds of his activities in commerce in marijuana. That inference depends more upon the totality of the circumstances than upon an individual transaction.[8]

There was obviously more. Vignali Wines, the company in question, was Antonio Sergi's venture. Sergi, Pochi's brother-in-law, suggested that the Pochis should open a liquor business in Canberra and agreed to take a quarter share. He convinced his friend Robert ('Bob') Trimboli to also take a quarter share in the venture. Mr and Mrs Pochi were to take a half share. As reported by the case in question, the contract was signed on 17 June 1975. Antonio ('Tony') Sergi contributed $60,000. Trimboli contributed $60,000 in the first instance and more later. Antonio Sergi also contributed stock from the Griffith-based winery. When the venture was first being contemplated, Mr and Mrs Pochi had few liquid assets, yet they made their payments by gathering money from different sources, such as donations from friends and family, as already mentioned.

There, I felt distinctively a feeling of uneasiness. A noise in my head.

My grandmother used to talk about her brothers and sisters all the time. In particular, those like Zia Bettina, or Zia Teresina, or Zio Cicco, who had left for Australia and whom she did not expect to see often, or ever again.

'He was so much like my father, *u zi Ciccu*', she used to say. And she would cry a bit and show the most recent pictures she had, sent all the way from Australia. 'He has a bakery, there in Australia. It's the best bakery of Australia!' That came back to mind, as I recollected data and dates. Francesco, *u zi Ciccu*, was married to an Anna … *Sergi*, from Platì, in Griffith. Some small troubles with some other drug cases, I could find for him, *u zi Ciccu*. I wondered how much my grandmother knew, if anything. I wondered whether he was close to that group of people who had lent money to one another and how much he and his wife had also invested in the winery or other Calabrian ventures, in the late 1970s, in the years I was reading about. *I shivered a bit. Very close to home, this one.*

Tony Sergi and Bob Trimboli (misspelled Trimbole at times) were named as mafia bosses who had links to the Riverina's booming marijuana trade in the 1970s. The 1979 Woodward Royal Commission into Drug Trafficking named the two men – together with other Calabrians of Griffith – as the group who orchestrated one of Australia's best-known cold cases, the disappearance – and assassination – of Donald MacKay. The Woodward Royal Commission said that the death sentence for MacKay – a police informer who exposed a large marijuana crop being cultivated in nearby Coleambally – came from Tony Sergi and was executed by Trimboli.

Trimboli, fearing for his freedom as the Woodward Royal Commission was ready to make two arrests in 1981, escaped to the United States and died in 1987 in Spain. Tony Sergi led a life under the radar. A prominent winemaker, he died in October 2017, at which point newspapers called me to have me comment on the news.

'What does the death of Tony Sergi mean for the Australian 'ndrangheta?' The most obvious, unanswerable, question. (Who knows really?!)

'Do you really think that having a Dr Anna Sergi commenting on the death of Antonio Sergi is a good idea? Also, he has a sister also called Anna

… Sergi.' My response. *And they might be my distant relatives too* – I thought and did not say.

'Anna is a very popular name in the Sergi family', the journalist commented. Yeah, you have no idea. 'But frankly, I said, I do not want the attention, it's also a difficult moment for the family.'

'The "don of the dons" dies, aged 82, without being charged over Don Mackay's death', said the newspapers.

'The head of the Griffith underworld', he was called.

The head, possibly, of the Australian 'ndrangheta, at least for a while, they wrote.

Connected to the Calabrian mafia, the 'ndrangheta, the Honoured Society, since his arrival in Griffith, like his father before him.

And yet, Griffith's Deputy Mayor Dino Zappacosta, elected in 2016, also of Calabrian origin, told the media that Mr Sergi was a much-loved member of the community in Griffith.

> He's always been a very trustworthy person, very generous and kind and all the stories you hear of various people and innuendo and whatever, I find it very difficult to understand but, hey, there may be some truth in it.[9]

Fils rouges

One of the problems in researching migrant, allegedly mafia, families in Australia is the recurrence of certain names, which makes it really difficult – believe me! – to map groups. Remember the police agent saying 'there are good Sergis and bad Sergis'? Well, it's quite difficult to understand who is who when there are at least four original Sergi lineages, all from Platì in Griffith, with really big families, all intertwined, with various members named Anna, Maria, Elisabetta, Antonio, Santa, Giuseppe, Caterina, Pasquale, Rocco and a few others. Moreover, especially in the early days, women took their husbands' surnames. As in Calabria, also in Australia, people can often only be differentiated by birth date.

Antonio Sergi was born in 1935 and married Angelina Scarfò in Griffith. Antonio's father was Giuseppe and his mother was Maria. The family was – no surprise – from Platì.

Giuseppe's brother was Domenico, who was married to Anna. 'Domenico married Anna, the love of his life', narrates Santa Sergi (probably one of their children or perhaps a granddaughter), who was married to Portolesi (another Calabrian surname), as the family was portrayed in the centenary of Griffith as a foundational family of the town.[10]

Their story, like any migrant story, made me think. For Calabrian migrants, Australia was most certainly not a happy place, especially at the beginning.

Domenico and Anna arrived in Griffith in 1955 – after 30 days of travelling across the globe.

And I complain about my 25-hour plane journey in economy from London to Melbourne!

> Domenico worked at the rice mill working day and night shifts with only a push bike for transport. He would often have to ride in the middle of the night with only the lines on the road to guide him on the 8-km journey and Anna was always waiting for him to make sure he arrived home safely. The days he was not working at the mill, he spent his time working on the farms.

The previous text appears on the Griffith memorial webpage. And I hope the family does not mind my use of this story here for illustrative purposes.

In 1977, Domenico was awarded Citizen of the Year in the Australia Day celebrations for assisting charities and raising thousands of dollars. When he died, in 2016, the community only had fond words for him and his generosity.[11]

The question that haunted and hurt me – and still does puzzle me – remains the following: *How do you know? How can anyone know, who is who?* Family ties there are so tight, and we know that the mafia phenomenon is not made up solely of individual criminal liability but involves families, blood, connections, daily life. *How do we make the right distinctions?*

Why should anyone doubt that the reasons why Domenico was awarded Citizen of the Year in Australia Day in 1977 are indeed genuine? And – by the same logic – why should anyone doubt that the intelligence gathered to indicate the involvement of Domenico's nephew, good-old abovementioned Tony, in drug trafficking and possibly the murder of Don Mackay is indeed genuine, too? Once again, this is for illustrative purposes, with no claim to know more than any court of law.

How to reconcile the two, apparent or real, truths? This is the struggle, still.

There is another Administrative Appeals Tribunal judgement on Giuseppe Sergi vs Minister for Immigration and Ethnic Affairs, in 1979 – again on a deportation order, following Mr Sergi's conviction for drug trafficking.[12] This case also gives interesting insight into the life of this unit of the Sergi family:

> One last matter of fact which I should mention before dealing with the principles to be applied is that Mr. and Mrs. Sergi have retained much of the outlook and customs which they gained from the land of their birth. Neither speaks English well. Mr. Sergi is illiterate. The youngest daughter, Josephine, now aged 20 years, has remained at home without employment looking after her parents since leaving school at the age of 16. It was put to me that these facts show that

Mr. and Mrs. Sergi have not become assimilated into the Australian community. I would not draw that conclusion. That they are both still much influenced by the customs and attitudes which they learned in the country in which they grew up is not surprising. They are simple people who have led a simple life.[13]

This appears as a matter of sociology of migration before being a matter of law. I became particularly sensitive to this as I kept reading through the documents of that period. A criminal stigma started to creep into matters linked to migrants' families, paired with an acknowledgement that organized crime activities could be – should have been, *were expected to be* – linked to Italian migrants.

Counsel for the Minister said that Italians in Australia may be subject to pressure from criminal elements to engage in the growing of marijuana and that Italians had been particularly involved in this offence.[14]

Prior to the publication of the Woodward Royal Commission report, this statement was deemed inapplicable: 'it is not within my knowledge that the growing of marijuana is an offence peculiarly or particularly connected with persons in Australia of Italian descent', continues the tribunal in the Sergi case. And indeed, this Sergi was not deported. But the lenient and cautious view of the tribunal changed after the Woodward Commission report was eventually published. And, in fact, it led to the deportation of Saverio Barbaro in 1980,[15] as the Administrative Appeals Tribunal accepted the Woodward report into evidence for the deportation case.

Mr Justice Woodward found that between 1974 and 1977 there was an organisation comprised almost exclusively of persons of Calabrian descent which was engaged in the illicit cultivation, trafficking and marketing of cannabis. He named as one of the members of that organisation the applicant in this review [Saverio Barbaro]. He said that the organisation was responsible for a number of cannabis plantations and for the death of Donald Bruce Mackay. He said that a secret organisation known as the Honoured Society exists in Australia composed exclusively of persons of Calabrian origin. It has been involved in extortion and other criminal activity, the most notorious being the series of shootings described as the Victorian Market Murders.[16] (See Chapter 4 for a discussion of Australian cities, and specifically Melbourne)

This marks an acknowledgement of the existence of the 'ndrangheta in Australia – and not for the first time;[17] it also marks the need to distinguish between those Italians – Calabrians even – who had been convicted of a criminal offence, including drug offences, and those who, after the report of the Woodward Commission, committed offences as members of the Honoured Society and were recognized as such.

'He is not a person who has simply been convicted of a drug trafficking offence. He stands now as a person whose reputation and standing in the community have been affected [...] he is a member of the Honoured Society and a member of the organisation which has been involved in drug trafficking in Australia, has been involved in extortion and has been responsible for several murders', continues the tribunal in the Barbaro case.

In a report delivered 21 December 1979,[18] Mr Justice Williams – who constituted the Australian Royal Commission of Inquiry into Drugs – revealed that, between 1974 and 1978, of the cannabis crops discovered throughout Australia by police, 22 plantations were identified that resulted in the arrest and charge of persons of Calabrian descent. A breakdown of figures revealed:

1. Twenty-two (22) were born in the village of Plati, Calabria.
2. Eighteen (18) were born elsewhere in Calabria.
3. Two (2) were Australian born of Calabrian parents.
4. Three (3) were born outside Calabria, but were arrested on plantations with Calabrians. These three were born in Sicily, Genoa and Nice.

The report continues: 'The overall management of this group appears to have been carried out by members of the Sergi family [...] with the channelling of finance back to the Griffith end of the operation.'

It further noticed 'a surprising capacity in some Calabrians readily to obtain "loans", even from persons who would seem to be in quite poor financial circumstances. Such loans appear on the evidence to remain outstanding for many years, to be without documentation and, if repaid, to be repaid without interest. This evidence supports the view that there is in the Calabrian community in Australia either a form of the Honoured Society or at least an unusual community of interest and thought.' Mr Justice Williams suggested that such a circumstance might facilitate the development of criminal activities within the ethnic community.

All mafia ingredients seem to emerge. Ethnic solidarity meets 'ndrangheta structures, 'a hierarchy based on considerations of blood relationship, regional, religious, or similar affiliations which is independent of civil authorities', all through 'deliberate non-disclosure' of each other's identity.[19] That is *omertà*, through ethnic solidarity or perhaps masked by ethnic solidarity.

The mix is a short circuit. There are indeed good Calabrians and bad Calabrians – courts and tribunals in Australia came to learn – but individual liability must prevail, especially in criminal matters. Nevertheless, the mafia-type enterprise that had emerged in the 1970s would lead to a stigma on Italian migrants – Calabrians specifically, grouped by place of origin even more specifically (Platì and nearby Aspromonte villages) as if they were all involved or suspected to be involved in the 'ndrangheta. Collective liability, however, was not a thing in Australia; it was not, and it still is not.

Surely, other strange things were happening – from an Australian perspective – in those years in the Calabrian community in NSW.

Twenty-one-year-old Francesco Sergi, on 26 January 1967, surrendered himself at the Fairfield Police Station, Western Sydney, an Italian district of the city. He confessed to a police officer that he had shot his brother, Domenico, and sister-in-law, Caterina. The shooting was described by the Supreme Court of NSW as 'a crime of passion'.[20] Francesco had come to learn that his younger sister, Maria, who had recently married, had been accused by his sister-in-law of having lax morals. In particular, it was suggested that Maria had been involved in a sexual relationship with a young man prior to her marriage. Following these rumours, Vincenzo Cannistra, Maria's husband, had left and returned to Italy. This brought disgrace to the Sergi family.

The Supreme Court confirmed that Francesco appeared to 'have been distressed and to have felt, as the oldest male member of the family living at home, that he bore responsibility for remedying the damage that had been done to the family's honour'. It was in that context that the two murders occurred.

Francesco didn't have any prior convictions or arrests and the court, on that occasion, showed mercy for his 'good character'. He was then arrested again in 1993 and convicted for unlawfully producing a large quantity of a drug, *Cannabis sativa*, in Queensland.

The extended family of Francesco Sergi was, anyway, another of those families on the radar of an anti-'ndrangheta policing effort. His father Giuseppe was also involved with growing Indian hemp crops in Bossley Park, Sydney. I discussed Giuseppe's case earlier on, as the tribunal on that occasion did look at the whole family and their ways of living. Vincenzo Cannistra, husband of Maria Sergi, who eventually came back from Italy, was also arrested in 1983 for the supply of Indian hemp.

While I understand the reasoning behind the tribunal's judgement in 1967 for the double murder carried out by Francesco Sergi and the labelling of the two murders as honour killings, I could not shake the feeling that, indeed, there could have been more to see in that case.

Calabrian cultural norms too often overlap with 'ndrangheta ones, or so it seems. And this case is one of the most obvious. *Was the sense of duty that Francesco felt as the oldest son to rectify the family's honour a cultural heritage, as the tribunal assumed, or a mafia value?* If it was the former, the murder could have been a dramatic turn for the worse in a heated discussion with his brother and his sister-in-law. If the latter, the murder might have been necessary and required of him as the oldest son. Adultery brings shame to the family and the 'ndrangheta doesn't tolerate adultery, nor does it tolerate whoever brings dishonour.[21]

Whatever happened in that case and to what extent it amounted to criminal conduct of any kind was and remains a matter for the court to judge. *I wished I could ask more questions about this of the persons involved.* Nevertheless, it was interesting to see how a mode of behaviour – in a family that was already under scrutiny for other offences – could mean different things to me than it did to the courts.

Hess's words resound:

A number of disputes cannot be brought before an official court anyway. These are the cases in which one party demands from another a course of action in line with their subcultural norms, a course of action not covered by formal laws. Unless one of the two parties resorts to direct self-help, the only arbitrator who also has the power of enforcement is the mafioso.[22]

Wogs and roofs

During my first trip to Griffith, I spent a lot of time learning about the Sergi families, good, bad and unknown. And the visit to the cemetery also enriched the whole experience. The morning of our trip back to Sydney, it was raining a little, just the right mood to roam around graves.

An eerie goodbye to Griffith, indeed. I remember taking a picture of our car, our solitary, lonely car, in the parking lot. No one else around.

Right at the entrance were Giuseppe (Platì, 4-4-1909/Griffith, 22-7-1989) and Caterina (Platì, 20-7-1916/Griffith, 3-4-1969) Sergi. Caterina was also Calabrian, born Perre, her father Antonio, her mother Giuseppina Catanzariti. Another Sergi family, another story. There was a joint tombstone for Giuseppe and Caterina. 'They lived for the love of their family. They rest in the serenity of honest people. They live again in the light of God', says the epigraph. Behind their grave are tombs for a number of families: Zirilli, Trimboli, Romeo, Calabria, Colla, Catanzariti, Zappia, Carbone, Musitano, Madaffari, Labbozzetta, Calipari, Mittiga, Pangallo, Barbaro, Agresta, Marando, Violi, Perre, Papalia, Alvaro, Velardi, Vergara. I took pictures and notes on almost all of them. Calabrian names, so many people who took the chance and risk to go to the other side of the world. Some of them may have been 'ndrangheta members, while others may have been witnesses or victims of the 'ndrangheta. *Could any one of those, in these small communities, really remain indifferent, unaffected, especially in certain periods?*

Again, those questions: *how can you know who is who? Where does the criminal liability start and ethnic solidarity end? How to explain that? How to understand?*

The feeling of losing the point of my research after this first Griffith trip was getting annoying. It seemed like I was conducting – I did conduct, at least for a while – research on Italian/Calabrian migration down under. Unintentionally stepping into migration research, I was digging much deeper into Italians abroad than I initially intended.[23]

A couple of days after that Griffith tour, I met a girl from Griffith one night in Fitzroy, one of Melbourne's coolest areas to hang out. She told me, simply, 'Yeah, you grow up knowing the Italians, the Calabrians, are kind of keeping it tight, to themselves. They meet at school, they marry, they don't go away to study for uni – especially women – not sure why, but some of them do have a reputation – still. My father did not want me to hang out much with them as I was growing up.'

The Promised Land was judgmental of Calabrians, for sure. The picture that had emerged was starting to get pretty dark.

Now, my friend Marie is a *wog*, and she explained to me what *wog* means. In Australia, a wog is a descendant of Southern European or Mediterranean migrants. It is not a nice word, wog; it's a racial slur, like the word *dago,* which was specifically aimed at Italians. The use of these slurs, for decades, denoted ghettos and separation across children, in schools, in churches, or wherever people crossed paths daily. Wogs were not treated the same as Australians of English descent. Australia, it turns out, has not always been welcoming, and certainly it has been racist and exclusionary of Italians and other European migrants.[24]

Today's second- and third-generation Italians seem quite comfortable expressing their *Italianness* consciously and conscientiously.[25] Being a wog has turned into a positive heritage, something to claim back with pride. Second- or third-generation Italians are likely to label themselves with this term now, with a new positive meaning. Indeed, a relatively recent phenomenon of 'wog pride' is the product of the second generation of Italians as a measure of the generational transformation of Italians and other Southern European groups within Australian society.[26]

One evening, Marie showed me a Facebook status she had stumbled upon while looking for something else. The status was dated from some years earlier and was public; it seemed to be perhaps a song, shared by a young man of Calabrian descent from Griffith. His name could be considered indicative of proximity to 'problematic' families, as much as mine arguably could.

Wog pride is my mind, Wog blood is my kind. So step aside and let us through, because it's all about the Wog crew. Wogs love is all around, My fellow Wogs never let me down. So show your pride and say it's true, because Wogs blood flows through you. United we stand, divided we fall. You can shoot one Wog, but you can't shoot us all. We are Wogs, We are full of class, Mess with us, And we'll kick your ass!

After she pointed out this status, I spent hours researching people on Facebook, Calabrian-Australian families of Australia, from Griffith and other rural areas of NSW. *Who knows who, and what do they do together? Who's commenting on status and pictures? What hashtags are used most often?* The Catholic school, the church, the birthdays, the Catholic confirmations. Intruding into lives, as much as privacy settings let you, with the urgency to explore that world more. Videos of grandmas making tomato sauce with their nieces and nephews, *just like my grandmother did*. Family moments, gathering rituals – they looked just like in Calabria. But with English words and with some twists, typical of Australian heritage, like having Christmas in summer. Fairly strange, I admit. The distinct feeling of a parallel world, almost, an alternative Calabria, Calabria Beta version. Calabria 2.0.

Wog pride is one of the components of ethnic solidarity that can be exploited by mafia groups.[27] People from the same places, who stick together and work together and grow up together, might be more willing to protect each other, not out of criminal intent but simply out of 'care' towards friends and family. Especially when the stigma of Calabrians = mafiosi reaches someone, and the instinct is, naturally, one of (self-) protection.

It's like not seeing the whole of a painting as you're too close to it. You see details, but the bigger picture eludes you.

It's incredibly difficult, I realized, to draw lines between what used to be Griffith's 'open secret' – the presence and the activities of 'ndrangheta families in the 1970s and 1980s – and the natural metamorphosis in the next generations who still carry the same surnames and links of those families.

Coming back from Griffith and after having read about the history of the Italian community in the region, I thought about the judicial cases against some alleged 'ndrangheta affiliates in the past, about recurring surnames and about wog pride. There was something above it all, above the mafia, about Calabrian identity, around Griffith.

I would have learned by travelling and researching the cities of Australia that Griffith's significance stretches way beyond the local and rural boundaries of the Riverina Valley when it comes to mafia stories and history. There is nowhere in Australia – aside perhaps from Perth, partially – that mafia links to the Honoured Society don't go back to Griffith at some stage.

I needed to explore this further. And it wasn't going to be easy, as the level of abstraction and – let's face it – the lack of data on what remains largely confidential knowledge of mafia investigations in Australia might have clouded my mind. Yes, I was starting to *see things*, relationships, complex connections. The research was becoming overwhelming, I was almost crushed by the awareness that I couldn't be sure of anything, and yet I kept noticing probabilities, opportunities.

Surprisingly, this was a familiar feeling. That feeling, I knew, back when I was a child, of being surrounded by it and unable to see it clearly, the 'ndrangheta.

Yes, I needed to explore this further. Because I had started with Griffith, Griffith had to remain one of the terms of reference. And I needed to move to other places, rural and urban, that had a historical link with Italianness, and Calabrianness even, down under. And then, possibly, with the 'ndrangheta.

Then it hit me. When you are too close to a picture to see anything but the details, maybe you need to look up to change perspective.

It was not just a line across the various dots that I needed to draw, but rather a *dome*, some sort of *roof*.

I had the feeling that I was about to give birth to a thought, and yet it was proving extremely difficult to do it. All the *fils rouges*, the common threads, the entangled stories, were somehow taking undecipherable forms. I was trying hard to follow my own train of thought.

The 'ndrangheta, in Griffith at least, at first looked like a subcultural legacy imported from the motherland by migrants from Calabria. However, it also could have been a phenomenon specific to Australia, mixing Australian ways with Calabrian mafia subculture. The cohort of values and behaviours has been kept safe and almost trapped in that community also, thanks to a series of societal changes, migration processes and historical metamorphoses. Griffith's – and Australia's – history has safeguarded some of the 'ndrangheta's cultural traits, untouched as a negative side effect of the preservation of culture. Among these traits are a culture of honour, tight family structures, religious obedience and rituals.

While I could see traits of that preserved subculture, I could not clearly make out any organizational structure behind it that I could call a mafia association. And that was frustrating.

Building my own mind maps and consulting actual network maps, I started drawing parallels between Calabria/Italy and Griffith/Australia. In the two settings, the density of 'ndrangheta behaviours surely differs; dimensions of the phenomenon differ; even the mafia – its rituals and traditions – differs. But what does not seem to differ is the *roof*. Above it all – above the resilience of the 'ndrangheta phenomenon in institutional, public and judicial talks – there seems to be a roof that keeps everything sheltered. In the 'ndrangheta organization, Aspromonte is the roof for Calabria. Calabria is a roof for clans around Italy. *Could Griffith be the roof for Australia? That which preserves and protects the phenomenon and the organization?*

I wonder, could there be 'ndrangheta by chance or by mistake, because of historical and social processes? In addition to 'ndrangheta by choice, of course.

And mind you, I absolutely am not justifying any of the activities that have qualified and still do qualify as criminal, wrongful or harmful conduct.

But the group density that has been observed since the very beginning in rural NSW – which I could observe too, online and offline – facilitates connections, shared behaviours, cultural preservation. In rural NSW this has been the case more than elsewhere, as the result of convergent analytical and historical elements.

The partial isolation and rural nature of the territory.

The different degrees of the so-called integration in what was often perceived as a non-welcoming – at times racist – country.[28]

The multi-ethnic – and almost experimental – societal structure in the territory, where *Italianness* – *Calabrianness* – was the leading 'ethnic' – minority – identity for a long time.[29]

The fact that criminal wealth was one of the founding resources of a minority (the 'ndrangheta families, the families of the Honoured Society) within this leading identity/group.

The naturally occurring changes in second- and third-generation migrants everywhere in Australia and the mutating nature of the wog attribute together with their self-identity.[30]

The mafia presence, with its cultural and *social* legacy – before evolving into a criminal phenomenon – might have become a provider of a 'public good'. In economics, this refers to a good that is provided without profit to all members of that community, non-excludable and non-rivalrous. In practice, the 'ndrangheta gained a reputation, facilitated the reinforcement of local identity and acted as a supplier of social and cultural capital, even if by chance and inadvertently. Its presence could also reduce uncertainty in many other aspects of social life and interactions.[31]

Losing 'it'

Australia is massive. And it is difficult to coordinate knowledge and intelligence across police forces or in the field. Documents stored in the national archives show how such complexity has affected any attempt to coordinate any type of anti-mafia strategy.[32]

Nevertheless, police and investigators did try, and, as in the case of the Woodward Commission in Griffith, they did scratch the surface of the phenomenon on various occasions. The Woodward Commission did see the 'ndrangheta in relation to the cannabis business, and probably something more than that, as we read between the lines.

I was not prepared to accept the proposition that the twenty-two plantations discovered throughout Australia between 1974 and 1978, involving persons of Calabrian descent, were unconnected and the results of independent actions or that individuals or small groups all decided, without liaison between each other, to cultivate cannabis.

An analysis carried out by officers of this Commission in relation to some of these plantations, both intrastate and interstate, revealed in many cases, links between those arrested and the Griffith group of Calabrians.[33]

The ethnic link remains a suspicion, and a strong one, indeed, of mafia presence. Where else, then, did the ethnic question emerge, apart from the cities, apart from Sydney and Melbourne and Perth and Canberra? Were there other towns like Griffith?

On 16 June 2012, journalists McKenzie, Baker and McKenna reported for the *Sydney Morning Herald*: 'Three Mafia figures living freely in Australia and labelled "extremely dangerous" by Italian authorities have been sentenced in absentia to long jail terms for international drug trafficking.'[34] Vincenzo Medici, 47, of Mildura (Victoria), and Michael Calleja, 53, of Melbourne, allegedly helped Nicola Ciconte, 56 – from rural Victoria but living on the Gold Coast at the time – to smuggle cocaine into Australia.

Mildura had been presented to me as another Italian town in Australia. Less than Griffith, which was about six to seven hours away by car – another 'ndrangheta rural connection.

'Ciconte maintained contact with associates in Vibo Valentia [Calabria] supplying the materials for the trial containers in collaboration with Medici; Calleja [...] made several trips from Australia to Calabria to determine the details of the shipments and the payments.'[35] Their key contact in Calabria was Vincenzo Barbieri, a 'ndrangheta cocaine broker in South America. Barbieri was an associate of the Mancuso clan, considered one of the most relevant 'ndrangheta groups today – from *my father's hometown, incidentally, but that's a story for later.*

Operation Decollo in the second half of the 2000s uncovered how some 'ndrangheta clans played a key role in drug trafficking in Latin America. The operation also pointed the finger to Australia, to Vincenzo Medici in Mildura, and the link with members of the Mancuso clan in Calabria.

Vincenzo Medici, together with his brother Matteo, was also convicted in Australia in 2011, after a trial in Italy in absentia, for trafficking in methylamphetamine.[36] It wasn't the first time for Matteo. He had been convicted of cultivating marijuana on his Red Cliffs property together with his mother, Giuseppina Medici, who was also convicted of trafficking 93 kilograms of marijuana.

On a very hot summer day in December 2017 – *again I was struggling with the upside-down climate* – a local police agent in Mildura was talking to me about this case. I couldn't get it at first, who was he talking about?

'The Medici family.'

'Right, but I wanted to know about Vincenzo Medici.'

'Yes, the Medici family!'

There we go, pronunciation matters. For me it's Mèdici. For him it was Medìci. Got that, moving on.

Victoria Police detective Damian Marrett in 1992 infiltrated a drug network in rural Victoria and the Riverina Valley, the area that includes Griffith in NSW.[37] In Mildura, the group was headed by a local man, Matteo Rosario Medici. Those years had not been easy for the Medici family:[38] Rocco Francesco Medici had been found floating in the Murrumbidgee River near Griffith together with another man, Giuseppe Furina. Rocco's ears had been cut off before his body was thrown in the water. Griffith again. *Was that a mafia-style punishment, perhaps for a betrayal?* His cousin, and the father of Vincenzo and Matteo, Marco Medici Sr, was shot in the back of the head at his fruit block in Red Cliffs, on the outskirts of Mildura, in 1983. *Another mafia punishment? Death by firearm from behind usually indicates a death sentence for traitors, those who tried to play double roles: they deserve death without knowing or seeing their murderer.* His son Matteo was charged with the murder, but he was acquitted. *Interesting.* I wanted to see the full judicial case, but I couldn't find it.

Betrayal, huh? Or simply silencing. So many accounts of those murders can be read between news and books. That family remains of interest somehow.

'It's one of those families, some of them were, are, quite respected, people shake hands with them, they receive visits from interstate … why, you ask? I am not sure really, maybe respect for what they used to be?' – the police officer again.

Mildura neither feels nor appears as Italian as Griffith. Not at all. This doesn't mean the town is not holding on to its Italian legacy, of course. But it has a lighter touch than Griffith. Or simply a lighter heritage to uphold.

I drove to Mildura alone from Adelaide. Even if it's officially in Victoria, Mildura is closer to Adelaide than Melbourne, only a four-and-a-half-hour drive from the South Australia capital, quick by Australian standards. *In summer, a solo road trip. I loved it.* Bordering Victoria and South Australia, and facing New South Wales, Mildura, differently from Griffith perhaps, feels like a place *in the middle*, a place of transit.

The drive to Mildura was one of the best of my life. Alone, through changing green landscapes and a blue sky, with my music on – at least until the phone baked under the sun and shut down for a while – and a deserted motorway. Truly deserted: I stopped in the middle of the motorway to take pictures!

Mildura is part of the Fruit Fly Exclusion Zone, meaning fruits and vegetables may not be taken into the area (they can, however, be taken out). I was stopped underneath a massive billboard signalling the start of the Exclusion Zone and asked to eat my banana there and then or throw it away. The officials watched me until I was done eating. *Awkward.*

I had rented a car, a big one this time. I had not asked for it, it was an upgrade after learning I had to travel cross-country. At the rental service they told me it was 'in case you hit the road in the dark, you can hit kangaroos with this and still drive'. OK. Right. Not sure if 'still drive' would have applied to me. Thus, I decided to spend the night in Mildura, to avoid driving in the dark. In a motel, one of those where you park in front of your room and your room looks like a small, always unused, flat. With spiders. Lovely, Australia.

Anyway, this time I had no paranoia about using my surname, plus, as I entered the city, I did not see much *Italianness*, not at first sight at least. *Had Mildura evolved much faster or at least differently than Griffith, for what concerned Italian identity?* After all, in the 2016 Census, Griffith's demographics registered 17.6 per cent Italian ethnicity, vs only 1.1 per cent in Mildura. And Griffith has less than half the population of Mildura.

I spent that night in December fighting off mosquitos, spiders and flies in the heat and reviewing some of the documents I had collected in the archives. Crime stories in Mildura populated the news throughout the 1960s and 1970s. Arsons, assaults, murder, drugs. There seemed to be, at least in the media at the time, a clear understanding that there was mafia in Mildura; that it was, again, Calabrian; and that it was also connected to other parts of the country, especially Victoria and Melbourne. Many of the stories I was looking at had happened before or at the same time as the Griffith mafia dramas. A report from the Australian Security Intelligence Organisation (ASIO) in 1958 details (supposed) branches of the Honoured Society of Victoria in the rural towns of Mildura and Shepperton.

ASIO redacted a report from 1963 'concerning the activities of the MAFFIA [double f and capital letters in the original] in the Mildura district'.[39] 'Local meetings of the MAFFIA are supposed to be held in Mildura every twenty-nine days.' This was attributed to an informant.

Names of fruit growers and farmers of Calabrian origin appear in this document: Romeo, Tassone, Rullo, Scambiaterra, Cufari, Strangio, Italiano. Stories about the Cufaris from Mildura will be discussed later when we move this journey to Queensland.

'There is a MAFFIA tribunal being convened for Mildura on the 30th of June.' Wow, that was specific intelligence! 'Members of the MAFFIA from Melbourne and Adelaide will attend. At this tribunal cases will be judged – fines and other punishment will be passed on offending Italians.'

What had this turned into?

So, let's recap. In the 1960s, there was some intelligence about a mafia tribunal in Mildura. Those were times when mafia was not even properly understood in Italy, so that intelligence is even more powerful as a result. *How could I, or anyone, exclude the possibility that there were mechanisms of control and conflict regulation, typical of the 'ndrangheta, back then? And if that was the case, maybe if we don't see clearer traces of these mechanisms today this might perhaps be a sign that there is less or no conflict to handle?*

In my research, a lot pointed to the visible side of the 'ndrangheta – with connections to the Calabrian/Italian communities. It was again confusing, as I said, to discern data on migration and mafia studies. That was the way most information was recorded back then. *Was I the one losing the 'ndrangheta in this data or was there a matter of accuracy in recording information in the first place and, eventually, in understanding the evolution of mafia structures?*

> No 1. The Da Vinci Club was founded as a social club to keep alive the friendly spirit among Italians and our hosts.
> No 2. All political discussions are forbidden. Meetings conferences and functions pertaining to the above will not be tolerated.
> No 3. All members shall act as gentlemen and avoid any discussions or acts that would be detrimental to the club or its members.

The constitution of the Italian Da Vinci Club in Mildura was redacted in July 1958. The club was built, as noted on its website,[40] to give Italian immigrants a place to perform arts, in addition to being a social club. Hence, no politics, no bad spirit. Now it's a wedding and event venue, fairly close to the motel where I was staying, as I discovered when I went for a stroll. A place where the Italian legacy has been maintained, somehow, without much regionalism. Which appeared to be the case overall in Mildura.

I had Peroni beer and Calabrese pizza – code for pizza with pepperoni or spicy sausage, in Australia – at one of Stefano's restaurants. Stefano De Pieri, a famous winemaker and restaurateur in Mildura, from Treviso, in the Northeast of Italy, migrated to Australia in 1974; he also owns the Grand Hotel, a gigantic structure that takes up an entire block in the town centre and overlooking the Murray River.

That evening, in front of my pizza and beer, I again felt as I had felt after Griffith – like I was losing *it*, the vision of *it*. It felt like I was again chasing Italian migration clues, trying to find relevant dots and connect them, trying to make sense of Italianness rather than mafia mobility. I was demoralized that evening; I felt my head spinning; I could not focus.

And what about the Medici involvement then? That's fairly recent ... Could it just be occasional? I wrote in my research journal that night while getting ready for bed.

In every meeting with the police in Australia, I found extremely competent people who tried their best to answer my questions without obviously giving away confidential information. In the simple room where the police meeting was held in Mildura – with the heat outside becoming unbearable and the air conditioning way too high inside – the conversation was very different from the one I had in Griffith. *The 'ndrangheta in Mildura is something from the '80s*, everyone said. And yet some agents nodded when I shared with them some thoughts about what else I had learned throughout my research. How the mafia manifests, what the 'ndrangheta seems to be also down here.

It felt like everyone was looking in another direction from the one I was intrigued by – the necessity to understand how much of the structure from the past has been preserved and how much has changed and evolved.

Yes, there are some families. Yes, people travel intestate, even to Griffith. Of course, they meet for marriages, funerals, baptisms, in the Da Vinci Club here, or down in Adelaide, surely in Melbourne. Yes, the communities are tight between here and Griffith, we can say that. No, they are not mafia, we don't think so. Some criminal activity, yes, of course. They don't do much really, apart from that one time with the drugs import. Oh, and we found cash, too much cash, hidden at someone's place once, too. But no, here everything passes through, everyone goes through, you wouldn't really see any type of criminal control, not even from the Italians, no, sorry, Calabrians.

I left Mildura with more questions than I had when I arrived. I was unclear about structures, activities, criminal hotspots, mafia behaviours and norms.

Griffith was the *roof*; mafia behaviours, and structures, had been there for decades, protected, under the roof. Mildura appeared as a hub for various criminal activities, and, after a closer look, mafia behaviours seemed to have vanished or to be not systemic, at the very least.

That reminded me of something. It was something tangled up between memories and analysis, something about the *Piana* of Gioia Tauro in Calabria, and Aspromonte. Something that I would only later form into an intelligible thought. It was the feeling that the 'ndrangheta from the provinces of Vibo Valentia or Crotone or the area of Gioia Tauro *feels* different when compared with the one from Aspromonte; the places, the activities, the grip. They *feel* different, in part at least. Why, I still needed to unpack.

It would have taken a while for all of this to sink in. Travelling in rural Australia, for some reason, diluted the purpose of my research. Without crimes committed, or with very different crimes committed, far from the noise of drug trafficking, it had become difficult for me to recognize where mafia research ended and migration research started, again.

Lost 'it'

While the white rental car slalomed down from Perth to the valley, heading to Harvey, I couldn't help but smile. Now, *that* really looked like the Calabrian countryside, like the roads that climb up to Aspromonte. The same feeling of desolation, the same feeling of being increasingly cut off from the world. I am not sure what it was exactly, in the geography of that place, as obviously the countryside tends to be more or less the same everywhere. It was probably also because I knew that Harvey only has about 3,300 people, and the connection to my research was in the fact that some Calabrian families from South and Western Australia, loosely connected to 'ndrangheta families, appeared to have bought land there at some point. Data released in 2009 by the Italian antimafia commission's then president, Francesco Forgione, indicate that Harvey is connected to both clans from the Calabrian town of Siderno active in Perth and to the clans Strangio and Perre from San Luca and Platì. Not the most accurate or specific data, honestly.

There is nothing Italian in Harvey, let alone Calabrian. Nothing stands out. Indeed, there is nothing to see. With my colleague and friend Stefano, who works and lives in Perth, we travelled around, not quite sure what we were looking at or looking for.

In the middle of nowhere, in a field with only a few houses, there it was, probably the tiniest Italian Club of Australia, Harvey Italian Club. Closed. A little red house, shut down. It does exist, yes, but if you try hard to find it on Google, it has no website, no Twitter, no Facebook page, only a couple of mentions in the news in relation to an Italian Sausage Festival. I took a picture in front of the building; I was a bit puzzled, but not surprised. I had tried to dig out something more on those areas, Harvey, Bunbury, and found nothing. Most of my trip to Perth had been filled with a feeling that I was missing something. I will talk about this more in the sections dedicated to Perth in the following chapters.

Harvey Catholic Church used to be called Our Lady of the Immigrants Catholic Church. According to locals, it has been over 55 years, 1966, since the community started celebrating the annual Feast of Our Lady of the Immigrants, imported from Milan. There are clear connections to migration, and particularly Italian migration – not clearly defined by regions – in the history of Harvey.[41]

When the Second World War started in 1939, a large portion of Australia's Italian residents were living in Western Australia – the gold industry was booming, and it was supposed to be lucrative. This is why Western Australia has the greatest proportion of all interned Italians across Australia. The Harvey internment camp was one of the first sites of internment: over 700 Italian men were interned there.[42] Many were Calabrians, as Stefano and I could judge from the engraved names in the memorial shrine. The shrine is a painful reminder of a past that the territory seems to struggle to forget as much as remember.

Everything left of the *Italianness* of that area is concentrated in that shrine. Discrimination and fear towards Italians and the internees of Harvey was unfortunately a hallmark in most of the history of Western Australia. It's hard to see anything beyond the shrine.

The police in Perth, both state and federal, did mention something about that past, something about lands that decades ago belonged to Italian families around Harvey, internees who, once free, had tried to remain in the area.

But that land, differently from other places, had not brought any settlement, any real investment in the territory.

'Let's maybe see if there is an Italian restaurant nearby?' said Stefano, 'or at least a cemetery!' I wondered whether that place, and its farms and houses, could have been – maybe had been in the past – used to harbour fugitives – frankly, who the hell could even think to go and look for a fugitive in a remote place like that one, so silent and slow? Yes, I could see that.

Very scattered news and a very scarce presence of Calabria and Italy in Harvey. And some news related to the game of briscola!

'Harvey residents Joe Crupi and Dom Comito were the winning team who took home $500, which they have offered to donate a portion to fundraising events that the WA Calabrese Club and Figli di Calabria host.'[43] Briscola. I love playing briscola: it sounds like Italy and old men playing at the bars in Calabria, lazily, the whole afternoon.

But that was all there was. Nothing but scattered news. At most, criminal opportunities, some sort of self-fulfilling prophecy about the criminality of the place. It was not satisfactory, and, for a researcher, it was disorienting.

I kept on visiting those places mentioned in reports, maps, books, all supposedly linked to the Calabrian mafia in Australia. And yet I had the distinct feeling that I was losing *it*, losing the 'ndrangheta. Harvey did connect somehow to Perth and Siderno, in the same way – more or less – in which Mildura connected to Adelaide and maybe Melbourne and Aspromonte. But things were very indistinct; I could not put anything clearly into focus.

Not only had I lost my object of research, my focus on the mafia, in Harvey, but obviously I had to ask myself, what exactly was I looking for, going to a place like that, in the middle of rural Western Australia? *What was I expecting to find, if not a confirmation of some circumstantial data that – I had already learned – clearly lacked territorial and cultural depth?*

3

Aspromonte, the Roots

The 'ndrangheta stole my doll

There is a time in every child's life that remains suspended. In what seems like an eternal present tense, memories and dreams and nightmares all mix up, for a future self to store and reorganize. I have a strange memory that comes back to me when thinking of that suspended childhood time. It's strange in the sense that I was unable to place it in time and space for a very long time, yet it's extremely vivid, like a feeling crawling under the skin.

It's late afternoon. We are in Dad's car. I am sitting on the back seat, wearing light clothes, must be warm outside. I am five or six or seven years old, I cannot be sure. I have my hair in a sort of bob cut, which I used to have at that age. I remember a light blue t-shirt but that I think it's not really part of that memory, I'm not sure why. I cannot recall whether my sister and my mum are also with us; odd, isn't it? I am very tired, I do remember that, almost snoozing. *Drive, Dad, drive. Where to?* By the time we arrive, it's dark, it must be very late. Lots of lights from cars around us, while we stop in a little square; there is a fountain, so typical of the villages of Calabria. Fresh water always streaming down to God knows where. People outside, I see from the car windows, are agitated; I still feel quite confused, maybe I had fallen asleep just before. I hear my father's voice. *Stay in the car, Anna. What if I have to …? Stay in the car.* His voice, so firm, his order, so final, as always. I stay in the car for what feels like eternity. Something is happening outside, I cannot quite see, but I am aware of cars' headlights. I grab my doll, a Barbie, half naked like all the Barbies I used to have – I kept losing their clothing, for some reason. I am playing with the Barbie. I hear commotion, people moving, my father still in sight, tense, while speaking with someone in uniform, a carabiniere I believe. It feels like forever. The car door opens, my father makes a gesture, something that looks like 'come on', but not towards me. *Towards the Barbie. What does he want with my Barbie?* 'Give me the doll, Anna, dai.' Why? 'We'll give it to that little girl there.' He points to a girl with longish hair who's crying not so far from us, surrounded by a lot of people.

'Why is she crying?'

'She lost her dad. Let's give her the doll.'

I don't want to give up my Barbie, I don't understand. What the hell is happening?

A sense of ... impoverishment ... almost, fills me. She lost her dad, *did someone hurt him? Who?* My father finally takes my Barbie, slams the car door, goes to her. I am puzzled. He comes back, a while later, ready to go. He has a gigantic cell phone, his first cell phone, and he is talking – I hear some words before he gets in the car ... "ndrangheta ... yeah, the feud ... no... he is dead, there is his head here, they were playing soccer with his head in the square, they told me'. We drive away, and I strangely know what a 'ndrangheta feud is.

Say, what?

There are discrepancies between my dad's memories and mine, so we cannot be sure whether the order of events is right. We used to drive around with those stories all the time. *But there was a doll and there was someone's head.*

And the 'ndrangheta stole my doll. Or rather I gave it away, but still, it sucked.

It could have been 3 May 1991, I would have been six. It is known as the *'mattanza'* – the slaughtering – of Taurianova. When I read about it years later, my memory lit up and lost puzzle pieces came back to the front of my mind.

Black Friday, it was called, the day when four people were killed in a single day: the first one at 12.30 pm, two others four hours later, and the last one at 8.30 pm. A feud between the Zagari–Avignone–Viola–Giovinazzo clan and their opponents, the Alampi–Asciutto–La Ficara clan. In less than two years, the feud had resulted in 40 deaths. At the core was the territory of Taurianova, a village of around 16,000 people, in between the flatland, *la Piana*, and Aspromonte, crucial for lucrative trafficking and hideouts. The trigger was the murder of Rocco Zagari the day before, on 2 May 1991. Zagari had succeeded Mimmo Giovinazzo in leading the homonymous clan. *What had gone wrong?* Giovinazzo had been a good mediator – ally to the stronger clan of the Piromalli in Gioia Tauro: he apparently managed illicit trades for the whole area, also on behalf of other families. He was getting some pushback from nearby clans over the management of affairs in the agricultural sector. Younger generations in the clans of Taurianova wanted new alliances and more drugs, violence and extortion. They were protected by the Versace clan, from the nearby village of Polistena, allied to the powerful Pesce family, from Rosarno, also in the flatland. *We'll talk about these clans later, tune in.*

Drugs vs land power. Giovinazzo was killed, but the expected new deal did not emerge. Zagari took his place as head of a clan with over 100 affiliates. But the clan had no external protection nor recognition, so it could not last.

Rocco Zagari died while at the barber, like famous Italian-American gangster Albert Anastasia. His death was avenged on 3 May with the murder of four people. One body, that of Giuseppe Grimaldi, killed in the afternoon, was severely mutilated.

His head is chopped off as he tries to escape.

His head is suddenly in the air, as one of the killers grabs it by the hair.

The other killer shoots at the head, which then crumbles down to the pavement.

It looks like a deflated ball. Someone kicks it. Someone, here, enjoys kicking a severed head.

Here, in and around the mountain, here in Aspromonte.

Bonasira

Bonasira, eu vi dicu a Vui, Madonna,
La gloriusa di Santa Maria.
Goodnight, I say to you, Madonna
The glorious Santa Maria.

My grandmother is immortal. She was one of those women who, on her shoulders, in her smile and in her daily gestures, carried the primitive forces of the universe. Nonna Mimma was the simplest of women and yet the kind of woman who could influence everyone around her, slowly, imperceptibly. She made the bed every morning, just perfectly, without a single wrinkle in the sheet – I never knew how she did that, never managed to do it myself – and she believed that one must not speak evil of others because bad luck will come back at you. *Fora gabbu signuri.* Which kind of meant 'God preserves us from bad luck', sort of. She tried to negotiate for the price of vegetables every single day: the man came to sell his produce door to door with a three-wheeled car – *whose motor you could hear the moment it turned up the road to enter the village, so loud and so old it was.* And Grandma urging us to run outside to stop him while she grabbed her purse. And she was also the kind of woman who gave food to the white stray cat that daily came outside the house and patiently waited for Grandma to feed her. That cat came to the house, patiently waiting, for days and weeks after Grandma died; she probably couldn't accept her death, either.

A la matina: bongiornu, bongiornu,
Vui siti Patruna di tuttu lu mundu.
And in the morning, good morning good morning,
You are the Patron of the whole world.

The summer in Santa Cristina d'Aspromonte, one of the 30 or so villages around the mountain, is your ideal summer, if your ideal includes time that stays still, hot weather during the day and a fresh breeze at night, food from the kitchen garden brought daily by Grandpa or bought off the man with the three-wheeled car. And you only share it, the summer, with about 800–900 people, the overall population.

The days went on pretty much the same: wake up around 8 am, have breakfast and watch some TV, make up the room. On Wednesdays you run to the weekly market to get mozzarella before they run out. And they apparently run out at 9 am. *So why don't they just bring more mozzarella?* The question. Every. Single. Wednesday. At 10 am, Lina and I used to meet on our adjacent balconies, while she was cleaning up her room and I was cleaning up mine. We are second (or third or fourth) degree cousins and we are the same age. We played and laughed and grew up together, with my sister and her brothers and sisters; through the years, we moved from talking about cartoons to talking about boys, as you do. The summers in Aspromonte were pretty much all the same, year after year. Every time, it felt like jumping into a beautifully crafted alternative reality, very different from my winter days and so very cosy and familiar. It was comfortable because it was timeless, I realize now.

And the mountain, oh, my mountain. Too big, I always thought. *Does it really fit in here?* I used to wonder, pointing at the map.

Every year, right after my birthday on 15 August, a strange feeling filled the air in that tiny, always half-asleep village. Summer was almost over, storms were behind the clouds, we looked for warmer pyjamas. Nonna Mimma took out the red shawl from inside the wardrobe. And the white plastic chairs – normally placed outside when chatting with the neighbours at sunset or after dinner – were put back inside every night, for fear of showers. *I had a very cute chair, very small, baby-size, just for me, I was so jealous of it; it was Anna's chair for everyone!*

> *Supra a l'artari nc'è na gran Signura,*
> *Maria di la Muntagna ca si chiama.*
> On the altar is a Great Lady,
> Maria of the Mountain she is called.

With that shawl and the white chairs, for nine days, from 24 August to 2 September, we used to walk up the street, reaching out to the large water fountain where Aspromonte natural park officially started – there was a rusty billboard saying 'Welcome to Aspromonte Park' – and we would be sitting there, in front of a statue of the Madonna di Polsi. The little shrine where the Madonna of the Mountain sat, holding fresh flowers and a baby Jesus, would be open for the occasion of the *novena*. For those nine days – hence the name *novena* – after dinner, without a precise time, more or less around 9 pm, we would be getting ready. We opened the door and waited for everyone else to walk up. It was the only time we were allowed, as children, to be out after dinner anyway, so that was exciting in itself. The older women of the *ruga* – the street – would move first, dictating the timing, of course. Rosina, Catuzza, Angelina, Giuseppina, Mariuzza and Nonna Mimma, everyone was someone's aunt or grandma anyway. It wasn't the greatest setting to pray for the Madonna – sat across two lines of chairs – we essentially were in the middle of the road, and there were cars going by. First would come the Rosary, already setting up that sort of trance recital. It was followed by the Colloquia. Yes, you would not just pray to the Madonna. You would *talk* to her, in nine Colloquia that told the story of the Madonna in the valley of Polsi, all finishing with a short chant.

Tu che il rumor di tante	*You broke the noise*
Ampie città spezzasti	*Of many large cities*
Qui di seder amasti	*and yet you settled here*
Di un'erma valle in sen	*in this lonely valley*
In questa valle ancora	*In this valley, still*
Il nome tuo si onora	*We honour your name*

The third chant was probably my favourite; like a lullaby, we used to sing them every night for nine nights. They gave me goose bumps. I learned the words of the Colloquia before I understood what they meant; I looked at the adoring eyes of those women staring at the Madonna – yes, the novena was mainly made up of women, apart from occasional male children following their mum or grandma. Those women adored that simple and young Maria, they *really* talked to her. Not that I understood the depth of that, but it was certainly something very powerful. This is why I felt so proud when, aged seven or eight, I was asked to read during the novena. After that, Lina and I would split the reading. One night I would read the Colloquia and she would lead the Rosary, and then we would do it the other way around the next day. It was a great honour to be the reader. Everyone else, especially the veterans, would know instantly if you made a mistake. Those words were sacred, you had to have the right tone, the right gravity. Unfortunately, at home we did not have the little booklet with the burgundy cover, with the chanting and the Colloquia; I remember yearning for it for some reason. I wanted to have my own. We all shared the available booklets eventually during the novena. Finally, each novena night, there were songs. Two or three per night, the songs of Polsi, always finishing with the Bonasira, the goodnight and goodbye song. It was a slow serenade, whose words could easily be drawled from one line to the other. Rosina's pitch was too high, Catuzza's was out of tune, the rest of us, almost sighing, were just following the lyrics. Then it was over, we would wrap things up and go back home while the other novena, *d'abbasciu,* in the lower side of the village, would still be singing. They always sang more than we did, who knows why, and I was jealous of that.

> *E la Madonna si vota e ndi dici:*
> *vajiti, bonasira e santa pace.*
> *And the Madonna turns around and says to us*
> *Go now, good night and peace.*

The Madonna of the Mountain, the Madonna of Polsi, is the pulsating heart of Aspromonte, beating within and around the villages and for the people, at times very fast, and always very deep.

Worshipping

Polsi is the symbol of Aspromonte. It is a sanctuary towering 860 metres above sea level, swallowed by the mountain, which, around the sanctuary, reaches almost 2,000 metres. It is a simple building, the sanctuary, but the nature surrounding those simple-looking walls is breathtaking. The river Bonamico, crossing through the villages of Platì and San Luca and ending up directly in the Ionian Sea, cuts the valley open. The white church in the middle of Polsi, surrounded by stone buildings, gets overcrowded with people flocking to greet the Madonna of the Mountain in the summer, every summer. It's a difficult image to render in writing, that of men, women and children chanting, laughing, singing, shaking, dancing, crying, *feeling*, while sharing narrow spaces on the balconies around the square. They make room to let the Madonna statue breathe when *She* passes through during the procession on 2 September.

Going to Polsi, my grandmother used to tell me, was not like it is now, *bella mia* (that was her 'sweetheart' to us and ours to her). People used to – still do – go to Polsi as a pilgrimage, and that, for decades and decades, required walking for at least 12 hours from the village. Now you can go by car and then maybe walk for three hours from the kiosk in Montalto – if you still want to feel the pilgrimage experience. Or you can almost drive up until the last minute and then just join the other worshippers at the top of the sanctuary. I never walked there; I promised myself that one day I will do the pilgrimage, for her, for Nonna. Even if now, on Google Maps, it looks like from the village of Santa Cristina to Polsi you can draw a very short line, Polsi was always too far and too difficult to reach when I was a child and stayed with Grandma, even though it was always mentioned and talked about. There are no proper roads to get there, apart from the main one on the other side of the mountain that goes through the village of San Luca and another one that goes from Gambarie. And even then, it is not an easy ride at all. *No, wait, scrap that.* This doesn't accurately describe the feeling of total loss and utter dismay about the trip that one does from the Ionian side to Polsi, or even from Reggio or Delianuova, through Gambarie, with a normal car. Your phone loses its signal, the roads should never be called roads in the first place, as they are at most paths ... to nowhere, really, swallowed by the mountain. You have no clue how long it will take you.

'Am I going in the right direction to Polsi? The road down there is interrupted.'

'Sure! Just to the end of the road, turn left, you can't miss it!'

The 'just to the end of the road' is a two-hour drive up and down, down and up, up and down, down and up, through the most uncomfortable curves, between precipices on your left and falling rocks on your right, cars coming in the other direction and you thinking, at the same time, 'Ok, good, they must be coming from somewhere!' and 'How the hell are we both going to fit in this road?!' You are at the point of giving up when the sanctuary appears, deep down, so deep and so down you cannot believe that is the path your car will have to take to get there. It feels like descending to some sort of inferno, not ascending to the Madonna.

Paradox.

'This is the first time I see a sanctuary so deep down a valley. Normally, don't you ascend to visit the Madonna?' notices Alberto, my partner, grinning and sweating because he is the one driving; it's the first time we have gone there together.'

According to the legend, Polsi was founded after a shepherd who was looking for a lost cow, or a lost calf – depending on the version – found the animal on its knees in front of a cross that had been unearthed from the ground. At that point, the Madonna appeared and asked the shepherd to build a sacred place there. This is the valley of Polsi, in the deepest throat of Aspromonte.

I wonder how they actually managed to bring what was needed to build this down here.

I was already a bit older, and it was already midway through the 2000s, the first time I went to Polsi. I don't remember much besides the heat and the discomfort of being in an overwhelming crowd. And some girls dancing. Everyone chatted about the girls, one of them was someone's – *someone not good* – daughter: she was so graceful and beautiful while moving to the rhythm of the tarantella. It seemed like everyone knew her. It seemed like everyone simply knew how to behave in that place.

The thing is, there was a code of behaviour in Polsi; there probably still is. The place is sacred and the celebrations for the Madonna must not be disturbed. Everything must stop when the Madonna di Polsi rises every year, no feuds, no blood, no shooting, no killings. It's a holiday also for the 'ndrangheta, and this is not really a strategy; it is mostly about faith, or a twisted sense of faith, that is. People in those areas feel the Madonna in a way I have never experienced or seen elsewhere. That devotion is real, so of course it does influence, powerfully, everything around it, the 'ndrangheta included. Polsi is the centre of the faith, including the *'ndranghetist* faith. In Polsi, at the time of the festivities in early September, everything should rest, including 'business', including 'crime'. You meet and shake hands about things already decided elsewhere. The 'ndrangheta is a devoted Christian and a Marian worshipper. After all, 'ndrangheta is a feminine noun and its various rituals often evoke the force of a divine feminine.[1]

The legend says that the 12 *tables* of the 'ndrangheta are kept at the sanctuary of Polsi in San Luca; they describe the 'ndrangheta's rules and behaviours and sanctify the new baptisms. The Mamma of San Luca, the Madonna from Polsi, is the epicentre, the belly, the pulsing heart of 'ndrangheta power. The umbilical cord between Calabria and its mafia is here. This doesn't mean all *'ndranghetisti* have to go to Polsi all the time – in the same way a Catholic doesn't go to the Vatican all the time, or ever – but Polsi is there when one *needs* it. And believe me, I say it once again, once you experience the level of devotion that Aspromonte villages have for the Madonna della Montagna, you understand what this actually means. *From within.*

There is a cross in Zervò, on the road connecting the east and the west of Aspromonte, 1,100 metres above sea level. From Santa Cristina, on the way to Piminoro, facing Oppido Mamertina, you have Platì, San Luca and Polsi to the left. Near the cross is an old military fort, used in the 1990s by the Cacciatori dell'Aspromonte, Aspromonte Hunters, a special squad of the carabinieri. The cross is a reminder that Polsi, Aspromonte, has been *terra franca* – a free zone – where many of the unspeakable horrors of Calabria have gone down. The Christ of Zervò is the Christ of the kidnapped victims. When the sun sets on Zervò, it fills the ruins around the old military base with a red sun and an orange sky. Beautiful. Creepily beautiful.

Aspromonte is indeed a beautiful place, but it is also a place, let's remember, where at some point *someone enjoyed kicking a head.* And not only that.

The monster mountain

That Aspromonte is a monster mountain is now visible to anyone, even first-timers in the area. After all, a monster – *monstrum* in Latin – is something or someone that evokes fear and wonder, a prodigy as much as an evil omen. Fear and wonder, indeed, a bit like religion. As a child, I never quite understood how something could feel so infinite as Aspromonte.

I am not quite clear on what my grandmother meant when she said '*staci 'ndranghitiandu*' – he/she is – and a verb that means 'acting in a cocky, arrogant way'. It is probably a reference to the arrogance and the hubris of the clans that drenched the rocks and the vegetation of Aspromonte with blood, during some of the most shameful pages of Calabrian, and Italian, history.

Just at the feet of the Madonna della Montagna – in Polsi, as pictured and narrated by novelists, journalists, historians, photographers and filmmakers – the clans did kidnap, torture and kill, in the name of power, through fear, and for money through ransom.

In a study from 2007,[2] Calabria recorded the second highest number of kidnappings in Italy, over 150, after Lombardy – where kidnappings had different motivations, some of which were linked to mafias – mainly the 'ndrangheta and Sicilian Cosa nostra. It is estimated that around 800 billion old Italian lira (today €400 million or more) was paid for the 694 kidnappings carried out by criminal organizations in Italy between 1945 and 2007: more than half of those, it is said, went into the 'ndrangheta's pockets.[3] It is estimated that clans from Aspromonte have been responsible for over 200 kidnappings since 1945, primarily between the 1970s and the 1980s.[4] The peak, across the country, was 1977, with 75 kidnappings. Differently from other criminal organizations, the 'ndrangheta's signature move was to keep the victims hidden in Aspromonte, where no one could find them. People kidnapped in the North of Italy were dragged down to the Calabrian Mountain, unseen and unheard. Aspromonte is impenetrable; police, carabinieri, the army, would all converge in the throat of Aspromonte just to be swallowed up by the utter impossibility of the task of finding anything or anyone in those territories. Only in 1991, at the end of the 'ndrangheta kidnapping season, was a special squad set up. They were called – still are called – the Cacciatori, the Hunters, whose motto is *'Vigilantia de cielo, coercitio ex terra'* (surveillance from the sky, coercion from the ground). They are supposed to be the keepers of Aspromonte.

I used to love getting lost in the nature reserve of Aspromonte, whose green colours deepened and darkened the more we got into the summer. I could trace my steps back solely because I was paying attention to all the blackberry bushes. Every once in a while there were strange stone buildings, skeletons of houses, no doors, no windows – some were shelters for the police or the carabinieri; did they ever get lost? Just there, in the middle of the grass, kissed by rays of sun in between the trees. It always felt like I was about to walk into someone else's scene, somewhere I was not supposed to be. The silence around, always. Creepy. Beautiful.

During the trials that in the mid-1990s identified some of the *'ndranghetisti* who had orchestrated the kidnappings,[5] two things emerged. Firstly, the monster mountain had a crucial role, and it was indeed strategic. It wasn't just accidental or even just convenient for the victims to be held there: it was necessary, the safest bet, for the plan to work. The kidnappings were a proper industry – a well-oiled mechanism that was as profitable as it was precise. The clans made plans, shared the work, knew where and how to hide the victims, how to conceal the cages – usually natural caves or holes in the ground but also literal cages in these caves – learned how to negotiate and interact with the victims' families and the authorities.[6]

Secondly, as the kidnappings were, of course, a form of capital accumulation for the clans involved, they did attract other 'supporters'. Local communities in Aspromonte villages around Natile, Platì and San Luca were involved in the daily management of the kidnappings, directly or indirectly.[7] Victims were in the custody of fugitives hiding in the territories; young affiliates were running errands in an attempt to climb the criminal ladder; food and water, clothes and blankets were provided by someone's aunt, mother, father, sister, brother or cousin in the village. What seems clear is that a portion of the ransom did enter the economy of the villages, especially to be used for the construction of houses and for fixing up existing buildings. Someone probably thought that a kidnapping was something everyone could benefit from. Neutralization techniques – 'victims don't risk their lives'; 'they are well fed'; 'they are taken care for'; 'we only want their money' – were probably resounding loudly in some people's minds.

Distant memories I hold of helicopters buzzing above my head, and the carabinieri's military green station wagons rushing up the hill just outside my bedroom window. A curfew was in place, not sure whether it was formalized or not by any institutional decree, but it was certainly upheld by Grandma who asked us to be home at sunset, no derogation of any kind. Especially in summer, that wasn't easy. It gave an idea, just a feeling, of something sinister, but I couldn't possibly understand what.

You are taken while you are entering the car with your mother, or just saying goodbye to your son or husband, or as you've just woken up on a Sunday after partying with your friends and you are having breakfast, or while you are getting back home after work. In a split second, you are pushed inside a car, the smell of men around you, the hands of one of them on your mouth and then blackout. Up to an 18-hour drive, maybe hidden in the trunk if you are kidnapped somewhere in the North. Or just a 15- to 30-minute drive, it's all it takes, if you are already in Calabria. The car speeds through the narrow cobblestone roads to reach Aspromonte as soon as possible. In any case, at some point, the monster mountain swallows you, them, the car, your freedom crushed, in an instant. You are drowsy and they don't show their faces; you are not sure what you see. They all wear the same clothes and face masks; you are blindfolded now; their voices are muffled by the vegetation that gets thicker around you. They make you hide for hours that feel like days, they give you cheese and some bread. They barely speak, you hide, and you have no idea where you are. You feel the wind through the trees and the foliage, hear some birds chirping ... or not, no, they are helicopters buzzing over you, far away. You feel like you want to scream, but your throat fails you; the monster mountain stole your voice. And you feel you are moving very slowly, almost not moving at all. Then, maybe when you are almost passing out, in and out of sleep, a guy who looks like he is in charge shakes you, *We've got to move.* It's colder now, probably the sun went down. *If it's dark then we can move,* he says. You move now, quickly, they push you, rush you. It's dark and you can now go unseen, go where they will keep you for the night, or for several nights. If you are one of the lucky ones you will go into a cave, no more than a metre and a half high, you cannot properly stand, unless you are a child … If you are less lucky, they will push you down into a … a hole in the ground, smelling the grass, to get to a basement, or underground, surrounded only by soil and wood. No light, no sun, no contact with the outside. You'll stay there – in the cave or the hole – as long as it's a safe hiding place; it could be weeks, or months; if they move you, you won't know why – *are you finally getting freed? Or are they just moving you somewhere else? What day is it?* You can try and guess, as they left you a calendar. And they bring you magazines, at times newspapers, if the news is not about you, your family, the ransom money and negotiations. You are an object of negotiation. You. You cry until you stop feeling things. And then you probably start giving names to your kidnappers: 'the Journalist' – who brings you the newspapers; 'the Tall One' – as he cannot enter the cave/ basement/hole; 'the Bird' – as when he speaks it sounds like he tweets. They are not always nasty with you. Sure, you are chained, literally, more often than not. You cannot move and you cannot ask about your family or what is going to happen to you. But they don't usually hit you. They feed you, they give you a hot meal every day, generally at lunch – soup or pasta – then for dinner cold cuts and cheese, as we are used to doing around here. You can wash yourself once a week – they'll bring you water and soap – but you might not feel like washing your hair if it's long. It's cold down there, it won't dry, and you'll catch a cold. Better not. The days go by, and seasons change. They give you an extra blanket. You sleep when it gets dark – if you can see the outside – and wake up at dawn. Or just wake up in the middle of the night and wait for dawn. The days go by, and you confuse silence with peace. Your freedom, after 10, 100, 200, or 300 days, comes always too late. They will bring you somewhere and leave you on your own to reach someone or something. You can't even run. Maybe they leave you in a barrack to be found by the carabinieri if they are looking for you; you hope they find you in time. You haven't washed your hair or beard for weeks, you look scruffy. Your eyes are not adjusting well to the sunlight. Your muscles are not used to walking anymore. You say your name when the carabinieri ask. *Does it mean anything to them, do they know who you are? How long have they been looking for you?* At home, flowers and pastries, the whole village is celebrating your return. *How much were you worth eventually?* This thought creeps into your head. *The*

Juventus won the cup? That's great. Will you now manage to properly wash your hair? And how are you going to look back at that monster mountain again?[8]

All of this, at the feet of the Madonna di Polsi. Polsi that protects, Polsi that condemns all this and yet did not deter. It's a heavy burden for the church to admit that in those years all this horror happened right in the middle of the sacred valley, protected by the sacred valley. Efforts have been made – especially by the local bishop[9] – to detach the cult of the Madonna di Polsi from the 'ndrangheta – and rightfully so, of course – but can all of this ever be forgotten? Don Pino Strangio, at one point rector of the Sanctuary of Polsi and recently priest of the village of San Luca, was convicted in first degree to 9 years for mafia association.[10] Things around here are difficult to read. To trust.

Stages of denial

The stories of the kidnappings, of men, women and even children, have been told by newspapers and books at the time and ever since. Notwithstanding the knowledge, there is something about the cruelty of those years that gets erased from the minds of many Calabrians.

In April 2015, my father and I accompanied a small cohort of people developing the Australian Four Corners documentary on the 'ndrangheta down under for ABC/Fairfax Media. In the dense colours of Aspromonte in spring – between the dark brown and the thousand shades of green – Nick's light Australian complexion, blue eyes and accent did stand out – he was the reporter in the documentary. When we got to Oppido Mamertina, in the big square so beautifully embraced by the monster mountain, we had to come up with a reason to justify our – *their* – presence there – not to attract even more attention.

The story that Four Corners wanted to tell was about a Calabrian man from Messignadi. This man was allegedly involved in a series of mafia activities in Calabria in the late 1970s and early 1980s, including a kidnapping. He had later migrated to Melbourne, where he had been found guilty of other mafia-type criminal activities. One of the folk songs dedicated to the Madonna di Polsi goes '*i Messignadi si ndi chianunu puru a pedi*' – *from Messignadi they can climb up on foot* (to the sanctuary). Messignadi is a small village, part of Oppido Mamertina, where we went. From there, Aspromonte is indeed within walking distance, as it is from my grandparents' village, Santa Cristina, which is nearby.

The official story was suggested by my father: the *forestieri* (foreigners) were there to shoot a documentary on the kidnappings. Just that. Because, apparently, talking about the kidnappings at the time (2015) was more acceptable than talking about the 'ndrangheta between Calabria and Australia. I realized on that occasion that the kidnapping season is labelled as a black page of Calabria's history, and that history is over and done, the page has been turned. *But how could it be gone, almost forgotten, if even I remember it? If it was not that long ago that we heard updates from the monster mountain in Calabria on national TV?*

It was almost a process of denial of harm, like those that follow conflicts, war crimes, crimes against humanity or genocide. *Could this be a collective denial process that has pushed the kidnapping season deep down in memories, locking them away from people's daily relationships with their villages and their communities?*

Sociologist Stanley Cohen, in his 2001 book *States of Denial*,[11] identifies three types of collective denial: literal, interpretative and implicatory. *Literal* denial is the blatant rejection of facts: this never happened. Interpretative denial does not reject the facts but rather offers a different interpretation of what happened: it's not that nothing happened, but what happened, it's not what you think or what it looks like or what you call it. Lastly, implicatory denial involves various forms of 'rationalisations': it's got nothing to do with me; what can an ordinary person do now? It's been dealt with, or someone else will deal with it. Implicatory denial is basically an evasion from, and minimization of, the psychological, political, social and moral implications that follow harm and violence.

The kidnappings? Clans of the 'ndrangheta, yes, but a long time ago. Things have changed now. It has nothing to do with me/us.

Transitional justice is a form of justice applied in territories after violence, conflicts, atrocities or human rights violations. This justice seeks equilibrium between denial and acknowledgement. On one side is the drive towards justice, truth discovery and reconciliation with the past; on the other side is the compelling need to bury and silence that hurtful past and just move on. Transitional justice often works in the form of truth and reconciliation commissions, such as the ones in South Africa after apartheid, or in Colombia after the agreement between the state and the FARC. Noticeably, in these complex contexts, when elements of the past are *contested*, not fully acknowledged – let's take the Troubles in Northern Ireland as an example[12] – there is little desire to break with said past and even less willingness to unpack its effects on the present. In settings with a contested or controversial past, there is a shortage of acknowledgement and almost a 'crisis of memory':[13] a widespread sense of insecurity in relation to how the past interlinks with the present.

In the Calabrian context, there has never been a formalized process of truth and reconciliation. After all, no one ever considered the period of the kidnappings a conflict or a massacre. In Calabria, on the one hand, the history of the kidnappings is 'secured': there is agreement that the kidnappers were 'ndrangheta families – who, in some cases, were put on trial – and that the kidnappings increased in the 1970s and 1980s to benefit said 'ndrangheta clans. On the other hand, a lot is still contested: there are competing interpretations about the legitimacy of the state during the kidnappings; different insights on whether the ransoms were paid and how much was eventually paid and to whom. There are different ideas on the identity of the 'ndrangheta of the time – *was it a fully formed mafia organization or less than that? Was there a brain behind this?* And finally, the degree of the actual involvement of the population – in the villages of Aspromonte, in the industry of kidnappings – is also controversial. A lot has remained unsaid, which is no surprise, considering the degree of misunderstanding of the 'ndrangheta phenomenon and the underestimation of the strength of mafia power in Calabria until the late 2000s.

The politics of memory of the kidnappings is still marshalled in the attempt to secure the past, for example by civil society's – NGOs' – and magistrates' efforts to clarify what happened and to attribute guilt to the 'ndrangheta organization as a whole and not just the single individuals. However, these attempts have more twists and turns than expected, as new truths emerge. Reporters and investigators are still lifting veils from the different stories of kidnappings 30 or 40 years later.[14]

Truth itself, as we know, can get politicized, and truth-seeking can give birth to new conflict.[15]

An unaccomplished acknowledgement and reconciliation process characterizes Calabria, because any kind of truth would be inherently divisive for local communities. *In this context, silence assumes meaning. Yes, the perpetual silence of the mountain.*

The memory of those days of violence simply slipped away. That violence – perhaps because it was self-inflicted or perhaps because it was indirect or perhaps because the victims were often too close to the perpetrators – has remained and still is in the background, as if it doesn't relate to the villages, the people, Aspromonte.

Violence that is not openly acknowledged and dealt with might remain trapped inside, like a quiet stream that grows imperceptibly. Until it becomes normality. A make-believe normality. Violence trapped inside remains like a distant echo, normalized, but it's still violence.[16]

Calabria is a difficult land, it's well-known, *it's normal.*

In Calabria, things will never change, *it's normal.*

In Calabria, politicians, administrators, thinkers, will disappoint, *it's normal.*

In Calabria, trade, commerce, politics, finance, could be hijacked by the mafia, *it's normal.*

Expectations of inadequacy and failures are, in Calabria, *normality.* A form of immutable fatalism that dates back to the Southern Question.[17]

Aspromonte today bears the existence of its violence hidden inside. If visitors still perceive it as an ominous and yet beautiful monster, it's also *normal.*

It's difficult to understand the effects of violence on a territory where fear, blood and tears have wounded many corners.

Memory, however, has different ways to keep trauma alive, even collectively, even when it's hidden. And the make-believe normality is the result of the missing acknowledgement of the past. With acknowledgement, in fact, often comes disidentification – a separation of one's identity – from the territory,[18] which becomes difficult to live in or with. A make-believe normality instead, even if it is a compromise with memory, allows identity to remain unchallenged.

The TV in those days of the late 1980s, early 1990s, was not functioning well. My grandmother and grandfather only had a small one in the house, in the dining room. Often the image was blurry, often only in black and white, the signal was habitually disrupted or not clear. I remember, when I was four or five years old, a woman with a violet jumper on TV, uncombed black hair, the images of her running every day on the news, for days. The Anonima Sequestri ('Kidnappers Anonymous') – that was the name given to the perpetrators at that time – had taken her son. At times my memories are of her holding a poster – with a handwritten message – in what looked like countryside, surrounded by journalists. At times she had chains. She had passion, fiery eyes, sad looks, and she was emotional and powerful. She could not avoid leaving a mark on memories.

That woman talked about her son Cesare, the victim of one of the longest kidnappings in the history of Italy. That woman tried to defeat the *normality* of Calabria; she tried to shake and unearth the heads buried in that denial-removal that still endures.

Madre Coraggio

Sono la mamma di Cesare Casella. Sto aspettando mio figlio da 17 mesi. Cesare deve trovarsi in Aspromonte. Non mi muoverò dalla Calabria finché non mi restituiscono mio figlio Cesare.

I am the mother of Cesare Casella. I have been waiting for 17 months for my son. Cesare must be in Aspromonte. I will not leave Calabria until they give me my Cesare back.

The newspapers at the time reported widely on the trips that Angiolina Montagna made in Calabria in summer 1989. She was coming from Pavia, in Lombardia, where her son Cesare had been kidnapped on 18 January 1988. The previous message was printed on the cardboard she carried around on her Calabrian trips. Written all in capitals, immortalized in a symbolic black and white picture of her at the entrance of San Luca. You can Google it, you'll find it.

My father was gone for days, and my mum remembers how much I was missing him, while I don't remember much. All I knew was that he was in Locri. And at that time, I had never been to Locri. I didn't even know where that was, near, far, why wasn't he coming back at night? Locri was a bad place for me, it kept Dad away.

Madre – Mamma – Coraggio, Mother Bravery, she was called. A tiny woman, with a different accent than women and men in Calabria. Mamma Casella arrived in the region to wear the chains she imagined Cesare wearing and to see the places where he was probably kept, in the depths of the monster mountain.

At that time, I had never been to Locri. I didn't even know where that was, near, far, why wasn't Dad coming back at night? And for how many nights, I cannot quite remember, but I do remember that he brought me back gifts – some clothes, a pair of trousers, which for months remained 'the Locri trousers'.

The first time I went to Locri was also the first time I saw the sun *in the wrong place*; accustomed, as I was, to seeing the sunset on the sea, it felt very strange to have the sun on the water at midday instead and to see it back down behind me, facing the sea, at sunset. I must have been 13 or 14 when I went to Locri, to the seaside, for the first time on the *other* side of the coast of Calabria. And the place looked normal, a bit indolent, yet beautiful, with its rich archaeological heritage.

Mamma Casella arrived in Locri in June 1989. Locri is the municipality where both the church and the tribunal responsible for the territory of San Luca are based. It is also one of the largest villages of the surrounding area, called Locride, even if it barely counts 13,000 people. What she was planning to do was to cry an appeal, an appeal to the 'ndrangheta, an appeal to mothers and fathers, an appeal to the church and an appeal to the state, months after that January 1988 when her 18-year-old son had been taken. In her desperation, journalists – and my father too – found a story to tell, a story to follow; images of her chained to the town hall, images of her visiting San Luca, then Polsi, then Platì. She was knocking on doors, carrying the chains around her neck – *a symbol of her chained son as much as perhaps a symbol of a chained region*. And she addressed mothers – to ask them to feel what she felt – and she also wanted to address the criminal minds and hearts behind the kidnapping of her son.[19]

Powerful images of Angiolina Montagna, Madre Coraggio, when she cries out for help, to the 'good people' of San Luca. Some of those images I remember from TV, as if they were a dream, far away. Some others I have conjured through my father's memories and his tales and videos and images of the time.

There she is in San Luca. Important people in the village heard her plea, and something, maybe, could happen, if only one of the women Mamma Casella was addressing eventually talked to her husband or father, who knows?

In Platì, instead, she met little or no solidarity; the little town received Mamma Coraggio with mistrust, defending its people, too often accused of mafia involvement, and not deserving the bad reputation. People were looking at her, doubtful of her motives as they doubt everyone; *after decades of violence and oppression, can they trust any* forestieri *(outsiders)?*

A young woman caught my father's attention during those days in Platì and his memory has become mine. She was not sure what was happening, she was there temporarily; she was 22 years old, and her parents had moved from Platì to Australia before she was born, over 40 years earlier. 'Do you know what the mafia is, here in Platì?' – my father asks. 'They say there is mafia here in Platì, yes' – she answers shyly – 'I've read about it in Australia, a drug lord, Robert Trimbole in Griffith, was from Platì'. *Remember him from Griffith, in the previous chapter?* This reference would obviously mean something to me much later in life.

From San Luca to Platì and finally to Polsi. Mamma Casella prayed on her knees to the Madonna della Montagna; she knew the 'ndrangheta's rules would not help her; there is no compassion in this mafia, they told her. She could only pray to the Madonna, because the 'ndrangheta worships the Madonna. The newspapers, and the public, were obsessed with this woman, whose tears and chains were louder than any Calabrian tears and chains back then.

'Look, here, at this corner. There is Platì over there, beyond the mountain, here is where they freed Cesare Casella, here in Natile. God, it was so cold that day.' My father's voice, while we were in the car, years later. He was driving a journalist friend somewhere and I just happened to be there. I had never been to Natile, but that was the first time I went to Platì with my father. I must have been 11 or 12 – I had just started secondary school – and Platì looked deserted, almost abandoned. There was no light in the church, how about that? My friend Marie, the one in Australia, told me that there was also no light in the church when she went there in 2017; perhaps it was a coincidence.

The courage of Mamma Casella was not in vain. The kidnappers lowered the ransom request – *after all, the Casellas were not even rich!* – and freed Cesare on 30 January near Natile. A man, Giuseppe Strangio, already sentenced to 27 years' imprisonment for another kidnapping, had started cooperating with investigators. Other kidnappings organized by a group of people from San Luca had gone wrong in the previous months. Freeing Cesare Casella was a way to get rid of a case that – in part because of the media attention – had become too problematic to handle for a group of 'ndranghetisti who were already feeling pressure from the authorities.

Upon release, Cesare seemed almost fine, he seemed to have managed it well; the newspapers of the time even said that he had put on some weight! He had been kept for 743 days, the second longest kidnapping in Italy.

The longest kidnapping, in fact, was that of Carlo Celadon, taken one week after Cesare Casella, on 25 January 1988, also 18 years old at the time. He was released on 5 May 1990, after 831 days and, they say, a payment of around 7 billion lira (€3.5 million). Celadon's was a cruel case with similarities to Casella's – the young age, the northern origin, Aspromonte. However, there are also many differences between them. Celadon was not well fed – he was often left for days without water and food; no cleaning water; mice in the hole with him, biting him and his food. He would count up to 22,000 each day before falling asleep. When they finally freed him, he had lost 30 kilograms and could not even stand properly. He looked like a ghost and could not even speak.

The media focus on Cesare Casella and his Madre Coraggio drew people's attention to Aspromonte; as a result, authorities were questioned, consciences were shaken, and resolutions and answers were demanded. But all this didn't make the lives of kidnapping victims like Carlo – outside that cone of media attention – any better. For them – at least six or seven of them kidnapped in the same months as Cesare – the whole area around their hiding holes and the caves, Aspromonte, the area around Locri (the Locride), was just an endless night without the moon. For Giuseppe Bertolami (taken in Lamezia Terme, in December 1989), the moon never appeared again, as he died while a hostage.[20]

Kidnapping season is over

The kidnappings in Calabria finally stopped when a new law allowed authorities to freeze the bank accounts of the victims' families. Law No. 82 of 1991 provides for the mandatory freezing of assets belonging to the victim, their spouse (also de facto), their relatives or any other person who could be involved in the ransom through a judge's declaration after the public prosecutor's request. Before this law, it was left to each magistrate to decide on similar provisions, case by case, which led to confusion and manipulation of the system. Moreover, centralized policing units were promoted so that investigations wouldn't spread across different forces and authorities, wasting precious time.

Until the new legislation was fully in force in 1993, the kidnappings did not stop completely, and there are surely several reasons for that.[21] In 1992 and 1993, six more kidnappings were carried out, but they were not 'ndrangheta-led.[22]

By the time I went to secondary school, in 1995, the kidnappings were over; they were barely talked about in school, too shameful and too recent to properly discuss. However, my family's experiences, between my father's job and my grandparents' location, had amplified my perceptions about those years. Aged 13, Aspromonte, albeit temporarily, was once more under the spotlight. Another kidnapping victim, Alessandra Sgarella, was being kept hidden in the monster mountain. And that was the 'ndrangheta again. And that time I became much more aware of it all and started asking questions.

Alessandra Sgarella had been taken in Milan in December 1997 and was freed nine months later, in September 1998, in Locri. For her freedom, and notwithstanding the new 1991 law, a ransom seems to have been paid – around 5 billion lira (€2.5 million) – as the documents for the perpetrators' arrest showed. No payment could be tracked; the hypothesis was that the money had been transferred using foreign bank accounts. Eleven people were later convicted of the kidnapping; investigation files show that the perpetrators were disappointed to receive only 5 billion lira, when they had initially asked for 50 and later negotiated for 15 instead.[23]

At the end of June 1998, when investigators closed in on seven affiliates of the Lumbaca clan, from Oppido Mamertina, the situation became tense. That summer Aspromonte went back to what it had been at the end of the 1980s: an impenetrable space that authorities' cars, helicopters and special squads were trying to dominate in order to rescue Alessandra Sgarella. The sirens alerted us to the ongoing search. Everyone agreed at that time – my grandmother most of all – that Aspromonte wasn't safe and I – we – really shouldn't go into the woods alone or when it was approaching sunset. For the whole summer – in between homework and a teenage crush on some boy in the village – there it was, normalization again. It became somewhat *normal* to think that someone – a woman – was hidden in the mountain and that the 'ndrangheta – whatever the 'ndrangheta was for me or anyone at that time – had taken her.

Important clans were involved in the kidnapping of Alessandra Sgarella: affiliates of the clans Perre, Strangio, Papalia, Barbaro and Giorgi, between San Luca and Platì, were indicted and convicted. Apparently, a boss from the Barbaro clan intervened from prison to coordinate the negotiation.[24] These clans' businesses were split between Calabria and Lombardia, just when investigations on the 'ndrangheta in the North of Italy were starting to surface, to finally emerge as an anti-mafia priority in the mid-2000s.[25]

It *felt* different, the Sgarella kidnapping, not only because it was an outlier and happened much later than the other kidnappings, but also because by that time the 'ndrangheta's shapes and forms were much clearer. The process that saw the clans of Aspromonte evolving into a proper criminal organization was on its way to completion, if not already completed. The perception – the knowledge, perhaps – and the fear, at the time of the Sgarella kidnapping, was not only that Aspromonte had been home to atrocities, but that the 'ndrangheta had taken a much more defined form. During a hearing in the Italian Chamber of Deputies that same year,[26] MPs requested clarifications from the justice ministry as to how the Sgarella kidnapping was approached: *was it true that the state had negotiated with the 'ndrangheta? Was it true that Giuseppe Barbaro, boss from Platì under strict prison sentence, handled the liberation from prison? And how to explain the ransom payment? Did the prosecutors know? Could anyone ever explain?* Some of these questions still don't have firm answers.

The kidnapping of Alessandra Sgarella could perhaps be seen as an artificial breakwater in the history of the mafia in Calabria. One of the last acts motivated by the traditional drives of the clans from the mountain, before the 'ndrangheta definitely sets foot on the global stage, or at least before it visibly does so. Careful, though, there is no separation between an old/traditional 'ndrangheta and a new/contemporary one; anyone who says otherwise can say that only for analytical purposes.[27] The 'ndrangheta of the kidnappings is at the same time the 'ndrangheta of 'sacred' rituals and that of power; these traits remain even when the organization fully commits to cross-border or high-end illicit business. The 'ndrangheta remains a conservative force that feeds off the territory. Even when it developed new formulas to protect itself and promote investments, as in the city of Reggio Calabria, as we will see. Even when the clans' alliances change. Even when new coordination structures emerge, and rankings change. The 'ndrangheta – the one of the hinterlands of Reggio Calabria – is protected, still, by the fortress-prison of Aspromonte. Its criminal reputation today is an echo of its reputation back then. There is a *reserve of violence* that the clans can count on today. We see proof of this in the way some clans still manage to engage in extortion by simply whispering words, without explicit threats, intimidating just by being present.[28] This contextualized, situational form of extortion is the product of a collective recollection of the violence that once was, now rooted in the communities. The 'ndrangheta of today is the natural development of the 'ndrangheta of then.

The malleability of memory

The monster mountain was never ominous to me. Even in front of the cross for the kidnapping victims, right up on Zervò from Santa Cristina, the mountain taught me silence, patience and time bending. Hushed mornings and sunny afternoons, quiet nights and slow weekends. The summer in Aspromonte was a dance of faces you didn't know and yet ended up recognizing anyway, year after year. So many people in an infinite series of short movies, where the village was the set and Aspromonte was the background.

I had brought a bicycle with me from the city; it was the first bike I had bought with my own (saved) money. It was a mountain bike, and it stayed at my grandparents' house for two decades. A symbol of summer, of things that never really changed in that village, for me. It was normal – even if I only did it for two or three months per year – to bike up in the mountain, stopping for the usual flock of sheep and the lonely, slow cows. No one touched or bothered the cows, they were 'sacred' – they still are; they might belong to who-knows-who. 'If you meet a cow in the woods, don't be scared, let her cross your path; don't cross theirs.' And the familiar voice of my grandmother finishing that phrase, as many others, with 'you never know who could be watching'! 'Where, in the mountain?' I would ask, not that convinced. 'Everywhere, *bella mia*, the mountain has eyes everywhere!'

The cows represent opulence. I wonder now whether the holiness of those cows also relates to the relationship that part of the region has with meat. *Yes, meat.* Some of the juiciest sausages I have tasted came from Aspromonte. The calves that are sacrificed to the Madonna in Polsi are chosen from among the best, the plumpest calves the family owns – only the best should be offered to the Madonna. My grandmother's words, again. She would often tell me – a bit emotional and a bit nostalgic – about her father, who was relatively well off, because he was a butcher: 'We always had meat, you know?' And that meant they were richer than others.

The emotional distance I now yearn for to analytically approach this subject is often in contrast with the emotional attachment needed to embrace my memories and dig deeper into the subject.

A famous report on the 'ndrangheta redacted by the Parliamentary Antimafia Commission in 2008 says that 'in Santa Cristina d'Aspromonte two families are active, Madafferi [or Madaffari] and Papalia'.[29] Since these are the surnames of my grandmother and grandfather, these two lines stood out for me when I first read them. *What did that mean? That I was close – within, around – mafia families and I never knew? The village has less than 1,000 people!* Sure, I had heard stories dating back to the 1930s about my grandfather's family; someone had confessed to an attempted murder charge to spare his brother from further retaliation in a farmers' feud. Awkward comments I heard made by some relatives on the connections with people in Platì with dubious reputations. And I had wondered why, at the funeral of a member of my grandmother's family, the church was so packed. People had come from so many different places, yet the dead relative was senile and hadn't been able to speak properly for years.

Some branches of these families had been in the village for a long time, and they were more or less prosperous families. *Did their wealth and old lineage bring them more respect than others? Would that make some of their members the natural interlocutors of criminal powers, or did they become criminal powers themselves due to their social prestige?*

Not much, after all, in my childhood in Aspromonte speaks of 'mafia'. The people in and around my family, close or distant relatives, Mum's cousins, their wives, children, uncles, aunties, Grandma's and Grandpa's brothers and sisters and families, all lived unassuming lives, more or less well off, average for the place, their lives more or less revealed to others, as it happens in small villages. Many of them, especially of my grandmother's generation, had never left the village, except to go to nearby villages. Some had gone – maybe only once in their lifetime – to visit relatives far away, sometimes very far away, in Australia or Lamerica![30] Every summer, the village would welcome its many migrants, from Australia, Canada, the United States. They looked like celebrities, the foreigners; they walked the streets with a flair of extravaganza. And whatever *u zi Ciccu* (Uncle Cicco) or *a za Lina* (Aunt Lina) were doing in Australia or America was not really of interest. Everyone was just happy to hear stories about where they lived, how they were, and how their children and grandchildren were. I knew who they were only because Grandma would send me to strangers' houses (*strangers to me*) to bring them coffee, sugar or even candies as a welcome gift, as a 'remember-me' token.

'Who do you belong to, little girl?' – the question was asked at least 30 times each summer, by various people. *A cu apparteni?*

'I am the granddaughter of Mimma Madaffari and Bruno Papalia, daughter of Sisa, not the one in America, the one in Cosenza!' Like a litany. 'Grandma says hi and sends you this [coffee, sugar, candies].'

People, families, had lived next to one another for decades and yet they still gave each other the '*voi*', the formal 'you' plural that in Calabria is a sign of respect; people knew little of each other, even when they were family, even if everyone was somehow connected to the neighbours and the rest of the village by either blood or endogamy. Conversations were about everything but intimate topics; mostly they told each other stories about family members who lived far away; news arrived through letters, phone calls, postcards. Everyone was very eager to learn what was happening to migrants far away. Being reserved and not displaying your family or personal business outside the house has always been praised as a virtue there. It's difficult to explain how close and yet how distant individuals and families looked to me back then. It's difficult to analyse ex post something that you were not really collecting data on.

And what about the mafia?

The 'ndrangheta was, back then, distant and imperceptible, probably because it was so close and everywhere around us. One might wonder how people, *good* people (as opposed to *bad* mafiosi), can tolerate mafia in their territories, especially when mafia kills and tortures as the 'ndrangheta clans did.

Some might wonder to what extent having mafia businesses nearby might eventually turn out to be *convenient* for a village. Mafias do, after all, bring protection and some sort of order:[31] that seems to be the only rational explanation for any degree of tolerance. *When mafias are around you can leave your door open, the car with the keys inside, the bike unlocked. Isn't that convenient?* But the social costs of protection and order might eventually be higher than they appear, in terms of social control and expectations on the community. A 'debt of security' towards these actors develops within the community. Someone will owe *them* something, and this unbalances social relations.

It has always been easy – too easy – to say that the 'ndrangheta's strength is in blood ties: this is why surnames do mean something in this criminal system, why I must wonder about the surnames in my family. However, it is difficult to avoid approximations; they distort the reality of those territories with pre-made judgements around blood ties and surnames. Let's not forget that in big families, such as those in many villages in Aspromonte, surnames are often just ascriptive ties: just an objective link between people. Very much like my surname links me to the many Sergis of Australia, good or bad. The risk of deforming this ascriptive tie into prescriptive data, indicating '*mafiosity*', is real and concerning.

And yes, the village protects as much as it entraps.[32] The proximity that geography forces on people is mixed with the impossibility or unwillingness to move elsewhere. The distance from one another and the non-involvement with neighbours' and families' lives turns into a survival skill. It's not that people don't want to see or that they tolerate the mafia, it's just that it is one thing to *know* (maybe see someone getting arrested) and another thing to *guess*. Guessing can hurt people, the same people you share your territory with, your blood, your communal existence, your daily survival. *Omertà* is not only intentionally aiding and abetting crime; at times it's just doing the best you can.

The village protects and quells tensions.

When the 'ndrangheta finally claimed its name and identity through the 1990s, the violence and the torture of the kidnappings got too close – 20 to 30 minutes on foot – to the village to be ignored. My father told me that one of the kidnapped did knock at my grandma's door once; she sent him to the police. She knew who that was. The suspicion that this type of criminality was not happening far away or elsewhere but was already in people's houses and in local families was becoming a certainty.

How else would you survive your daily life if not by crafting a mix between denial of what might hurt you and a renewed trust in what you feel you know?

What you know is what is close and what is in sight. What you know is the village and its pre-negotiated and unspoken boundaries. What you know is what protects you. What if you had a suspicion that [any name] was involved in a kidnapping? You knew him as a kid … and he was a good kid!

It's difficult, yes, to overcome these judgements in the enclaves of these villages. Incidentally, this can indeed become full-blown *omertà*, when it turns into the inability or unwillingness to denounce, with the desire to protect criminal activities.

It is difficult to disentangle the individual memories of a distant past in my childhood from the memories acquired later as an adult. Indeed, information available to us today about past events can not only trigger memory but can also change the way we store our own memory.[33] Memory is fragile and error-prone; it is a reconstructive process, inaccurate and distorted, at times straight up wrong. But the reconstructive nature of memory supports the development of self-identity; its *malleability* can also transform initially disparate reminiscences of various people into full recollections shared across different individuals. This is also why autobiographical memories are firstly reconstructed to be unique – distinct – from other people's memories but, at the same time, converge with those of others because of social interactions. Collective memories, therefore, are a combination of individual memories shared thanks to several socio-psychological processes.

My memories of the 1990s in Aspromonte are not just mine; indeed, if they were just mine, they would not be sufficiently specific or rich to turn into stories. Merged into the collective memory of my family, and more broadly of my region, my individual fragmented memories can be reconstructed and shared to become part of the collective narrative of places and times I refer to in this chapter.

★★★

During the 2015 trip with Nick, the Australian journalist, I took a picture in front of the cross in Zervò that later became the cover of my monograph.[34] It is a beautiful shot of the sunset over Aspromonte, Oppido and Platì down the valley, San Luca in the corner, Santa Cristina on the horizon. We stayed up there for hours waiting to shoot that pink and red sunset. The intellectual effort I made on that occasion was intense. I wasn't trying to explain Aspromonte to them – I wasn't and am not the best person to do that, from both a knowledge and a memory perspective. I don't know enough about the place, and I don't recall enough about the 1980s and 1990s to be a witness to mafia events. Rather, I found myself trying to have them *feel* the intensity of my experience as a child; shared memories I had gained as an adult, about those places, emerged forcefully. Explaining the kidnappings as I remember *feeling* them, *growing* to know about them. My father's recollections, writings of the time and even more recent studies enriched the stories I told them and helped me reframe both memory and analysis.

The monster mountain was never an ominous monster to me. Finding a way to explain why that is the case to anyone who saw or read of the monstrosity, the violence, the bloodshed in that mountain, has been the journey I have embarked upon since that day in Zervò. I did not quite know then that my Australian journey had also actually taken a forceful turn that day in Calabria.

At the centre of the Australian documentary production, as I already mentioned, was a man in Melbourne whose surname, Madafferi, brought me right back to the mountains and to my grandmother and the village.

From St Kilda to Kings Cross

Sydney Kings Cross

There are songs that brand entire experiences or entire periods of your life. For me, in Sydney, that song was 'From St Kilda to Kings Cross',[1] by Australian songwriter Paul Kelly. One of those songs everyone seems to know in Australia. And the lyrics I can still recollect: 'From St Kilda to Kings Cross is thirteen hours on a bus | I pressed my face against the glass And watched the white lines rushing past | And all around me felt like all inside me | And my body left me and my soul went running.' This is the song I listened to the first time I went there. And at the moment when I realized that Sydney never quite conquered my heart.

Unlike Paul Kelly, the first time I went to Sydney, it was by train and not by bus, from Canberra. It was October 2015 and I had been in Canberra for a week or so. A 'week or so' in Canberra equals three months. I don't get that city. Large avenues, few cars, many shopping malls, the smallest city centre ever, hidden in between malls, no one around, everyone inside massive buildings, shops, houses. *Is this how Australia is run?* For three days I couldn't even find a proper restaurant because I was living in the southern part of the city, far away from what they call the Civic Centre. You cannot properly walk in Canberra; the roads are meant for cars. It is all large white buildings immersed in their own green lawns. Yes, Australia's Capital Territory is white and green. Canberra was the first city in Australia I landed in, the first Australian city I ever visited. And I will never forget it, because it gave me the impression that will long live inside me: a first impression about Australia, as a white, green and large land, some sort of quiet place, but with a secret.

Little did I know then that they would make a TV series about the underworld of politics in Canberra precisely called the Secret City. Go figure.

How to get to Sydney from Canberra on a day trip? Easy, on a coach that takes you there in around four hours. Seemed like a simple instruction, if only it wasn't so complicated to get to the bus station early Saturday morning. It was difficult not to notice the train station in front of the hotel where I was staying. Being European, I am bound to think that taking the train could be the simplest solution. *There must be a train.* It's basically as far as London to Edinburgh or Milan to Rome. Great, I'll walk into the train station; online things were confusing for some reason.

Is there a train to Sydney, and back, on Saturday? Canberra train station. A capital city train station. On a Friday afternoon, completely empty. A sales assistant behind a shining orange and white counter smiles and asks me whether I need help. Yes, I do. 'I'd like a return trip to Sydney for tomorrow, Sydney Kings Cross.' I chuckle as Kings Cross to me remains London King's Cross; I had only recently learned Kings Cross is an important Sydney station. The sales assistant stares at me and says: 'Are you sure? You know there are direct buses to get to Sydney from the Civic Centre? And flights?' 'Yes, I know, but I'd like to take the train.' 'The train is not direct, and it takes four hours and a half.' 'Do I have to change somewhere?' 'Yes, in Sydney Central if you want to get to Kings Cross ... but the train stops everywhere in the middle, no one takes the train from here to Sydney ... are you sure?'

I did take the train, notwithstanding the disbelief of the sales assistant; it was much cheaper than the coach. *What?* Coming from England, where train fares are so high, that was a weird thing.

Queanbeyan
Bungendore
Tarago
Goulburn
Bundanoon
Moss Vale
Bowral
Mittagong
Campbelltown
and Sydney Central.

Not that many stops after all, on a train that was half-empty and had a configuration that made it look like we were travelling during the 1950s. Those stops and the countryside where the train cut through. So much Australia, in one single train ride, in between the most English heritage – the little covered stations, straight out of the Victorian period – to the beautiful and funny-sounding aboriginal names of some of the towns. So much Australia, in between past, super past and present.

Once again, that song from Paul Kelly in my head:[2] 'Have you ever seen Kings Cross when the rain is falling soft? | And if the rain don't fall too hard | Everything shines just like a postcard | Everything goes on just the same.' I could not forget that first trip to Sydney, which was for leisure and not for work. The first time one sees Sydney Harbour, the Opera and the promenade opposite. No, that cannot be forgotten. You feel like *all around is all inside you*, as the song says. All that water and the bridge, monumental; that is what you feel, *monumental*.

But Sydney never quite conquered my heart.

Power clubs

When, almost two years later in August 2017, I managed to spend more time in Sydney, for research, I remember how I sat silently the first night in the dark blue of Sydney Harbour. An eerie night, windy and dark. A deep blue that I had never seen in a city. In a way, feeling out of place made the air feel more ominous than it was. I woke up in my hotel room the next morning, in the sticky, humid weather of a summer that wasn't supposed to be summer, ready to meet with my friend Marie and roam the Italian neighbourhoods of Sydney: Fairfield and, of course, Leichhardt (the official 'Little Italy') and Bossley Park. There is, as I understood it, a variety of so-called little Italies in Sydney, like Five Docks and Haberfield: the variety of neighbourhoods claiming the title perhaps shows the vivacity of the city's urban mobilization. On the one hand, Italians used to be concentrated in certain neighbourhoods; on the other hand, they were, they are, everywhere.

The Club Marconi in Bossley Park was one of my target destinations. I lost A$10 in the slot machines the first time I went there. And, in front of a beer while playing briscola, I talked to a man who had migrated from Veneto the second time around; that went better. A very nice man, Mario: he let me win.

The Club Marconi is an impressive building; it is green, yellow, blue, white and red. It hosts a soccer club and provides social entertainment for its members. It has a reputation in the suburban context of Sydney for its cosmopolitan staff and its link with the Marconi Stallions football club. It has been argued that 'Marconi's promotion of modern ideals of leisure, recreation, and community involvement contributed to its easy incorporation into the suburban context'.[3] And that building shows exactly that. Australian overall, but *speaking* Italian, nevertheless.

The Club Marconi historically has been immersed in the Italian community with money and power. When ethnic links meet enterprise, I learned in Australia, power is likely to last longer. In my 'ndrangheta research in Australia, the names of various individuals gravitating around the Marconi club have appeared. Not necessarily 'ndrangheta-related, not at all, but it's interesting that they have come out while researching mafias. There is a fine – dangerous – line between ethnic ties and mafia ties, always.

Beware, reader, what follows is a very intricate set of links and medleys of names and locations, Australian and Calabrian. It made my head spin; it might make yours spin too.

A former president of the Club Marconi, Antonio 'Tony' Labbozzetta, for example, was mentioned in a newspaper article in 2009.[4] The investigation sustained that in late 2003, three Italian businessman, Pat Sergi – *yes, another Sergi!* – Tony Labbozzetta and Nick Scali, engaged in a campaign, with politicians and within the Italian community, to assist Francesco 'Frank' Madafferi to obtain a visa, apparently in exchange for political donations to the Liberal Party. Frank had been in Australia since 1989; his brother Tony had arrived much earlier. Frank had overstayed his visa, married and had children; in the mid-1990s his immigration status was eventually questioned. In Italy he was expected to serve prison time after a criminal career that had eventually led him to escape abroad. Investigative journalists offered even more details on these events in a 90-minute documentary in 2015 by Four Corners/Fairfax Media.[5]

Now, remember what I wrote in the previous chapter, about the trip with Australian journalists who were following the story of a man who had moved from Aspromonte to Melbourne? That was the documentary and that man was Frank Madafferi. When he was still in Calabria, Frank had been involved in investigations related to a kidnapping; in 2008 he was arrested in Australia and in 2014 he was sentenced for drug trafficking in Victoria. The Australian journalists I met in Calabria in 2015 were there to follow this individual and his family. The investigation focused mostly on the Melbourne side of the story – the importation of drugs and the 'ndrangheta links in the criminal syndicate. There was also a Sydney component to the story.

It is all very intricate in Sydney, when politics meets ethnic groups and when there is a fine line between unethical behaviour, clientelism, favours, corruption and friendship. Things are clearly not easy to unpack and can be manipulated when you play at very high levels in the community.

Tony Labbozzetta, Pat Sergi and Nick Scali are indeed often mentioned together in the news as a powerful trio of Italian businessmen in NSW – friends or colleagues – who, at specific points, shared – allegedly – some interests: obtaining the visa for Francesco Madafferi; doing business together for charities and social causes; supporting, also through opaque circuits of donations, the Liberal Party. Union is strength and strength might lead to 'unchecked' privileges, and then to abuse.

In 1999, a manager of the Club Marconi,[6] Peter, declared that, during a hearing by the Liquor Administration Board, he received threats, probably aimed at discouraging him from talking to the board. The board was investigating matters concerning the Club Marconi and Mr Labbozzetta. His assistant manager, Forrest, had also been attacked.

'Take what happened to Forrest as a warning and don't rock the boat. It could be unhealthy, keep your mouth shut, and give the liquor people nothing.'

And then the man holding a gun said:

'We like you Peter, we don't like anything to happen to you. Be careful what you say to the Liquor Administration Board.'[7]

Peter initially did report this to the police but eventually he was unwilling to identify who made the threats, as he knew him to be a close friend of Labbozzetta, another Calabrian man named Quattrone. 'Better to resign than to upset these Calabrians.'

Mr Labbozzetta himself was eventually banned for a short while from the Marconi Club. This followed a judgement.[8] He had derived a benefit from the club, a benefit that was not offered equally to other members, which included some tangible things – inaccurate books and accounts, for example – but also intangible things: the ability to approve building contracts without calling for tenders; gifts to the General Secretary of the Federation of International Football Associations (FIFA); and serving club liquors outside the premises of the club.

And so what? While I was in Sydney this name, or rather surname, Labbozzetta, kept popping up. And so did the people around him and around the Marconi Club. There was a grip around that club and its Italian/Calabrian membership that kept pushing me to ask questions.

Mr Labbozzetta himself spoke out after a 2009 portrayal of him and his group of friends came out (including Pat and Domenic Sergi, and Roy Spagnolo, from Griffith) following the news about the visa lobbying for Frank Madafferi.

> When it comes to anything to do with Italians ... It seems if your name ends in an i, e, o, or a, then you must be a criminal [...] What is happening is disgusting, offensive, almost criminal. It is wog bashing, simple as that. We are back to the bad old days when people looked down on Italians in this country, called us awful names.[9]

Some of Mr Labbozzetta's relatives were – apparently – involved in mafia-related activities. In particular, a combined reading of an Australian police intelligence document of the mid-1990s with an intelligence note from the Italian anti-mafia district prosecutors in Reggio Calabria gives an interesting set of details: a relative of Mr Labbozzetta, also living in NSW, together with a cousin, living in Reggio Calabria, are said, for example, to have set up two travel agencies, one in Reggio and one in Western Sydney. These agencies were allegedly also used in the 1990s to arrange travel to and from Italy, facilitating drug trafficking for the Alvaro and Italiano clans, among others, operating in Calabria and Australia. The Alvaro clan and the Italiano clan are very well-known clans in Calabria, operating in Delianuova, Sant'Eufemia d'Aspromonte and Sinopoli. According to documents, Agostino and Carmelo, two cousins of Tony, who married within the Alvaro family, had been accused of conspiracy to sell drugs along with others in the Alvaro clan in South Australia.

Certainly, one doesn't choose one's family, that goes without saying, and there is no guilt in having relatives convicted for crimes. But the intricacy of certain connections sometimes makes it very difficult to appreciate – and remember – boundaries. In the details shared by the Italian police on family ties, mafia connections and links of a dubious nature across Italy and Australia, there are also apparent connections with people in Canada in this case. Additionally, there is a note that the director of one of the two travel agencies – Frank, the one in Reggio Calabria – is still an Australian citizen and used to act as special ethnic adviser for former NSW minister Eric Bedford. Frank also worked closely on immigration matters with the late federal immigration minister Al Grassby, who was suspected of doing favours for mafia families in Griffith.[10] Frank allegedly travelled to Italy with Grassby on several occasions and apparently lobbied on behalf of several Italians who had been denied visas to enter Australia. From politics to travel agencies – *phenomenal versatility, it would seem.*

Oh, and the travel agency in Cabramatta, Sydney, was also curiously called *Marconi*, like the Club. *Wheel of names!*

Pat Sergi, a property developer in Fairfield, was said to have been a party to this intercontinental travel agency arrangement. Mentioned in the Woodward Royal Commission as being part of Robert Trimboli's Griffith drug network, he apparently chose to flee the country using an airline ticket under a false name obtained from the travel agency of Mr Labbozzetta's family in NSW.

Yes, indeed, another Sergi. In this case, we have a person who was – in his lifetime – awarded an Order of Australia *and* named as a money launderer – buying and selling properties to launder the proceeds of crime for the Griffith mafia clans. A cousin of Tony Sergi, from the winery in Griffith, and married into the Trimboli family, Pat's friendships with politicians and businessmen have been under scrutiny on various occasions.[11]

Another man, Nicodemo (Nick) Scali, is mentioned in regard to the political donations and the scandal over the visa for Madafferi. Italian authorities were also interested in him for an alleged attempt in 2008 to corrupt an Australian-Italian politician with a A$3 million bribe on behalf of former Italian premier Silvio Berlusconi's party.[12] The investigation was then archived. The Italian President of the Republic, Carlo Azeglio Ciampi, in 2005 nominated Scali for an award as a 'prestigious Calabrian abroad'.

I heard a lot about Mr Scali while in Sydney, where he is well known as the founder of Nick Scali Furniture – one of Australia's largest importers of premium furniture, now under family management. He is also from

Calabria – from a tiny village named San Martino di Taurianova, in Aspromonte; there doesn't seem to be any obvious – open, direct – evidence of a mafia connection for him. Scali has been investigated in Operation Credo by the Independent Commission of Anti-Corruption (ICAC) in NSW, for suspicious political donations in 2014/2015.[13] The news of his dinners with politicians and developers – including Pat Sergi – is in the public domain.[14]

Operation Credo by ICAC involved another member of the Club Marconi, Joseph (Joe) Tripodi, a Fairfield MP. Also from a Calabrian migrant family, Mr Tripodi became of interest to ICAC and to the courts on a number of occasions. For example, in 2017 ICAC recommended charges of misconduct in public office against Tripodi (which did not proceed any further).[15] ICAC found that Mr Tripodi had engaged in seriously corrupt conduct as he used his ministerial position to try to award a government water contract that would financially benefit the Obeid family.[16]

Notably, his friendships with Tony Labbozzetta, Pat Sergi and Nick Scali were also scrutinized on different occasions. For example, between 1996 and 2000, when he was an up-and-coming NSW Labour MP, he had shares in Sergi's Westside Property Developments, which bought and sold government land. Famously, in his inaugural speech in 1996, Mr Tripodi praised Mr Sergi as a 'friend to keep for life'.[17] They were all involved, somehow, in the proceedings related to a 'feud over a dilapidated one-room club', which was 'engulfing prominent members of Sydney's Italian community', as reported by the *Sydney Morning Herald* in 2012.[18] The dilapidated one-room club in question was the Calabria Community Club, in a case that ended in front of the NSW Supreme Court.[19]

Now, the case was complicated. Obviously, it caught my attention because of the involvement of the Calabrian community. And indeed, the usual group of Calabrians was there. The club had, at the time of the events, fewer than 100 members, including, of course, Nick Scali, Pat Sergi and Tony Labbozzetta.

A Google search revealed that the Calabria Community Club was still operational in Fairfield, Western Sydney. Its president, in late 2021, was Rocco Leonello. In the case of almost ten years ago, he was siding with a Mr Joe Giglio (still on the board, too) and had the support of Mr Tripodi, for whom he had previously worked as a ministerial staffer. Against them was property developer Pat Carbone, also of Calabrian origin, who was backed by Tony Labbozzetta and Nick Scali. The controversy was around a potential A\$200 million rezoning proposal that had led to the value of the club's land increasing tenfold and a A\$100 million property development funding deal being on the table.

Mr Tripodi was not a member of the club at the time, nor was he directly involved in the story, except that Mr Carbone said that Tripodi was indeed the puppeteer – the 'shadow director' behind it all.

The court heard of a set of back-door arrangements, informal loans and lies following the rezoning of the club and the funding deal in favour of two 'friends'. Two Vietnamese businessmen were put in charge of the redevelopment of the club, and Mr Carbone was thrown off the board. Mr Carbone, at the time, spoke out against Mr Leonello's plan to finance the investment and for that, he claimed, he was distanced from the board. While all this was happening, Mr Tripodi allegedly intervened to persuade him to approve the deal, even if it was a 'shit deal', to please the board.

But the proceedings were dismissed, notwithstanding the alleged secret and urgent nature of the politics around the deals finalized by Mr Leonello and notwithstanding the exclusion of Mr Carbone from the affairs of the club, which was accepted as unlawful. It proved difficult, eventually, to demonstrate that Mr Leonello, under the alleged guidance of Mr Tripodi, had acted out of private interest.

> An attempt was being made to paint Mr Tripodi as some kind of puppeteer who manipulated the affairs of the Club. No more was established than that Mr Tripodi – who by the time of these events had left Parliament – was a respected figure in the relevant community, to whom many – on both sides – resorted for advice. It is only fair to Mr Tripodi to say that there was not the slightest evidence of any impropriety on his part.[20]

And with this soft caress – that to many could almost sound like a description of many old respectable men of honour – the Supreme Court concluded its judgement.

While this case was still under judgement, the newspapers reported tensions and back-stabbing as voting for the board of the club approached in 2013.

'You are not even Calabrian!' shouted supporters of Mr Leonello to Peter Jones, Mr Carbone's adviser.

'I am Sicilian!' he replied. But he was lying, he was not even Italian! Perhaps he thought that Sicilian meant something … *more.*

Among those elected to the board, then-vice president Filippo Occhiuto proposed the (successful) nomination of Antonio Rizzotto, who was 80 years old at the time. Mr Rizzotto and his co-accused Antonio Calabria, a Griffith farmer, were released from jail in 1999 after serving six years for managing a drug crop worth A$8 million on an isolated property near Cobar. A very interesting mix of men in the Calabrian community, and a more direct reference back to the 'ndrangheta, one of the very few.

As already mentioned , Mr Tripodi was not a member of the Calabria Club. He was, however, more than just a member of the Club Marconi. The proceedings regarding the Calabria Club went on roughly at the same time as his attempt to become president of the Club Marconi.

'Make Marconi "first again"' – that was the slogan for his candidacy.

'Make Marconi "first again" and let's cut waiting times for pizzas, coffees, and gelato.'

His priorities were clear, but the impact of the Supreme Court case did perhaps affect his candidacy. Tripodi lost by 681 votes to 471, with Vince Foti winning the presidency. Foti, who is from Sinopoli, in the core of Aspromonte, is another Calabrian success story in Australia. He never lost sight of his birthplace either, as we will see later when we move the narration to the city of Reggio Calabria. More problems arose for Foti in 2021 when a former CEO of the Marconi Club, Tony Zappia, another Italian–Calabrian sounding name, was involved in a strange case of payments authorized from the club to pay for non-existent services, with a suspicion of self-laundering.[21]

How did I even get to all of this? What a phenomenal train of thought, leading … nowhere? I remember stopping at some point while walking around Leichhardt, after another day of circling newspaper articles, reading court documents, underlining the same names over and over again.

How did I end up here? And what does this have to do with the 'ndrangheta? Sure, there are some dubious, tenuous connections, dated and limited, and so what? What am I seeing here?

I had lost it.

Once again, I had started chasing names and connections; I found what seemed to be *chambers* of power, but I had completely lost my research object.

And all around me felt like all inside me, as Paul Kelly would sing.

Calabrian claustrophobia

'At some point they all start to be called Joe.'

At the table in a large room of a Sydney office, during a meeting with federal police, NSW police and other institutions, I was surrounded by a group of people – analysts, investigators – who all had a lot of experience and interest in my field of research.

'At some point some of them [clan (sur)name] start to be called Joe. Joe [surname]. Even if until the day before they were called Pasquale or Rocco or Domenico.'

'It could be a sign of respect', I hear myself say. 'After all Giuseppe, Joe, was the old *capo-bastone*, the family's head.'

That meeting came after a week spent in Sydney, after travels and chats at the Marconi Club, and too many newspaper articles from decades ago.

Everything had started pointing back to Griffith again, directly or indirectly. I made some sense of it only later when I was back in Melbourne.

Drug traffickers and money launderers on one side: that was the easy part, the criminal enterprise. But, on the other side, what Sydney left me with was mostly a claustrophobic circle of people, Calabrians, prominent members of the Italian community, businessmen of the western suburbs of the city, gravitating around local politics.

How much of what I discussed then, how much of what I was reading, was actually part of my research? What was background only? What was just irrelevant for a criminological analysis of the 'ndrangheta in contemporary Australia?

A troubling question started pounding in my head. *Was I also playing into some sort of stigmatization of Calabrians? News of alleged misconduct, relationships that are based on favouritism, instrumental and natural friendships, ethnic solidarity, business logic, might not be 'mafia' after all?*

The 'ndrangheta was almost never there. And yet it was always in the background, somewhere far behind, forgotten, popping out here and there but not too prominently. And beyond the occasional link to the drugs – through someone's cousin, brother, second-degree uncle – what exactly was all this about? Sure, there were references to what used to be the normality of a Griffith-based portion of the Calabrian community – involved in organized crime in the roaring 1970s and 1980s. *But wasn't it true that many of the Calabrian individuals named in the news in Sydney had indeed left their past, their Calabrian heritage and 'problematic' families behind? And even if that was only people's perception, and not the truth, wasn't that something to consider anyway?*

'Without doubt Pat Sergi is one of the most remarkable people I have ever met. His selfless contribution is certainly worthy of the recognition and thanks of the NSW Parliament.'[22] By 1997, when former NSW minister Reba Meagher said these words, many had forgotten that Mr Sergi had apparently lied to the Woodward Commission, 20 years earlier, about the origin of the funds he had used to buy properties in Fairfield and his family links with Sergi and Trimboli.

But indeed, one can leave the past behind.

The problem with the 'ndrangheta is precisely that it never really dies; it adapts and modifies just as its culture of origin does. It appears as a collective subject that promotes a subcultural model of norms, values, beliefs, behaviours, and that feeds into, and twists, its culture of reference. The 'ndrangheta's quintessential feature is to create networks, based on gratitude and trust and voluntary subjection to a recognized boss or leader. *Just do one favour, or two, just make 'friends', you never know when you'll need to cash in on one favour and who you are going to need.*

In Sydney, I took notes on random things that popped into my head. I felt surrounded, crushed at times, by Calabrian *flavours* and *references*: places of origin, names of villages, family surnames, marriages, ethnic bonds, families' stories of migration, stories of success or failure, cultural traditions, long-lost traditions. I left Sydney feeling a strange mix of pride – for my Calabrian roots – and mistrust, too.

But something was off. As if something was lurking behind the walls of a dressed-up 'normality'.

Calabria is full of proverbs, sayings from popular culture, that many Calabrians still use to express their thoughts in relation to recurring situations in life.

Some proverbs came to my mind one night in Sydney while I was having dinner in the hotel; things that my Nonna Mimma used to say to me or that I heard while growing up. I noted them down; they somehow resonated with what I was reading and learning about Australian-Calabrian circles. There are many ways to twist culture.

> *Mentiti cui megghju i tia e fanci i spisi.*
> *Go with those who are better than you and pay for them.*
> There is always something to gain by advancing favours to those
> 'higher' than you.

This could be twisted as favouritism, even clientelism, trafficking of favours, corruption and particularism.

> *Aundi cantanu tanti galli, 'un fa mai juarnu.*
> *Where many cocks sing, nothing gets done.*
> If there are too many people willing to lead, nothing gets done.

This expresses the need for strong leadership.

> *'A chiavi d'oru japri 'i porti 'i bbronzu.*
> *The golden key opens doors made of bronze.*
> There is no door that cannot be opened, with the right amount
> of 'gold'.

The 'golden key' might not be the most obvious one, but there is always a way in.

> *A carni cchiù ccara si 'ccatta, cchiù dduci si mangia.*
> *The more expensive the meat, the sweeter it tastes.*
> Investing in something expensive leads to more satisfaction.

The greed for something expensive might justify unethical practices.

> *'Nda vucca chiusa non ci caca musca.*
> *In a shut mouth no fly can shit.*
> It's better to keep your mouth shut.

Silence can hurt as much as it can protect.

Cu' non si faci l'affari soi ca lanterna va cercandu guai.
Whoever doesn't mind their own business is seeking trouble with a lantern.
Whoever doesn't mind their own business is asking for trouble.

Yes, silence can hurt as much as it protects.

Seeking self-improvement by making the right friends; offering people 'above you' (or perceived as such) unrequested support 'in advance', by being 'at one's disposal' [in Italy, the *'messa a disposizione'* is considered by the Supreme Court as conduct akin to affiliation to the 'ndrangheta[23]]; doing favours and playing through servitude will benefit you in the long term; investing in risky businesses leads to more enjoyable results; working well together with others requires clear leadership; keep your mouth shut and don't go looking for trouble. All of this can be part of some Calabrians' mindset (and the 'ndrangheta's too), enough to generate proverbs; some of these things I saw in the stories in front of me.

Was I reading too much into things? Am I still?

The Sydney trip made it even more obvious that I needed to return to Calabria, its composite culture, its educational values, the few discernible traits of its shared mentality, even knowing how much of what we call 'culture' is impossible to pin down and generalize. I consulted the work of anthropologists such as Fortunata Piselli, and historians such as Piero Bevilacqua, and their analyses of Calabrian villages, emigration, social relations and the mental frameworks of different generations of Calabrians. This is necessary, I believe, to understand the roots of the social behaviours that made up – still do – Calabrian self-identities; to question how these self-identities could be preserved abroad and whether – or rather, to what extent – they still shape and influence relations in the migrant community. And eventually feed a criminal organization and its formal or informal structures.

Ethnic enclaves, machine politics and ethnic entrepreneurship were the concepts spinning in my head as I tried to make sense of what I had learned about Sydney and especially about Fairfield, one of Sydney's western suburbs. After all, it was Fairfield, and not Griffith strangely, that was primarily known as the New Platì in the Italian chronicles of the 1980s.[24] Fairfield is still today the twin town of Platì, as said.

Migrant communities have different needs when they arrive at a destination, primarily economic subsistence and social identity. Social identity is the concept of the self in the social space – stretched between the place of arrival and the place of origin.[25] Long-distance migration – such as from Calabria to Australia – often weakens social bonds with one's culture and place of origin.[26] Migrant groups either fully assimilate with the host population or form hybrid, plural, ethnic enclaves. These enclaves, which often concentrate in, or otherwise connect to, specific geographical areas (in our case Fairfield), are based on an individual's economic base and group identity. Basically, the perpetuation of social bonds – which are the basis of a group's identity – is tied to economic subsistence. Being Calabrian – and choosing to belong to a group that places Calabrians within a trusted circle – provides benefits from an economic perspective: people will support each other, use each other's services and products, vouch for each other. The economy is *embedded* in concrete social relations.[27] Those economic benefits perpetuate social bonds and might eventually facilitate further social relationships, including political alliances.

There is nothing inherently wrong with this, of course.

However, if an ethnic group comes to depend on a restricted few for their economic livelihood or progress, the ethnic enclave will tend to preserve old patterns of behaviour for longer. This could happen, for example, through favouritism and exchanges of favours; elite business deals; abuse of trust and power; monopolistic control over commerce and trade within the ethnic community; or even corruption to benefit those restricted few. It could be that the restricted few want to actively promote those behaviours and patterns to reinforce their position in the community. Among these patterns could be mafia-type behaviours – use of intimidation, systemic corruption and others – naturally promoting favouritism in social exchanges.

It is not difficult to see how such spaces of ethnic self-identity prosper in line with ethnic political machines. Self-identities in the social space, based on shared origin and solidarity, can, in fact, also build and reinforce political machines. Political machines, especially in urban contexts and through social clubs – like the Marconi and the Calabrian clubs, for example – serve several interests for ethnic groups.[28] Across ethnic groups, in fact, there might be different types of communities and individuals. Merton has defined them as subgroups:[29] some people might feel deprived of possibilities; some might feel like social mobility is not within their reach; some might push for their own *legitimate* businesses; others might push for their own *illegitimate* ventures. The promises of social mobility and wealth, legitimate or otherwise, are clearly alluring for many. Ethnic enclaves operate as (usually elitist) political machines; they can pave the way to those promises, in exchange for votes and support.

Furthermore, machine politics in ethnic communities can promote entrepreneurship. Some roles and economic mobility in the host society might be inaccessible for migrants; the ethnic enclave offers a protected niche – made up of contacts and cultural mutual recognition – that might facilitate entrepreneurship.[30]

Ethnic enclaves, machine politics and ethnic entrepreneurship exist everywhere, albeit differently, across various migrant communities and host societies. It's obviously not just about Italians in Australia.

In Sydney, in Australia, these concepts can explain a lot of the relationships I have seen in the chronicles of those powerful Calabrians.

But where is the 'ndrangheta in all this?

It is in some of the very murky bonds that first defined social ties and self-identities in the migrant communities of Fairfield, as much as Griffith and other Australian localities. It is, as well, in some of the behaviours within Calabrian enclaves: at times pursuing the interests of the few can be leveraged on ethnic solidarity, in between ethnic entrepreneurship and urban machine politics.

The 'ndrangheta is a collective system that shares many of the values that make up the Calabrian cultural milieu. From within this milieu, it promotes subcultural values; it is a driver of cultural preservation. Using practices and behaviours from shared places and cultures reinforces mutual recognition and strengthens mutual obligations. The 'ndrangheta is based on ideals and behaviours that are nothing but twisted interpretations of some Calabrian values. The recognized superiority of tradition; the superior value of what is close and culturally homogeneous over what is foreign and outside one's circle of family and friends; the willingness to improve one's financial and social conditions, if needed by cutting corners; the nourishment of a culture of particularism, where personal favours and privileged channels of communication are more successful than transparent and universal rules of engagement; the idea that, in order to succeed in society, rules can be broken and investments can be made in advance, because support given is support gained.

There is only tenuous evidence of the 'ndrangheta as an *organization* in Sydney, but some of the 'ndrangheta *behaviours* are well ingrained in certain sectors of local ethnic enclaves. And these behaviours partially reveal the organization.

Which is why they, these enclaves, felt claustrophobic.

But, then again, Sydney never quite conquered my heart.

Leaving Sydney and heading towards Melbourne, Paul Kelly's song still echoed in my head:[31]

> I want to see the sun go down from St Kilda Esplanade
> I'd give you all of Sydney Harbour
> For that one sweet promenade.

St Kilda Esplanade, Melbourne's finest, conquered my heart.

Lygon Street Meltdown

Yes, I am in love with Melbourne. And for Melbourne I do have a special song. It starts like this:

> Things were getting hot in the night,
> And the air wasn't feeling right,

Word is out the mighty could fall,
Like so many empires before,
Rivalry was cutting deep,
So many vendettas; how could they sleep?[32]

I heard this song in the summer of 2017, on Spotify, while looking for Melbourne-based songs. Since then, the Melbourne Ska Orchestra has been part of my playlists and 'Lygon Street Meltdown' has become my Melbourne anthem.

'Of course you'd live in Carlton!', chuckled Greg, the senior police officer who came to pick me up at my accommodation in Melbourne, the first time I visited in 2015. Carlton was, used to be, maybe is, the most Italian neighbourhood of the city, especially Lygon Street, Melbourne's Little Italy.

I lived in Carlton, between Faraday Street and Lygon Street, every time I went to Melbourne. There's no other place that feels just quite Carlton to me. On Lygon Street, a spritz arrives with a proper aperitivo. Wine shop on one side, delicatessen on the other, different Italian products proudly sold to Melbournians or whoever else. A Sicilian bistro, a Tuscan restaurant and then another bar and a wonderful pizzeria. Italians of all ages: some have just arrived down under, others have been there for decades. Depending on how much they 'feel' Italy as a part of their sales, you can guess how long they have been there. Some integrate Italian products into Australian habits; others sell them as unique, different, better, gourmet products, made in Italy.

Yes, in Lygon Street the spritz tastes of Italy. And yes, Italianness in Carlton is very visible, between the Italian Museum, the Brunetti Bar that always looks like it's Sunday morning, the smell of pizza with buffalo mozzarella. But it's more than that. Carlton's character is messy. There are many things 'out of place' in Lygon Street, as in any Little Italy, some shops and restaurants that are Lebanese or Indian or Greek, for example. And the Italian character of the Piazza Italia looks like a dated sepia postcard. Carlton is wearing its legacy like a necklace made of pearls and pasta beans, half precious, half popular; a legacy, the Italianness of Carlton, that just conquers you, not because it's easy and shiny, but because it's worn with authenticity, with no attempt made to disguise the mess of history.

Greg drove me around Carlton before taking me to a meeting. He told me stories of the past, of clandestine bars where the Carlton Crew – a mix of individuals of Italian descent, and their Irish and Australian allies – used to rock the nights. *Bars that today even have a fancy rooftop terrace and are all hipsters' spots!* Melbourne, like every city of similar dimensions, has a past, and that past is filled with the names of past gangsters.

The Carlton Crew included, among others, Alphonse Gangitano, Mick Gatto, Jason and Mark Moran, and Mario Condello, some of Italian origins, some born and bred in Melbourne. The stories of the Black Prince,

Gangitano, of his mafioso attitude, his underworld activities, drugs, the violence of 'gangland Melbourne', and eventually his murder in 1998, are still a very vivid component of the city's image. To the point of being in my favourite song on Melbourne, 'Lygon Street Meltdown'.[33]

> Tonight the Prince is losing his crown
> Here comes the Lygon Street Meltdown
> He recalled his mother's words
> 'Crime will never pay'
> You cross the line, then you will suffer.

Between 1998 and 2010, 36 underworld figures were killed in the so-called Melbourne gangland war. And yes, the song went further in describing this 'war' and the Carlton Crew:

> Lygon Street Meltdown
> Underbelly bubblin' up
> (We hear the) Carlton Crew is getting rough.[34]

Retaliatory murders and interconnected feuds across different criminal groups, from the Honoured Society (*hint*, the 'ndrangheta) to the Carlton Crew, from the Moran family, associated with the Painters and Dockers Union at the waterfront, to the Williams family. Murders shook the city and painted the reputation of Carlton in blood. Or we should say, tinted *again* the reputation of Carlton in blood.

'Not that this would have been the first time, anyway', added Greg while he showed me where Mick Gatto used to go for lunch every Tuesday. 'Have you heard of the Victoria Market murders?'

And yes, of course I had.[35] In the 1960s, they were the reason why the FBI sent Jack Cusack and Calabrian authorities sent Ugo Macera, both in secondment to the Victoria Police, to write a report (1964) on the Honoured Society in Melbourne. Almost at the same time, agent Colin Brown made a similar effort for the Australian Security Intelligence Organisation (ASIO), in 1965.

The story goes like this. Domenico Italiano, known as 'the Pope' and considered the head of the 'ndrangheta – *Honoured Society, Black Hand, yes, at the time names varied* – died in 1962; Antonio 'The Toad' Barbara (misspelling of Barbaro) died right after that, of natural causes, too. In the vacuum that their deaths created, Calabrian-born Vincenzo Angilletta and Vincenzo Muratore entered a power struggle. Their deaths in 1963 and 1964 became known as the Victoria Market murders. It is said that the 'war' was eventually won by Victoria Market stallholder Liborio Benvenuto, aka Mr Big, considered the highest-ranking member of the 'ndrangheta in Melbourne, one of the highest-ranking in the whole of Australia, until he died of cancer in 1988. A simple Google search on 'Liborio Benvenuto' still yields a number of results in terms of books, 'Underbelly' TV shows and investigative enquiries.

The Queen Victoria Market, QVM, at the lower end of Carlton coming from the city centre, is today a paradise for the senses. Stalls and stalls of various types of produce, from artisanal products to vegetables, from gourmet coffees to fresh pizza, from meat and poultry to books; you can get lost for hours. I have walked several times in the QVM, especially when, in 'my summer' 2017, I lived in Melbourne and the market held winter Tuesday night events. Fully embracing Italian and all sorts of ethnic products, surrounded by the colourful skyscrapers of the city, you'd struggle today to imagine a time when the market was a place for criminal cartels, extortion, bloodshed.

Around the QVM murders there are, of course, many little stories: a disturbing trend of violence seemed to linger around men of Calabrian origin working there. Other shootings, in fact, preceded and followed the murders of Muratore and Angiletta. Stories, once again, of migrants, of struggles, of a mafia-dense past in Calabria that couldn't quite be forgotten. In the many stories of those years kept in the national archives, I bet anyone can find one that speaks to them. And the following is my choice.

> Antonino Monaco, son of Giuseppe Antonio and of Giuseppa Condello, born in Santa Cristina d'Aspromonte In June 1924. In his township of origin, he exercised the trade of mule-driver. Domineering and violent, he consorted with the worst criminals of the town and he himself boasted that he belonged to a family of 'mafiosi' (his sister is at present living as the de facto wife of Giuseppe Antonio Italiano, recognised as the head of the 'mafia' of the area and also subject to special surveillance by the Public Security authorities). Married, with three dependent children, in November 1950 he emigrated to Australia where he still resides.[36]

For many, including my grandparents, in Santa Cristina d'Aspromonte, Giuseppe Antonio Italiano – Peppe 'Ntoni – was the '*cumpari*', which literally means godfather or a person who has been an important witness at your wedding. The term is also used out of 'respect' for someone, often mafia-related but not always. The *cumpari*'s de facto wife, or fiancée – who lived near my mum's teacher (what anecdotes you find while researching) – was then eventually dumped before becoming a lawfully wedded wife. This was a bit of a scandal in the village, as my great-aunt still recalls, 'that poor girl, dumped like that!' Circling back home again, touching lightly on the history around me.

The Assistant Secretary of the Entry Policy Branch in the Ministry of Interior, S.R. Lewis, reported in 1964 that Monaco was one of four men shot in Melbourne earlier that year.

Giuseppe Carbone, son of Pasquale and of Maria Cambrea, born in Delianova in February 1920. In his township of origin, he exercised the trade of agricultural labourer. A violent and domineering type, he consorted with previously convicted persons in the town and was associated with local criminality.

Michele Carbone, son of Giuseppe and of Saveria Papalia, born in Delianova in March 1907, he exercised the trade of agricultural labourer; slandered by public opinion for various crimes, lazy and a vagrant, he frequented public places in company with the best-known criminals ... he was without means of support, he spent freely and it is therefore to be considered that he lived on the proceeds of his crimes.

Ferdinando Carbone, son of Francesco and of Francesca Romeo, born in Varapodio in January 1925. [...] Ex-university student, in his township of origin he enjoys a good reputation. He has no convictions of any kind and he has caused no incidents by his conducts.[37]

All four men came from small villages next to one another in Aspromonte, villages where I went to visit a relative, or to a wedding, or, in the case of Delianova (Delianuova), where we used to go and buy my birthday cake every year. Three men out of four had criminal records. Three out of four also allegedly had connections with the local mafia. Once more, 'Lygon Street Meltdown' was the anthem of those days:

Back stabbin's outta control
No one to trust with what you know
Homicide here in the street and you know it will repeat.[38]

Surely, anyone who listens to this song and these lyrics will have a fairly good idea of what that period was about:

Gangland wars in town
It's a Lygon Street Meltdown.[39]

Now, the Australian authorities probably – I would dare say most certainly – did not know that the Calabrian men's places of origin, surnames and family relationships could have framed these murders as old 'ndrangheta grudges.

There does not appear to be any degree of relationship between the abovementioned persons. This is how the report on these four persons ends.

Truthfully, what triggered inquiries into these people at the time were allegations that various Italian nationals, including the abovementioned four, had entered the country illegally thanks to forged documents – illegal landing permits or illegal re-entries. Antonio Barbaro (commonly misspelled Barbara), an immigration agent in the early 1950s, was found lodging sponsorship applications in the names of Italians living in Victoria – usually without their knowledge – with the help of two other departmental employees, a Calabrian and an Australian. Barbaro/a was Calabrian, *from Platì*. He was also believed to be one of the mythical three founders of the 'ndrangheta in Australia in 1922. The legend of three founders of the Australian 'ndrangheta aboard the King of Italy ship, which arrived in Fremantle on 18 December 1922,[40] echoes the legend of Osso, Mastrosso and Carcagnosso, the three Spanish knights, founders of the mafia in Italy. Barbaro/a was considered by Victoria Police as 'a leading figure in the Black Hand group in Melbourne'.[41] He was eventually charged on counts of forgery and uttering but the main prosecution witness was reluctant and failed to testify, possibly out of intimidation. *Mafia method?*

Family dynasties

There does not appear to be any degree of relationship between the abovementioned persons.
  I believe some connection would have emerged by looking at the stories of those four men shot in Melbourne back home. Different times.
  Cumpari Peppe 'Ntoni Italiano – who lived *'more uxorio'* (unmarried) with the sister of abovementioned Monaco – was considered the patriarch of the Italiano *'ndrina*, still a well-known surname in Delianuova, with his son, Giasone, supposedly leading the family today, in partnership with the Alvaro clan from nearby Sinopoli and Sant'Eufemia d'Aspromonte. An informant to Australian police detailed in 1989 that a 'very dangerous mafia man came to Australia from Italy. His name may have been Giuseppe or Antonio and his last name Italiano […] This man was brought to Australia by two other men, "Little Domenic" Sergi and Frank "Little Trees" Barbaro. "Little Domenic" Sergi drove Italiano from Mildura to Griffith, then later to Sydney […] Italiano is an old man. He may have just come to Australia to give a report or to get a report. This is not uncommon with the mafia.'[42]
  During this trip, Peppe 'Ntoni is believed to have also visited Liborio Benvenuto, just a few months before he died in 1988 in Melbourne. This would confirm the criminal ranking of both individuals and the interconnectedness across families.
  Italian antimafia documents of the early 1990s confirm that, on 22 July 1990, there was a 'ndrangheta meeting in the town of Ardore, province of Reggio Calabria.[43] For Australia, the representative of the clans was Domenico Sergi (aka Little Domenic), which would explain why he was the one to escort Peppe 'Ntoni Italiano in Australia. Little Domenic Sergi is the cousin of the more famous Tony Sergi, and he was apparently 'constantly involved with drugs […] he never stops',[44] which

would confirm the prominence of the Sergi clan for the drug trade in Australia and in Italy. Little Domenic married Elisabetta Agresta in Melbourne in 1963. He died in 2020 in Griffith during one of the many Australian lockdowns due to COVID-19, surrounded – as it's expected, normal and desirable – by his loving family, where Calabrian ties have been well preserved. Even if the migration of the families from rural Griffith to either Sydney or Melbourne had in fact already started in the 1960s, Griffith remains home. Elisabetta's brother, Pasquale Agresta, was apparently Little Domenic Sergi's associate in Melbourne, where he was detained following the discovery of a marijuana plantation, the largest found in Australia (31.5 acres in Coleambally).

Fast-forward to 2017, Turin, Italy. Domenico Agresta – who at the time was 29 years old (born in 1988) – has become a witness for the prosecution, an informer. In so doing, he has lost his family and endangered his life: he is expected to be in prison for at least 30 years for murder and mafia membership, as boss – the very young boss – of a 'ndrina in Volpiano, near Turin, connected to the clans in Platì. Domenico Agresta, aka Micu McDonald, talks about his family, about Platì, the North of Italy, the drugs, and about Australia.[45] In particular, he says, his relatives in the 'ndrina Agresta have 'helped to form' two different locali (geographical consortia of 'ndrangheta clans, 'ndrine) in Australia, one in Victoria (possibly Melbourne) and one in NSW (possibly Griffith or Fairfield).

I was based in Melbourne when this testimony came out,[46] in summer 2017. I wondered whether Micu knew that Pasquale and Giuseppe Agresta, who were both his distant relatives, were identified in the early 1990s by confidential police investigations as mafia leaders in Melbourne, in the years when the leader was Liborio Benvenuto. Micu did confirm what was already known thanks to other declarations of pentiti (collaborators of justice) and informers. To understand what the involvement of the Agrestas in the foundation of a locale in Australia means, one needs to understand the locale of Platì first.

> In Platì, there are four families [...] who all respond to Barbaro Rosario and before him to Barbaro Francesco, known as 'u castanu' [...]; there are four families represented in Platì who recognise Barbaro Rosario as their boss. In Platì, in the locale, they are a family. Trimboli, Agresta, Perre and Barbaro, they are all a family. Sometimes even with different surnames, but they are all a family.[47]

So, in Platì in Calabria, in Volpiano near Turin, and in Australia, with all due differences in time and in space, the 'ndrine of the locale of Platì holds onto what counts the most: surnames, marriages, family connections. Actual criminal intent comes after all these other elements.

These four main families in Platì, also tight with other local mafia clans such as Sergi, Papalia, Musitano and Perre, have branched out in the North of Italy and, let's not forget, in North America as well.

In January 2022 13 people belonging to the clans Barbaro and Sergi were arrested in the province of Pavia, in the North of Italy, for drug-related crimes.[48] The operation showed how, with some tribulations due to the pandemic, the locale of Platì still handles the distribution of cocaine in the northern region of Lombardia and Piemonte. But Calabria remains the polar star. 'If my father gets into a fight down there (in Calabria) because of you, mind you, your mother, your grandmother, my father-in-law, I'll slaughter everyone!',[49] Rocco Barbaro says, intercepted, to someone who is causing trouble with payments in the North. This Barbaro was born in 1995.

A family model that seems to have overcome the challenges of intergenerational transitions. A family dynasty.

Family dynasties have a lot in common with mafia families, or the other way around: mafia families are also family dynasties.[50] We can scrutinize the entrepreneurial character of some 'ndrangheta clans, their attachment to blood ties – while still conducting business with everyone else – and their intergenerational resilience through the analytical lenses on dynasties.

Ownership – *how much of the family business is actually owned by family members?*
Succession – *who is the leader and who is going to succeed them?*
Size/form – *generational evolution or involution.*
Management structures – *hierarchical, coordinated or horizontal?*
Family relations at large – *who marries or divorces whom, who dies, who falls out with whom?*

These factors might help explain the build-up and nature of a family dynasty,[51] including a criminal dynasty. Many of the resources in family dynasties are not financial: they have been referred to as 'familiness' or f-factor.[52] Familiness includes evaluations on how family interactions run and on the roles of family members. It can lead to reflection on cultural changes,[53] including the evolution of family relations brought by marriages, funerals, births, divorces, migration, social obligations and so forth. The key consideration is that *familiness* clearly affects business.[54]

In an attempt to draw a parallel between business dynasties and 'ndrangheta dynasties, it firstly appears obvious that (criminal) business across many of these families remains mostly anchored to certain evergreen crimes – including drugs, extortion, murders, intimidation, threats and money laundering. Furthermore, a lot of what these family branches have been doing far from their place of origin is coping with family stuff; this has eventually affected their business ventures. A lot of what is known about mafia families in Australia is *not* their criminal activities but their movements, their travels, their marriages, their disappointments, the wrong or right choice in the selection of a partner or in making an investment. This is why a lot of what appears as 'mafia-related' in reality could also be read as (migrant) family-related.

Each dynasty has a series of decisions to make:[55] business forms, modes of control, strategies and governance structures, survival mechanisms.

In terms of *business forms*, the dynasty will have an 'office' for the holding companies and various workplaces for the family branches, if the business contemplates branches. For example, in the Barbaro clan, in addition to the 'main office' in Platì, we have had an executive Italian branch in Lombardia and Piemonte, an Australian branch in Griffith and other business offices, for example, in Melbourne or in the Gold Coast.

Secondly, in order to sustain profitability and generate wealth, the dynasty will need a *strategy*: family trust, endogamy, face-to-face meetings and risk-taking attitudes. These choices are all clearly interlinked with the survival of the family venture. 'Little Domenic' Sergi travels all the way to Calabria for a face-to-face meeting: he attempts to keep the family business clearly visible to others. His marriage with Elisabetta Agresta should confirm the dynasty's choice of endogamy across the same families over and over again.

Thirdly, maintaining governance requires choosing relationships with outsiders – a necessity for any family-based clan. It also requires the creation of boards – coordinating structures – to address conflict and any arising issue. Deciding who, in the criminal families of Griffith, is going to welcome the visitor from another 'ndrangheta clan of the calibre of Peppe 'Ntoni Italiano would be, for example, something that needs agreement. Similarly, understanding how to present the family to the outside requires a prior agreement – albeit informal – on how to handle 'externals' ('*ndranghetisti* or outsiders).

Between Australia and Calabria – especially taking as the example the *'ndrine* from Platì – one can see family dynasties where blood is part of the social capital, which benefits criminal businesses, as it nourishes trust. The creation of a coordination mechanism and a conflict resolution system are meant to manage the inevitable interference of familiness in business. Such mechanisms could also provide protection and be used to present the families to the outside as if they were just about business.

These are family dynasties that have maintained executive 'offices' in Griffith or Melbourne but nevertheless seem to respond to a corporate – a *brand* – identity that remains anchored to Calabria. A mix between cultural codes from Calabria and family/personal resources only shared by a very select few characterizes these dynasties. Outsiders are seldom all in and are often included only on the basis of opportunistic (business) reasons. All of this makes some of these families more resilient. But – perhaps more importantly – it's the *familiness* of their criminal venture that we keep calling *mafia*, in Calabria as in Australia, the social and private dimensions. At times, it's only through family relations and what these relations imply that we identify what we then call mafia/'ndrangheta.

It's at times confusing to realize you are actually looking inside families when researching 'ndrangheta clans. It's disturbing to realize, especially when looking at mafia mobility, that one of the dimensions of the mafia's business success is about very normal things, like visiting relatives on another continent, calling your uncle every other week, breaking a mother's heart by moving abroad, travelling six hours by car to attend a wedding, making an effort to solve family disputes or just giving in to your rage when something goes wrong in your world. When I read obituaries of people I have heard so much about, for their 'ndrangheta career, I do feel human pity and sorrow.

Intercontinental dynasties

Two more things emerged while researching the 'ndrangheta in Melbourne. The first was the existence of mafia powerhouses, maintaining the connection to the *organization* of the 'ndrangheta in two different ways. A first way is to report back directly to Calabria and to the mother clan there. A second way is to report back to Griffith, like a local executive hub for Calabrian criminal ventures in Australia.

The second thing that emerged was that some criminal dynasties endeavoured to get and maintain power. This had become clear when looking at ethnic enclaves and at the attempts to foster networks of instrumental friendships in public administration, business and politics, as already observed in Sydney.

And then maybe there was a third thing, overall. A lot was not about Melbourne, but in Melbourne, somehow, it resonated.

In order to discuss these points, it is important to properly introduce a family, the Barbaro clan. In Australia – between Melbourne, Sydney and, of course, Griffith – this clan not only preserves Calabrian links, but it has also been willing to increase the autonomous power of the 'ndrangheta down under.

Premise: one of the first bits of news that anyone learns when approaching the study of the mafia presence in Australia relates to the so-called world's largest ecstasy bust in 2008.

When I first travelled to Melbourne, in October 2015, I had lunch with a federal police agent in a café in the business district. We were both featured in the documentary *The Mafia in Australia* run by Fairfax Media in June 2015. As said, for this same documentary, I had driven around Aspromonte with journalist Nick and his colleagues, discussing, among many things, the events around Francesco 'Frank' Madafferi. The police agent in Melbourne had worked on Operation Inca, codename for the 'world's largest ecstasy bust' (at the time). His knowledge of the 'ndrangheta in Australia was from the field.

Over 4.4 tonnes of MDMA (ecstasy) shipped from Europe (Italy) were seized in the Port of Melbourne in August 2008, hidden in tomato tins, with a street value of A$440 million and leading to the arrest of 20 people across Australia. Behind the shipment was a criminal network based in Melbourne, with contacts in South Australia and New South Wales, affiliated to Calabrian mafia clans in Australia and with partners in Italy. The head of the network was Pasquale 'Pat' Barbaro, as the person responsible for, and the financier of, the 'job'. His main partner at the time was Francesco 'Frank' Madafferi.[56]

The circumstances of both men are of interest when looking at Melbourne and the 'ndrangheta. Indeed, the whole network is of relevance. Arrested with Barbaro and Madafferi were other men of Calabrian descent: Salvatore Agresta, Pasquale Sergi, Saverio Zirilli and Carmelo Falanga, sentenced for their role in the 'importation of border-controlled drugs in a commercial quantity'.[57] In particular, Zirilli and Barbaro travelled into and out of Griffith; Madafferi, Sergi and Agresta were already in Melbourne; Falanga came from Adelaide. As the court found:[58]

> Barbaro, at the apex of the conspiracy, the financier and main organiser together with Falanga, who is equal in terms of criminality with Barbaro although in terms of the organisational structure may be considered not as overtly involved. Zirilli who was in a very similar but slightly lower position than Falanga, being the right-hand man of Barbaro and able to substitute for him when he was unavailable, but it would appear acting upon his instructions. Agresta and Sergi appear to be the foot soldiers of the conspiracy, in that they do not have a decision-making or decision-influencing role, even allowing for the call urging Barbaro and Zirilli to return to Melbourne that was made by Agresta.

The network – even when counting on other local men, Rob Karam, Jon Visser and John Higgs – clearly had a Calabrian connotation, as it pivoted around Pat Barbaro.

Pat Barbaro can be considered the 'ndrangheta's golden boy, one of the sons of Francesco, Frank, 'Little Trees' Barbaro and Elizabeth Sergi, another sister of that Tony Sergi we mentioned earlier. *A strategic marriage between the two main 'ndrangheta clans of Australia and of Platì*. Pat was born in Griffith, his cousins being Sergis, Agrestas and Zirillis, and he had a substantial number of relatives still in Calabria, in Platì. Frank Little Trees Barbaro (born in 1937), Pat's father, is considered a first-class member of the 'ndrangheta. Born in Platì, 'Little Trees' belongs to the Barbaro branch *'u castanu'*. One of his cousins in Platì, Francesco as well (1927–2018), had been recognized as the *capo-locale*, the head of the families, under the Barbaro–Papalia 'regime' in Platì. It is no mystery that Francesco Barbaro and Antonio Papalia, the two regents of the family in Calabria, were among the most industrious criminal minds of the 'ndrangheta in the North of Italy, in Canada and in Australia. Since the 1970s, judicial chronicles in Italy have indicated the heavy involvement of these clans in kidnappings and their investments in the North of Italy, especially linked to drugs, in Lombardia and Piemonte.[59]

Frank 'Little Trees' Barbaro was mentioned by the Woodward Royal Commission, along with Antonio Sergi and Robert Trimboli, as a senior member of the criminal organization that controlled a vast drug distribution network and was also considered responsible for the disappearance of Donald Mackay in Griffith in 1977. Little Trees' kinship and friendship with Little Domenic Sergi and with Liborio Benvenuto in Melbourne and the fact that he was the target of many of the anti-drug operations in the 1980s seem to confirm the criminal stature of the man.

There was an interesting story in one of the confidential documents I consulted, which not only added some clarity about who is who in the mafia in Australia, but also gave me some insights into the weight of criminal legacies for someone like Pat Barbaro. I will summarize the story here, trying to stick to those facts in the narrative that are not confidential or are proven in a court of law.

At some point in the early 1980s, Anna, one of the daughters of a man named Giovanni, married Angelo, on the basis of an understanding between the two men about the assets that Anna was going to receive as her dowry. After the wedding, Angelo apparently became increasingly demanding of his entitlements on his wife's assets. Giovanni, with the help of Little Dominic Sergi and Frank Little Trees Barbaro, devised a scheme to get rid of Angelo. The scheme consisted of arranging a trip back to Calabria for the married couple and having someone kill him there. This was arranged through phone calls to Platì and was executed there when the couple did travel to Italy. Eventually, Giovanni had to travel to Calabria himself to bring home his widowed daughter and pay for the contract killing. While in Platì, Giovanni met with the man who had arranged the murder and who was the *capo-bastone*, the head of the clan, then: Frank 'Little Trees' Barbaro's brother, Rosario, aka Rosi. Rosi Barbaro, who married Maria Agresta in Platì, was one of the most important 'ndrangheta men in the Barbaro 'ndrina and in the 'ndrangheta overall; a *capo-società*, to be specific, representative of those affiliates carrying the highest ranking in Platì. For a long time, Rosi was the recognized boss of the families in Platì in the Barbaro–Papalia group, including Trimboli, Agresta, Perre and others, especially since the arrest and detention of Francesco Barbaro '*u castanu*' in 1989.

The Barbaro–Papalia clan's involvement with the kidnappings is also a known fact. Italian police showed how some of the proceeds from the kidnappings orchestrated by men of this clan were sent to Australia in the 1970s and 1980s to buy land and invest in Indian hemp plantations.[60] This was done through prearranged trips, including those of key figures like Vincenzo Trimboli, relative of Bob Trimboli, Aussie Bob, who was involved in the killing of Don McKay in 1977. Or Domenico Barbaro (born 1937), aka 'the Australian', who travelled at various times down under in the 1970s, and who, according to the police, used to carry cash directly on his person. *If this is not a family dynasty, enjoying a decent amount of success …*

Business dynasties, including those with a criminal business, are often families with considerable political influence. And, as I said earlier, the Barbaro clan is interesting also because of their attempt to develop their 'will to power' down under.

Indeed, the story of Pat Barbaro has another angle that needs some scrutiny. It comes with Barbaro's partnership with Francesco 'Frank' Madafferi. Frank's brother Antonio, Tony 'Blondie' Madafferi, is a successful entrepreneur but is repeatedly referred to as an 'alleged mafia boss' by newspapers and police files.

Now, remember Frank and his visa scandal? Yes, the one that links back to Sydney circuits of Calabrian men, Nick Scali, Tony Labbozzetta, Pat Sergi. We are at that again.

Wayne Bastin, Sergeant of Police at the Organised Crime Squad in Victoria Police, gave a statement in 1998 in the case *Francesco Madafferi vs Department of Immigration and Multicultural Affairs*.[61] In this statement he detailed how Frank Madafferi had been lying to authorities in Australia about his criminal past in Italy, where he had served time for mafia-type conspiracy and involvement in a kidnapping, among other things.

> I am also aware that Francesco Madafferi is the brother of Antonio Blondie Madafferi […] Antonio Madafferi was the subject of a National Crime Authority probe into the extent of Italian organised crime in Australia.
>
> It is my belief that Francesco Madafferi belongs to a crime family involved in Blackmail, Extortion and Murder and if allowed to remain in Australia will continue to carry out acts of violence on behalf of an organised criminal syndicate.[62]

And that was 1998. Let's go back to Melbourne, and the vicissitudes of some Calabrian (and 'ndrangheta) families, in the Melbourne 'underworld' and 'upperworld'.

North Carlton

The Reggio Calabria Club is in Parkville, on Brunswick Road, northwest of Carlton, Upper Lygon Street. The first time I went there in 2015, the club was closed. On the way back, I stopped for a cannolo in the Gelobar and met the nice Calabrian man who, as I said a few chapters back, reminded me of the '*caffè pagato*'.

Two years later, I do it again. I walk up all of Lygon Street and stop at the Melbourne General Cemetery. It's a bit creepy and yet beautiful, almost romantic, to walk around all the graves overlooking Melbourne from the hill. So many Italians, so many Calabrians, have their final rest in Victoria, their engravings in Italian, or even in dialect.

' 'Dassa 'ndo duluri a famijjia tutta. I lacrimi e i sorrisi si li tinni u Creaturi.' (She leaves the whole family in pain. The tears and the smiles all got the Creator – [*sic*]). Assunta, from Oppido Mamertina, Calabria.

I get to the Gelobar again. Things feel different this time around. A Melbourne lawyer of Calabrian descent, Joseph 'Pino' Acquaro, was shot dead on 15 March 2016 as he was walking to his car after locking up his restaurant and cafe – the Gelobar precisely, there on Lygon Street. The event shocked Melbournians. On his head – the court heard, and the news reported – was a contract killing, apparently linked to the 'ndrangheta.[63] Specifically, Acquaro could have been part of a group of lawyers – including in particular Ms Nicola Gobbo – passing confidential information to the police. The Royal Commission into the Management of Police Informants, also known as the 'Lawyer X case', was launched in late 2018 to investigate the alleged mishandling of lawyers-informants by Victoria Police, centring specifically on Gobbo.[64] Anyway, a man, Calabrian as well, not linked to the 'ndrangheta, or at least not directly, was charged in 2019 – pleading not guilty[65] – for the murder of Acquaro, allegedly motivated by personal frictions.[66]

Acquaro was also a former director of the Italian Chamber of Commerce and a former head of the Reggio Calabria Club. *The clubs, once again; the grip, again.*

The case rekindled public curiosity about the role of some individuals in the Calabrian community in Melbourne as well as questions about the 'ndrangheta's criminal and political interests. Indeed, among Joe Acquaro's clients, it was heavily reported, were top 'ndrangheta men, including Pasquale Barbaro and Frank Madafferi and the others of the so-called 'Tomato Tins Drug Syndicate' (as they are also known). Tony 'Blondie' Madafferi, Frank's brother, was at some point even suspected to be behind the contract killing.[67] Although the client–lawyer relationship between Frank Madafferi and Joe Acquaro ended in 2013, Frank Madafferi asked for a review of his sentence considering the case of 'Lawyer X' and the alleged involvement of Acquaro as one of the police informants.[68] Madafferi wasn't the only one: Pasquale Barbaro, Carmelo Falanga, Salvatore Agresta, Rob Karam, Saverio Zirilli and Jan Visser all did the same because they had all been clients of Nicola Gobbo, Lawyer X.[69]

The Chief Commissioner submitted evidence that Acquaro did talk to Victoria Police in 2014, as reported in a 2021 case to review Frank Madafferi's sentence.[70] In fact, Acquaro initiated contacts when his professional relationship with Frank Madafferi was already over.

> [Acquaro] initiated contact regarding concerns for his sons [who] had become aligned with and [were] committing criminal acts under the direction of Frank and Tony Madafferi.[71]

Acquaro's reason was recognized as a justification to make sure his declarations would not be made public. *If this was mafia, there would be punishment for those who talk against it.*

> The risk to Mr Acquaro's children is said to exist notwithstanding that they have a 'close relationship' with the family that controls the relevant criminal enterprise that would seek to enforce the code of silence.[72]

The Madafferi brothers tend to appear in the same phrases. According to the evidence, 'later, Acquaro referred to his need to "get rid of these people" and he was told by the police that their priority was to lock up "the Madafferi boys", "Frank and Tony as well"'.

In July 2021, the media reported that Frank Madafferi was close to being deported to Italy, expelled from Australia before the court could rule whether his conviction for drug trafficking should be overturned amid allegations it was tainted by his solicitor Joseph Acquaro's work as a police informer.[73] The newspaper *The Age* noted: 'The successful deportation of Madafferi would mark the culmination of a two-decade saga by law enforcement and immigration officials to revoke his residency visa for his reputed involvement in criminal activity in Australia and serious criminal history in his native Italy.'[74]

Yes, saga is a good term. In December 2021, Frank Madafferi was denied bail, after having been denied parole.[75] He is still expected to be released in 2024.

If, instead of walking up towards the Gelobar from the cemetery in Carlton, one goes straight down Rathdowne Street, the pizzeria La Porchetta is there. *As a side note, the Calabrese pizza there is not great, to be honest, but then again, on pizza I might be biased.* The founder and owner of the pizzeria chain La Porchetta is Tony Madafferi, who also owns the Market Europa grocery store in the Melbourne suburb of Noble Park. Mr Madafferi clearly has a name in the food industry. Politically engaged and supported by prominent members of the Italian community in Melbourne and Sydney (including Nick Scali and Pat Sergi, just to never forget about them), his family as well as his personal and business relationships have been under persistent scrutiny due to mafia allegations.

While we were in Calabria in April 2015, during the production of the documentary for Four Corners, the journalist, Nick, told me about some of his research into certain ('ndrangheta) family dynasties in Melbourne. We were up in Aspromonte, parked on a hill, watching a pink moon rising, waiting for the sunset to peak so they could shoot some scenes over the valley. A perfect time to chat. Family connections; interlinkages of individuals within the Italian community; interests in the Italian Chamber of Commerce; the proximity to political figures: all emerged as interesting nodes of a very complex story. The story that Nick was choosing to air related indeed to the scandal over the visa for Tony Madafferi's brother, Frank. A web of political donations run through expensive fundraising dinners and pressure on authorities was exercised from various angles within the Calabrian elite community. It was all exposed in the documentary and in further news reports.[76] Knowing what I know today, probably my expert testimony in that documentary would have been different, less absolute, less certain, more dubious on the nature of mafia ties in Australia, and more cautious on the conduct of certain characters involved. Because boundaries are difficult here.

One must learn in order to … learn.

The visa scandal became front-page news because it involved immigration ministers, multiple senators and Liberal MPs. Frank Madafferi was eventually granted a visa, just a few months before being arrested with Pasquale Barbaro over the MDMA shipment. Never convicted of anything, Tony Madafferi's reputation was clearly stained by footage of his meeting with his brother Frank and Pasquale Barbaro in 2008 prior to the MDMA bust. In 2015, the police commissioner banned Tony Madafferi from the Crown Casino because of his alleged organized crime connections. Later, what the press said about Tony Madafferi's alleged involvement in the murder of Joseph Acquaro did not help his reputation. It was more than just news on the case, though: various confidential police reports, since the mid-1980s, had referred to him as someone gravitating towards the Calabrian boss Liborio Benvenuto, and later involved in different crimes, albeit not necessarily directly.

'It is the belief of myself and other investigators that Antonio Madafferi is the head of an organised crime syndicate operating within, or associated with, the Melbourne Fresh Produce Market. Investigators also believe that Antonio Madafferi is an enforcer for this syndicate.'[77] This is Sergeant Wayne Bastin who, in 1998, details a number of murders, incidents and aggressions related to the Melbourne Fresh Produce Markets that remained unsolved cases and somehow indicate the involvement of Tony Madafferi.

Newspapers reported different stories in relation to Tony Madafferi, but obviously, without any conviction, mafia allegations remain (rightfully so) problematic to mention. *The Age* published an apology to Mr Madafferi in 2016.

The Age acknowledges that Mr Madafferi is a hard-working family man who has never been charged by the police with any criminal offence, and has no criminal convictions. To the extent that any of the articles might have suggested the contrary, *The Age* accepts that such suggestions are false and apologises to Mr Madafferi.[78]

On 8 August 2017, in my rented flat in Faraday Street in Carlton, while I was lazily having coffee, I got a call from an Italian journalist friend in Melbourne.

'Have you seen the news?'
'Yeah, briefly ...'
'Would you care to comment?'
'I'd rather not.'
'Oh, why not?'
'I am not sure whether this Lobster-Mobster news is mafia or just ... politics?'

It gets *really* real *really* fast: all these people, their businesses and affairs, their connections and alleged misconduct. *I know the main characters now; I know where places are; I learned a bit about the cultural milieu they exist in. I doubt things.*

The 'Lobster with a Mobster' clever pun refers to a dinner that Matthew Guy, state opposition leader in 2017, had with alleged mafia boss Tony Madafferi.[79] This dinner, which became the object of considerable media attention, was hosted in a venue of Melbourne's dockland owned by one of Madafferi's friends, who was also at the dinner. A dinner that Madafferi's cousin paid for; the cousin is also Calabrian and a Liberal Party donor, involved in the scandal of the visa for Frank Madafferi as well. The purpose of that dinner was officially to discuss public policy issues in relation to the vegetable-growing industry – the main business of many at the table. As reported by *The Age*, 'it is understood the diners discussed the move of the Victorian Fruit and Vegetable wholesale market from Footscray to Epping. Traditionally, Mr Madafferi and other greengrocers exercised significant influence at the Footscray market.'[80]

Some months later, in April 2018, *The Age* revealed that a Liberal Party figure – appointed by opposition leader Matthew Guy to lead the state's property development agency – personally promoted an alleged boss of the Calabrian mafia in Australia to a prominent business body. President of the Italian Chamber of Commerce and Industry in Melbourne Tony De Domenico was appointed in 2014 as chairman of Places Victoria, the precursor to Development Victoria, responsible for developing state government-owned buildings and land. He had allegedly supported Tony Madafferi's application to become a chamber member with his business Europa Market. *I stress the word 'allegedly' here.* Nevertheless, this called for the intervention by the Italian embassy to block Mr Madafferi's membership because of his notorious, albeit unproven, mafia reputation. The news – which even led to expectations of the resignation of Mr De Domenico – was later retracted and unpublished. *The Age* issued another apology, this time to Mr De Domenico, who 'has no, and has never had any, personal or commercial relationship with any mafia figure, did not personally assist any mafia figure, and is a fit and proper person to be a member of government boards and agencies and is otherwise a person of good repute.'[81] Actually, Mr De Domenico, like many others in the Calabrian/Italian communities, was awarded a Medal in the Order of Australia at the Queen's Birthday Honours List in 2018 for his contribution to urban planning, research and development in Victoria.

Aside from the political ethics and morals of the individuals involved, the proximity of (usually wealthy) individuals of Calabrian origin to people in power remains a trait of both Melbourne and Sydney.

And that makes you wonder, how much of this is mafia? And according to whom? How much of it is politics instead? How much is it about migration mechanisms and the ethnic enclaves around family dynasties and how much is it just chance, mistake, a wrong place, wrong time kind of thing?

Hidden in the dusty archive my father still keeps for his 'stuff from the 1990s', an article written by former Judge Agostino Cordova.[82] *He wrote 'Everyone knows that mafiosi not only can vote, but, more importantly, make other people vote' (...) 'the phenomenon of the mafia vote resembles a phoenix: everyone says that it exists, but no one really knows (or wants to know) where it is'.*

One day in 2019 I walked all the way up to Lygon Street, past the cemetery and the Gelobar, and turned left towards Brunswick to finally reach the Reggio Calabria Club (RCC); I remember it very vividly. There was a statue of the Madonna di Polsi behind a glass door in a shed in the parking lot of the club. A reminder that in early October the RCC still organizes the festivities for the Madonna of the Mountain, to whom many Calabrians in Melbourne are still devoted. The RCC, the Marconi Club in Sydney, the Victoria Market in Melbourne, perhaps even the Italian Chambers of Commerce: these spaces have effectively substituted for the public squares in Calabrian/Italian villages. They offer spaces of cohesion and preservation of language, norms, history and traditions, as Calabrians – myself included – are very proud of their heritage and their migrant culture.

How memories overlap all the time.

In 2008, in the same parking lot of the RCC, Frank Madafferi, Carmelo Falanga and Pat Barbaro were waiting for someone; they were expecting a drug shipment at the Port of Melbourne and they suspected the police had seized the containers.[83] In 2009, Frank Madafferi and Pat Barbaro were charged with the attempted murder of Fedele D'Amico in the RCC parking lot, probably considering him responsible for the lost drugs.[84] Frank, everyone apparently knew, was an irascible man ('Mad Frank' he was nicknamed) who seemed to think that Melbourne was his ground and who had no problem doubting his own friends' loyalty as well.

> Non cujjuniari assai cu mia, capiscisti?
> Ti para ca fuckin' Melborne esta u fuckin' u toi?
> Non esti u toi, understand? [inaudible]
> Mannaia santu fuckin' Roccu!
> I am fuckin' indispensable for fuckin' Melbourne.
> Melbourne esti u meu non esti i fuckin' i Pascali.[85]

> Don't mess with me, understand?
> Do you think that fucking Melbourne is fucking yours?
> It's not, understand?
> Goddamn St. Rocco!
> I am fucking indispensable for fucking Melbourne
> Melbourne is mine, it is not Pasquale's.

Even in the latest 2021 court case to review Frank Madafferi's sentence,[86] there are references to his irascible character and intimidating behaviour.

> There was a fight at the Gelobar when Madafferi turned up 'really angry and agitated', 'jumped' him and 'knocked him out'. Madafferi and his brother Tony had made a threat to Acquaro's life and spread the rumour that Acquaro was Lawyer X. Furthermore, Madafferi was 'collecting money at the market' and was in the company of an unknown male who was carrying a gun. Acquaro showed police a picture of the gun. The police notes of this meeting state 'the week Frank goes in something is going to happen'. [Acquaro] is alert but not worried.

These words, these behaviours – threat, intimidation, anger – together with the degree of respect that Pat Barbaro showed to both Frank and Tony Madafferi, could justify why authorities questioned the hierarchy of power, why they wondered what these behaviours and this form of respect meant. If Frank was more than just a business associate of Pat Barbaro – or even Tony's shadow, as was suggested at some point – it would cast doubt on the role of the greengrocer entrepreneur Tony Madafferi.

And this doubt doesn't seem to leave him.

★★★

In February 2020, Operation Eyfhemos in Reggio Calabria opened a window onto the world of some alleged mafia associates from the village of Santa Eufemia d'Aspromonte who had visited relatives in Melbourne.[87]

Obviously, intercepted conversations among mafia affiliates are to be taken with a pinch of salt, as they might just be the result of boasting or exaggeration, or simply inaccurate.

This was a potentially explosive operation, detailing the 'ndrangheta connections of the Alvaro clan in Santa Eufemia d'Aspromonte with members of the local municipality – including the mayor and deputy mayor – with officers of the town councils, with entrepreneurs and with covert Masonic lodges.

One of the men involved, Cosimo Cannizzaro, who is said to hold a high-ranking position in the 'ndrangheta *locale* in Santa Eufemia, had gone to Australia to help resolve a situation related to an affiliate there who had 'misbehaved' and, for that, could be sanctioned. *Interesting how the face-to-face contact remains crucial in certain families.* In the interceptions, Cannizzaro recounted a 'ndrangheta reunion with someone named Diego Luppino and someone named 'Ntony [*sic*] Madafferi, referred to as the *'ndrina* boss of Melbourne ('the capobastone down there!'[88]), to decide what to do about the case.

> We don't respond to them ... they are from our village, they are friends ... they can call on me, I said – one day I'll go to Australia and they'll free a space for me.[89]

He means that a 'ndrangheta spot will be 'open' for him.

The operation detailed a series of relationships, stories about Melbourne, by people belonging to a *'ndrina*, the Alvaro clan, that in Australia holds an historical role. *Remember Tony Labbozzetta in Sydney and the alleged involvement of people in his family with the Alvaro clan and their drug trafficking operations? Remember Peppe 'Ntoni Italiano in Delianuova and the partnerships between the Italianos and the Alvaros still today? Things connected, nodes on a giant spider web in my mind.*

> One night we were at his house, seven of us, we were counting money. Seven! Men and women, we are holding a tablecloth, from its four angles holding the money from the market ... all the money he gets ... He also has something like 18 parking slots, in the supermarkets, in the markets ... everywhere! [...] in the centre of Melbourne, he is building a ... something ... 26 floors! He has wedding venues, a villa ... When I go there, I have to fight with my brothers ... with my sister ... I must go there ...[90]

He, in this case, is identified as Italian-Australian entrepreneur Diego Luppino, whose origins can be traced back to Santa Eufemia, and whose past and present see a series of successes in Australia due to his business acumen and entrepreneurship. *Another successful Italian/Calabrian, another honourable career.* Friend and colleague of Tony Madafferi – the two even shared a business years ago – Luppino as well ends up on the news because of Operation Eyfhemos,[91] even though neither of the two men is accused of anything.

Many publicly recognized men, entrepreneurs, their successes, and their friendships, as in Australia, so in Calabria. Have you noticed?

A world of very archaic rituals, where respect is not just used as a criminal tool but also it is also rooted in family honour and history. This is the world of the Alvaro clan, described in Eyfhemos. A world where, if someone with high social status, like Luppino or Madafferi, is mentioned, it means something for the authorities, aside from any criminal conduct. The 'ndrangheta, its glue, its values, its internal machinery, is indeed not all about crime.[92] In fact, keeping the *organization*, to some extent, detached or distant from criminal activities is a feature of the 'ndrangheta's secrecy and power. It is eventually what keeps the 'ndrangheta resilient and alive: *being able to compartmentalize.*

In August 2020, *The Age* reported that – as confidential police documents released as part of the Gobbo royal commission reveal – the police had at some point considered Tony Madafferi as the man who ordered the hit on Mario Condello.[93] Condello, Calabrian, a drug trafficker, loan shark and money launderer with close links to the Australian 'ndrangheta and other crime families of Melbourne, was killed in 2006, but they never found the triggerman. Now, I can only imagine what kind of conversations keep going on between Mr Madafferi and the journalists that call him to comment on this kind of news!

'What is there to comment about? Go and find a job. Where does this bullshit come from? It has nothing to do with me,'[94] Tony Madafferi replied to the journalist asking for a comment about his alleged role as *capo-bastone* of Melbourne, after Operation Eyfhemos. These criminal scenarios have indeed nothing to do with him, from an Australian perspective, for sure.

Bombs, Bridges and Gold

What a city, Adelaide. 'The city's asleep and the church is bare', someone said to me once about Adelaide. I never quite knew where this quote came from; I did Google it and couldn't find it! A fitting description, the warmth, the sleep in between churches, Adelaide.

'What kind of Italian are you?'

What do you read in this sentence? Probably nothing, really. The meaning, as is often the case, is given by the context, and by the sender. This was a message I received in my inbox in July 2019 – I was in Montreal. I ignored it.

'You must be the cop-lover traitor kind of type'.

A follow-up message, same person, in December 2019, months later. *Why? Why would someone you don't know send you unsolicited messages like this one? Someone you know only by their family's surname; someone that you know that they know who you are and what you do for a living.*

I guess to some people these messages could sound provocative or just like a nuisance. For me, they were about *recognition. He knows that I know who he is* and he counts on that when sending a few words that are not just provocative, they carry a pinch of intimidation.

This was the second time I got unwanted attention and 'friendly' warnings from someone *allegedly* close to 'ndrangheta clans. Of all places, in Adelaide, a city where nothing much seems to happen.

The first time I had this unpleasant experience, it was my first time in Adelaide. I couldn't really believe then that someone would tell me to 'start doing something else' and that my surname 'attracted attention, you know?' and 'What? You think they don't know you are poking your nose into their affairs?' I couldn't really believe that was happening to me, I didn't really know anything about anyone, I had just started my research! *Ah, how the optics of what you seem to do and know count more than what you actually do and know!*

It was October 2015 and I fell in love with the sunsets over the beach in Glenelg.

Sunsets

When the sun sets each day at the end of October in Adelaide, one cannot be sure what year they will wake up in tomorrow. On that terrace at the Liberty Towers in the suburban area of Glenelg – *what floor was it?* – I got completely lost in the pink sky, the Barossa wine and the fresh breeze from the ocean, all by myself. I never enjoyed being alone so much as during October 2015 in Adelaide.

Adelaide. It sounds so much better if you pronounce it in the Italian way. *A.DE.LA.I.DE.* All the letters, all of them. Such a smooth sound, smoother than the rushed English 'Adelaide', where you lose half of the word. *Adleid*, that's how it sounds.

With only 175 years of history, now perhaps 180? – the capital of South Australia wasn't there in 1800. *Can you believe it? In our world so old.* And yet Adelaide is not even remotely new, parts of it look like the nineteenth century. With the sun that touches everything, everything feels *young* anyway.

There are women wearing hair clips like the ones you could see on the cover of a 1960s magazine, on a Sunday morning in Glenelg. And the colours of dresses are almost always pink or some shade of pink.

There are men waiting silently by the little, almost deserted stations outside the city, to get on the train to the centre, under those cute Victorian roofs over the platforms, white or light green or yellow, with those squiggles that Queen Victoria clearly liked. They are wearing just swimwear, those men, they might just go for a quick swim; *everyone seems just about to go for a quick swim here in Glenelg, by the sea, in South Australia.*

Adelaide is self-contained. Like one of those snow globes, though without the snow. The Victorian market right in the city centre, the University of Adelaide, beautifully old-looking, near the Museum of South Australia. The museum of immigration, with the history very much revisited, where the story of an Australian free colony and the White Australia policy become intertwined, in between political correctness and shame. Oh, and the opals. *Who knew Adelaide had a love affair with opals?*

The dolphins, I saw them right at sunrise swimming around while I tried to set foot in the freezing cold ocean water of mid-spring. I so wanted to try to swim in that ocean and I lasted for two whole minutes; too cold. And the flies coming out of the water. No one had told me about the weird behaviour of flies on the beaches in Australia, it's like they have iron legs or wings or whatever. You just can't shake them off, they get glued on you. *What the hell …*

In Glenelg, there is a pier that helps you look into the horizon. I walked almost every day right over the edge of the pier, where the horizon helped me think. I walked for kilometres on the beaches from Glenelg, east, west, wherever.

And then the animals of Adelaide: just a few kilometres outside the city centre there are parks and animal reserves, like Cleland Wildlife Park, with koalas and kangaroos eating out of my hands or chewing eucalyptus leaves right in my face, pretty much stoned. *Look*, they say, *we can just stay here and chill*. This was the first time I saw kangaroos – grey, brown, red! – and koalas.

Adelaide was the second city, after Canberra, that I visited in Australia, before Melbourne even. For the first couple of days, I had to remind myself that I *actually* was in Australia. *How far is Australia? And I was there.* It felt like I could leave things behind in the strange slowing down of the hours. Most of the day, everyone I knew back in Europe was asleep; what a sense of freedom.

I learned lessons the first time I went to Adelaide. Many Italian, Calabrian, families have lived at the side of the mountain there, west of the city, for decades. I remembered Nonno Bruno, my grandfather, telling me stories about the times after the war when people left the villages of Aspromonte to go to Australia. 'It couldn't have been worse than Calabria', he said. 'I was supposed to go to Adelaide, but then I got injured and stayed, I wasn't good enough to work in the farms there.'

In between the pink and orange sunsets, the soft red wine, the squared clean streets of the city centre, it was easy to forget that Adelaide had a dark past. A bit like Calabria, where underneath an apparently beautiful and unassuming surface, there run deep and shameful truths.

Wine

Little by little I got used to the pink and orange and purple and red of the sky in Glenelg, day after day, for 12 days saying Adelaide in Italian, in October 2015, while drinking wine, all by myself. Oh, the wine of Adelaide, the wine of the Barossa Valley, which I managed to properly visit only in 2019.

That the Barossa Valley is wine heaven is indeed a well-known fact. Certainly, South Australia's relationship with wine is a very successful love story. There are many wine tours you can book, where a happy tour guide in a van will take you and other guests around the valley for you to sip delicious wine and try locally sourced cheese and fruit. My friend Bea and I chose the tour that had the most packed into one day. That weekend in March 2019 was my holiday weekend, no research, no 'ndrangheta, just endless fields of violet, blue and yellow, my best friend, wine and cheese. However, when we reached the third winery of the day, already a bit dizzy and cheerful from the wine we had already drunk, there I was back again into facts and knowledge related to organized crime, or *alleged* organized crime, or mafia, in Australia.

Peter Lehmann is a famous winery in the Barossa; in 2016, it was acquired by the Casella Family Brands, from Griffith, NSW.[1] Anyone who has ever set foot in a shop in the United Kingdom that sells wine will have seen the Yellow Tail Australian wine, with fluo colours and a kangaroo on the label. Yellow Tail is the Casellas' best-known wine, but the family owns several other brands and many companies across Australia. They are also the sponsors of local Italian festas and local sports teams in Griffith. *Yes, Griffith again.* Due to the location of their business, their Italian (Sicilian) origin and one of the three brother's involvement in drug cultivation, the Casella family has been suspected on a few occasions of mafia proximity.[2] In 2009, someone tried to extort money from the family in exchange for not revealing secrets about the alleged involvement of Filippo Casella, the patriarch, in cannabis cultivation and in the murder of a cousin in the mid-1980s linked to the local 'ndrangheta clans.[3] Marcello's (one of the three brothers) links with a drug network in the Riverina Valley,[4] headed by Luigi Fato,[5] also attracted media scrutiny. Fato was jailed for 16 years in 2016.

'It's all happening. It has taken this long, but it is all happening. And Marcello is real keen about doing his thing', Fato was intercepted saying in 2013.

Marcello Casella was accused of offering funding, equipment and knowledge of irrigation – which he, as a winemaker, could indeed offer – for the cultivation of cannabis. He pleaded guilty to a lesser offence – concealing information – and he got a six-month non-custodial sentence. The charges laid out in February 2014 against him, together with other Griffith locals, including two other men of Calabrian descent, Saverio Ciampa and Pasquale Sergi,[6] were not the first ones for him, either, as he had been convicted and had served a sentence in Queensland in the mid-1990s; he also had problems with the law for his Bronze Wing Ammunition company.[7] Marcello Casella resigned as director of Casella Family Brands in February 2014 because the family business could not be associated with such criminal charges. However, while he was standing trial in the NSW District Court in 2018, he was still using his skills in corporate governance to benefit business ventures he shared with two other men, a local politician aiming at federal politics and a local entrepreneur. Around the companies the trio was involved with, which Casella funded, doubts about transparency emerged, including shady donations to the Liberal Party.[8]

Shadows of dirty business and concerns over the true meaning of the family's philanthropic endeavours can be considered somewhat normal when it comes to family dynasties like that of the Casellas; maybe drugs less so. But the Casellas are a family whose business keeps growing – as their acquisitions in South Australia show. This is a family that clearly pairs business acumen with a strong influence over the territory of Griffith, to which it is tied through fundraising, sponsorships and many other social and financial investments.

Suggestions of mafia behaviours and mafia proximity, with these preconditions, are quick to emerge due to the history of the territory of Griffith. In the Italian community of Griffith, everyone knows each other, and even winemakers have worked with one another. For example, John Casella, now managing director of the family's winery, used to work for Tony Sergi; surely things can get messy, if journalists or analysts try to make sense of such connections.

In fact, John Casella sued Fairfax Media in 2011 for an allegedly defamatory article in the *Sydney Morning Herald* that insisted on his connections with Tony Sergi, Marcello's criminal past and the mixed reputation of the family.[9] In that case, the Supreme Court considered the article not defamatory because guilt by association does not exist in Australia.

> The article as a whole is capable of suggesting that the plaintiff is one of a close Italian family in control of substantial commercial operations, members of which have a criminal background and against whom allegations of criminality have been made. However, in my opinion, the guilt or involvement in criminal activities of the identified family members provides no rational basis for the inference that the plaintiff himself is involved in the criminal organisation, the Mafia.

That day in the Barossa Valley, once again, I had a very familiar feeling, of circling back to Griffith every time something with a potential criminal dimension involved the Southern Italian community. *Was there – is there – a problem with news reporting, or is there also something about the … slipperiness – Is that the right word? – the ambiguous nature of these matters in Australia?*

And, moreover, where do we draw the line between mafia behaviours and any other crime, such as business or financial crime, especially if it involves (Italian-descent) family dynasties?

Bombing

In August 2019, the Supreme Court of South Australia heard another case about adverse publicity in which various articles in the media seemed to associate a man, Domenic Perre, with the 'ndrangheta in more or less direct ways.[10] Domenic Perre, on trial for drug trafficking on that occasion, contended that the adverse publicity could deprive him of a fair trial and amounted to an abuse of process. Overall, the court found, the articles associating Mr Perre with the 'ndrangheta were not as detrimental to him as some other facts reported in the news about his past drug convictions and about the 1994 events at the National Crime Authority (NCA) bombing.

The NCA bombing, another thing that everyone in Australia knows about. I had no idea to what extent this was the case until I met with a very nice man,

Michael, who was writing a book about it in Adelaide; he shared with me his doubts, concerns, experiences. *Oh, and he was the one who told me about the opals!*

The story of Domenic Perre is unique because it involves this cold case, the so-called NCA bombing in 1994, and, incidentally, touches upon another important case as well, the assassination of AFP Commissioner Colin Winchester in Canberra in 1989. Let's go in order.

At just after 7.00 am on 2 March 1994, an employee of the NCA collected the NCA's mail for the day at the General Post Office. A red card in the post office box said that there was a package waiting to be collected from the counter. He collected it, a red, white and yellow Express Post package, addressed to 'NCA, Geoffrey Bowen'. The sender appeared to be 'IBM Promotions'. Geoffrey Bowen arrived in his office on the 12th floor at 9 am, called the post office downstairs and asked whether a package had arrived for him. He was expecting some exhibits to use in a trial against a man named Perre the next day. He was told a package had arrived, but Bowen recognized that he was not expecting *that* package, nothing about computers! Bowen joked, tragically, 'it might be a bomb'! As it was unsolicited mail, the package was scanned, but the scan didn't show any anomaly. At 9.15 am Bowen opened the package.

> There was a loud crack, like a rifle shot or something similar, and I remember Geoff letting out a strangled-type cry, a yell, and falling sideways, and then – it must have been almost instantaneously – then there was an enormous buffeting of – like wind buffeting and an enormous sound that I can only describe as very very loud static. That is what it was like. I was immediately blinded. That was the last thing I saw.[11]

These are the words of Peter Wallis, solicitor with the NCA working with Bowen, who was severely injured in the explosion. Detective Sergeant Geoffrey Bowen was killed. Nine days later a man, Domenic Perre, was arrested and charged with the bombing.

Perre, from Platì (*again!*), had arrived in Australia in November 1962 with his family and, at the time of the bombing, was already known to Australian authorities because he had been involved, since 1980, in trafficking cannabis.

The NCA bombing case proceeded schizophrenically. In early September 1994, the director of public prosecutions entered a *nolle prosequi* in relation to both charges against Perre: not enough evidence. But the state coroner of South Australia carried out a new inquest in 1999. A lot of the coroner's inquest revolved around the behaviour of Mr Perre before and after the bombing:[12] his aversion to Bowen had become almost an obsession, they said. There were so many lies told to the police back then.

There was, for example, a letter by Perre to the owner of Central Firearms, a place where Perre was a regular. Perre was asking for support in claiming that another man, a gunsmith at the Central Firearms, was responsible for mailing the bomb, and that that man had confessed to him, Perre, but was afraid to confess to the police.

> Don't be afraid, cooperate, you will be doing the right thing and I will look after you as my brother and my lawyer will help you any time. He did it and I will surely die in jail if you my friend do not help, please if you believe in God and Jesus help me this man is evil. Your friend Domenic – GOD BLESS YOU.[13]

The whole inquest is full of these pleas. The coroner eventually concluded that Mr Perre was indeed responsible for the NCA bombing.

> I find, pursuant to Section 25(1) of the Coroners Act (1975), that the circumstances of the death of Detective Sergeant Geoffrey Leigh Bowen were that he died when he opened a parcel bomb, sent to him by Domenic Perre, and the bomb exploded in his hands.[14]

The vicissitudes surrounding the Perre family since the NCA bombing have obviously been subject to public scrutiny. The involvement of members of this family in the drug trade has been the most recurrent element of such interest.

Firstly, in September 1993, Northern Territory police found a crop of cannabis comprising 10,000 plants at a remote location in the Hidden Valley worth a total value of over A$40 million. Francesco Perre, Domenic's brother, was arrested together with 12 other people, including other Calabrians. Among them was Antonio Perre, uncle of Domenic and Francesco, who was in Australia on a tourist visa at the time. Antonio Perre, from Platì, had entered Australia after falsely declaring he had never been charged with a criminal activity: in truth, he had been sentenced for murder and had spent 12 years in prison. For the Hidden Valley operation, he was sentenced to 18 months' imprisonment and was eventually extradited back to Italy in 1994. After the raids in 1993, it was suggested that the people arrested at the scene in the Hidden Valley were just one part of the criminal enterprise. The investigations confirmed that Domenic Perre and others in Adelaide were the importers. The *Sunday Territorian*, on 30 October 2016, reported that at the time investigations had looked at the involvement of Calabrian 'ethnic organised crime', the mafia, the Honoured Society, the 'ndrangheta, call it as you may. Incidentally, this is the article that Mr Perre has been complaining about, as he found it detrimental to his reputation.

When NCA agents carried out a search at Perre's house in 1993 – and among them was Detective Bowen – they also found equipment for telephone interception, which was also seized. The search was carried out while no one was home, something that, understandably, would have upset anyone. Surely, Perre was very annoyed. He identified who had actually entered his house and complained about them stealing stuff, including his firearms. This grudge would be recorded later as significant, during the coroner's inquest in 1999 and the trial in 2020.

In fact, on 1 March 2018, Domenic Perre was again arrested and charged with the murder of Detective Sergeant Bowen and the attempted murder of Mr Wallis. In February 2020, Perre pleaded not guilty.[15] The trial in the Supreme Court started in November 2020 and lasted until summer 2021, one of the longest trials in Australia's history. The verdict took longer than anticipated, such was the complexity of the case. In March 2022 the verdict was still pending. It will be very significant whichever way it goes. I was asked to serve as an expert witness on the case on matters related to Calabrian culture and mafia culture. *Is there a way to link Calabrian culture and mafia (sub)culture, to argue that someone's behaviour is in fact linked to both?* That was the prosecutor's question to me. *Imagine that. One of the most difficult things I have ever done. I doubted myself several times and cursed the interpretative nature of social sciences.* The case of the prosecution rested on the assumption that 'regardless of whether the accused identifies as a member of 'ndrangheta, he and his family have been raised and lived in that culture'.[16] They continued:

> Those cultural attitudes have a bearing on the assessment of a number
> of aspects of the evidence of the case including … the importance and
> sanctity of family … the role of women … the distrust of authority,
> particularly law enforcement … the culture of silence.

Throughout the years, his involvement in drugs had not stopped. In 1997 and in 1998, Domenic Perre received six-year and four-year sentences in both South Australia and the Northern Territory for drug offences (production of amphetamines). The media at the time reported that Mr Perre had resorted to drug production because he was broke: the costs for the NCA bombing defence case and the Northern Territory cannabis crop charges had been too much.[17] He requested legal aid. Other members of his family, his brother Francesco and Francesco's wife Rita, were at different times charged with drug and firearms offences.[18] Domenic Perre himself was convicted again, while in prison, for drug and firearms offences in September 2020,[19] just weeks before the NCA bombing trial started again. Lawyer Anthony Perre, Domenic's son, and his wife Emma were convicted of stealing electricity and possessing equipment for growing cannabis in 2017 as well, all of which was reported in local news.[20] A A$6,000 fine and the suspension of

Anthony Perre's certificate to practise for only six weeks 'outraged police and fellow lawyers who felt his conduct tarnished the profession and should have warranted a more severe sanction'.[21]

Clearly, this family has been attracting quite a lot of attention due to the NCA bombing case and their involvement with illegal drugs. It is indeed understandable that a high-profile murder case, an explosion in the city centre, could be seen as a direct attack on the institutions, almost as a terrorist message. The connection of the Perre family to this case, their record of criminal activities and the confrontational attitude of family members towards the authorities have all been considered echoes of mafia-type behaviours. These echoes, paired with the ethnic origins of the family, from Platì, and their family ties to Griffith (Domenic and Francesco's close relatives – aunts, uncles – with their same surname are married into the Barbaro family/clan in Griffith) and to other people of interest to the NCA, might clarify why a 'mafia doubt' was cast upon them. This also poses questions, *de relato*, about the true meaning – intimidation and power affirmation perhaps? – of the NCA bombing if Perre in the end is convicted for it. *Was it revenge? Was it to show off, an affirmation of power? Was it a message to someone else? Was it the 'ndrangheta? And, if so, Australian or Calabrian, or both?*

Excellent murders

Now, what if I told you that another high-profile cold case in Australia – the assassination of AFP Assistant Commissioner Colin Winchester, in January 1989 in Canberra – also seems to have links with Adelaide and, indirectly, to the Perre family? Wouldn't you feel, as I feel, that sense of claustrophobia once again, as things seem to intersect and connect to one another oddly on this 'ndrangheta trail?

The Winchester case is also quite complicated after decades of judicial back and forth. Public servant David Eastman was convicted of this murder in 1995 but 20 years later, in 2014, following a Commission of Inquiry ('The Martin Report')[22], a court effectively ordered a retrial and reopened the case.[23] Other investigative paths had not been fully explored; some things had been actively buried. There were also some so-called 'Calabrian leads'.

The Martin Report described how Mr Winchester was perceived as a corrupt police officer by some families of Calabrian extraction who were involved in drug production. An AFP report in 1989 had advanced the hypothesis that these families might have believed that Winchester had failed to protect them – as he had promised to do – thus leaving them exposed to police scrutiny in Operations Bungadore 1 and 2. Significant was a declaration of the Australian Bureau of Criminal Intelligence in December 1990:[24]

The murder of Assistant Commissioner Winchester on 10 January 1989 was committed by, or on behalf of, an organised group of Italian residents in Griffith and Canberra to protect the assets and liberty of those persons involved in the past and continued large scale production and marketing of Indian hemp in Australia.

Once again, the Griffith connection. *To note: this essentially would mean that three major cold cases, and murders, in Australia, of Donald MacKay, Colin Winchester and Geoffrey Bowen, could all be connected to the 'ndrangheta somehow? OK, breathe.*

Exhibits in the Eastman Inquiry that dealt with the Calabrian connection mention the usual suspects: members of the Barbaro family in Griffith and Melbourne; known Italian/Calabrian organized crime figures with Calabrian surnames – Pelle, Nirta, Alvaro – all extremely well-known mafia clans in Calabria, all intertwined in family and business networks as exposed by Operations Bungadore 1 and 2 and other investigations of the time in NSW, ATC (Australian Capital Territory) and Victoria.

Remember from the previous chapter the man Luigi Pochi, Tony Sergi's brother-in-law? Heavily involved in the Griffith area Indian hemp production? Well, he was also of interest of the authorities in this murder, considered as a high-ranking member of the 'ndrangheta.

An AFP report of 1989 acknowledges that information received from Italy and during Operation Seville (a joint operation by AFP Canberra and NSW Police in the early 1980s into production of Indian hemp within the Italian community) point to two individuals, Bruno Musitano and Giuseppe Ielasi, who *may* have been brought over from Italy to commit the murder.

I was asked in 2017 to provide an expert statement to the defence team of Mr Eastman. When the case was reopened, the defence team wished to re-establish the narrative around the events of the Winchester murder and put the 'mafia' lead back on the stand. The Italian evidence stood out to me. Italian authorities, Carabinieri, on 25 January 1989, had sent the AFP information about Bruno Musitano leaving Italy two months earlier to go to Australia to perform a deed to 'redeem his family honour'.[25] Italian authorities had warned that 'Bruno Musitano is renowned for his 'ndranghita [*sic*] associations' and considered a 'dangerous person due to his family background'. Also, he was a capable weapon handler. On 12 June 1989, Italian authorities sent further information, advising that Musitano had been sent to Australia to kill Assistant Commissioner Winchester and that arrangements had been made for him to remain in Australia and marry an Australian resident. According to the files, Bruno Musitano had been to Australia before, in 1985, to pay the corrupt 'chief of police' (that would be Winchester) to allow drugs to go through. Musitano had to return to Italy but, when Winchester did not accept the bribe, Musitano came back to kill him. This, in summary, was the information passed on by the

Italian carabinieri. These were the findings included in Operation Peat (1989): 'Suspicion of Calabrian Organised Crime Involvement the Murder of Assistant Commissioner Colin Stanley Winchester'.[26]

I'll repeat it. *Italian carabinieri sent this information.*

How is that possible that this information had not turned the whole case around? The AFP found 'no firm evidence obtained to support the information received' even though 'the Musitano/Ielasi information has been the most positive indication to date that the murder was arranged and executed by Calabrian organised crime elements'.

No kidding.

Bruno Musitano had relatives in Melbourne – in the Barbaro family – and in Adelaide – in the Perre family. Ielasi, the other man cited by the Italian authorities, remained in Melbourne; Musitano went to Adelaide. Now this is a bit of a merry-go-round of names. Bruno Musitano married into the Pollifrone family. For Australian authorities, the Pollifrones have known 'ndrangheta ties in Adelaide.[27] Musitano also has more links with the Perre family. Sam Catanzariti is Musitano's cousin. Catanzariti was also an associate of Domenic Perre targeted in Operation Zoom, which led, in 1996, to the arrest of Perre, Catanzariti and others for setting up an amphetamine factory.[28] Additionally, in 1993, Bruno Musitano was among the people arrested in the Hidden Valley raids, involving Antonio, Frank and Domenic Perre. Musitano was sentenced to four years' imprisonment on that occasion.[29] Even in this case, as we have seen in Melbourne and in Griffith, criminal association and conspiracy are determined by family ties and interfamilial vicissitudes, rather than just by shared ethnicity: there is something more about being in a Calabrian mafia family than just being Calabrian, of course. There is affinity, there must be.

Cerberus

Ten kilometres north-east of Adelaide city centre is the suburban area of Newton. The area is commonly known to host a significant population of Italian origin. I went there in December 2017, when I took the car to drive from Adelaide to Mildura. It was boiling hot, the phone had died from overexposure to the sun in the car and I decided to stop in the first place that had parking.

Caffé Settebello in front of me. I could have an early lunch, which wasn't too bad. After a pizza with a strange taste – *garlic perhaps?* – but nevertheless okay, I decide to walk around. Broad streets, so typical in suburban Australia, low trees, and houses. No one around, everything looks very *large*. The Italianness of this place is in the names of restaurants and bars, pretty much as in Griffith and in Mildura. No. 1 Flotta Street, a ten-minute walk from the cafe, is a broad empty space with a nice villa.

It's not difficult to imagine the past sometimes.

On the evening of Saturday, 2 September 1989, in a garage at 1 Flotta Street in Newton, about 20 males of Calabrian descent attended what appeared to be a secret meeting. Conversations intercepted at the time by the AFP led them to suspect this was a 'ndrangheta meeting. The host was Umberto Pollifrone, who at the time lived nearby in Newton. Umberto Pollifrone was the father-in-law of Bruno Musitano and was allegedly involved with other 'ndrangheta members in Canberra, Griffith, Sydney and Adelaide, according to the authorities. The police managed to listen to the conversations in the garage at 1 Flotta Street thanks to a hidden listening device. Raids followed on the houses of Musitano and Pollifrone, looking for illicit firearms that had been mentioned in the meeting.

Located in a wall cavity of a shed in Pollifrone's backyard, the authorities found a small notebook containing a 'ndrangheta code of initiation rituals.[30] Two years earlier, in Nailsworth, another suburban area of Adelaide, another code of the 'ndrangheta had been found in the possession of Raffaele Alvaro.[31] In and around Adelaide, 'ndrangheta rituals were known and shared. This is a sign that the *organization* of the 'ndrangheta – with its rituals, its lifeblood – was alive and tenacious. *Were these rituals used to glue together an existing organization or to 'engineer' one? So far from home in Calabria, was keeping the 'ndrangheta alive a choice, could it be done 'artificially'? I noted this thought down back then, worth reconsidering.*

Without the rituals, the identity of the organization is difficult to recognize.[32]

Cerberus was the mythological three-headed dog that guarded the gates of Hades. The allegory was used for Operation Cerberus in late 1980s and early 1990s, a joint-agency task force led by the NCA looking into Italo-Australian organized crime, mostly the 'ndrangheta. *I wondered whether it was a reference to the 'ndrangheta's special relation with the number three, with reference to a 'trinity', forming this mafia.*

The 'ndrangheta's heads can be looked at from various perspectives: *crimes, behaviours* and *organization* are the three heads that I managed to identify.[33] These three heads – as analytical dimensions – need to be seen all together to understand the 'ndrangheta phenomenon in its entirety. It is, however, often the case that we can see elements pointing to one of these dimensions alone. In Adelaide, and in Australia overall, we have often seen the *crimes*, usually drugs, as well as some recurrent modes of *behaviours*, including family ties coming *before* ethnicity and social ties; disrespect for authorities and police; low-profile licit activities; small-scale entrepreneurialism; preservation of cultural traditions; and others. The *organization* is what allows us to appraise these crimes and behaviours as manifestations of a criminal association. The organization is less visible – the rituals, the rankings – due to its inherently secretive – and often misunderstood – nature. Only the reputation is clearly visible, of the organizational elements.

Operation Cerberus tried to map the families and their associations, across the whole of Australia. The operation's findings were in fact updated in 2003 and several times since then.

One of the impressive things about Cerberus was the analysis of the networks based on a mix between family ties and criminal ties. In the case of the Perre family, for example, Cerberus identified another interesting connection with 'ndrangheta members. This was the connection with Bruno Romeo, aka 'The Fox' – married to Domenic Perre's cousin. According to police files, Bruno 'the Fox' Romeo was either the boss of South Australia or close to being the boss. *Is that relevant information to know? Looking at the way the 'ndrangheta family bonds work, it might be.*

Certainly, Bruno 'the Fox' Romeo was one of the protagonists of Cerberus and so was his family. Their activities ranged from South Australia to Queensland, primarily drugs related.

In the words of a prominent police informant in Cerberus in late 1980s *(keep him in mind for later ...)*, Bruno Romeo had been involved in the drug trade for at least 15 years (at the time), had properties in South Australia and Queensland, and used to do labouring work to 'fake' a normal income. According to the informant, Bruno Romeo's close friend was Dominic Sergi – *remember him? 'Little Domenic' Sergi whom we talked about!* Considered a very senior member of the 'ndrangheta, Romeo consistently carried out extortions and organized major drug-related activities and other activities, including fox skin trade between Tasmania, Victoria and New South Wales. Interesting characteristics, behavioural traits of the man, emerge from this portrait:

> Romeo has always had other people take the blame and to go to gaol for him when his operations have been discovered. He has never been locked up and he pays a lot of money for protection [...] He never takes any risks himself, always has other people take the risks for him.[34]

We are talking about a man who was born in 1929 and was in his fifties and sixties in the 1980s; thus, a first-generation *'ndranghetista.*

Romeo seemingly had over a dozen people go to jail for him in Adelaide, but also in Shepperton and in Canberra. For example, a man, Antonio Perre, who went to jail for him in Canberra was apparently too scared to speak out against Romeo to the police, so he took the full blame. This was the case of the Katunga Crop in 1981, when people in the Sergi clan, in Shepperton, Victoria, were arrested; among the suspects were also Romeo's wife and his sons Domenico, Giuseppe and Bruno Lee.

All three of Bruno Romeo's sons have seemingly continued on the criminal path, especially involved with drugs, beyond South Australia. Bruno 'The Fox' moved to Queensland and started investing in building properties as well as organizing drug trades from there. His son, Bruno Lee, followed in his footsteps and in 2003 was considered 'the only Queensland based IOC identity identified previously by the Cerberus Task Force that according to QPS data is still active in criminal activities'.[35] Another son, Giuseppe, remained in Adelaide, but he seemed to maintain his heroin business through contacts with traffickers in Sydney and in Perth, where he was eventually jailed.

Note: one of the associates of Bruno 'The Fox' Romeo was a man called Antonio Rizzotto, a Sydney-based man involved in the heroin trade in the 1980s and 1990s and considered a senior member of the 'ndrangheta. *Remember that name from the previous chapter?* He was a senior member of the Calabria Club in Sydney.

Calabrian claustrophobia much, anyone?

More connections to heroin and to drug traffickers in Sydney run in the Romeo family.

In the 2000s, Giuseppe Romeo was apparently working with local *'ndranghetisti* within the Perre and Carbone clans and the Sergi clan in NSW. Among his associates, in the network reconstructions of Cerberus, were also outlaw motorcycle gang members, such as Tony Sobey, vice president of the Gypsy Jokers in Adelaide. Bruno Lee, Giuseppe's brother and associate, was often seen with another man of interest, Frank Barbaro.

Another merry-go-round of 'usual' names.

According to the 2003 findings of Cerberus, this Frank Barbaro, who was 40 years old at the time, was one of the most important men of the 'ndrangheta.

Another Barbaro tale.

Sunshine State

He maintains strong associations across so many states and groups. He regularly travelled by vehicle and plane around to facilitate these contacts and activities. He showed particularly strong travel patterns between Canberra, Melbourne, Brisbane, Adelaide, the Gold Coast and Sydney. It is assessed that a number of the common links may not be able to be maintained without him, at least initially, without his continued shuttling between states.[36]

We are in the 2000s and 2010s. Based in NSW, Frank Barbaro's plan was to move to the Gold Coast. He owned car dealerships and night clubs in Canberra, so he travelled often for his legitimate businesses. He attended funeral services every other week, no matter where they were. Out of respect for the deceased's family and for networking, said the authorities. *And mind you, in Australia you really have to travel by plane if you want to go anywhere fast; it's difficult to travel by car, let alone train; too long, too slow, too far.*

An interesting man, Frank Barbaro. *His father, well … his father is a whole other story, and we'll get to that a bit later.* But Frank was both a man of honour *and* a next-generation *'ndranghetista*, say the authorities.

> He was observed to use notions of honour and respect as a point to initiate standover and intimidation. He was aggressive in demanding respect. He used instances where he claimed to have had his honour or respect violated as jumping off point for threats of violence and demands for 'fines'. These demands for fines seemed to relate to a system of being able to fine other members of the IOC [Italian Organised Crime] milieu if they were proven to have breached particular codes.[37]

Perhaps Cerberus in 2003 had stepped onto something without properly recognizing it. Even though further intelligence of this system of *fines* was not developed, it seems like it could be a sign not only that the man held a high rank in the organization, but also that perhaps he held one of the three functions that make up the *Copiata* in a locale of the 'ndrangheta in Calabria. The *Copiata* is made up of three functions: the *contabile* (taking care of money); the *crimine* (directing criminal activities for the locale); and the *capo-locale* with the *mastro di giornata* (the head and vice-head of the *locale*). Someone who has the power to resolve controversies, to fix problems, to sanction and to re-establish the 'ndrangheta order and keep its traditions safe could be a prominent person in one of these three roles.

Crucial functions in the 'ndrangheta are indeed attributed to those who have the 'right' family lineage and the 'right' type of connections, who is accepted by everyone else as reliable and prestigious. The capacity that Frank Barbaro seemed to have to broker contacts, maintain promises, travel, keep honour and respect as key aspects of his lifestyle, are all signs that he might have had an important function in his 'group' or *locale* and in the overall organization.

It is understandable why. Frank Barbaro's father, Pasquale, aka Peter, aka Principale, Barbaro, was not only one of the most senior members of the 'ndrangheta of his generation, but he was also the first *pentito* of the 'ndrangheta in Australia (at least of a significant level that we know of).

Remember the prominent Cerberus informant? It was him.

Another Barbaro tale.

A cousin of Frank 'Little Trees' Barbaro, Pasquale married one of Little Trees' sisters, Anna, in Platì, while one of his brothers married within the Sergi clan. Pasquale Barbaro, 'Principale', initially claimed that he was no mafia member but that, yes, he knew the Honoured Society and some mafiosi, as he was surrounded by them. This claim was later proven false, as his knowledge was too specific for a simple bystander; he was too involved to be just an observer.

It was 1989 in Brisbane when 'Principale' Barbaro started talking. His son Frank's plan to move to the Gold Coast was in line with his father's choice. *I went to the Gold Coast in July 2017.*

It was the first time I drove an automated car, from the airport in Brisbane onto the five-lane motorway towards the coast. It was late evening going into the night and I remember having one of those moments of realization that *wow, I was driving in Australia!* The arrival in the Gold Coast felt like jumping into a video game. In between a small Las Vegas (not that I ever went to Nevada ...) and a city on the Italian Riviera. LEDs and neon colours, slot machines, casinos, way too cheap or way too expensive tourist restaurants, hotels, skyscrapers, lights, compulsive entertainment, nightlife.

It felt like driving into a video game where the goal was, apparently, to find ... parking!

Gold Coast peak season meant that I had to book a motor inn 20 kilometres away from the conference venue. 'Keep away from that path, there are snakes', was the lovely warning of one of the housekeepers. Also, I had to drive back and forth for three days and each time I struggled to find a parking spot. *What a nightmare.* I was ready to pay for a parking space, like any human being in an Australian city, *if only I could find one.*

The surfing waves of the ocean that almost bang onto the skyscrapers; an amazing walk on the beach, with fine white sand, leaving the city behind and walking into the sea, with the sounds and colours of the night as background. *The Gold Coast is a paradise for investments and for partying.*

They had told me that Queensland doesn't have any 'ndrangheta.

'Just some Sicilians, no Calabrians', a colleague of mine had said on a purely anecdotal basis. And this was also confirmed, to some extent, upon meeting some of the authorities there, apparently clueless about this whole Honoured Society thing – 'isn't that in Melbourne or ... where was it? ... Riverina?'

Historical archives reveal that Queensland had actually been the first to identify the 'ndrangheta.[38] Authorities called it *'camorra'* or *Black Hand* (as *camorra* indicates the extortion of money and the Black Hand was an early name of the mafia – running extortion rackets – in America too) and studied how it impacted the Italian community. The Black Hand extortion rackets in the sugar cane fields were recorded before 1945.[39] Notwithstanding this early bloom, in the past decades Queensland has often been forgotten and is almost never mentioned when it comes to the 'ndrangheta. Sure, there might be business, and sure, individuals from New South Wales have always displayed connections to Queensland, especially to outlaw motorcycle gangs (OMGs) for drug distribution. There are some Barbaro men over there too, such as Harley Barbaro, a biker, nephew of Frank, often mentioned in the 'underworld news' up to March 2022. Frank Barbaro, whom we just mentioned, in the 2000s was said to have a strong relationship (business partnership and godfather to his twins) with Arthur Loveday, the president of the North Coast chapter of the Bandidos in Port Macquarie. Loveday's wife is the sister of Alex Vella, of Maltese origin, national president of the Rebels. The links with other groups, including OMGs, are not sporadic for many Calabrian mafiosi, especially in Queensland. In Queensland there is money laundering as well, say the investigators, which is linked to the huge opportunities for investments in construction and entertainment that the Sunshine State offers.

Queensland also seems to have been a welcoming place for various individuals seeking to leave their old lives behind, maybe to start again. Pasquale 'Principale' Barbaro had moved to Queensland after his divorce. His discussions with his wife Anna over their son Giuseppe, constantly in trouble with the law, led him to leave.

Yes, for Pasquale Principale Barbaro, Canberra wasn't quite right anymore – and yet he had been, allegedly, the boss there for decades. In Queensland he eventually remarried; in Brisbane he was shot dead in 1990, probably for having dishonoured his family and the whole 'ndrangheta.

Anyway, Principale's choices did not much influence the destiny of the family dynasty. In addition to his son Frank, his nephew Pasquale Timothy Barbaro (the son of Principale's son, Giuseppe) also followed the mafia lure.

Let's go, another Barbaro tale! But let's back up a moment.

A quick Google search for the Barbaros in Australia yields two main recent results: first, Pasquale 'Pat' Barbaro (son of Frank Little Trees Barbaro, born in 1961) was arrested and sentenced in Melbourne for the 4.4 tonnes of MDMA shipment with Frank Madafferi and others in 2008; second, Pasquale Timothy Barbaro (born 1981), son of Giuseppe Barbaro and grandson of Pasquale *Principale* Barbaro, nephew of Frank Barbaro (born 1963), was killed in Sydney in 2016.

Gangster-looking, tattoos, expensive clothes and selfies on Instagram: a well-known underworld figure. A TV show about him aired in 2021 called 'Australian Gangster' (no, I haven't watched it … yet!). The murder of Pasquale Timothy Barbaro was the object of public scrutiny.[40] At the time I wondered whether that was a mafia murder and, if so, if that meant retaliation was next. But there was no retaliation, this wasn't a mafia murder. The media looked at his associates – various individuals from all different criminal groups in Sydney, from bikers to drug networks – and obviously at his family. A surname, that of Barbaro – *we know by now* – that is both a curse and a blessing in the underworld. In December 2021, four men, bikies, were convicted for the murder of Pasquale Tim Barbaro, whom one of them called 'the dog', just before describing killing him as 'the best … loved the feeling'.[41] *No, this was not mafia-related. And yet.*

Already in 2003, Pasquale Tim apparently was not getting along with his family. Intelligence records reveal how he was in the process of setting up his own drug distribution network in the Australian Capital Territory (ACT) area, especially for MDMA. But because he was trying to undercut the local market, his quest for independence would have clashed with the family business and effectively made him a rival of his uncle Frank.

Family can indeed become a burden in someone's quest for independence, also in crime.

Cerberus revealed at the time: 'Their "dispute" appears to be under review by the "Mafia" heads in Griffith NSW, as both Frank and Pasquale are claiming the other is a police informant.'[42]

However, the surname 'Barbaro' made Pasquale Tim what he apparently had become. Greedy and risk-prone, highly confident and intelligent in his business choices, he had managed an MDMA distribution network in NSW, ACT and Queensland since early 2000s, seemingly related to his family's (and especially his uncle Frank's) network and trusted associates across Australia.

The power of a surname indicates that a mafia dynasty can be trusted; it is bound together by certain codes of conduct with which all members abide. It's a *'reserve' of reputation* – a prime characteristic of the 'ndrangheta – that still separates some mafia families from others and creates some sort of unspoken and unwritten, but still recognizable, hierarchy among them, based on respect and the weight of history. Reputation is money to mafia groups, as it saves directly on production costs, as well as transaction costs of whatever illicit commodity or service they provide.[43] The more robust their reputation, the less the group needs to use other costly resources, such as violence, to establish their business. Mafia families, especially mafia dynasties, become *known* for the services and activities they carry out. They are also visible in the underworld as people able to be in charge; this brings them *generalized favourability* as they are able to embed themselves into different markets and networks and are resilient.[44]

Mafia reputation, mafia links, or rather, criminal ties among certain individuals of Calabrian/Italian descent in Australia, run deep and far across generations in the country. This is the social capital of mafia groups down under,[45] in between external connections, social embeddedness and recognition.

Ain't no sunshine

Sunshine State Queensland is recognized as a welcoming place to those who want to start over; another man who seemingly wanted to take this chance was named Pasquale Cufari.

This story is about Queensland as much as it is about Adelaide and Mildura again. And Calabria, of course. I heard the details from the news and was later asked to reflect on them as an expert witness in a trial. This is not clearly linked to a proper mafia story in Queensland, but its background might be. The details of this story emerged because of a food safety crisis beginning in September 2018, when numerous punnets of strawberries grown in Queensland and Western Australia were found to be contaminated with needles – needles were found in the punnets.[46] All over Australia, strawberries were recalled from supermarket shelves; farmers were forced to throw away their crops. After a series of investigations, in November that year, a farm supervisor was eventually arrested in Brisbane and charged with seven counts of contaminating goods in relation to one of the initial cases of contamination. Charges were dismissed in mid-2021.[47] I like to think I contributed to this, as I had served as a witness for the defence to identify patterns of corporate sabotage and other possible lines of enquiry. *No, it did not seem mafia-related.*

When Mark, a journalist I had met in Brisbane – *in front of a glorious pint of beer on the Southbank of the city* – called me up about this story, I had no idea how this could even be related to any mafia stuff. Mark told me how Donnybrook Berries, one of the farms at the centre of the contamination scandal, had slowly become the region's largest producer of strawberries and how this farm had an interesting past. After Mark briefed me, I talked to my friend Marie, who was also interested in this story.

'Pasquale Cufari, from Mildura, he owns Donnybrook. He still lives in Mildura but goes to Queensland once or twice a year. Where did we hear that name?' Marie quizzed me.

Media scrutiny followed, because journalists love unearthing a mafia connection even when it doesn't relate to the actual event.[48] They revealed that members of the Cufari family, from Platì and nearby Natile in Calabria, were believed to have been involved in several mafia-related activities in the 1980s and 1990s. The family was already recorded by ASIO's 1965 Brown report as part of the locale of Mildura, with Pasquale's father, Francesco, being one of the leaders for Red Cliffs.

'Oh, and they have always been citrus or fruit farmers, like in Calabria!' Marie chuckled.

Pasquale Cufari's uncle, Tony, was involved with Joe Arena – a renowned mafia member in Melbourne close to Liborio Benvenuto. Cufari helped Arena to legitimize large sums of money; he was eventually jailed in 1992. And Pasquale himself had served a five-year jail sentence in the mid-1990s for trafficking cannabis. According to the updated findings of Operation Cerberus by the NCA in 2003, Pasquale Cufari was believed to be an associate of Carmelo Loprete's network in Adelaide. Carmelo Loprete was one of four individuals arrested in Operation Decollo in Italy – and never extradited from Australia – as broker to 'ndrangheta clans in shipping cocaine from South America to Australia via Italy between 2002 and 2004.[49]

'Adelaide to Mildura is four-and-a-half hours; you might live in Mildura but, often, your affairs are in Adelaide', was the comment of a Mildura police agent with whom I discussed the 'mafia' in the area.

After the events of the 2000s, Pasquale Cufari wanted to turn a page and invested in Queensland, where he founded his company, Sylina Pty Ltd, exporting citrus fruit and grapes. While nothing suggests that the strawberry needle sabotage was a deliberate act against the Cufaris, not even the Sunshine State could bury the 'ndrangheta-related story from the past for long. Too juicy, for some newspapers, to point out how Queensland has been a welcoming place for former or current alleged *'ndranghetisti* wishing to invest and/or change their lives.

Hide and seek

There is *continuation* in the 'ndrangheta. We are talking in fact about a *permanent* organization. The past merges into the present, informs new generations and allocates blame and success. It is difficult to escape from the 'ndrangheta; reputation matters as much as family. I am reminded of what the *capo-bastone* Girolamo Molè was intercepted saying to his nephew, reminding him of what the 'ndrangheta really is, even when clans start fighting:[50]

> You cannot destroy history … if you want you can be our ally, if not you go on your own, but whatever you do you need to know your place. History counts for something, sacrifices, jail, everything counts, we respect the past and we respect history, we respect it all and we won't be wrong!

Powerful words to be reminded of on my way to Perth.

If there is one thing that Perth and Brisbane share, it is the sun. The Sunshine State of Queensland and the Golden State of Western Australia are embraced by warmth and ocean waves.

Perth is *too* shiny; *you know what I mean?* It's polished and full of bright lights everywhere, sunny, yellow and blue. In summer 2017 I had enough time to fall in love with the carefree lifestyle of Perth and with the breathtaking red skies over Fremantle at sunset.

Who knew that an entire port could become pink and orange? It's probably there in the port of Fremantle that I learned to love colourful containers.

'Why on earth would you even go to Perth? Nothing ever happens there!', one of my journalist friends in Melbourne had told me. *Genuine stupor.* I learned that a four-hour flight from Sydney or Melbourne is apparently enough to forget that the capital of Western Australia is still in Australia. Yet life in Perth seems pretty good. I could see why someone would choose to settle there.

The only way to escape a 'ndrangheta past is probably to set yourself free.

When the news broke about the arrest of Bruno Crisafi in June 2017,[51] I had not been to Perth yet. You can hide in the 'ndrangheta, yes, you can decide to fly abroad where your relatives will hide and protect you, give you a job as a pizza-maker and help you keep a low profile. You can hide, sure, but you cannot escape. Crisafi had been a *latitante*, a fugitive, in Australia since his arrest in 2015; the man had been convicted of mafia association and drug trafficking and sentenced to a total of 20 years in 2016 in Rome. He was on the run but suddenly decided to go back and surrender to the authorities as soon as he landed in Rome.

What a strange decision; I wondered what prompted it.

Crisafi wasn't the first and certainly will not be the last 'ndrangheta affiliate to go into hiding and disappear in Australia. Family protects and forgets, after all. Affiliate to one of the most important clans of Calabria, the Giorgi clan, aka Cicero, from infamous San Luca, Crisafi was involved with large-scale importation of cocaine into Rome from Colombia and Morocco; he acted as a broker with South American narcos. Learning that a fugitive in the 'ndrangheta had been harboured in Perth might not mean much in itself; after all, it is a matter of family protection, it is predictable, expected. However, it did mean something in my overall trip to Western Australia.

When I drove to Harvey, south of Perth, with my friend Stefano at that time, the feeling that 'someone-can-hide-down-here-and-no-one-would-ever-find-them' was just too real. Around there one could hide fugitives, investments, interests, whatever.

Perth was the last trip I made that summer of 2017. And in so many ways, it was full of elements of oddity in my 'ndrangheta research down under, full of insights and peculiarities that pushed my understanding of the Australian context much further.

It is commonly said that Platì is the mind of the 'ndrangheta and San Luca is the heart. San Luca holds the keys to the rituals and the spirituality of the 'ndrangheta. The village, in Aspromonte, hosts the sanctuary of the Madonna of Polsi, the Madonna of the Mountain, and it is also home of some of the most historical and powerful clans. Those clans that keep the rituals, those that keep the tradition alive.

In the Australian 'ndrangheta, the clans from Platì dominate, with their family dynasties and their history, from Griffith to Melbourne, from Sydney to Canberra, from Adelaide to Brisbane. But in Perth something was different; not less Calabria, but certainly a little less Griffith.

Less Griffith meant less Platì, for the first time, in Australia.

It's not as if there were no clans from San Luca in Australia elsewhere. Indeed, case law shows that, also in 1980s, members of clans from San Luca were involved in the drug trade in other parts of Australia.[52] Domenico Nirta, from San Luca, was believed to be a *capo-bastone* in Canberra in the 1970s and 1980s. In Perth, however, the presence of San Luca clans is felt more than elsewhere in Australia.

Platì and San Luca clans have been connected for decades, of course; the two villages are about 20 kilometres away from one another, which, in the roads of Aspromonte, means about half an hour by car. Historically, the Nirta–Strangio–Romeo clans are linked to the Barbaro–Papalia from

Platì by marriage and blood. The San Luca-based Romeo *'ndrina*, known as 'La Minore', is composed of associates from the Giorgi, Morabito, Pelle, Romeo, Pipicella, Pizzata, Strangio, Giampaolo, Femia, Cua-Ietto, Calabrò and Trimboli families, all from San Luca. The intricacies of surnames here is impressive. The Romeo clan, historically, is linked to the Barbaro clan in Platì as well as the Nirta clan, called 'Scalzone' or 'La Maggiore', comprising Giorgi (aka Cicero), Mammoliti and Nirta-Strangio subgroups. This group has been present in Australia, in Perth and in Canberra especially, since at least the late 1980s, according to Italian police documentation. A crucial element to understand here is the connection of San Luca clans to clans from Siderno, notoriously active in the drug trade internationally. However, in the historical mapping of Australian 'ndrangheta clans, Perth did not feature as an interesting case; things in Perth were probably not seen to be as important as those in Griffith or were not perceived as clearly organized.

Bridges

When, on 15 August 2007, my father received a call from his editor-in-chief, our day at the beach – *to celebrate my birthday, by the way* – was, of course, ruined. There had been a multiple killing in Germany: the 'ndrangheta was on the front pages of international news. The Duisburg massacre involved the death of six people, five of them under 25, in front of a pizzeria, 'Da Bruno', in the city in North Westphalia, Germany. A small figurine card featuring Saint Michael was found in the pocket of one of the victims – *it was his birthday, too – what a coincidence*; the investigators thought it was a sign of an affiliation ritual. A 'ndrangheta affiliation ritual, as the victims were all from San Luca and all part of known 'ndrangheta families.

In San Luca, a feud had erupted in 1991 between the two main families: Nirta–Strangio on one side vs Pelle–Vottari on the other side. Other clans, bearing the same surnames, were not directly involved but had family members who were; things became very tense. Associates from both families, and from their satellite supporter clans, killed each other across the years, including the murder of a woman, Maria Strangio, wife of Giovanni Luca Nirta, on Christmas Day 2006. After this murder, there was Duisburg and a series of anti-mafia operations targeted both *'ndrine*. The Duisburg events, it is commonly believed, woke up Germany, and Europe, to the presence of *'ndranghetisti* outside Italy and their ability to move money and exercise violence abroad. Duisburg is also considered one of the mistakes of the 'ndrangheta that exposed the whole organization to the world and obviously led to increased scrutiny by law enforcement in Italy and abroad.

'We had a chance after Duisburg, a chance to really hurt the heart of the 'ndrangheta. We blew it.' My very first interview for my PhD in 2011 with a former chief prosecutor in Calabria, Salvatore Boemi. I will never forget this statement.

Many people left San Luca in the 1990s also due to this feud, settling in the North of Italy or in Germany, Switzerland, Belgium, the Netherlands and some in Australia as well, looking for new opportunities, going into hiding, looking for family members already abroad who could help them hide, or simply move on, if allowed. In Perth, many arrived from San Luca; some stayed, some eventually returned to Italy.

Sal is almost 40 years of age.[53] He was born in Western Australia, in a suburban area of Perth, known for its nightlife and up-and-coming dining scene. His Calabrian parents had arrived there not long before he was born. He is Australian but his Calabrian roots fascinate him – he is a wog, after all. In Perth he is already known to the authorities for drug trafficking and arms possession. His associates are from various groups, people he grew up with, wogs like him, friends of his family, people with whom his parents speak in dialect. He has never been to Calabria nor Italy. He has heard so much about it. His cousin used to live there, then moved to Germany; now he lives in Perth where he has a successful food business – he is good at all things sweet! His cousin talks about Calabria and about San Luca, what a beautiful place! Their common place of origin, such strange nostalgia. In Germany, his cousin says, the only good thing was that there were relatives; no, he didn't like living in Germany. Perth is cool, he will stay, but Calabria must be one of a kind. His cousin had gone to Perth for a holiday, a holiday that is still ongoing after many years. If Sal wanted to leave, he could go to Europe, indeed, Germany – he still has relatives there who could help him with the language – or he could go to Italy, Calabria, family will welcome him with open arms, a family he has never met! A friend in Perth, also with Calabrian parents born in Siderno (30 kilometres from San Luca), is his associate in business – drugs, weapons – it's good money. They both engage with the main clans in Perth, some Calabrian too, connected to two brothers who run some sort of farming and meat business in the city, while arranging for drug distribution. At times they link up with associates in Adelaide and once even in Melbourne, carrying drugs all the way to Perth from there!

His friend has good contacts in Siderno; sometimes, they send drugs from Europe to be sold in Australia, usually through the port of Hamburg over to Fremantle; other times, they send people, from the village or nearby towns, and all Sal and his friend have to do is to make sure these new arrivals are provided for – find them a job in a pizzeria or in a gelato shop and help them navigate Australian society, without attracting attention.

Eventually, Sal and his friend travel to Calabria; there could be an opportunity to get more involved in some business there, make more money. They go to San Luca first, then Siderno. 'Look, the Australians!' That's what they call them. 'You speak English, that's useful!' They tell them. They meet relatives, who introduce them to people. 'Go to Rome, then Milan, then Germany and the Netherlands; you'll meet who you have to meet there, they are from the same village.' 'And when you come back, bring back the money'; also, 'You are good at tech stuff, help us figure out these special devices.' Sal was supposed to stay away for a few weeks but ended up staying longer. After all, in Perth he has the authorities breathing down his neck; here, in Calabria, in Siderno – which is a bit bigger than San Luca – and it also has the sea! – here, he is among people who protect him and involve him; he is part of something. When Sal gets arrested in Germany, while acting as a drug courier, he realizes he might be tried for mafia association in Italy. It's a large operation, Operation Pollino (aka European 'ndrangheta connection[54]) where Europol, Eurojust and some police forces in Europe have cooperated to arrest over 80 people in 2018. He resists arrest and displays problematic behaviours towards the authorities. Sal challenges the legal system and its values in Italy; he wants to go back to Perth now, be tried there. This wasn't that great, coming to Italy, but in San Luca, as well as in Perth, his family, at least, was proud of him.

I created this profile while driving back from Osborne Park, a suburban area of Perth. There I stopped for ice cream in a shop also run by a Calabrian family; common surnames, such as Calabrò and Giampaolo, run in that family.

The founder arrived in Perth in late 1980s and the business seems quite good. Strange flavours indeed, one of my scoops tasted like bubble-gum!

Historical intelligence indicates that a family member, who was also living in Perth, was extradited to Italy in the early 1990s in connection with an alleged involvement in a heroin-trafficking syndicate operating between Italy and Turkey, with a base in San Luca, as well. Eventually, he returned to Perth in the early 1990s; authorities believed he was still involved with other local 'ndrangheta families within the San Luca *locale* in Western Australia. But then again, he left the past behind.

How many more examples would I be stumbling upon of 'ndrangheta shadows mixed with Calabrian migrant entrepreneurialism?

The San Luca angle was a bit of a surprise in Perth; the recurring surnames of mafia affiliates from San Luca – Pizzata, Crisafi, Pelle, Strangio, Pipicella – have some echo with suspected mafia affiliates involved in drug trade and other crimes in Perth. Across the years, individuals involved with 'ndrangheta families from villages in Aspromonte have converged in Perth for various reasons: some with the need to hide, others wishing to reconnect with families, and others even for the willingness to climb the criminal career ladder faster than they perhaps could have done in Calabria.

A bridge between Perth and this side of Aspromonte seems to have always existed and it doesn't involve the rest of Australia very much. *How does that work?*

Perth appears on one side, very dynamic: clans' names and individuals in charge alternate – with some families that authorities consider to be 'ndrangheta families, which do not seem to rely on historical criminal pedigrees in Calabria. On the other side, however, some Perth-based 'ndrangheta clans are authoritative and historically powerful, connected to Calabria, and wealthy in Australia, involved in illicit as much as licit activities through the usual investments in food, cash-intensive commerce and socially acceptable businesses, feeding off and exploiting Italian communities.

I realized that, after all, I already knew about the different character of the 'ndrangheta in Perth when compared with the rest of Australia. That Western Australia doesn't appear anywhere in the earlier mapping of the Australian 'ndrangheta, nor is it acknowledged that in Perth there might have been 'ndrangheta-type activities, I found indeed strange from the start. There are, however, some archival sources that do indicate some mafia activity there in the 1960s, but much less than anywhere else in Australia by comparison.[55] Perhaps there is an even stranger element to this absence: among the latest events that point to the existence of the 'ndrangheta in Australia, from an Italian perspective at least, Perth is actually the principal centre of interest.

Organizing thoughts

When I put the Siderno Café in Stirling into Google Maps, another suburban area north of Perth, I had no idea that I would find myself driving on what seemed to me like a road trip in the US Midwest. *Not that I have ever been to the US Midwest, but my movie imagery was triggered.* Large roads, with motels on one side, petrol stations on the other, and just land and land all around. I had chosen the Siderno Café because of its name and the reference to the Calabrian town of Siderno, the village in the province of Reggio Calabria, Ionian coast, that is so present in 'ndrangheta chronicles. And because Stirling a few years back had been part of one of the 'ndrangheta 'scandals' that Italian authorities were very keen on investigating.

While I was sitting at the Siderno Café, which is curiously run by Sicilians and not Calabrians, and eating meatballs, I was reading a book on serial killers,[56] about 'organized' serial killers – socially competent, with an ordinary life, usually of average or high intelligence who kill because triggered – and 'disorganized' serial killers – socially incompetent, with below average intelligence, who kill opportunistically.

Fun fact, serial killers were my first 'criminological' love, however creepy that might sound, I realize.

At that time, reading a book about this made me think of an apparent dichotomy, in what was at the time a very imprecise, half-baked, thought. On one side, in Perth, I was learning about one mafia clan – I cannot mention their name/surname for confidentiality issues – that appears very '*organized*' in the serial killer sense: they have high social respectability, they are employed, they are 'normal'. They do not seem interested in keeping much contact with Calabria or elsewhere, they are locally very embedded. They are Calabrians, and they selectively – opportunistically – use Calabrian 'ndrangheta codes for affiliation, but they are not part of any 'historical' 'ndrangheta clan. They are carefully selecting their activities; they seem in control and completely flying under the radar. They have made just a few mistakes, dictated by what we can consider *triggers*, which eventually have ended up exposing them to the authorities – not enough to be prosecuted though. On the other side, I was also learning about individuals belonging to different families who have well-known 'ndrangheta surnames; they are, by contrast, somewhat '*disorganized*' within the serial killer typology. Even with the right starting tools (the mafia surname/affiliation and the network attached to that) they are not always able to further their success as '*ndranghetisti*; they make mistakes in their criminality, which remains low-level compared with the others, they are greedy; even when they aim higher – maybe they want to be working with associates and family members abroad – they still remain fairly anchored to the local when it comes to criminal capability. They don't seem in control.

I wish I could show you the scribblings I made on the napkin right there at the Siderno Café, to organize my thoughts!

In relation to the first, apparently *organized*, group, the questions I posed to myself were the same I had asked already in relation to the role of rituals in keeping the 'ndrangheta alive in South Australia: *to what extent are 'ndrangheta cultural components inherited, transmitted or engineered as recruitment tools?*[57]

With so much 'free' publicity as to what the 'ndrangheta is about today, could it be possible to instrumentally use 'ndrangheta rituals, heritage, traditions and legacy to push forward a specific plan?

Can anyone create – engineer – an organization that identifies with and mirrors the 'ndrangheta if it's beneficial for affiliates to do so? After all, the 'ndrangheta 'know-how' already contributed to the formation of brand-new criminal organizations, such as the Famiglia Basilischi in the region of Basilicata in Calabria.[58]

Saying it differently, *to what extent can those who run a criminal clan-based enterprise use the cultural elements of the 'ndrangheta to create a sense of identity and attract new generations/recruits? And all of this abroad?*

The sense of a *'ndranghetist* identity might be lacking due to distance from Calabria, but it is somewhat yearned for in the same way in which many Calabrian migrants yearn for a Calabrian identity. There is a widespread sense of *nostalgia* accompanying new generations of Italians/Calabrians in Australia, paired with a sense of betrayal towards some parts of the host Australian society[59] – *could this be a good enough drive for some wannabe* 'ndranghetisti*?*

These questions are not easy ones to answer, because answers require more data than what is available to me. I intuitively sensed that perceptions of Perth as an insular city might shape the narrative of any research into Western Australia.[60]

This also led me to another set of questions in relation to the second, apparently *disorganized*, group. Perth's connections to Calabria, and to the 'ndrangheta in Calabria, manifest in the travels, the choices to move abroad, the harbouring of fugitives and the willingness to keep the communication channels open, mainly with San Luca or Siderno clans or other Calabrian 'ndrangheta cells. We often hear that this is the modus operandi of the 'ndrangheta, to keep the channels open.

But what if, in Perth, this is also exacerbated by the insularity of the place?

What if it's easier to keep the channels of communication open with Calabria than it is to keep them open with the rest of Australia?

What if heirs of 'ndrangheta clans find that they have more in common with the Calabrian mafiosi than with Australian ones?

What if the bridge to Calabria is safer than other bridges to Australia overall?

These questions do accompany me still, and clearly not only in reference to Perth.

Crossing bridges

The waiter at the Siderno Café was also the owner or manager, I don't remember; he was Sicilian, and Sicilian was the menu. In Stirling, however, the presence of the Calabrian community is tangible, as is *Italianness* overall. According to census data from 2011,[61] 19.2 per cent of the population of Stirling is Italian or of Italian descent (almost five times more than the 3.8 per cent of Western Australia and the 3.3 per cent overall in Australia); 10.8 per cent speak Italian in Stirling, compared with only 1.4 per cent in Australia overall. Stirling sounds and looks more Italian, and also more Calabrian, in the banners, posters, names and surnames on the doors, businesses and so forth. It isn't surprising that they had an Italian mayor between 1997 and 2005, for example.

21 August 2009

Domenico Antonio 'Tony' Vallelonga, born in Nardodipace, in the province of Vibo Valentia in Calabria, but resident in Gwelup and mayor of Stirling, WA, from 1997 to 2005, is in Siderno, Calabria. He goes to a laundromat, Ape Green, owned by Giuseppe Commisso – who will later be convicted as head of the 'ndrangheta in Siderno. Authorities have bugged the laundromat. Vallelonga goes in to introduce himself, presented by Carmelo Muià. *We will 'meet' Carmelo Muià again, when we talk about Canada!*

Tony Vallelonga apparently received over 80 per cent of the votes in Stirling when he was elected mayor; he was made an Honorary Freeman of the City of Stirling in 2009; he invested in property development. His family is closely tied to the Italian club in Perth and very well known in the Italian community. He is also a 'good man', according to his guest, Giuseppe Commisso.

These interceptions are part of Operation Crimine,[62] which is one of the main investigations into the functioning of the 'ndrangheta run between 2008 and 2010. The men in the laundromat discuss a problem with an affiliate in Australia, who is seemingly going against the 'ndrangheta rules. *This is, at least, the reconstruction of the prosecutors.* This man had gone to Calabria, bypassed the 'ndrangheta rules in Australia and attempted to interact directly with the Calabrian clans instead of the Australian clans.

Vallelonga:	… I knew he came here … I tell you the truth, if someone has any intention of giving him something [meaning the dote or similar 'ndrangheta recognition/ranking], at least it has to come from our branch.
Commisso:	Did you tell him that?
Vallelonga:	I did … now that I am here …
Commisso:	Who gave him that?
Vallelonga:	He went there … nah, in Siderno that cannot happen, in Delianuova, I spoke to people there and that didn't happen …
Commisso:	Who did he gave it to … the butcher? […] and what did he give them?
Vallelonga:	The last one. […] now Pino told him 'if you have it, we will recognise you'.
Commisso:	They sent me a 'mbasciata [a message] […] we agreed that we will talk … they sent it from there, from Mico Italiano [from Delianuova, living in Australia].
Vallelonga:	Yes, exactly!

Commisso:	He sent it to them, they sent it to me and then there is another family, Pizzata, they wanted to invite him in San Luca.
Vallelonga:	Yes.
Commisso:	I said to them … it's so and so, so they are not inviting him anymore … it's bad!
Vallelonga:	I swear, I was just so … I haven't called him again, I am a peaceful man.
Commisso:	But this is bad … it's bad … here, from Siderno to Australia, we cannot operate like this, if you are not good there, you are not good here either.
Vallelonga:	Definitely. And this is why I came to talk to you …

The conversation goes on. It persuaded the prosecutors to ask for an extradition with a mafia association charge against Tony Vallelonga, which was never granted by Australian authorities due to the lack of reciprocity of the mafia offence and, more importantly, insufficient evidence for other charges. Mr Vallelonga has never been accused of anything and denies the accusations of the Italian authorities.[63] This conversation, for him, was not about the mafia in any way; he doesn't even know what the word mafia means, as he declares also in the interceptions.

Commisso:	This is a wicked one …
Vallelonga:	He is detached … [meaning perhaps that he left the main group].
Commisso:	Again? For how long?
Vallelonga:	Four days […] He said that he wants to call on you and on me and I said to him that, officially, he cannot call on anyone, I call on him, he cannot do the 'man' like this anymore.
Commisso:	And why would he want to call me?
Vallelonga:	… he says 'I'll go and demand my place in Siderno' and I reply 'Siderno … You don't respond to Siderno!'
Commisso:	But he stays there or comes here?
Vallelonga:	No! He asks for his place in Siderno so he responds to Siderno as locale. He wanted that the locale of Australia …
Commisso:	Who the hell says these things? […] we cannot allow these things … if you are not good there, you are not good here!
Vallelonga:	About the locale, I did tell him, 'you, in a locale? As long as I am alive you don't get a locale and that's it!'

Whatever the correct interpretation of these words might be – whether or not in line with the thesis of the prosecutors – we will probably never know. It was not the first time and won't be the last time that words that mean something in the 'ndrangheta do not mirror in behaviours of the 'ndrangheta or, rather, provable charges.

A thought at that time. Could there be a 'ndrangheta without crimes of the 'ndrangheta? A question that Italian authorities would never accept, but that we must ask when we are abroad and see the complications of trials, awareness, investigations, understanding.

This conversation between Vallelonga and Commisso shows, at the very least, that there are still connections between Siderno and Perth, with travels arranged and agreements reached. As already mentioned, Giuseppe Commisso, 'Il Mastro' (the Master), was eventually convicted of mafia association and is considered one of the main 'ndrangheta men in Siderno, and of the 'ndrangheta overall. He references men in Australia, the rules for the formation of a *locale*, specifically in Perth, and he is talking about people that Mr Vallelonga seems to know. From the words of Commisso, it seems that some individuals in Perth are linked to the Italiano clan in Delianuova (*Mico Italiano, mentioned above, is a relative of that Peppe 'Ntoni Italiano whom we talked about in the previous chapter – remember him?*); they have family links with the Alvaro family also in Delianuova (*those we mentioned in relation to Melbourne and the latest Operation Eyfhemos*) and the Pizzata family in San Luca. According to the intercepted materials and the reconstruction of the prosecutors, all of these people are operating on the basis that the Siderno clans have a higher governing power over them, at least in Perth. This seems to have been partially confirmed in arrests made in 2021 with Operation Ironside,[64] where men of Calabrian descent operating in South Australia also seemed to be connected to Sidernesi in Western Australia and Calabria. Additionally, Operation Platinum in Western Australia between 2019 and 2021 developed around the drug network of an individual named Pizzata, his connections through another man, Lupoi, in South Australia, and the involvement of an accounting firm run by other local (Calabrian-born) well-known entrepreneurs in Perth.

Once again, after a week in Perth, I was overwhelmed by the flow of documents, the Calabrian names, their correlation to one another, the circularity of it all. Nothing was well in focus, though, as usual.

I drove back home the last night there after hours of talks about all of this once more and, without realizing it, I crossed half of the city without switching on the front and rear lights of the car. I could have easily had an accident if it wasn't for the streetlights. It was all way too much, as always. And driving in the darkness, perhaps, was way too corny, yet strangely accurate, as a metaphor for my feelings back then.

Again, questions pounding in my head: *What if it's easier to keep the channels of communication open in Calabria than it is to keep them open with the rest of*

Australia? What if some people here have more in common with the Calabrian mafiosi than with Australian ones? What if they have more in common with mafiosi elsewhere, outside Australia, outside Calabria? What if there is the 'ndrangheta without the 'ndrangheta crimes?

I started thinking of Canada.

This is, after all, what the Siderno Group is supposedly about, a bridge between Siderno, Perth and Canada, offering channels of communication. For many, these channels elude and replace those in the country of residence – in Australia; they are completely self-serving and utterly self-sufficient.

Yes, Perth leads to a Canadian story, this time.

North American Hybrids

On 22 July 1990, Domenico Sergi (Little Domenic, from Griffith, remember him?) – representative for Australia; Vincenzo Trento and Anthony Cipriani – representatives for Canada; and Eliseo Lazzarino for Belgium, met in Ardore (Reggio Calabria province). It's defined as a 'ndrangheta meeting.[1]

10 August 2009, Apegreen Laundromat, Siderno.[2]

Giuseppe Commisso: Here is a friend who came from Australia, he is from Nardodipace ... please come in ... *compare!* He is a friend of mine ...

Domenico Antonio Vallelonga: Pleased to meet you, Tony Vallelonga.

Carmelo Muià: Pleasure is mine, Carmelo Muià ...[3]

Churches and funerals

'Are you going to go there just to see a church?'

'I have to start somewhere, that's one of the addresses in the arrest warrant at the very least!'

A friend of mine in Toronto was genuinely questioning the rationale of that trip. *But ... I have to see the places, I need to see the spaces.*

It was April 2017 and I was staying in Toronto. It took me pretty much two hours to travel to the site of the church on public transport; I hadn't rented a car. I wish I had. I wouldn't have had parking issues anyway, as in front of the St Clare of Assisi Catholic Church, on 150 St Francis Avenue, in Woodbridge, a large suburban community in the city of Vaughan, just north of Toronto, there is no scarcity of parking space. It was windy, just a few days earlier it had snowed in Montreal, and Toronto was ice cold, or at least it was for me, in April ... *one should feel spring, right? Right.* Anyway, I had bought a new pair of snow boots, insulated and furry inside, so I was ready to face what to me was definitely still winter.

Being in Woodbridge at the time was somewhat strange. In fact, I didn't really know what I was expecting to see. I arrived at a scenic bridge, crossed it and found shopping malls and a variety of commercial venues. The roads became larger the farther behind I left the shopping area. St Clare was a massive, white and brown building that looked very polished and very new. A lot of Woodbridge looks very polished and very new.

I am not religious, but I have always found churches are good places to visit, to do some people watching, to understand communities' vibes. Certainly, St Clare of Assisi wasn't any different, on a festive day in April in Canada, around Easter. Woodbridge is considered one of the most densely Italian areas in Canada, with a population that is 31 per cent Italian according to 2016 census data.[4] Being surrounded by Italian voices, at the end of what must have been a mass, it felt surreal, on that cold April day in Ontario. And yet, it made me smile, it felt familiar.

If there is one thing I learned across all my travels for research, it is that a sense of familiarity can surprise me when I least expect it. In the parking lot outside a church, hearing people chatting after a service in Vaughan, Ontario. On a residential street on the outskirts of Adelaide, in South Australia. In a restaurant in Mildura, Victoria.

Now, I haven't said why I chose St Clare of Assisi as a place to visit in Vaughan, I realize.

Operation Acero Connection (which means 'Maple Connection', incidentally – Italian antimafia authorities are funny that way),[5] in 2015, is one of the latest investigations related to the Siderno Group of Crime, one of many since Operation Siderno Group in 1992. A very popular 'mob' story, that of the Siderno Group – as old as 1920s New York City – reported even by Wikipedia.

Operation Acero Connection painted a bleak picture of what Italian investigators were observing between Siderno – *the Calabrian Ionian coast town that we mentioned when talking about Perth* – and Ontario, Canada. Almost as bleak as the findings of Project Ophoenix for the Royal Canadian Mounted Police (RCMP) that same year. Both investigations, from different angles, looked at the 'ndrangheta cells of the Siderno Group and their Canadian connections.

Yes, I realize I still have not said why I decided to go to that church!

On 29 April 2014, a funeral was celebrated in St Clare of Assisi at 150 Francis Avenue in Woodbridge. It was a commemoration for Carmine Verduci, killed at the nearby Regina Sport Café on 24 April 2014. *I couldn't find the bar, by the way.* Two other victims were shot, including a woman, born in Canada but originally from a Siderno family, married to another man from Siderno; two other Italian men were hurt as well. A bloodbath; the media feasted on it.

The murder of Carmine Verduci has been at the centre of inquiries in both Italy and Canada; around his death there are changing alliances, trust issues and strategic mobility. And, in the way in which many things in Australia seem to be connected to Platì, in Ontario a lot of 'mafia stuff' seems to revolve around individuals from the town of Siderno.

During the ceremony at St Clare of Assisi, Canadian authorities were watching, and taking pictures, as Operation Acero and Project Ophoenix showed up one year later. They took pictures of the *Crimine* of Toronto, the chamber of control that the Siderno clans have established in Ontario.

Surely, the first time I went to one of the RCMP offices in Toronto, in April 2017, I was expecting the murder of Verduci and his funeral to be a prominent topic of discussion. I had walked down a wide road – *unnecessarily wide, to be honest* – exposed to the wind and the rain, for like half an hour that day. The bus didn't go as far as I needed and there wasn't an Uber or a cab nearby. It seemed like I was walking into a secret location – not a headquarters, not a branch office; the receptionist barely knew what the RCMP was and where their rooms were. I was in no mood for finding that amusing, as I was soaking wet because of the rain. Shamelessly, I spent 20 minutes in the bathroom drying my clothes – especially my tights – before getting into the meeting and curse the day I had chosen to do this job and engage in research in Canada *amid a snowstorm with whirling rain. You know, one of those days.* Anyway, the meeting eventually went very well as I started diving into yet another country, another 'ndrangheta story, another cultural and policing approach to mafias.

During Verduci's funeral in 2014, the authorities photographed what they believed to be the heads and the associates of the so-called Siderno Group of Crime in Ontario. A who's-who list of participants in the funeral – shaking hands and sharing grief, sorrow and disbelief – was drafted and became part of the intelligence work. The RCMP worked relentlessly at this, you could tell.

As in Perth, the so-called Siderno Group is yet another slice of the 'ndrangheta. Mind you, it is still the 'ndrangheta, probably one of the most important 'ndrangheta(s); some of the most influential clans of the Calabrian mafia are around Siderno and respond to the Siderno 'society'.

But we need to step back and start with the first investigations into the Siderno Group as an autonomous 'ndrangheta entity. It's the 1990s and we are already in North America.

Brooklyn blood

We start in New York, in Brooklyn – to be precise, 6403 14th Avenue, corner of 64th Street. There is not much to notice there today: a laundromat on the corner, those fire escape metal stairs that I absolutely adore in New York; the usual Brooklyn feeling, a mix of 'Chill out even if it's the end of the world' and 'When is the garbage going to be collected?' kind of thing. Brooklyn is not my place in New York. I am a Harlem person; that's where I choose to live when I am in the city. It's a long way on the D train from Harlem to 62nd Street in Brooklyn. You should take the time to get a coffee and a pastry in one of the nearby bakeries, in Brooklyn, they all are in between hipster and rundown, and they are delightful.

Files from the Drug Enforcement Administration in the late 1980s describe a man, Nicodemo Ciccia, as being associated with individuals involved in international drug trafficking. He was also suspected of distributing heroin for organized crime syndicates. He was murdered on the late evening of 2 September 1991, by five gunshots, in front of 6403 14th Avenue in Brooklyn.

Nicodemo Ciccia was also president of the Marco Aurelio Social Club, which was at the time precisely there, at 6403 14th Avenue in Brooklyn.

The murder investigation revealed that most of the members of the Marco Aurelio Social Club were originally from the area of Siderno, near Reggio Calabria.

> Research revealed that some of the members of the social club were documented in the files of law enforcement agencies in the United States, Canada and Italy as suspected international drug traffickers.[6]

In an extremely alarmist fashion, the DEA further declared:

> The Siderno Group ... one of the many factions or groups that constitute the N'DRAGHETTA [sic] – has a history of interfactional disputes that often result in assaults and murders. In the past there have been times when the Italian government has virtually lost control of large segments of the country's Southland to rival gangs.

The authorities at the time discovered that intelligence data on the Siderno-based clans date back to at least 1958, 'when law enforcement sources in the United States reportedly advised the Canadian police that elements of organised crime in the United States were planning to form a group in Toronto to be known as the "Toronto Locale".'

The *locale* is the prime territorial 'ndrangheta structure, and it was understood as such from the start by law enforcement. Clearly, at the time authorities focused on the Italian–American La Cosa Nostra, or as they call it, LCN (*no comment on this acronym ... how much I laughed the first time I read LCN and connected it to the Sicilian 'la' (the) Cosa Nostra!*).

By the 1970s, the Siderno Group was extensively documented in both Canada and the United States, with *locali* in Albany, New York City, Detroit, Miami, Chicago. Something, however, was clearly recognizable for American law enforcement: the clans were connected to other, more well-known families of Italian–American extraction. The Magaddino–Todaro family in Buffalo, the Bonanno family in New York City, for example.

He reported that he was put in the middle of a circle of members and some words were said. When the ritual was concluded they all kissed and hugged each other, and the subject's name was recorded in a book so that every other soldier and family would know that he had been made a soldier. A fee of $27.50 was reportedly paid to the organisation by the newly made soldier.[7]

This information was sent around to law enforcement agencies in the United States in the 1990s. Over a coffee near One Police Plaza in Lower Manhattan, I am showing this document to a retired police officer who has kindly agreed to have a chat with me about the *good ol' days* of his detective work.

He doesn't seem too impressed: 'initiation fees, never seen that, and for that amount?' He asserts that, if the Siderno Group existed in NYC, then it must have been some sub-unit within LCN. 'If it was organised crime, then it was within our traditional organised crime.' He means the Mob, as there is a wonderful juxtaposition in the narrative of law enforcement in North America whereby *ethnic* organized crime, which means Italian mostly, has become *traditional* organized crime by default.[8]

But anyway, while the DEA was compiling its report in NYC, the police in Reggio Calabria were busy with Operation Siderno Group, precisely between 1992 and 1994.[9] Let's compare some notes.

The identification in Canada, the United States and Australia of entire communities of Calabrian origin involved in international drug trafficking has allowed authorities, throughout the years, to build an (incomplete) map of the criminal organization called the 'Siderno Group'. This organization, made up of individuals from the province of Reggio Calabria who immigrated to the abovementioned countries at different times, has transplanted to those places terrorist and violent methods typical of the Calabrian 'ndrangheta, reaching such levels of dangerousness that Canadian and Australian authorities launched internal investigations. The name 'Siderno Group' has been given by the Canadians, and it refers to Siderno because many affiliates, if not most, came from Siderno.[10]

This was the Italian authorities in Operation Siderno Group. Their information, at least for Australia, was slightly incorrect, as it was not for the Siderno Group clans that internal inquiries were launched in the 1970s and 1980s. Nevertheless, the elements for the identification of the Siderno Group are all there: the names of families, the surnames, the feuds and the marriages, the migration routes and the business activities as well. One name that stands above all is that of Antonio – 'Ntoni – Macrì, aka the *king of three worlds*, killed in 1975.

There seems to be a before and after *don* 'Ntoni Macrì; the before was the 'real', 'honoured' society, almost a project of unification of Siderno clans in the world; afterwards came kidnapping, drug trafficking, violence and money. This is not uncommon in the history of mafia; there is often a perceived *old* mafia of honour and respect, which gives way to a violent, bloody *new* mafia[11] – it is mostly a series of generational issues turned into mafia history.

> During November 1976, information was received that persons going to Italy for heroin must first go to Reggio Calabria. The heroin customer would then be referred to member of the Sicilian Mafia who in turn would make arrangements to finalise the drug transaction. In recent years N'DRANGHETTA [*sic*] wholesale heroin suppliers have established connections directly to traditional organised crime customers in the New York area. [...] The N'DRANGHETTA now has the ability to supply both heroin and cocaine. It has been reported that some N'DRANGHETTA groups utilise the wives of members to transport large amounts of money to Canada to pay for monthly shipments of fifty to one hundred kilograms of cocaine. In contrast, other investigations revealed N'DRANGHETTA involvement in highly sophisticated operations. Money used as payment for cocaine shipments was transferred to Swiss banks. The money was subsequently transferred to banks in the United States and ultimately redeposited into South American bank accounts.[12]

And these were the American authorities, NYC-based, pretty much in the same years and months.

The DEA went through the entire membership list of the Marco Aurelio Social Club, with names, addresses and phone numbers. Real estate records revealed that the club's building was owned by a Giuseppe Prochilo. Prochilo's home address was the club's address. Prochilo had been president of the club before Ciccia, but that was not why his name resounded to the authorities. There were, in fact, two other reasons. Italian law enforcement had made several requests for updated intelligence relative to a man named Giuseppe Prochilo. In the early 1980s, in Calabria, a judge received a letter from someone in Queens, New York, referring to the arrest of a man, Vincenzo Coluccio, in Italy. Coluccio – said the letter – was supposedly preparing to become a drug supplier in New York City, for Domenico Coluccio (a food importer) and Salvatore Ricupero, a travel agent in NYC. The group, said the letter, was working with Giuseppe Prochilo, 'the chief representative of the Siderno Mafia in Brooklyn'.

Reading through the intelligence related to the murder of Ciccia in front of the Marco Aurelio Social Club in Brooklyn, the surnames were surely all Calabrian, and the place of birth was mostly Siderno or nearby villages. However, the key element of that intelligence was the hybrid nature of whatever the Siderno Group was, at the time, in New York City.

For example, the abovementioned Salvatore Ricupero was considered the second man of the Siderno *locale* in New York, the one who facilitated drug trafficking in the United States by handling the money on behalf of the bosses in Siderno. He was employed by World Premier International Travel as a travel consultant. This travel agency was well documented in DEA files, because a business record check identified the owner as Anthony Anastasio, a 'soldier' in the Gambino crime family of NYC. Ricupero's business card was found on the body of Nicodemo Ciccia outside the Marco Aurelio Social Club. Another member of the Marco Aurelio Social Club was John Grillo, suspected member of the Siderno Group and suspected member of the narcotic trafficking organization associated with Roberto Pannunzi. Pannunzi, a celebrity in drug trafficking investigations between the 1970s and 1990s, was a major heroin trafficker who could organize and act as broker for large amounts of heroin shipped to New York via Canada. Pannunzi enjoyed the support of both Don 'Ntoni Macrì and Gaetano Badalamenti, Cosa nostra leader for drug trafficking between Sicily and New York. Pannunzi was moving heroin from Palermo to Siderno to then ship it to North America via France.

It was the 1980s and, in North America, the Siderno Group was anything but ethnically tight. Working with other groups, especially within the Sicilian–American mafia, was business as usual. Or at least this was the perception of New York authorities. The hybridization of the 'ndrangheta on one side and of the Sicilian Cosa nostra on the other side in NYC has perhaps hindered comprehension of both phenomena. Even today, talking to the New York Police Department or the FBI, identifying which mafia are we talking about, if there is any difference at all, proves complex. *Or perhaps, there is no real difference? I wonder.*

According to police in Reggio Calabria, the connection between the mafia clans in Palermo, Sicily, and individuals in high positions in the 'ndrangheta in Siderno in the 1980s and 1990s, was meant to support heroin and cocaine deliveries throughout America. Among these individuals were Vincenzo Macrì, in Siderno, and his brother Antonio, 'Toto', living on 66th Street in Brooklyn, both identified by Italian authorities as 'prominent Members of the Italian Organised Crime Group known as the N'DRAGHETTA' (sic!).[13]

During the 1990s, however, things in Siderno changed fast following a feud between the Commisso and Costa families and the succession of men of honour in charge. This is a long story that cannot possibly be narrated here. We can use the voice of a police informer reporting on the situation at the beginning of the 1990s.[14] He discusses murders, alliances, misunderstandings and violence in Siderno, and then says:

> As I have said, Cosimo Commisso is the unchallenged boss of Siderno, where nothing moves unless he wishes so. He owns houses, companies, land, commercial activities, and controls every business activity even when not directly controlled by him. Public work in the area is also controlled by him. His rise to power after the death of Antonio Macrì ('don' 'Ntoni Macrì) has been almost automatic as he was privy to narcotics and trafficking, at the time already becoming the real business of mafia clans. Commisso was already handling the drug trade together with Vincenzo Macrì, don Antonio's son. Vincenzo could have been the successor of his father, he had the ability to do so. But he was arrested in New York for drugs and he got almost 20 years. Another Macrì, also named Vincenzo, also into drug trade, didn't have the 'substance' to be a leader, he liked the good life, and gambling, and he didn't inspire power. Therefore, it was almost natural for Cosimo Commisso to take over the Siderno clans, as he had a strong family behind, while Vincenzo is now marginal to the organisation.

It seemed clear at the time how New York events influenced Siderno and how Siderno events affected both New York and, eventually, North America. The meeting in Ardore, Calabria, at the beginning of this chapter, is one of many happening in those years.

Surnames first and place of origin second: this is the 'ndrangheta recipe for mobility. The clans from Siderno and surrounding areas appear *hypermobile* – capable of handling fast movements, of people, investments and relations, facilitated by the global nature of transports, markets and networks. Hypermobility is an intense mobility, where people not only travel a lot, move from place to place, but also move a lot in between places, as a life choice or for business; this makes it possible for these individuals to build up network capital faster. They acquire extra skills or extra social status and privileges, as they can count on their experiences and contacts more than others.[15] Clans and individuals belonging to the Siderno Group have, in fact, demonstrated a peculiar capability and willingness not just to move, adapt and settle elsewhere – their businesses and their families – but also to give back to Siderno from wherever they are and to connect among places as well, Canada, Australia, the United States, Belgium.[16] In the Siderno Group, it's not just Siderno that remains in the middle – cradle and grave – starting and ending point of the 'ndrangheta. It's also that events in one place influence other places, too, including Siderno. This calls for quick changes, flexibility in leadership and coordination, and it causes confusion – for authorities and observers. It is said, in Italian documents, that the *Società* of 'ndrangheta in

Siderno has over 90 *locali* around the world, which would make these groups effectively the most international and probably the most resilient abroad. And there is the Commisso *'ndrina*, above them all.

Crowds and wrinkles

Carmelo Muià, the man who apparently met Tony Vallelonga in Commisso's Apegreen laundromat, was killed in January 2018 in Siderno. He was believed to be a man of honour of a *'ndrina* carrying his surname. His brother Vincenzo started looking for the people responsible for his death. The Muià *'ndrina* is active in Siderno as an associate of the larger Commisso clan, in the town district called Ferraro.

Imagine you book a table at a restaurant but, instead of giving your surname, you give the name of the *contrada* – city district – you live in. This is how the 'ndrangheta in Siderno manifests. Not just through surnames, but exceptionally through district names, much like the mafia families in Palermo, Sicily, and similarly to what happens in Reggio Calabria, a much bigger city.

'Ndrina of district Donisi, *'ndrina* of district Landa, *'ndrina* of district Ferraro, *'ndrina* of Siderno Superiore, *'ndrina* of district Salvi, *'ndrina* of district Oliveto. Mostly responding to one of the town's locali or the local *società* but increasingly growing and differentiating their degree of autonomy and organizational features.

Yes, this is the *Società* of Siderno, where hegemony is in the hands of the Commisso clan, the uber-clan to which all others, including Muià and Figliomeni, are connected. They operate above others. Near Siderno, in Gioiosa Ionica, the Ursino–Ursini and Jerinò clans are both associates of the Siderno Costa–Curciarello clan and they also have projections into Canada; the Commissos are widely recognized as superior.

The morphology of the 'ndrangheta in Siderno mirrors the town itself. The first image I can conjure of Siderno is the very long sea walk. One street, many bars and activities on the side. Very much like its criminal society: one uber-clan, stretched from one place to the other, many *'ndrine* on the side.

'It's mafia-crowded, Siderno' is what a prosecutor in Reggio Calabria told me during one of our chats. It must be difficult to navigate, a town that is *mafia-crowded*.

When Vincenzo Muià, Carmelo Muià's brother, and his cousin got on an Alitalia flight with their children from Rome to Toronto at the end of March 2019, the reasons for the travel were not straightforward for the anti-mafia prosecutors who were 'following' them.

> 'I am going to Toronto to my relatives.'
> 'Don't get into trouble please.'

'No! I am just going to see my relatives. I even bring my son! […] I'll go
  for a tour, my cousin is there …'
'Yes, I wanted to ask: did things calm down there or not?'
'Seems like it; we'll see.'[17]

In Operation Canadian Connection, in July and August 2019, authorities
made 28 arrests between Siderno and Toronto. This operation looked at
the intense mobility – *hypermobility* indeed – of 'ndrangheta clans from the
Siderno area between Calabria and Ontario and also how the ups and downs
in the management of power in Canada profoundly affect Calabria, in the
same way as *crowded* Siderno might affect regimes in Toronto.

'The brigands, I want to go and meet them. They called on me; they told
me to go. I'll see …'
'Sure, but it's war now … It's a disaster there, it's worse than here!'[18]

Toronto might indeed be a *disaster* but, nevertheless, from Siderno,
Vincenzo Muià seems to believe that he must go to Toronto to understand
who killed his brother Carmelo. The brigands are in fact the Figliomeni
brothers, Cosimo and Angelo, who are 'hiding' in Ontario following their
convictions for mafia crimes in 2017 in the trials for Operation Acero
Connection in Italy. Eminent members of the Commisso clan, the Figliomeni
brothers must know what is happening in Siderno as in Toronto. The so-
called Chamber of Control in Toronto, the *Crimine* – say the prosecutors in
Operation Canadian Connection – is headed primarily by the Figliomeni
brothers and by Francesco and Rocco Remo Commisso. They are said to
hold a conflict resolution management role and a sanctioning role as well,
which is the *Crimine* function. The Chamber of Control of Toronto is tied
to Siderno, but Siderno does not impose any 'ndrangheta ruling on Toronto.

Vincenzo Muià's travel is an example of how *familiness* – the vicissitudes
of a family dynasty – can be influential in mafia business. In his attempt
to find out who gave the permission or the order to kill his brother, and
who in fact is to be held responsible for the murder, Vincenzo spends
months meeting with all the most important and influential members of
the 'ndrangheta in Siderno, both in Calabria and in Canada. He needs to be
sure about what happened, so that he can also be sure about how to avenge
the death, according to the prosecutors. His obsession. However, in May
2021 and in May 2022, the prosecutors' hypotheses were not confirmed in
court: Vincenzo Muià and the others of the Siderno Group moving between
Canada and Italy were found not guilty of mafia charges.[19] So, once again,
we look at different interpretations of judicial narratives.

Still, certain things remain better said and handled in person within the mafia
world. No matter how evolved the 'ndrangheta may be, there are still occasions
when its traditional heart imposes face-to-face contacts. We also find a lot of
the 'normality' of men and families of and around the 'ndrangheta when they

travel to meet face to face. In their conversations, we see how normal it all can be, how regular, how uneventful, most of the time. *And I wonder, is this really mobility of crime, or even hypermobility, or just people's lives? Both?*

Vincenzo Muià was hosted by a man, Luigi Vescio, also hit by Operation Canadian Connection.[20]

In Woodbridge, down the road from St Clare of Assisi Church, on Weston Road, the Vescio brothers' funeral home is a flourishing business.

On the first night, Luigi Vescio had everyone over for dinner, Vincenzo and his son, cousin and sons, together with Angelo and Cosimo Figliomeni. The dinner was recorded, through phone interceptions: the anti-mafia prosecutors in Reggio worked with York Police to make sure that surveillance could be carried out in Canada. This was also part of Project Sindacato for York Police. At dinner, in between discussions of the reasons why Vincenzo Muià has come all the way to Toronto, other topics seemed to have been on Angelo Figliomeni's mind.

Luigi:	[T]his is very expensive, like 400 or 500 bucks, but they all use it, actors and actresses … I'll give you some tonight!
Angelo:	For these wrinkles? […] I bought a small one, just for the forehead here.
Luigi:	[I]t's also for the eyes.
Angelo:	I haven't used it yet […] when it's time I'll go for a lifting. … in 10 or 15 years.
Vincenzo:	Look, I came here for you, I wouldn't have come otherwise. I won't tell you again. I came just for you. We'll meet in due time … when you want … but I wouldn't have come, why would I have to?
Angelo:	We'll meet every day. Let's see.
Vincenzo:	Yes.
Luigi:	[S]ee, this is the cream, here underneath the eyes …
Angelo:	Do I need to massage it? Just here?
Luigi:	[T]he whole face!
Angelo:	I have the beard!
Luigi:	… even the neck … ah you see, old age! This is the best cream!
Vincenzo:	… not to look old, Angelino! Don't you know you're getting old anyway?[21]

It doesn't get more normal than discussing face creams at dinner when one of the guests is enquiring about his dead brother. Even (alleged) 'ndranghetisti get old and worry about appearances. And mafia wrinkles must be tough to conceal.

In August 2019, following Project Sindacato, York Police arrested Angelo Figliomeni and charged him and eight members of his 'family' with money laundering, directing or participating in a criminal organization, fraud, loan sharking and illegal gaming. Police also seized cash, luxury cars, houses and other goods. One of the things that emerged clearly from Project Sindacato was the leadership role of the Figliomeni brothers in Ontario. Project Sindacato collapsed before reaching trial due to procedural errors.[22] However, in Sindacato, the police could observe how the so-called Siderno Group operates in the area. The senior members of the Commisso–Figliomeni group are very locally entrenched, never leaving the area of Woodbridge; their role seems more one of management and bridging across people and businesses; they are said to have contacts with the Hells Angels; they seem respected by others in the underworld; they also seem to be particularly attached to traditions and to the expectations that come from their 'ndrangheta connections beyond Ontario. Their reputation seems to precede them in the community, including the Italian community, within which they are embedded business-wise and, of course, socially. Construction, waste disposal, restaurants, online gaming, bars, extortion in food services, loan sharking, charities. They don't seem that interested in any specific political or public administration role, though.

Some other members, including lower-ranking and second-generation individuals, would handle the drug trade more directly; they would travel more often back and forth from Calabria. *Would they be delivering messages? Would they be taking care of different sides of the criminal enterprise?*

They seem to have a split group identity. On the one hand, from a Canadian perspective, we have a group that is heavily invested in local business, particularly able to exploit the 'Canadian way' of doing organized crime, powerful but among other powerful groups. On the other side, from an Italian perspective, we have a group that is still very attached to traditions, to the motherland, to maintaining its primary role and representing the highest ranks of the 'ndrangheta in Ontario. This ability to hold multiple identities is a peculiarity of the 'ndrangheta abroad, but in Canada it has probably reached more hybrid forms than elsewhere because of their longevity, paired with the peculiarity of the Siderno Group: international drug traffickers on the one hand but still aware that most things are handled in person, possibly while eating together.

Connectivity and isomorphism

Indeed, dining together in Calabria is a matter of huge importance. And it is no surprise that the 'ndrangheta meets and does business abroad in a restaurant or at a dinner party. The social aspect of the 'ndrangheta organization survives and is the key to understanding the phenomenon.

Earlier intelligence in the United States, Australia and Canada revolved around social clubs – as ethnic enclaves. Today's intelligence is also gathered through *social media*, today's best substitutes, perhaps, for those ethnic enclaves, clubs, of the past.

On my way to Toronto in April 2017, travelling five hours by train from Montreal, I was sorting my documents and coding data. Between procrastination and curiosity, I ended up digging into social media, Facebook pages, groups and Instagram profiles, of migrants and migrant communities abroad. I got emotional in doing that; as a migrant myself, the need to reconnect with people and with places of origin is something I understand. There are groups linked to various villages in Calabria connecting migrants from all over the world. Groups for migrants from Siderno or Marina di Gioiosa Ionica or other Calabrians in Toronto or Canada; many people seem to be able, and willing, to share with strangers the feeling of being in two places at the same time.

And I found that extremely beautiful and extremely relevant for my research. The feeling of *home*, as researchers have discussed,[23] is a multidimensional concept: home can be both sedentary and mobile. On one side, you fix one place as home, while at the same time you build up a life somewhere else, which also feels like home. Because it is not uncommon for migrant communities to develop decentred and multiple attachments and feelings of belonging in more than one place,[24] the use of social media groups that connect these communities in places of arrival has a fundamental role in defining and rooting the concept of home also in places of origin. In this *networked diaspora*, home can turn into an imagined community, a comforting thought that feels safe, even if distant.[25]

I couldn't help but wonder about the difference between these networked communities and the in-person ones. *To what extent are these networked communities enough for regular people? To what extent would people prefer meeting in person instead?*

And that was before the COVID-19 pandemic! Surely, during the pandemic lockdowns and travel restrictions, those networked communities, between Facebook, Instagram, TikTok and the like, must have acted as bridges. More bridges, mafia or not.

Of course, one could not generalize and assume that everyone who engages with a Facebook group for migrants would eventually want to go and meet people from the group offline, too. *I wouldn't.* Indeed, some people might prefer to keep 'real' contacts close and travel from one 'home' to another to do so; they might not be satisfied with online communities.

This train of thought led me to think about how 'ndrangheta families are said to need the face-to-face encounters to keep their relationships and business flowing. The face-to-face encounters are part of the *familiness* of many mafia dynasties.[26] *Is this just another normal trait of these groups, is it about secrecy or about the need for connectivity across migrant families ... or both?*

On one of those pages for Calabrians in Toronto, I was looking for advice on a good restaurant. I wanted something Calabrian, something not for tourists. Little Italy, in Toronto, is quite fake, as you can imagine: the usual street of pizzerias, Italian flags, dotted red and white tablecloths (*who on earth still thinks that is genuinely Italian?!*), strange words and misspelling in the menus (*seriously, can't people Google correct spelling!?*).

When I went to the pizzeria I had found online, the woman who waited on my table was a chatty woman from Calabria; she must have been 60 or 65 and when she asked me where I was from, I replied that I was from Calabria, too, and that I knew the place she was from; she was from Monasterace, just above Siderno. Postcards and pictures from the place covered the walls. *Her eyes almost filled with joy in hearing that; she brought me things from the kitchen to try just because I had made her smile by being from Calabria.* She told me part of her family's story: she had arrived in Canada when she was nine, she used to go back for a while, almost every year, but she had not been back to her village for about 15 years now. She knew everything that was going on there, anyway, her sister had moved 'back home', and they talked every week. She said it like that, that *her sister moved back home.* It was nice to hear: her Italian was not polished at all, and I could barely understand her 'new' dialect, but you could tell she was longing to speak dialect with someone.

I was left thinking of two manifestations of the mobility from Siderno and surrounding areas, not just for mafias but for migrant experiences more generally. On one side, there is the *online world*, where imagined communities of people connect with an imagined reality of the place of origin, where everything seems good and everything gets celebrated. On the other side, in the *offline world*, reality might be different – contacts might be more sporadic and people usually choose whether to stay connected with 'home' by travelling there often or to connect with *compaesani* at the place of arrival, where the new home is. In the world of mafia mobility and hypermobility, where long-haul trips are still required when you have things to fix and talk business, maintaining solid local and offline contacts, but also frequent communication across borders, seems to be the best choice to preserve both family and business connections.

> 'Oh Co' [Cosimo Figliomeni], who told you that we would come here to Canada?' (asks Vincenzo Muià)
> 'My wife!'
> 'And who told your wife?'
> 'Who do you think? Pino told his wife and she told her sister, my wife!'[27]

Naturally.
Connectivity and communication, to guarantee mobility and even hypermobility, runs in the family, even across borders.

Project Ophoenix, led by the Combined Forces Special Enforcement Unit in Toronto, reached its conclusion with the first trial against the 'ndrangheta outside Italy. Quite an achievement. On 28 February 2019,[28] the Ontario Superior Court of Justice convicted Giuseppe Ursino, from Marina di Gioiosa Ionica, near Siderno, as a local boss of the 'ndrangheta, associated with the Siderno clans in Ontario, historically linked with the clans near Siderno in Calabria. It was the first time that a non-Italian court sentenced someone for his 'ndrangheta role and connection, thus recognizing the 'ndrangheta as a criminal organization abroad.

'In America [meaning Canada] for those from our village as well as for those of his village … they are all under the Siderno people … he went and without saying anything, he gave a dote.'

'But you are not going to recognise that dote here will you?'

The boss of Siderno, Giuseppe Commisso, was (again) speaking in his laundromat, during Operation Crimine in 2010, about the relationship between the clans from Siderno and those from Gioiosa Ionica and Marina di Gioiosa Ionica.

Never had a laundromat had such a dynamic life!

The area is crowded for the 'ndrangheta there but, in Canada, Siderno rules *uber alles*. It doesn't matter whether, for business purposes, the clans must be flexible and hybrid and obviously mix with other groups. Within the 'ndrangheta, 'order' and 'procedure' still are said to mean something, or so it appears … So, there cannot be any recognition of a ranking – a *dote* – outside the rules. And this, once again, is a matter to handle in person, paying the right visits to the right people and doing the right thing according to tradition and regulations. *Oh, the importance of 'doing things right', so typical of mafia-type families in Canada!*[29]

> You want us to be friends and to respect each other and we go forward … but let's not kid ourselves, if we can't we'll stay in our own locale and that's the end of it. Things must be done properly, it's not like what is done there [Canada] is better than what is done here [Siderno]. There are people from my village there, as well as from Marina [di Gioiosa Ionica], so you can't just do what you want, no one can.[30]

The connectivity among different clans of the Siderno area, including those whose past has been belligerent in Calabria, remains one of the main characteristics of the Siderno Group. On the one hand, the distance between Canada and Calabria allows autonomous action: Calabria remains in the background of migrants' experiences on online forums as much as it remains in the background of mafia activities. On the other hand, connectivity offline, in-person meetings, trips to show goodwill, settling disputes over dinner, all helps to clarify roles and rankings in between Siderno and Canada. The reputation of the clans is Siderno is constantly enhanced and confirmed by their Ontario connections. And vice versa, the Ontario-based clans are powerful and resilient because they can count on the connection with Siderno. This also helps to understand the boundaries of any organizational *isomorphism* that the *'ndrine* exhibit abroad.

The process of isomorphism is the recognition of similarity between the activities or structure of one organization and those of another. This similarity can be the result of *imitation* or *independent development* under similar constraints.[31] Within family dynasties like the typical *'ndrine*, branches of the dynasty abroad usually take on similar organizational features of the family back home. Indeed, we can observe isomorphism across virtually all 'ndrangheta clans; they tend to replicate the organizational structures of a family within the projections of that family abroad. Usually the mother *'ndrina* remains anchored to its own *locale* and its own territory and coordinates matters with the branches abroad. But the Siderno clans are peculiar for two reasons.

Firstly, the representatives of the clans from Siderno abroad have been adopting an umbrella role like that of the *Crimine* or *Provincia* in the 'ndrangheta in Calabria: they coordinate various Italian/Calabrian clans, even beyond the Sidernesi. This is because, criminally speaking, they have been the most historically active and the most connected to other groups, especially the Italian–American La Cosa Nostra in the United States since the time of the famous operation Pizza Connection about heroin shipments.[32] They have gone beyond being the projected image of the *Società* of Siderno. Their isomorphism is dictated by the need for survival and connectivity abroad. More critically, we can assume that affiliates from the Siderno clans in Toronto have learned what the organizational needs of others are in the Canadian scene and have aligned their behaviour to that. This kind of isomorphism is the result of a process of natural and/or cultural selection that has taught the Sidernesi how to organize, not only by adapting to Canada but also to remain *'ndranghetisti*.

Secondly, in assuming an umbrella role, the Siderno Group in Ontario has transformed effectively, by imitation this time, into its own peculiar *Società*. The *Società* of Siderno operates in Toronto in the same way as it operates in Calabria. But it's also more than that. The representatives of the Siderno Group in Ontario, as mentioned, can even act *in lieu of* the main *Società* of Siderno, from Toronto and not from Calabria, as hinted at by Operation Canadian Connection. Imitation of norms, moving roles and overlapping isomorphic traits between the two worlds: all difficult to unpack.

'I cannot go against everyone!' – says Vincenzo Muià to an associate. He adds:

> For those here in Canada, for them, it's easier to speak because obviously here things are different. But this is reality, and they say: come

here, come to Toronto. If you cannot do what you must do there, then leave! But he [Francesco Commisso, in Toronto] was speaking in general … as it happened here [in Siderno] today, it can happen there [in Toronto] tomorrow. But he says and rightly so: you cannot forget the past; no one can. Are they here [in Siderno]? Okay! They can try and forget from there [in Toronto], because it does not touch them, but here you cannot forget.[33]

Here, in Siderno, and *there*, in Toronto. Through intense exchange of communication and shared criminal interests and values, there it is, a widely connected, hypermobile and isomorphic organization. Where no one, in the end, can forget to avenge a murder, for example.

Leaving Toronto in summer 2019, I was left with a question, a curiosity perhaps, as an earworm inside my head: what could be happening right now in Australia, and especially in Perth, if the Società *of Siderno is indeed so connected to the point of being also manageable, when needed, from Toronto? Is anyone paying attention to this? Who is taking care of those relations or new ones between Canada and Australia, if at all? Does it matter really, when it comes to the 'ndrangheta in Perth, if some of the power shifts from Siderno to Canada? Does it matter if we ask these questions?*

In 2014, the FBI and the Italian authorities arrested a few people, associates of the Gambino family and 'ndrangheta clans, in Brooklyn.[34] The case was about drugs and money laundering and was aided by an undercover FBI officer; it was dubbed Operation New Bridge by Italian authorities.[35] Different people, among them Franco Lupoi – a Gambino member but who 'had lived in Calabria' – organized the drug trade with the Siderno-based Ursino clan in Italy. The resourceful nature of the network showed very clearly how opportunity in the right context and with the right capability makes the connection between old-school Gambinos in New York and international Siderno-based affiliates not only possible but extremely likely. The Sidernesi can count on a wide network across North America, via New York or Ontario, due to their presence in Toronto, the interdependency between Siderno clans and Ontario clans, and the historical partnerships with Cosa nostra in Sicily and the United States.

In June 2021, a man, Salvatore Lupoi, was arrested in Adelaide as part of a massive anti-mafia, anti-organized crime operation that the AFP led together with the FBI.[36] This Lupoi, in Adelaide, was known to authorities for involvement in drugs and was also allegedly involved with local 'ndrangheta-like clans, including the Alvaro clan in South Australia and others from the Siderno area in Western Australia.[37] His name, and his arrest more generally, reminded me of the 2014 Operation New Bridge. An American–Australian connection, via Canada, that I kept seeing whenever there were Siderno clans involved.

Whenever Siderno is involved, I see the most hybrid and fluid borders.

Hybrid borders

> Homogenisation across organisations does not just happen; in the initial stages of their life cycle, organisational fields display considerable diversity in approach and form. Once a field becomes well established, however, there is an inexorable push towards homogenisation.[38]

Homogenization – or integration – might be a result of a quest for stability, to sustain that reputation gained thanks to isomorphic processes. This, I thought, could help explain 'traditional' organized crime in Canada, meaning 'the mafia'.

Between Ontario and Quebec, and especially in the Niagara region at the border with New York State, isomorphism of Italian mafia groups – both 'ndrangheta and Cosa nostra, or even others – has generated interesting hybrids.[39] Firstly, the heavy legacy and reputation of LCN – the Italian–American mafia – has probably led many groups, including 'ndrangheta groups, to imitate 'the Sicilians', Cosa nostra – or whatever Cosa nostra was supposed to be in certain periods, between Hollywood myths and reality. Gangsterism, opulence, the glamourization of criminal life and the idolization of charismatic leaders became the common mafia traits across Calabrian as much as Sicilian clans in Canada as in the United States.

This, at least, seems to be the established organizational field of mafias in the Niagara region: multiple identities, depending on context; opportunistic ties and integration with others; and hybridization of structures. There could be a difference between the formal structure of criminal groups and their informal decisions. Different groups might have adopted the same organizational form, or they wished to appear as if they had.

The harsh repression of LCN (*yes I got used to calling it LCN!*) at the US border, paired with the enduring power (or rather perception of rising power) of the 'ndrangheta and the Siderno Group especially, led to a breakdown of formal identities across mafia groups in Canada. For a long time, the distinction between Calabrians and Sicilians seemed to be a matter of the past – of the 1970s fights in Montreal between Cotroni-Violi and Rizzuto, for example. On the other hand, a return to *regionalization* of mafia groups,[40] which amounts to an apparent distinction between Calabrian and Sicilian factions, and their respective identities as 'ndrangheta or (La) Cosa Nostra, seems to have recently rekindled animosity across old alliances.

'He [Natale Luppino] was going with the Sicilians, you know … the way I understand it, they hang around with the Sicilians.' And the 'Sicilians' are against the Sidernesi, he added.[41]

This is Vincenzo Muià talking, again, in Siderno about his upcoming trip to Ontario. He is talking with a relative of Luppino about a recent murder in the family in the city of Hamilton, Ontario, and the implications and reasons for it. They, Luppino, *were going with the Sicilians*. And he probably meant the American (La) Cosa Nostra family, on the other side of the Niagara border, in Buffalo.

There is a mafia war in Hamilton, one could read in the news.

Where the hell is Hamilton? I had to admit to ignorance when I was planning my first trip to Canada in 2017. I did visit Hamilton that year. I was researching the 'ndrangheta and I asked myself, *had Hamilton anything to do with the 'ndrangheta?* I was not sure. I was so wrong.

I went to Hamilton when the killings had not yet multiplied, and the situation was not yet as confused as it became between 2018 and 2022.

Hamilton is a bit over an hour from Toronto by public transport, 50 minutes by car. The bus trip was smooth, still too cold for April. The bus left me on the main street; I went straight to the harbour because I do love port cities; *waterfronts make me feel like I can breathe better, right into the sea air.* Hamilton is … *regular*. Squared, even. It was windy and cold, as the snow and the rain of the previous days had frozen the air. The city is green and open, the harbour embraces the streets downtown; the shopping districts look, to me at least, like a small Toronto.

Pasquale 'Pat' Musitano was killed in broad daylight in a shopping mall in a Hamilton district, Burlington, on 10 July 2020. His brother, Angelo, had been killed in the driveway of his house, in May 2017, right after my trip there. Pat had already survived an attempt on his life in April 2019, so underworld observers in the media agreed that he was a 'dead man walking'.[42]

Who wanted the Musitano brothers dead?

This is surely a question for journalists and authorities, of course. But, from an analytical perspective, I also tried to form my own picture of the situation. Angelo and Pasquale Musitano were the sons of Dominic Musitano, descendant of Angelo Musitano (senior), known as 'the beast of Delianuova'. Delianuova is a small town in Aspromonte – with the Italiano and Alvaro 'ndrine. *Were these brothers 'ndrangheta?* Yes, if we consider the legacy of territories and surnames, as the links to the village of Platì through the Delianuova part of the Musitano family have been ascertained in Italy on various occasions. And yet, probably not, not 'ndrangheta, not really.

Angelo (junior) and Pasquale Musitano, the story goes, were part of a *traditional* criminal organization in Hamilton – which essentially means an Italian mafia-type organization. In the 1990s, they had opted to join forces with the Cuntrera–Caruana family clan from Montreal. Headed by Vito Rizzuto, whose story is a stand-alone mafia story, this branch of La Cosa Nostra in Montreal maintained links both to Sicily and to New York through the Bonanno family. Now, to be of value for Rizzuto and to side with him – still the story goes – the Musitanos got rid of Johnny 'Pops' Papalia, boss of another Hamilton mafia family, also of Calabrian descent, and enemy of the Montrealese Rizzuto, over a matter of debt and honour. Indeed, this seemed like a boss vs boss kind of situation. The Musitanos were convicted of Papalia's murder in 2000. Yes, this is how the story goes.

Hang on a second; does that mean that we have here a 'ndrangheta family that chose – is 'chose' the right term? – at some point to switch over to La Cosa Nostra? And what does that mean in practice? How did they handle the animosity with the Papalias, considering they were from the same village, Delianuova, a village of around 3,300 people?

A lot of mafia *flags* in Canada, between 'ndrangheta and La Cosa Nostra. There, in Hamilton, over the Niagara River, I confirmed how mere ethnicity cannot be the only common denominator to mafia mobility. *Isn't it the behaviour that counts? Isn't this what I always say, anyway?*

Pat Musitano was described as 'Tony Soprano before Tony Soprano was on television'.[43] A gangster appearance – wearing suits, custom-made items of clothing, dark sunglasses – and his preference for luxurious cars and good restaurants. *He certainly seemed more of an American mobster than a Calabrian 'ndrangheta capo-bastone.* Since his death, new groups have already emerged: new group identities, new alliances with New York and the rest of Canada.

Similarly, after Johnny Papalia's death, the family seemed to have died with him, as his brother never retaliated and in fact stepped back from the whole mafia business.[44]

'When Johnny left, all the power left with him. You may be in during the glory with the boss, but when the boss goes, you disappear with him', said a retired detective in Ontario to the media.[45]

A look at Hamilton again – squeezed between Montreal, Toronto and Buffalo, NY – confirms how Italian mafia groups there, whether Calabrian or Sicilian, tend(ed) to imitate 'the Mafia' (capital M, the spelling I hate) that *ought to be*, trying to imitate the American 'Mob'. And chasing that is a bit like chasing witches; a mafiacraft, some have called it,[46] like witchcraft, where I had to identify voices and silences to interpret the presence and absence of this 'thing' called mafia.

Papalia. That surname could not go unnoticed. It is in fact my mother's, thus my grandfather's, surname. Delianuova is 20 minutes away by car from Santa Cristina, where my mother grew up, where I spent months of my childhood, my Aspromonte village. Relatives in Aspromonte, I now know, do travel between those villages as they travelled to North America. Whenever my grandfather's sister, also a Papalia, came back to the village with her family from Rochester, NY – also in the Niagara region – the village celebrated them almost as survivors – *what had they survived? Migration? Or the United States? Who knows, but such was the perception. Treat them well, they had such a long trip!*

Johnny 'Pops' Papalia is one of those mafia characters who has books written about him.[47] Originally from Delianuova, his mother was from the Italiano crime family (clan) – *that of Peppe 'Ntoni Italiano, remember him travelling to greet friends and family in Australia?* – and his father had links with the Barbaro–Papalia–Sergi in Platì – *yes, the same Barbaro and the same Sergi we have already mentioned throughout this book.* Cousins of Johnny, Domenico in Calabria and Antonio and Rocco in Lombardia, near Milan, are considered among the most influential men of this clan in the past couple of decades. *Just Google them, really.* Surely, if Johnny 'Pops' Papalia was 'ndrangheta, he was of the highest calibre. In fact, judicial chronicles reported on the role of the Papalia family in the kidnappings, their role in the cocaine trade between Calabria and Lombardia, in Operation Nord-Sud, for example, in the mid-1990s; they had a role in supporting and shaping Barbaro's and Sergi's activities as well, beyond Italy and probably into Australia.

And yet, in Hamilton, they were not really 'ndrangheta. Or at least not only. Business-wise Papalia was in fact close to the Buffalo-based Mogaddino–Todaro family and close to the New York LCN too. Buffalo is really around the corner from Hamilton, about a one-hour drive across Niagara Falls and the US–Canada border. Must be a great place to drive to, by car; sadly, I haven't done that yet.

Whatever happens in Buffalo might be considered influential for Hamilton and vice versa. Borders do not really matter, and seemingly neither does ethnicity, when territorial proximity is so significant. The border also plays a role in shaping hybrid – borderland – identities.[48]

When Giuseppe and Domenico Violi were arrested during Project Otremens in late 2017, both the FBI[49] and the RCMP[50] found more than what they were expecting.

> The reason why we're here is from this day forward, you're gonna be an official member of the Bonanno family. It's already – from this guy, this guy, this guy – everybody approved it, so from this day forward, you're a member of the Bonanno family. Congratulations.[51]

An undercover agent from New York on one side, and a video-recorded induction into the mafia on the other. The newly initiated agent played a key role in a trafficking case involving the Violi brothers from Hamilton. Forging new alliances and revamping old ones.

The Violi brothers are the two sons of deceased Paolo Violi, a mafia boss killed in Montreal during the quest for power of the Rizzuto family in the 1970s. They come from the old-school Calabrian 'Honoured Society'. Paolo Violi was linked by blood to the Alvaro clan. Paul's aunt was Rosa Violi, married to Cosimo Alvaro, historical *capo-bastone* in Sinopoli, Aspromonte, Calabria. *Various nephews of Cosimo Alvaro migrated to South Australia, by the way.* Two of the girls in the family, Concetta and Domenica, married brothers Agostino and Carmelo Labbozzetta. The two brothers were cousins of *that* Tony Labbozzetta, whose reputation has been such an issue in New South Wales, and were involved in the drug trade in Australia. *Remember him?*

According to a confidential file of the Italian anti-mafia prosecutors from the late 1990s:

> From the results of checks we have carried out, it is reasonable to maintain that the criminal organisations in both Platì and Sinopoli can be connected to the Australian ones also through the abovementioned subjects, including the Violi in Canada.

The world of the 'ndrangheta and of Calabrian mobility, like dots connecting around the world, is at times very small.

Following the Montreal mafia war that killed their father, the Violi brothers moved with their mother to Hamilton and, the story goes, they were welcomed into the Luppino (crime) family, to whom they were related by blood. Giacomo Luppino, 'the head of Hamilton ... with a strong influence in the 'ndrangheta in the Toronto area',[52] was the father-in-law of Montreal-based Paolo Violi. The Luppinos are Calabrian, with a solid 'ndrangheta lineage: Giacomo Luppino was a prominent member – founder – of the so-called Chamber of Control of the 'ndrangheta in Ontario. However, the Luppino–Violi in Hamilton historically have always been linked to LCN in Buffalo.[53]

Yes, head spins, I know.

Dom Violi, during Project Otremens, confirmed that he had been made the underboss of the Buffalo LCN and seemed proud that no other Canadian before him had been so high up in an American–Italian (crime) family. Both Dom and Joe were arrested during Otremens; interceptions and surveillance reveal how both brothers were looking after their alliances both with Buffalo (Dom) and possibly with the Bonanno in NYC (Joe); they also reported to their uncles Natale and Rocco Luppino, heads of the family. They were, essentially, maintaining hybrid organizations, a mix of old (expectations, traditions) and new (businesses, alliances), crossing borders, crossing identities, using different mafia flags.[54] They adapted, they survived, they mutated.

Of course, looking at Hamilton in 2021–2022, questions remain about the Violi brothers' return to Hamilton following the end of their prison sentences. While Joe's release is further way, Dom's release will come much sooner; his day parole has already raised eyebrows among underworld observers.[55] *With the current scenario in Hamilton, with new families and new violence, is anyone able to rule at all there? And what about the violence?*

The US–Canadian border between Buffalo and Hamilton seems to blur the lines between 'ndrangheta and American LCN: a mafia borderland identity.

But I wonder, *was there ever a real separation of identities? Has the identity of origin ever mattered there? Is this even 'ndrangheta anyway? Or rather, is the 'ndrangheta that people 'remember' here really a criminal entity? Or perhaps some sort of social club, a nostalgic and sepia-coloured postcard from Calabria?*

Indeed, ethnicity is not what matters in and around Niagara, behaviours do. And, again, family and the perception of the 'right way' of doing things.[56]

> Dom Violi stated that Joe Todaro was right; he should have been told that Iavarone and Caputo had been straightened out [allegedly in the Gambino family in California], because it was in Todaro's area.[57]

★★★

On 13 February 2019, Vincenzo Muià is talking to a man, considered a *'ndranghetista* as well, Giuseppe Macrì, in Siderno.

> 'My condolences for … your nephew, is that right, your nephew? I was told … was he the one married to Gisella's daughter? I didn't know […] what the fuck happened? Did they go inside to kill him?
> 'Yeah, probably they didn't know him, they had to go to the house, in the street … to shoot.'
> 'I have to go to Toronto … on the 30th.'
> 'Where the fuck are you going? It's worse than here (in Siderno) … it's a mess there (in Toronto).'[58]

The nephew was Cece Luppino; he had been killed in Hamilton in January 2019. Son of Rocco Luppino, considered the head of the Luppino family, Cece was not interested in a mafia life but was bearing the weight of his surname and origins.

> J. Violi stated that Cece told his father he watched his father struggle for 30 years, and that Cece does not want to struggle for 30 years; and if he does have to, then he doesn't want it.[59]

Now, if the Siderno clans in Calabria have family in Hamilton and they operate through the Siderno Group and its Crimine *in Toronto, is there a line connecting Toronto and Hamilton? It surely seems like there is, according to Calabrian mafiosi.* But I couldn't confirm or deny this in my research. Who knows, really? Conjectures are quick to come, these days.

As a researcher, and not an intelligence analyst (*which, in another life, I would have loved to be!*), these questions remain at the level of curiosity; the data is too incomplete. And yet I cannot help but wonder, while lining up individuals, names, places, and putting everything on one or the other side of the Canadian–US border, *how easily can you convert from one mafia identity to another? What does one lose, what does one let go of, if anything at all, in switching mafia flags, mafia identities? In a world where Calabrian mafia families have imitated American gangsterism, just because that was in vogue around them at the time, can the trend be reversed? Or is there adaptation of the 'ndrangheta even today?*

While keeping up with the news about Vaughan, Woodbridge and Hamilton and their apparently quiet suburban life, and remembering *crowded* Siderno, I wondered: *now that Canadian authorities are paying attention to the 'ndrangheta, now that the 'ndrangheta is even spelled correctly abroad, what's next? Are the Siderno clans really expanding – and will they attract more attention because of that? Or are they struggling – and therefore attracting more attention because of that?*

Are they hypermobile, from Siderno to Perth, from Siderno to New York, from New York to Toronto and now over to Hamilton, or are they just … scrambling to survive?

While research data is genuinely not enough for any prediction or conjecture, my intuition tells me that, one way or the other, the rule of survival of the fittest will apply. Many will continue being hypermobile, finding contacts, rekindling connections across the world, travelling from Australia to Canada to Europe. Some will fail, some will barely manage by rearranging the mafia-type group around rituals, rules, sanctions, crime. Others will be jailed in the process; others will go free thanks to procedural hiccups. Siderno will be home, but many outside Siderno still might not know what exactly this means yet. New clans, from Calabria – from the Vibo Valentia province for example – have consolidated their position in Ontario with an understanding, it appears, that the *Società* of Siderno remains superior in Canada. The Sidernesi are – *make* – home, far from home, for others too.

It can be useful to have a place to call home, from a mafia perspective, when the world is spinning, and criminal identities can get bloody and hybrid. After all, as I said at the beginning, places of origin, for migrant communities (including mafia ones), are often imagined communities, holding a symbolic significance – the attraction of a potential, one day, 'return'. We shouldn't underestimate what 'home' means, even for the mafia.

Hypermobility and reputation

Montreal is, for me (and others for sure), Leonard Cohen. My first vision of Montreal was in the lyrics to *Suzanne*: 'Suzanne takes you down to her place near the river | You can hear the boats go by, you can spend the night forever.'[60]

If you didn't know the face of Leonard Cohen (*weird, but hey, it can happen!*) you definitely will after seeing two giant murals in the streets of Montreal. They are like sudden slaps on your eyes, one in Crescent Street that follows you through the road while crossing, the other on the side of the Cooper Building on St-Laurent Boulevard, which you basically stumble upon pretty much by mistake.

Montreal is the waterfront, the old port, the plateau, the stupid need to climb a mountain to get from one side of the city to the other. And the streets are so long, with the house numbers going to 10,000 or 11,000. And Leonard Cohen, for sure.

Montreal is nothing like Toronto, nothing like the rest of North America. Everyone says it's the French legacy, and that is surely true, but I think it's the mix between Italian, French, the old port city, Canadian law, American dreams, the sheer cold, the pale green roofs and the gothic houses. It's the whole mix.

Italian authorities, after Operation Acero Connection in 2015, kept saying that the violence around the Siderno Group in Canada was due to their will to expand into Montreal following the unrest and power void after Vito Rizzuto's death in 2013. They were wrong, or at least partially wrong, as the 'war' was between different 'ndrangheta factions – between the Figliomeni and the Coluccio, apparently.

No one from outside Montreal can enter Montreal, let alone rule it. Everyone was very adamant about that when I first started asking in 2017. Montreal is self-contained, criminal groups work together, and the Rizzuto name is still high-value currency.

End of story. Seriously, no one ever even fathoms anything different in Montreal. 'Italians [Italian antimafia authorities] should stop saying that the Calabrians wish to take over Montreal, they cannot', I was told by various law enforcement agents.

Once you set foot in Canada, if you are researching organized crime, there is only one name that will accompany you from day one. That of Vito Rizzuto.

Vito Rizzuto is another of those characters who deserves a book on his own and, indeed, various books have been written about him, his criminal career, his life.[61] His name, his legacy, still affect the perception of mafia in Montreal – whatever is left of Cosa nostra and its Sicilian roots – as well as the perception of mafia and organized crime around the whole of Canada and western/upstate New York.

Even if the events around Rizzuto have always somehow fallen outside my scope of research – as they are not, after all, strictly about the 'ndrangheta – I couldn't avoid learning about him, his family and their struggles to keep their powerhouse solid even today. Talking to the authorities about Project Colisée in mid-2000s and Project Cadenza later,[62] both targeting the Rizzuto family and their criminal activities, gave me the necessary background to understand the scope of the mafia phenomenon and reach into Montreal and Canada overall.

Rizzuto was a mediator, a broker. He was able to offer his services with a view to benefitting himself. He had a certain aura about him that enabled him to ensure that everyone followed his directions. As investigator, Eric

Vecchio, *with whom I would speak on the phone in 2019 while sitting in a police station listening to a chief of police explaining the current situation of the Montreal mafia, that was fascinating ... anyway* ... as Vecchio declared to the Commission of Inquiry on the Awarding and Management of Public Contracts in the Construction Industry Schemes (Charbonneau Commission, whose report is from 2015),[63] 'Mr. Rizzuto sells his credibility to make deals, sells the possibility of finding a resolution to the dispute.' The essence of the mafioso, according to pretty much everyone.[64]

The Charbonneau Commission found that members of the Rizzuto clan were enlisted to settle disputes among construction companies over contract bids and that they collected cash from them – mafiosi are known to favour agreements and facilitate cartels between businessmen.[65] Nick Junior, Vito Rizzuto's son, was shot and killed in 2009. Vito was subpoenaed to testify at the Charbonneau inquiry but died of lung cancer in 2013 before he could appear.

A man of honour. And surely not only in Montreal, as his associates, in life as much as in business, were also in Ontario, the Cuntrera–Caruana, the Commisso, and in the United States, where his connection to the Bonannos was notorious.

He was one of those whom everyone imitated or wanted to please, in Hamilton, in Toronto, in Buffalo and in New York.

Indeed, the glorification of the boss is *not* a 'ndrangheta feature as much as it has been a trait of Cosa nostra in Sicily and in the United States. Charismatic leaders of Corleone, for example (Riina, Bagarella, Provenzano, to name a few), and individuals like John Gotti or Vito Genovese in New York, are part of the public understanding of what a mobster is, was or is expected to be.

Vito Rizzuto, in Montreal, was surely one of the glorified ones. His legacy left big shoes to fill for his sons, who might have his surname but not necessarily his charisma.

At a bar in Petite Italie in Montreal, whose themes were sports and old-style Italy, while having a cappuccino and looking at vintage pictures that the owner proudly kept on the counter for everyone to see, I played the curious-yet-clueless-girl card, in my not-good-enough Quebec-French.

'Isn't it around here that Nick Rizzuto Jr was killed?'
'Sure thing.'
'Did they come here a lot, the Rizzuto?'
'All the time. We couldn't keep them out, could we? Plus, you wouldn't
have found a more polite and respected man than Vito, I tell you, never
a problem with him around.'

The reputation of a man of honour leaves many people puzzled; *isn't the mafia bad anyway? How was he a nice person?* But many often confuse charisma with respect, assuming that the latter must follow from the former and also vice versa. And this is the big win, one of many, for *any* mafia.

★★★

In Montreal, you breathe Canada like nowhere else. Walking down the Old Port, *le Vieux-Port*, with the giant panoramic wheel over the water, the feeling of a spur-of-the-moment festival with street food, walks and laughter pervade you. In March, in the snow, as much as in July, in the summer heat.

Down Rue de la Commune, at number 1000, right where the port road starts – authorized access only – is where the pedestrian walk around the old port ends. Just outside where the fenced part of the port starts in front of the Saint-Laurent River is a series of luxury condos in what looks like a giant concrete box. In 2015, the Charbonneau Commission found that various business interests linked with Rizzuto and other organized crime figures in Montreal converged in 1000 de la Commune. Raynald Desjardins, a very notorious organized crime member – at one point close to the Rizzutos, then in a feud with them, but also close to other criminal groups in the city, including the Hells Angels – was given an apartment and a garage in the building without paying for it, for example. Desjardins, by the way, was 'presented' to me as a boss with the former Calabrian faction of Montreal, with the Cotroni–Violi. *I resist pigeon-holing groups and factions in Montreal, or Canada.*

Anyway, Vito Rizzuto had agreed to act as enforcer for financial services and businesses ongoing in the building; one of the entrepreneurs involved, Toni Magi, had entered business with Nick Rizzuto Jr, too. Rumours followed both Nick Jr's death as apparently linked to Magi, too, and Magi's death in 2019 as well, apparently linked to the Rizzutos also.

If you walk down the Old Port promenade, leaving 1000 de la Commune behind you, for 40 minutes straight towards the Port Authority, you experience Montreal unfolding on your right, in the old city, and on your left, into the sea. With *poutine* in your hands – French fries with cheese curds topped with gravy, bought at the nearest kiosk over the promenade – you can feel the city all around you. Strangers do not shy away from making eye contact – *it is apparently all right in Montreal to do so, who knew.* In the old town, dance halls are weirdly populated on a random weeknight – *I entered one by mistake and was pretty much forced to stay for half an hour not to be impolite!* Music is often heard coming out of buildings; the underground city – over 30 kilometres of underground tunnels! – makes you feel like a caged mouse but is a blessing with the snow outside; the cathedral towers on your left; an abandoned warehouse, an urban designer's dream, attracts on the right.

Montreal is poetry and music; I am sure you have heard that before. But it is also one of the most corrupt cities in North America, as the Charbonneau Commission found, and with a high density of criminal activities. A variety of groups, from outlaw motorcycle gangs to the Rizzuto family allies, to street gangs, all seemingly live and collaborate in the underworld of the city.

Contradictory and artistic, Montreal. Irresistible.

I walked for hours, in June and July 2019, the last time I was there. I doubt there is somewhere reachable from the city centre that I have not walked past.

Back and forth from the port of Montreal, on which I was doing research in summer 2019. A long strip of land, somehow never fully kissed by the sun, always basking in a strange white light.

Music in my ears, almost every day, sitting across Notre Dame, in loop. There was a song, 'Cathedrals' by Jump Little Children,[66] whose lyrics have essentially become my memory of Montreal, its Notre Dame, the solitary walks I had then, the wind, the port, the sea. It goes like this:

In the shadows
Of tall buildings
Of open arches
Endlessly kneeling
Sonic landscapes
Echoing vistas

And unexpectedly, while listening to this song on loop, I was struck by how much it mirrored my feelings of seeking home during my travels, especially in its last notes:

A final moment
In the dead of night
In the Cathedrals
Of New York and Rome
There is a feeling
That you should just go Home
And spend a lifetime
Finding out just where that is.[67]

Yes, there was a feeling that I should have just gone home. And unfold my mind.

Home, back to Calabria.

7

The Port, the Sea and
the Wrong Sun

The port

The port of Gioia Tauro was always there, yet was never there, in my youth. Something so big and yet so out of place.

No one seemed to be working at the site of the port of Gioia Tauro on a Monday morning in November 2017. I had driven by the port fences many times before but that time I stopped. Where was everyone? At 12.00 on a Monday morning, shouldn't it be buzzing with activity? It struck me as an anomaly that one of Italy's busiest ports, as far as I knew, was so deserted.

I didn't know much about ports then. I did not know how containers were moved from one place to the other; I didn't *really* know how drugs were moved through containers either.

In summer 2018, on the beach of San Ferdinando, in front of a €4 Aperol Spritz as orange as the falling sky over the sea, on the left there it was, the port again, with the cranes over the water, the arms of global trade over the sea, as I would learn visiting other ports from 2019 for research on drug importation and organized crime on the waterfronts and harbours around the world. It's strange how certain things, even if they are always there, impossible to miss, eventually get missed.

It's difficult to unpack in my head why the port of Gioia Tauro was always there and yet was never there when I was a child. A self-contained world, that of a port, in the middle of three towns – Rosarno, Gioia Tauro and San Ferdinando – that looked completely out of place in comparison with the surrounding territory. The port is progress and international trade. The triad of Rosarno, Gioia Tauro and San Ferdinando – part of the so-called *Piana*, the flatland – is historically a territory linked to agricultural sectors. *Lines and lines of olive trees and citrus groves here.* The asymmetry between the port and the land behind it; the lack of a city behind the port; the clear disparity and tension between internationalization and attachment to the local, between progress and self-preservation.

It's always there and never there, the port of Gioia Tauro, yes. It's one of those secrets everyone knows, that the port of Gioia Tauro was built and sustained, especially in its early days in the 1990s, with the money and in the interest of some of the most important clans of the 'ndrangheta of the *Piana*.

In the famous verdict for the trial named 'Porto',[1] which started in 1998 and finished in 2000, the defendants were tried for a plan to extort the Medcenter Container Terminal (MCT). Since 1995, MCT has managed the transhipment activities at the port of Gioia Tauro. The Piromalli–Molé clan in Gioia Tauro and the Pesce clan in Rosarno were placing an extortion tax of one and a half US dollars for every container moved in the port by MCT.

Mr Bianchi (alias for a broker of both clans with MCT)
Mr Lugli (vice president of MCT)
Early 1990s

Mr Bianchi:	'We are there … watching … we have been watching and waiting for this, for this change […] We are there, we live there, we have past, present, and future there. Our request is that for every container there is something for us, we consider this logical, fair, a reciprocal exchange, correct and civil, … Our request is that we ask for a one and a half dollar for every container that gets offloaded, because in there, you have 80, 85, 90 dollars, I don't know how much, for each container. It's just crumbs that we ask for […] This is our request, evaluate it, bring it forward …'
Mr Lugli:	'What I can do is to bring this forward to the administrators, first thing. Obviously, working with a certain tranquillity and the fact of being on a territory that we know it's difficult … eh! We did not come down here thinking that Calabria was paradise!'
Mr Bianchi:	'Yes, you know where you came … and from our side, we can give you all possible guarantees, when we make an agreement. I tell you again, we are by your side all the time, anything you need, that nuisance or problem you might have we will be able to solve it in a snap of a finger, if we make an agreement. If we cannot make an agreement, you'll work on your own and we will work on our own.'[2]

Sure, Calabria is not paradise, the investors knew that, and they were ready to adapt to the extortive request. This is because it was not an extortive request after all, as much as it was a protection offer, gladly accepted by the entrepreneurs, and clearly proposed by the mafiosi. *Who are these mafiosi anyway? What's their deal?*

Their deal, quite literally, is mostly drugs. And the *Piana* is where they reign.

Gioia

For a long time, Gioia Tauro has been considered a cocaine hub, as the arrival of the narcotic on the shores of the Calabrian port remained solidly linked to the local clans, main importers and high-end distributors too.

> An articulated criminal group, working at various levels, including units of port workers, able to move huge sums of money and false documents to facilitate the movement of the associates in foreign countries, with the scope of committing various criminal offences and in particular of procuring, purchasing and importing (from Panama ports of Cristobal and Balboa), transporting to Italy through cargo ships belonging to the Mediterranean Shipping Company, Hamburg, CMA-CGM arriving in Rotterdam, Naples, Salerno, Genova and, primarily, Gioia Tauro.[3]

In Operation Puerto Liberado,[4] whose arrests date back to 2014 and the end of the trial to 2019, the role of employees of MCT was considered pivotal. A script pretty much like this:

> Offload the container from the cargo ship.
> Identify the number on the container, which was communicated to you, something like MEDU9130190.
> Move the container to the designated truck.
> Get the container out of the port.
> Get the cocaine out of the container, usually in a nearby warehouse.
> Stock the cocaine for later cutting and distribution.

This happens pretty much in every port, but in Gioia Tauro one thing is always peculiar. The money that bought the drugs in the first place comes from the same territory where the drugs arrive and are initially distributed. The 'ndrangheta clans invest, import and receive, as well as distribute wholesale. And it is not always like this, not even for the 'ndrangheta clans active in other places.[5] The cocaine investors are not always the distributors, but in Gioia Tauro they are. This gives them a powerful grip on both the cocaine and the territory. Such must be the habit of managing key nodal points of the supply chain in Gioia Tauro that at times, even in other ports, the clans send someone to make sure that nothing goes wrong.

Or at least this was the case when, in October 2015, during Operation Panda, the Guardia di Finanza in Genova, Liguria, arrested three people for international drug trafficking. Among them was Giuseppe Bellocco, affiliate of the Bellocco–Pesce clan, the primary 'ndrangheta group in Rosarno. Even as a fugitive, which he was at the time, he thought that he had to supervise the 148 kilograms of cocaine arriving in Genova.

According to the Direzione Nazionale Antimafia,[6] the port of Gioia Tauro remains one of the main entry points for cocaine in Italy, notwithstanding a decline in its importance recorded during 2017–2018. In fact, whereas, in 2017, 80.89 per cent of the total amount of cross-border seizures of cocaine in Italy was seized in Gioia Tauro (for a total of 1,912.22 kilograms of cocaine), in 2018 these seizures went down drastically, to only 217 kilograms overall in Gioia. This mirrored the overall losses of the port, which in that period faced a 30 per cent decline in commercial activities, mainly due to changing routes: for example, the South America East Coast route (SAEC) route from Brazilian ports no longer saw Gioia Tauro as the first stop; it became the last stop, after Genova and Livorno, which means that cocaine, if any, could be collected in those two ports instead. In 2019, however, the business of the port of Gioia Tauro picked up again. In fact, in 2019 around 2,200 kilograms of cocaine were seized in Gioia Tauro,[7] confirming a primary role for the port and the clans around it. In 2020, seizures went beyond those of 2019 and grew to unprecedented levels again in 2021, notwithstanding the COVID-19 pandemic. This is why, perhaps, the geography of the clans in the *Piana* is particularly complex. The fact that the port, in fact, sits above Gioia Tauro, Rosarno and San Ferdinando has created the need to coordinate activities in these territories. The *Società* of Rosarno, which is a very large *locale*, is made up of the Piromalli–Molé, Bellocco, Pesce and Oppedisano 'ndrine. Each 'ndrina then operates in a single area of interest: Piromalli–Molé in the towns of Gioia Tauro and San Ferdinando, Bellocco in San Ferdinando, Pesce and Oppedisano in Rosarno. And they work together with others, of course, at the border between the Reggio Calabria and the Vibo Valentia provinces.

When you arrive near the port of Gioia Tauro, whether it's from Rosarno or San Ferdinando or Gioia Tauro itself, at some point you see a sign saying 'to the port', and you suddenly realize it's there, it's been there all along. *I have been to many large seaports during my research, and never have I experienced something so hidden in plain sight. Or perhaps it could be that I grew up around it and am used to it? Perhaps this is what happens when something is around you, but you never see it intentionally. A bit like the 'ndrangheta.*

Yes, when you arrive near the port of Gioia Tauro, you are suddenly reminded that the port is there. It's like someone dropped it from the sky, a port without a maritime city behind it, out of nowhere. With 30–40 years of history, the port is linked to the land that hosts it and also designed to suck up and dry out its resources.

Inside, the port looks like any other container port – gigantic cranes, majestic cargo ships docked over the 1.5 kilometres of docking area, full of colourful containers. But it's not Montreal with the Old Port over the Saint Laurent district. And it's not New York on the docks of Brooklyn. It's not Genova with the Lantern over the old port terminals, and it's not Liverpool with the city wharf. Gioia Tauro is surrounded by a territory that does not match the intent and the hopes of its port, its capacity, its reach in international trade.

And in the container that you were waiting for on the cargo ship from South America, the bag with cocaine contains an extra seal to replace the one that you had to rip to open the container in the first place. You must be ready, more than ready, because when the container arrives, whoever is on duty is going to open that container, replace the seal, get the bag with cocaine into a car just outside the port and move it away from there. Or sometimes they rip open the door of the container directly, without even breaking the seal, to just put it back later, if they can. And, yes, you got 15–25 per cent of the whole shipment, often paid in cocaine, too. What a treat.

Scripting the activity, again.

But what if you are not from around the port area?

If there is a family, let's say the Alvaros, who has a shipment coming into Gioia Tauro, it's not them who can get it out, so they have to ask … they must ask someone who is already inside, and they pay around 20%, either in cash or in cocaine …[8]

In Operation Provvidenza, in 2018, a series of arrests hit one of the main criminal dynasties of the area of Gioia Tauro. The Piromalli-Molé *'ndrina* demonstrated their grip over the ports, with their drug imports to Calabria and Genova and their business of inferior-quality olive oil exported to North America. Their *hubris*, their arrogance, has been picked up many times before and after. In 2021, Operation Geolja[9] and Operation Nuova Narcos Europea[10] showed how the families of this large clan still have a grip over entrepreneurial activities in the *Piana*, the extortion rackets in Gioia Tauro and in some cities in the North of Italy and, of course, drugs throughout Europe.

An intercepted call in 2007 between Gioacchino Arcidiaco and Aldo Micciché shows this hubris, reported in Operation Cento Anni di Storia (One Hundred Years of History).[11] Arcidiaco, who is a good friend of Antonio Piromalli, at the time in jail but still *capo-bastone*, head of the *'ndrina* in Gioia Tauro, was supposed to meet with Marcello Dell'Utri, a senator – later convicted for mafia offences – and for years right-hand man of former Italian Prime Minister Silvio Berlusconi. Arcidiaco, to prepare for that meeting, sought guidance from Aldo Micciché, a former politician who had moved to Venezuela; this chat related to some business to be fixed for the Piromallis. Micciché seemingly had no doubt how to approach this.

> The Piana, the Piana is our thing, let him get that. The port of Gioia Tauro, we did that! Did you get it? Let him understand that in Aspromonte, everything that happens up there happens because of us, through us, got it? You need to know how to do politics. Let him understand that in Calabria, whether he moves across the Tyrrhenian routes, or the Ionian one, or in the middle, he needs us … got it? And when I say us, I mean Gioacchino Arcidiaco and Antonio Piromalli, am I being clear?[12]

'Be careful who looks at you', my uncle – who still lives in Gioia Tauro – used to say, 'no one here [in Gioia Tauro] will bother you, they don't know who you are, and in not knowing, they wouldn't dare to make a mistake.'

I spent weeks of my youth in Gioia Tauro visiting my uncle and auntie who lived there. *Zio used to drink red wine with tonic water or soda, that used to make my father flip. And Zia wanted us to go to the beautician, it was a proper thing for a lady, even when aged 12!*

Gioia has always been, for me, a place where I was, at the same time, a little bit *freer* than I was at home with my parents and a little bit more *disciplined* than I was at home with my parents. *How?* There was the sense of freedom connected to being at the seaside, of being able to walk the streets without a care in the world, of going to the sea alone, even when I was 13 or even ten, of not having a sleep curfew, because it was often summer and we used to go and walk in the town centre or, even better, along the sea, the *lungomare*. Yes, that was freedom. *And eating ketchup and drinking Coca-Cola, both forbidden at home.* But being with uncle and auntie, their life, their organization, their rules, gave me a different kind of discipline, more of a military-style get-up-get-dressed-clean-up-go-to-the-sea-come-back-eat-lunch-sleep-two-hours-go-to-the-sea-again-or-just-stay-downstairs-and-play-or-whatever-else-eat-dinner-go-out-sleep-repeat. It was fun, I loved it, I loved *them*; I used to love going there year after year throughout my childhood and my teenage years. Sometimes, when it was raining or the weather wasn't good enough to stay out, I would join uncle in his shop, a huge warehouse of shoes and bags and luggage – the first one you saw upon entering Gioia Tauro. In front of it, the Annunziata shopping mall – a bit of a competitor – which later, in 2015, was seized because it was linked to the Piromalli clan.

Occasionally, you heard things. Someone's uncle was *hiding* in France for a while and they came back and got arrested; someone had to go to Germany to visit another brother who thought it was better to stay there, as it was *safer* than Gioia; another one's cousin was sent to jail *for no apparent reason* (that was the comment), damned *sbirri!* (derogatory term for carabinieri or police); the money for the local festival was being eaten away by the usual *people* instead of being managed by the local committee. *Is the shop/activity safe? Who did they ask for a loan?* Yes, common chit-chat in a Calabrian town of the *Piana*.

Vague memories of a very little me, aged five – I would have reconstructed later – recalling turmoil on the beach, having to come back to auntie's home earlier than usual – hearing the word 'faida' (a 'ndrangheta feud) and knowing more or less what it was perhaps for the first time ever. It was August 1990 and someone had been shot on the beach,[13] *right down at the marina, where people sunbathe and go for a swim. Actually, three someones, I would learn, a father and his two sons, they were looking for trouble, they were pissing someone off. Wait, what?*

Years later, it must have been mid-August, around my birthday. A teenage me, constantly unhappy, frustrated, I felt misunderstood as you do at 16, you just want to be left alone. I went to the beach by myself. On the way back after a quick swim, the road I used to take to walk back was blocked. Another murder. Another faida? *Yes, something dated, which someone decided it was time to settle years later. What the hell, I think. I had to walk a whole other route, be late, be reprimanded, suffer the heat. What the hell, the heat, that – the heat – was my problem.*

Indeed, Calabria is not paradise; investors know that, politicians learn that, and people too. In the land of the Piromalli–Molé clan, history is heavy, and hubris is at home.

The reason for the hubris manifested by the Piromalli–Molé clan is indeed rooted in their history. Their reputation peaked in the 1980s and 1990s when they were considered the interlocutors of the Sicilian clans of Cosa nostra in Calabria, at a time when Cosa nostra was just approaching its most cruel stage – the terror of the early 1990s.

In Operation 'Ndrangheta Stragista,[14] the Piromalli–Molé clan had a prominent role. The trial started in 2020 against affiliates and non-affiliates of the clans, with accusations of favouring the terror strategy of Cosa nostra. This operation exposed not only the links across criminal groups – with the Sicilian clans often referring to the Calabrian ones for directives, in the shadow – but also across criminal groups, deviant Masonic lodges and powerful elites. This investigation is bound to rewrite Italian history. The appeal trial started in January 2022.

If the Sicilians, of the likes of Nitto Santapaola and Totò Riina, had to send an important message to Calabria, they would have reached out primarily to the Piromalli-Molè, with whom they had a privileged relationship. After all, at that time, the Piromalli-Molè was the most powerful family in the Calabrian 'ndrangheta, and they exercised their dominant influence even on clans that were outside their territory, outside the Piana of Gioia Tauro.[15]

I would also say that if I were one of the Sicilians, I would send any message to the Piromalli. I say this because, even if the 'ndrangheta from Reggio Calabria is very important and geographically operates close to Sicily, at that time the Reggio clans were coming out of a mafia war [which ended in 1991] that had shed a lot of blood in the capital city and made equilibria less stable. It was not clear yet who could be the privileged interlocutor there. On the other side, the Piromalli at the time enjoyed stable and unchallenged power in the Piana of Gioia Tauro and they were one of the most important families of the 'ndrangheta, thus they were best placed to receive the Sicilians.[16]

The Piromalli–Molé were, in fact, also stronger on the war side: they had – always had and still have – weapons.

With monthly meetings between the Corleone-based clans of Cosa nostra and the Piromalli family in Calabria, the elite of the 'ndrangheta at that stage not only 'discussed' the terror strategy with the Sicilians but also strengthened networks in Calabria and the rest of Italy through access to selected Masonic lodges, such as the infamous P2 of Licio Gelli,[17] and invested in the port and the motorway in Calabria.

Gioia Tauro is not a pretty town. Together with Rosarno and San Ferdinando, the three towns around the port, this is one of those places that struggle between natural beauty – the sea and the mountains behind it remain gorgeous – and the brutality of men's ineptitude. *Stuck in an ugly shell, too deep to rub off.* But in the eyes and words of most Gioitani I met, pride in the town and its beauty are common. I noticed, because it was not always common in the other places I usually visited when I was younger. *It was the opposite of Santa Cristina, for example, where many people seemed apologetic that they even lived there!* The Gioitani were proud of the livelihood of the town, the nightlife at summer, and primarily the waterfront that had been redone and was the pride and glory of the locals. The *pontile*, the pier, now exists in between rundown streets and the usual frame of unfinished red-brick houses and unpaved roads. I remember when that was inaugurated during one of my summer vacations, how everyone was proud of that waterfront and that pier. They still are.

In summer 2020, Operation Waterfront in Reggio Calabria[18] revealed that, since the years 2013–2014, public works at the waterfront were allegedly subcontracted to families close to the Piromalli. This is a conversation between a prosecutor and a defendant:

'For the work at the waterfront there were conflicts, as the Molé family, as the cousins Nino (one born in 1990 and one in 1989), sons of Mommo and Mico, were back in Gioia Tauro … so they wanted in the waterfront works. They went to talk to Morabito … and he told them to talk to Cosimo …'

'So the Molé wanted in?'

'They wanted to get in the works.'

'Even in the maintenance of a building, if one can get in ...'

'So Morabito said that his contact was Cosimo ... the person linked to the Piromalli?'

'Yes, that is what I knew.'[19]

Whether it was a form of pride that reached the extreme of parochialism or simply love for what was near, close, and became an identity qualifier, I cannot quite say. Echoes of the amoral familism ethos proposed by Banfield come to mind,[20] with all the criticisms that this theory has received since it was first published in 1958. Banfield's main postulate was that rural communities in Southern Italy would 'maximise the material, short-run advantage of the nuclear family and assume that all others will do likewise'.[21] This was certainly something that, upon first sight, one can observe in many places in Calabria, especially in the *Piana*. However, for many, Banfield's approach was stereotypical and simplistic: it disregards completely the historical development of the South and advances unproved generalizations.[22] An incorrect functioning of the clientele mechanism in public administration,[23] rather than the presence of amoral familism, might be the reason for the lack of infrastructure in the rural community that Banfield studied in Southern Italy. Surely culture – in the form Banfield assumed was linked to families – cannot be solely responsible for the backwardness of institutions and the faulty development of economic and social life: this approach leads to assumption and stereotypes.[24]

So, what to make of Gioia Tauro? We line up a pronounced parochialism – where the town is the centre of commerce for the whole *Piana* and therefore *better* than all the other villages; the perseverance of religious feelings – there are many, many altars to the Madonna in private gardens and houses; the widespread mistrust of everything that is outside Gioia – as national and regional politics seem far away and uninteresting. Indeed, it is a difficult balance: on one side there is a tendency towards mistrust of formal authorities and promotion of in-group favouritism and parochialism;[25] on the other side, there is low adherence to social norms and *particularism* that is celebrated in various facets of individual and social life. Particularism means that you need to assess every specific situation on its own, including public ones. And you cannot trust the same results to follow in similar situations. The need for trust, therefore, might be met by others on the territory,[26] the *'ndranghetisti* with a particularly charismatic presence, like the Piromallis. They can both abide by the particularistic nature of relationship in the place and offer trustworthy results most of the time.

It does require competence and ethnography beyond this book to assess all of this properly. However, mafia power stems from all these elements – the exploitation of tradition, the mistrust of rules and authorities – *because authorities don't seem to uphold or respect the rules themselves anyway* – plus the promotion of particularism for self-preservation and identity promotion.

Flatland and motorways

When you bind people to ugliness, they might struggle to believe that ugliness is not their fault but the system's fault, beyond what is local and familiar. Many end up feeling powerless, incapable of reacting, stuck to their destiny, stuck to their place that they both endure and adore.

All the things a little girl could hear back then.

Who are you marrying? Careful, their brother works for 'them'.

Who the hell did you get into business with? Don't you know who is giving them money for this?

So, they are struggling? We know who to ask for support and a 'gift'.

And are you sure you like the mayor? Wasn't he arrested? Sure they said not guilty, but can you still trust him?

Politicians, they are all 'cornuti' (despicables, untrustworthy).

Preja u Signuri e futti u prossimu.

Pray to God but fuck with men.

Hypocrisy.

While the waterfront was one of the key spaces, I don't remember the port at all in my childhood days in Gioia Tauro. Instead, I remember the port from all sorts of different angles but not in Gioia; mostly, it was from the beaches of the beautiful bay of Capo Vaticano, at night. Just sitting by the shore, looking at the bright lights of the port, far away on the horizon. I remember the port appearing on the side of the car when driving, down the motorway. The citrus trees and the port behind them. On the motorway, the infamous Salerno–Reggio Calabria, the A2 (also European E45), the motorway of the Mediterranean, it's called now, used to be the motorway of the sun.

The history of this motorway, too, is a tale of the Piana.

The citrus tricks you into believing that it is always summer or spring or late autumn; winter is difficult to come by around here. Winter is gloomy and hopeless on the *Piana*, when the sea gets angry and the waves darker, along miles and miles of coast. The sea here gets really black.

The A2 or E45, motorway of the Mediterranean, cuts through the *Piana* of Gioia Tauro, which comprises dozens of villages all the way up from the sea to Aspromonte. The pulsating heart remains the port, bridging the province of Reggio Calabria and the nearby province of Vibo Valentia, united in territory and destiny.

The trial for Operation Arca in the early 2000s revealed the system that the clans had set up to divide the profits from the public works on the motorway in the 1990s.[27] It was a whole-of-the-'ndrangheta kind of affair, a banquet, a buffet, where everyone could feast.

The families from the north-east of Calabria, in the area of Sibari and Cirò, had taken care of the northern part (from Mormanno to Tarsia); the families from Cosenza – my birthplace – had received the mandate from Tarsia to Falerna from the families of the *Piana*; the families from Lamezia Terme (especially the Iannazzos) had taken from Falerna to Pizzo – and we are already in Vibo province and the *Piana* area; the Mancusos took the bit from Pizzo to Mileto; the Pesces from Mileto to Rosarno; the Piromallis took the area around Gioia Tauro, of course; the Alvaro, Condello, Tripodi, Bertuca and De Stefano clans had the biggest slice, from Palmi all the way down to Reggio Calabria city. The usual parade of well-known surnames with their associates and satellite clans, all pretty much linked to the Reggio Calabria city factions of the super clan De Stefano. The organization 'ndrangheta at its most systemic. The system operated through subcontracts allocated to third parties working for the clans; that way, they could facilitate the employment of known individuals on one side and inflate the amounts of invoices and prices on the other. Thus, all competition was discouraged through intimidation or damage to properties of others.

It was supposed to be one of the region's main infrastructures.

The 'ndrangheta clans, perhaps all of them, have a love–hate relationship with the land. Land to control, land to grab, land to exploit, land to hide in, land to leave and to come back to, to kill in, to marry and procreate in. Land to possess. It's in the blood and in the passion of this mafia, perhaps many other mafias too, to love and hate the territory where they spill blood and money.

The territory gives prestige and recognition. Especially when you build on the land and what you built remains there for everyone to see, like a motorway. In the works for the motorway, the clans usually took a percentage, a fee, for the works carried out by whoever got the contracts. The Pesce family for example took 3 per cent.

'In one occasion, my brother-in-law showed me the machinery and the locations of all the works that the Pesce family did, on the motorway, near Palmi.'[28]

This is Giuseppina Pesce, the daughter of Salvatore Pesce (former boss of the Pesce *'ndrina*); she turned to the authorities and agreed to cooperate. She helped identify the structures and the activities of her family, in part resulting in Operation All Clean,[29] Operation Galassia later in 2014 and Operation Vulcano in 2016.

From what she said, the authorities realized it would be a mistake to consider mafia power as a granite-like and monolithic body.

On the outside the 'ndrina always looks granitic and solid. This obviously is so that they can be feared and respected more by the population and by the subjects they interact with time after time. However, it would be a huge mistake to think that this rocklike appearance showed to the outside corresponds to a real monolithic structure internally [...] All human aggregations, with time, are subjected to transformation, at times also violent ones, because they are nothing more than the mirror of the men that make them: tot capita, tot sententiae.[30]

Cages and fever

Giuseppina Pesce told the authorities what she could 'breathe' as the daughter of a mafia boss because she was also involved herself with the family business for a while. Her story is one of the few stories of mafia women who turned informants to escape the violence, physical and emotional, of their families. The stories of Giuseppina Pesce and of Maria Concetta Cacciola, her friend and distant relative, in Rosarno, have pierced the veil of the daily lives in some 'ndrangheta families, not just as a system of power, business, dirty money and corrupt politics, but also as a system of domestic abuse and gender violence. Some commentators have even argued that there could be a proper tactic of the prosecutors to turn more women away from the 'ndrangheta as a disruption mechanism against the organization.[31] But with the diversities within 'ndrangheta families, it is not often the case that a one-size-fits-all approach can work; people are always different, inside or outside the mafia.

Rosarno is another of those villages in the *Piana* that looks as ugly on the outside as it does on the inside with its mafia stories. A series of unfinished houses, pinkish and yellowish colours of brick all around, a sense of decay; a feeling, if possible, of time stuck as much as time running out. It feels slow, Rosarno, and yet it also feels like it's too late to do anything. It feels slow and it feels like giving up.

'I fear my family, as it is notoriously a mafia family', Maria Concetta Cacciola said to the authorities after she walked into the local carabinieri office of Rosarno in May 2011. She belonged to the Cacciola clan, associated by marriage with the powerful Bellocco that, together with the Pesce, rule over Rosarno and San Ferdinando, around the port of Gioia Tauro.

If my family knows that I have been here to talk to you today, they'll kill me.[32]

She talks, Maria Concetta – Cetta – of people who will later be arrested and convicted for loan sharking, mafia association and other crimes.

Giulio Bellocco and his wife Aurora Spanò, they live in San Ferdinando and one can say that the town is theirs, as everyone knows that for every investment, even to rent a house, one must ask permission to them in San Ferdinando. For example, 5 years ago my cousin wanted to move to San Ferdinando with his partner, who is a girl from abroad. The Bellocco, they didn't know that he was our relative, a relative of the Cacciola, so they went to him to ask how dared he to go live in San Ferdinando without contacting them first. I know because I have been told this story by my aunt and then my father got involved.[33]

Cetta was placed under protection by the authorities and moved from one secure location to another in the North of Italy. Her relatives called her, over and over, asking her to take it all back, to tell the prosecutors that nothing she said is true.

'Tell them, tell them it's not true.'

Her father suffered the consequences of what they all considered a betrayal.

Don't worry, come back home … Did I get mad at you …? Yes, for the sgarro,[34] I didn't deserve this sgarro. And I am sure that also your brother knows, and everyone else in Rosarno … I want you, my daughter, back home … remember who we are, remember that there is no one else and if I have to sacrifice something, I will, understood? You are my blood and if I have to be considered an infame[35] … [I will] … but you have to live your life … it's been twenty years, they don't need you to arrest me, right? I can defend myself [he screams] … No I am not screaming, I know what I have been through, I don't care, and I know I have been dishonoured … it's death … if you had not done this, I would have been happier, but it's ok now … all Rosarno knows that you have not said anything, rest assured, they won't believe what she [the prosecutor] says … in my house, people will know the difference between selling and buying!

These were recordings of interceptions I could hear as a journalist friend sent them to me. There are many angles, bits and pieces of the story of Maria Concetta Cacciola in Rosarno and that of Giuseppina Pesce that I learned but cannot recount here but that others have narrated.[36] My friend Marie had taken an interest in Cetta's story, empathizing with this young woman, barely 30 years of age, engaged when she was 13, used as a pawn in her family's mafia alliance, her life in between domestic violence and emotional strains. We talked a lot about Cetta, Marie and I, and how difficult it is to imagine a woman, more or less our age, in our time, in a 'normal' country, going through the things she went through.

I did have problems at home, no one understood me. My husband was in jail, they were jealous of me ... I had received some anonymous letters, so they used to beat me, they caged me at home, I couldn't get out, I couldn't have friends.

Some of the words that Cetta said to the prosecutors.

'The best thing in my life is my children who I will keep in my heart. I leave them with so much pain and sadness', she wrote in a letter to her mother, thinking she could trust her. 'I am entrusting my children to you, but I beg you. Do not make the same mistake with them. I want them to have a better life than the one I had.'

'Life has brought me nothing but pain.'[37] I got chills when I heard the recordings of Cetta. She spoke, her dialect, just like some of my cousins and aunts in Gioia Tauro. So familiar.

Maria Concetta Cacciola was found dead on 20 August 2011. She had ingested acid, a quantity that had melted her insides. They first ruled it as a suicide. But it was not suicide, it was a tragic family murder, as was proven at trial some years later.

In the *Piana* of Gioia Tauro, the 'ndrangheta can kill, and it murders women for infamy, for dishonour. Domestic violence, in the mafia, can become a double wound: it's not just gendered violence, it's collective violence too. The 'ndrangheta family lives by mafia rules of behaviour. It bends and distorts the desirable meaning of family, the love, trust and support we all wish we'd have in a family. A 'ndrangheta family does not forgive betrayal because betrayal brings *infamy* and the 'ndrangheta does not forget infamy – infamy destroys reputation and reputation is everything for the *'ndrina*.

Stories like these – of arrogance, hubris, entitlement, unchallenged power over 'weaker' family members – remind you truly of what mafias are about. Usurpation. And distortion of what is love, choice and self-improvement. And violence, one way or the other, always violence.

A couple of months before Maria Concetta Cacciola's death, another woman mysteriously killed herself by ingesting acid, in April 2011. Santa 'Tita' Buccafusca, aged 37 at the time, was the wife of mafia boss Pantaleone 'Luni' Mancuso, aka 'Scarpuni' (Big Shoe); he was arrested and convicted one too many times. She was a mother of a little boy, and she became afraid of the violence around her husband's side of the family. She had decided to talk to the authorities for the sake of her child but had then feared the consequences. She didn't go through with her cooperation; she went back home to Luni only to die one month later. The investigation into her suicide confirmed that the amount of acid she had ingested was unlikely to have been drunk by one person on her own, it was way too much. Operation Costa Pulita,[38] whose verdict of over 1,200 pages was made public in August 2020, intercepted close associates of Tita's husband, in the nearby town of Briatico, discussing the reasons why Tita might have betrayed Luni that way:[39]

> Sure, maybe you want to raise your child differently ... they are in over their head, right? But surely you can just go on your own, you'll get a new identity, they'll promise her that [...] they'll arrest us as well, though!

They were relieved when Tita chickened out of her initial intent:

> The fever is gone, all good, the fever is gone.

Tita was, after all, concerned that everyone would think that she was crazy. That was how everyone seemed to judge her and why a suicide was not ruled out.

How often is a woman judged insane and untrustworthy by men around her who use that as an excuse for their own violence? How often are women called crazy just to undermine their strength and credibility?[40]

This is already common, and disturbingly so, in all facets of society; in a mafia or 'ndrangheta family this is even more visible, as *mafiosi*'s masculinity creates a violent social atmosphere for women.[41] When women in mafia families are victimized – and not all of them are by the way, some women are perfectly integrated in the mafia system[42] – they are twice victimized: by the violence of men, and by the violence of the surrounding mafia (masculine) culture. Women's performance against violent mafia activity can challenge this masculinity – their acts of love towards their children, a new love interest, solidarity and self-protection can represent challenges. But obviously for such a performance to be successful – for the act to break the chain of violence – the sacrifice is enormous, and violence and masculinity are pervasive in mafias.

Differently from Cetta Cacciola, Tita's remains a suicide – *she remained one with 'the fever'*. I often wonder whether something more will come out on her personal hell and on her deathly cage. I do hope so, in the name of a higher sense of justice.

Tita was from Nicotera, where she lived and where she had a fish shop, which was also used – according to the authorities – to distribute cocaine in the hinterland of Vibo Valentia.

In Nicotera, I learned how to swim.

Just before the inlets and caves of Capo Vaticano, the town of Nicotera is especially pretty at night. With the view above the bay from the wide balcony opposite the old castle illuminated by that distinctive orange light. Vintage buildings include an old cinema right by the main square; brick walls, like a fortress, keep the town centre contained. Sure, one or two bars are owned by the ruling clan here, the Mancuso from nearby Limbadi, but that is somewhat normal around here. By word of mouth, you learn which one is which and you just avoid them. And this doesn't take much away from the beauty of the place.

Nicotera Marina, the part of Nicotera which is by the sea, is not particularly beautiful – certainly not as beautiful as Nicotera *paese*, the town above the sea. A wide and long sandy beach there and a green and blue transparent sea most of the time, with cute little waves perfect for children's play.

That is where I learned how to catch the waves.

That was before some of the local beach resorts were confiscated, owned by associates of the Mancuso; it was also before the Mancuso family reached the levels of notoriety of today.

The Sayonara Club, at the very end of the beachfront, was clearly different from the others. It was a gated space, made that way to convince people that entry was exclusive and to protect it from unwanted visitors and/or eyes from the street. You could still peek inside from portholes in the bricked walls. You would see a deep blue swimming pool, various lounge chairs at its borders, fake palm trees – *or were they real?!* – and the usual images of happy families with playful children. A slice of semi-luxury in a place, Nicotera Marina, that caters to all 'social classes'. We went to the Sayonara Club for at least a couple of years during our holidays; it was just more practical when we were kids, felt even safer. At some point, we stopped going. *As with many things that happened in my family when I was a child, I didn't understand why one day we went someplace all the time and suddenly we stopped, forever.*

Mafia infiltration, that is why. Learning that behind a restaurant, a bar, a beach club, were mafia money, interests, affairs. Once you know, you need to make a choice: stay (and accept) or go (and condemn). As my father always said back then, there is no grey area here; it's black and white.

Today, passing in front of the Sayonara beach club – which is still there under different management – I am struck by a sense of anguish. For the childhood things I didn't understand back then, for things I still don't get; for the misfortunes of places that used to look fun and shiny and today just look out of place or forgotten. There, in Nicotera, in that Sayonara Club, two 'summits', in summer 1991, were organized with mafia/'ndrangheta bosses from the whole of Calabria, who all met with emissaries of Cosa nostra, allegedly – or not, as has been repeated in different judicial files from Operation Arca to 'Ndrangheta Stragista – to organize the strategy of terror that Cosa nostra was willing to engage in and that would kill judges Giovanni Falcone and Paolo Borsellino, among others. A young Luigi Mancuso was hosting then; the Sayonara was lush.

It is one of those villages, Nicotera, where you find solace in the seafood and in the simplicity of the place and the people. And a place where you wouldn't expect a homicide in plain sight on a Sunday afternoon in mid-August 2018.[43] That day, I was in nearby Capo Vaticano, and the news travelled fast. It was about revenge, people whispered. It was payback for another murder and the violence of a few months ago, they said. It was about a dispute from the nearby town of Limbadi, pointed out the newspapers.

Limbadi, the domain of the Mancuso clan. And, incidentally, my father's birthplace.

Limbadi Beach

> Limbadi Beach
> Limbadi Beach
> Limbadi Beach-Beach-Beach
> U cors'i sutta, u cors'i subra
> E non t'incrisci mai[44]

Imagine me as a little girl, singing this local song up and down the high street. I can hardly picture it myself now.

Some folk songs remain stuck in your head for years – even those you don't like or considered lame when you were growing up. This one was the hit of summer in Limbadi, the village where my father was born, the village where my father was elected mayor in the mid-2000s, the village that my mother hated – she didn't try to hide it – and the village where we went on vacation for years when I was a child and then a teenager. The usual people just took the guitar and played 'Limbadi Beach' on the main square of the town, laughing and joking.

There is no beach in Limbadi, by the way. The nearest beach is Nicotera, about 10 kilometres away.

This song just celebrates the mindlessness of summer days, when the town is once again full, emigrants come back for the holidays and everyone just goes back and forth on the high street – as if they were walking by the beach – chit-chatting, just navigating the boredom, the slowness and the (perceived) routine of daily life.

The sinister side of Limbadi was always in the background for the young me.

I certainly did not care that my aunt lived in front of a beautiful and large villa, with wooden windows and a reddish roof; it almost always looked like no one lived there. To me, that house felt like a house of mystery, out of a movie, at the end of a long dirt street where only two houses – that villa and my aunt's house – were facing each other. I remember longing to enter that courtyard, or play with the children I sometimes heard from there, or go hide-and-seek, or act like there was a treasure hunt to solve.

That house, however – I could perceive it in the firm words of my father and the worrisome looks of my mother – was off limits. *Just play and act like it's not there. Just don't look at it. I learned to avoid looking at it, to ignore it, I wasn't sure why, of course, but I did.*

That house belonged to the Mancuso family, to Luigi Mancuso specifically.

'Who is that? His brother, 'Ntoni, he is nothing in comparison to Luigi. Yes Luigi is the youngest, the one who rules over the whole world, not just Italy. He is the roof of the world ... he is a 'lady' ... he is a good person, he is so intelligent ... he has two degrees!'

Giovanni Giamborino, alleged associate of the clan, sings the boss's praises as detailed in Operation Rinascita-Scott, at the end of 2019.[45]

'You don't have to ask him who rules Nicotera, Reggio, or this and that ... he has the roof of the world ... there's no one ... and if there's someone, he is always higher, right? [...] He has never picked a fight with anyone ... understood? In Tropea, Pizzo, Vibo Marina ... Reggio. [...] All round the world where there are these things, no one else is at his level. They talk about Australia, Canada, New York ... and it's always him, even if they don't know him. [...] Now with all these informants and all these events ... what can he do, the poor man ... they don't realise that if there's someone like him nothing happens, and people are safe ... you can leave your keys to the door ... they don't get it! They want the war, the police, the prosecutors, everyone ... why can't you leave him alone with his family after 25 years ... they keep following him, they don't get it, you won't change his head.'

Luigi Mancuso, born in 1954, is known in his circles as 'the Supreme'. He is the youngest of 11 brothers and sisters, and this only increases his appeal. The aura of power and authority surrounding him has built up through the years to sound unrealistic on the one hand and worrisome on the other. On one side, the personification of power in one man is dangerous; on the other side, perceptions are often mistaken for truth and that can eventually be even more dangerous.

When I was growing up, and as soon as I learned – albeit superficially – about the 'ndrangheta and the Mancuso clan in Limbadi, the generally accepted story was that *these people – they –* were not doing much in the village, their business was outside Limbadi. And frankly, I never had the impression that this was not the case. There was only one thing, thinking back to that time, that stood out.

This man, with nice hair but a harsh face, who was often sitting at the bar in the main square, and whom everyone referred to as U Santu, the Saint, or U Signurino, the Little Sir. Never accept the coffee from people around him, that was the rule.

Weird things to remember or process when you are six or seven years old. That was Luigi Mancuso in the early 1990s.

Was this grandeur or was there really, is there, a will to keep the peace on Luigi Mancuso's side? After all, the Mancuso family has known quite a long season of internal violence among the various branches of the family. To speak of them as one family is misleading in fact, as there are many fictions, many capabilities, feuds and differences across the various uncles, cousins, brothers, sisters.

But the surname, now, is a brand. No doubt about that.

While I was growing up, Luigi Mancuso was in jail, arrested in 1993 for mafia and drug offences between Calabria and Milan; he didn't come out until 2012, only to be arrested again in 2019. The reputation of Limbadi changed with this clan. In 1983, Limbadi was the first municipality of Italy whose city council was dissolved for reasons of public order linked to mafia, even before a law was approved that provided for the dissolution of councils for mafia infiltration in 1991.[46] At the time, the President of the Republic took the initiative after Francesco 'Ciccio' Mancuso came in first, elected to the town council, even if he spent the time of the electoral campaign in hiding, trying to avoid scrutiny.

'*Dinnu ca io su mafiosu, macara mi conveni essìri mafiusu.*'
'They say that I am a mafioso, maybe it's convenient to be one.'

Journalists at the time, my father included, remember him saying (in dialect):

'I am calm, if.the law is used to condemn, it's also used to absolve.'[47]

It's a strange story, that of Ciccio Mancuso. In 1979, he had formed a company to extract construction materials from a cave – a company where other people had invested their money. The initial capital was not sufficient for the work needed and that is when a guarantor from the Mammoliti clan – close to the Piromalli in Gioia Tauro – entered the business. Ciccio – previously only charged for *illicit grazing* – was on everyone's mind in Limbadi for these new friendships. He had turned from a small entrepreneur into a not-so-careful investor in a very short time. His relationship with his other brothers and the rest of the family was not a strong one then; history provides an image of him as an individual acting on his own, not because of his surname, not because of alliances, all the while attempting to climb up social and financial ladders. This was before the drugs and before the investments of the rest of the family, and it makes you wonder about the common approach of some entrepreneurial men to try and circumvent certain rules without thinking of the social and economic good and consequences. But, then again, there was a choice.

This was just before the myth of the Mancuso family developed.

The Mancuso family is an interesting mafia dynasty. Compared with many of the families of Aspromonte and the *Piana* of Gioia Tauro, they are something of a new mafia, having emerged relatively recently, around the 1970s. Their power was consolidated thanks to the involvement of some of the family members in the kidnappings in the North of Italy – which gave them credit before the 'ndrangheta clans from Aspromonte. But, also, their proximity to the Piromalli, Molé and Mammoliti clans and the interests in the building of the port of Gioia Tauro and the A2/E45 motorway were part of their ascension to independence and power.

In the early 1990s, when the Piromallis were interacting with Cosa nostra over the terror strategy the Sicilian clans wanted to adopt, Luigi Mancuso was already involved with the Piromallis, young and with a clear vision for the 'ndrangheta's future, before his arrest in 1993.

There are two main characteristics of the Mancuso dynasty that are worth considering. Firstly, there are different branches of the same family; same surname, slightly different specialisms. One family branch, 'The Nephews', is more violent; the other branch, 'The Uncles', is more for the pacification and coordination of the province. Furthermore, the Mancusos overall are extremely well connected. Their 'friends' are everywhere: in other provinces, with the clans of the province of Crotone; in the North of Italy, especially in Lombardia, Piemonte, Liguria and Toscana; in the capital city Rome; in Switzerland; in Latin America, with cocaine brokers in Colombia or Venezuela or Peru, as detailed, for example, since Operation Decollo in the 1990s and 2000s.

More importantly, the Mancusos enjoy the benefits of a special geographical position in Calabria: they are in the province of Vibo Valentia – thus close to the clans in Catanzaro – but their business is often linked to the clans of the *Piana* (nearby, but in the province of Reggio Calabria), Piromalli, Pesce and Bellocco. Nicotera, the town near Limbadi part of the Mancuso's territory, is the last town in the province of Vibo, right next to Rosarno, the first town in the province of Reggio. The Mancusos have, in fact, forged links with the 'ndrangheta clans from Aspromonte, via the *Piana*. They often acted as the point of reference for the whole province of Vibo because the family is recognized and recognizable in at least three provinces, Vibo, Catanzaro and Reggio.

Yes, everyone can benefit, or try to, if they are their friends. Which is why you freeze when you receive a letter from a relative in Limbadi, whom you know is a friend to some of *them,* and that letter warns you that 'there will be consequences for your family' if a certain real estate business transaction is not resolved soon in their favour. You freeze, not because you fear the relative directly; you know that their implicit, whispered, reference of intimidation is *them; that they are friends with them.*

They [clan X] followed a different order, they were not recognised by Polsi [the 'ndrangheta clans in Aspromonte]. They answered directly to the Mancuso. In particular, Luigi Mancuso is now trying to form a Province in Vibo Valentia, a Crimine of Vibo Valentia, with the approval of the 'ndrangheta in Polsi, so that he can fix all situations and recognise all the different clans of the area, which should all answer to him. Luigi Mancuso was happy for the good order in Vibo Valentia [...] he was pursuing a peace operation, trying to reunite all the clans, and his own family.[48]

In 2019, a former 'ndranghetista-turned-informant, during an official interview with the authorities in Operation Rinascita-Scott, detailed Luigi Mancuso's project of peace and unification of the province of Vibo. The 'ndrangheta in Reggio and from Aspromonte is the winning brand; it would be foolish for Luigi to miss out on that. The trial of Rinascita-Scott, started in January 2021 and dubbed around the world as the 'ndrangheta 'maxi-trial', is in fact a trial against the 'mafia order' in the province of Vibo Valentia, where the figure of Luigi Mancuso, together with other important alleged bosses and clans, towers. It is a very important trial; for the first time, the clans of the province of Vibo Valentia province, their interactions with one another, it's all pictured together.

If one was paying attention, the signs of success and impressive evolution of the Mancusos were all there from the start. From the sparse accumulation of capital, through several business endeavours (legal and illegal) of the 1980s and 1990s, from the hands on the port and the motorway to the business of cocaine, they learned from other clans and become an independent and recognized primary group. The Mancuso family has changed and evolved in the past decades, quickly and often unsystematically.

Their separation and distance, in spirit if not in space, from Limbadi is a thing of the past – if it ever was real at all.

When the marching band walks along the paved roads of the village on 27 July, the day of San Pantaleone, the protector Saint of Limbadi, the whole village is silent. Even those, like my father, who are not Catholic nor religious at all respect and celebrate San Pantaleone; it is a social celebration in addition to being a religious one.

Would you prevent a man, coming out of prison where he served time for mafia association and other crimes, from walking down to the statue of San Pantaleone, to help lift and carry it? In theory, that man has paid his dues to society, through the prison sentence; in theory, he should be welcomed back to the community; in theory, he should be treated like any other devoted citizen who wishes to pray to the Saint and offers to carry the statue as a sign of dedication. However, in practice, this is not quite the case. Everyone notices that man, everyone knows who he is, some wonder why he is doing what he is doing, some question his ulterior motives. Does he want to show off? Does he want to fool whoever is watching with a sanctified gesture? Does the man who was/is called the Saint wish to be associated with the actual Saint?

It didn't look right, I remember, when this scene happened; it must have been 2012 or 2013. I was watching the procession of the Saint around the church like everyone else who did not participate, that is, at the bar. It didn't look like everyone was comfortable at all with that gesture, but no one said a word. And frankly, when you see a known mafia boss carrying the statue of the Saint around, you wonder what that word – that no one dares to say – could be? What can anyone *realistically* say? *Stop praying to the Saint or God? Don't even try to show that you changed? Just go away?* It's difficult, in a place like Limbadi, where most of the 3,500 inhabitants just live a normal life or try to (at times by denying or ignoring what's in front of them), to shake off the accepted order like that, to push a single moment to a blast. And for what? Tension? Violence?

It's easy, or at least easier, to just go with the flow and let things be. And that is not *omertà*, it is just looking away. Indeed, *omertà* might imply an accepted *awareness* of how things work; but at times people *choose not to know, not to get involved* altogether to avoid guilty consciences. This is valid for various situations, from keeping silent when the mafia boss participates in the religious function to the choice not to get involved in asking difficult questions or to avoid reporting quarrels with relatives to the police when you know there might be more behind those quarrels and family is still family. No participation, no questions mean *avoidance*. Whether you can justify it or not is another issue.

Other times, you see willing participation and acceptance of the allure of mafia power, just an illusion that accepting it will grant you some extra money or other mild benefit. *You tell yourself that if the mafia business is flourishing, your acceptance doesn't matter either way. So what's the harm in getting a slice of the cake?*

You are 20–25 years old; you didn't really go to school – you didn't like it; you want to live a good life; school is too complicated and slow. Your family is just a regular family; mum, dad, brothers, sisters, grandmothers, grandfathers and so on. Everyone in your family has worked and still does, normally. But they have 'them' as neighbours who are 'friends'. And your mother wants a bigger house, and your brothers want a pool – like a big one, in the garden. You also like to go dancing and drink, and just have a jolly good time with your friends. You want a car or a motorbike. All these things you want, you know, will make you look cool, who needs school for that? As time passes, your mother gets the bigger house, your father gets the car and you get the motorbike too, your brothers get the pool, everyone is enjoying what they wanted and they know, there could be more. They always have 'them' over for dinner, a large table for their guests and a lot of food and laughter. They are not hurting anyone, after all. You are just opening your house for 'them', so 'he' can have his meetings, come for a drink, host his friends. At times, maybe your father is doing something for them too, delivering a package maybe; small favours, nothing big. And when 'they' ask you whether you can help place some of the white powder that makes them rich, you maybe hesitate – that is cocaine, if you are caught, that is jail time. But you might still say yes because you think that the risk is worth it and that, if you don't do it, someone else will.[49]

Neutralization techniques, those that criminologists have discussed in the theory of drift,[50] are powerful for those who become involved in mafia business from below – those who don't know, don't care – don't want to care – what else is there, if anything; those who think about their small advantages only.

Denial of Responsibility – I didn't do it, they are the mafiosi, not me!
Denial of Injury – I just hosted meetings and helped a bit, what's wrong with that?
Denial of the Victim – I did it for me, it's not like I *killed* anyone.
Condemnation of the Condemners – The judge is a *cornuto* (a dickhead).
Appeal to Higher Loyalties – I did it for my family.

How many times have I heard these sentences in normal conversations with relatives, their friends, their friends' relatives, in Limbadi.
  And it is all true when you are in the middle of it. Insignificant – disposable perhaps – for '*them*', but already too involved for anti-mafia authorities. The stigma of mafia proximity, in territories like Limbadi, is like fire. You get burned as you get closer, and the wounds remain somewhat open forever. Mafia, even when a jail sentence is served, is branded on the skin. And it stinks as much as it attracts.
  It's a big cauldron, the mafia of the Mancuso family. There is something in it for everyone. A big cauldron, a *caddara*. This is the name apparently given to the micro-structure, composed of a handful of people, including Luigi Mancuso, at the top of the 'ndrangheta in the province of Vibo Valentia. *Caddara* is the dialect word for the big cauldron where all the different parts of the pork are boiled together – it's a ritualistic celebration, the 'caddara'. In the words of a witness in Operation Rinascita-Scott in 2019:[51] 'It's the so-called "caddara", we called it "caddara", and that is what we said, all embraced together.'
  Poetic. Almost.

Donde estamos?

Limbadi, like much of Calabria, is a place of migration. Thus it is only natural that even in Limbadi, as it was for Platì or San Luca or Delianuova or many other villages we have mentioned, one could also trace 'ndrangheta routes abroad, exploiting the routes of migration. Different towns, different migration, different networks, different countries. Argentina, mostly.

Many people from Limbadi migrated to Argentina and very few to other locations. Chain migration worked especially well in the fascist period, when over 1,400 Limbadesi migrated to Argentina, following those who had migrated before them.[52] This is similar to the story in nearby villages in Vibo province – a different part of Calabria, different migration paths.

I went to Buenos Aires only in 2019, flying from Melbourne to Santiago, then Argentina. It was the first time that I set foot in that part of the world, and it wasn't for work. I say 'only' in 2019 because I could have gone much earlier. My father has gone there one to three times a year for many years to visit relatives. He loves Buenos Aires and never shuts up about it.

I wanted to meet my father's aunt, who at the time was over 90 and still very lucid, before she passed away, which she did some months later. She made gnocchi and cooked for five people every day; she stood proud at all her one metre and 45 centimetres height. She was like a second mother to my father, and Buenos Aires has been in our family that place that was always mentioned in connection with Limbadi, with Calabria, with the migrant experience and the tough times when these choices of going away for good were made.

I was somehow disappointed by the *Italianness* of Buenos Aires. I was used to Australia or Canada, where Italianness is celebrated and even differentiated by region.[53] In Buenos Aires, it looks like a much more dated Italianness, rooted in decades ago, never really developed, never truly evolved. In a way, it is in everything around you, but somehow it gets lost in whatever Argentina and Argentinians have turned it into.

Zia Rosina spoke the same dialect she used to speak in Limbadi, as if she had not really left 50 years earlier. Every once in a while, a Spanish word substituted for the missing Italian word she was looking for; her world was Limbadi in Argentina. It was there in her eyes, in her questions about people living in Italy with whom she spoke on the phone every week, in her salacious comments about the town of origin or the fancy district of Palermo where she had lived with many others from the village since her arrival in the city.

Palermo is buzzing with life; like a soap bubble, elegant, light and colourful, the district encapsulates both the quintessential Argentinian joy of life and the reminder of the Italian migrant community that has shaped the area across the years.

In Operation Magma in 2019–2020,[54] the district of Palermo was one of the places where anti-mafia investigations converged; among those arrested, two lived in Palermo and one of the businesses used for meetings was in Palermo, too. The connection – still under scrutiny – with the Bellocco clan in San Ferdinando and Rosarno, with interests from the Mancusos too, for cocaine apparently. Their meetings in Calabria, just outside the entrance to the port, in a restaurant where I have dined many times with family; *their seafood and their wine is so good*. Always close to home for the clans.

> 'I have two factories of artisanal Calabrian pasta … and I got a request here … those who requested it, you'll know them, the Pelle family, from San Luca … they have two restaurants here in Buenos Aires: one is the "San Luca" that used to be the "Caravaggio", in Puerto Madero … Now they opened up a new one, on the opposite side of the river. The Ristorante-Bar San Luca, previously Caravaggio, Giuseppe is there. The other restaurant, on the opposite side of the river, near the Cascina D'Onor. I went there to eat with Ruben, I saw him, he remembered me, and we talked about the pasta, he said "I pay, there is no problem", so I brought all the documents, the pictures of the pasta, the various pieces, how is it made, everything. I'll offer it to him and to others, this is good business!'[55]

Of course it is good business! Puerto Madero is the place where tourists and visitors, as well as locals, go for a bite or for a stroll in the capital city of Argentina. *What is wrong with importing pasta from Calabria, I wonder?* Apart from those who handle the business, who might be involved in other types of illicit activities, what is the *actual* problem with that? It seems like seizing globalization and the opportunities it brings. *Maybe*. Cutting lines, perhaps? I wonder how different this is from what everyone else does in similar industries across borders but without the 'mafia' label.

And yet the difference is in the behaviour, in the expectations of how certain social relations should be between Calabria and Buenos Aires, as emerged in another extract from Operation Magma.

> 'Well I need to refresh his memory. I am in a foreign country, where he rules, as you do. Do you understand me?'
>
> 'There are no rulers here.'
>
> 'No, I mean this is your country. As I come from another country, he has to tell me "Tomorrow morning, as you arrive, I'll come and pick you up, you come and eat at my place". Then I might not go to his house and eat, but you'll need to have the clean face (*la faccia lavata*[56]) – wash my face, be a hypocrite, but wash your face!'[57]

Between pasta and social expectations, the exploitation of migration is instrumental to the development of relations for business opportunities as much as for social opportunities. Migration of Calabrians from the area of Vibo to Argentina is surely not deterministic for the settlement of mafias. When there is mafia where there is migration, it is not because with migration there comes mafia, but because mafia needs to exploit migrants' relationships and their sense of ethnic identity. Migrant communities of Calabrians abroad are often in vulnerable places; the wish to be as welcoming as possible with fellow co-regionals or compatriots means that availability and kindness can be exploited without you even knowing. Or, when you do know, the possibility for extra profits, of an illicit nature, might indeed become appealing.

Often, when 'ndrangheta members are involved, what glues everything together abroad – what glues all the relations that then eventually bring different people to also do business together in, let's say, pasta – is actually *cocaine*. In Europe,[58] as outside.

You are a lawyer or a cocaine broker; you might decide to become the referent for the Bellocco: they need someone to handle cocaine imports from Buenos Aires or Uruguay, or to offer support with the local legislation if a Mancuso or a Morabito, fugitives, need documents to stay in Uruguay or defend themselves.

In Argentina, so far, it seems that the business of cocaine is one of the 'ndrangheta's main investments.

'Does this arrive in Gioia Tauro?'

'Yes, and the other one in another port, Le Havre, you know where it is, in Normandy, in France. Before I left, two French guys came with the Calabrians ... they said: "If you want to send stuff to France, we can assure you we can move it away from the port, 100%, from the international port of Le Havre". We have to go to safe ports now, Gioia Tauro and ...'

'Gioia Tauro is not safe! It's like an atomic bomb!'

'Sure, but in Gioia Tauro they bring 500 kg from one side and 400–500 from the other side ... do you get it? You still don't get it, those won't stop in Gioia Tauro, they are transiting through, but those in transit get caught in the port.

[...]

In Gioia Tauro stuff does not get into the port, it gets thrown out in the sea. Got it? Thrown in the sea before the port! Where the fishermen's boats then pull it up and bring it to the shore.'

'Who throws it off?'

'We bought people off – yes, in Gioia Tauro we don't open the containers ...'

'But where do they throw it off? Still in the sea of the port?'

'No, outside! [...] it's like 5–6 miles, even more ... The boats there can get to Sicily, switch off the GPS and the Guardia di Finanza won't reach you. You can even put a GPS on the package ...'

'It's not that easy.'

'This is not easy, of course not, let's be honest [...] but it is a new operation, these people are safe, to do something right you need the right ones.'

[...]

'All cargos start in Santa Marta, Colombia, then they stop in Santo Domingo; they put it [cocaine] in there and then when it goes to Le Havre or Gioia Tauro we are doing great.'[59]

It is somewhat expected that, as soon as the illegal business of cocaine brings more risk and becomes difficult to sustain, legal opportunities will be favoured – the pasta, for example, 'is a lot more interesting ... this is my intention, you know, to invest in something here'. The pasta or another business is another opportunity born out of the same routes and networks from which the cocaine business developed. And it starts with the Italians already abroad, those from the village near yours; those who still phone home in Italy to ask how everyone is doing; those who wish to show how well they are doing for themselves in Buenos Aires and how good migration has been for them, even if the bond with the village, with Calabria, has not really been severed and probably never will be.

Wrong sun, same sun

Between the port of Gioia Tauro and the misery of certain towns in the *Piana* and the province of Vibo Valentia there is a constellation of clans, with their occasional or stable mobility to the North of Italy or Europe, or with their connections to the more established clans for the importation of drugs from Latin America. Some of them are under trial, in the maxi-trial Rinascita-Scott for the Vibo area, for example, and others will be.

It seems easy enough to say that there are different *Calabrie* (plural). They appear plural, these territories. Different Calabrie with different geographies and distant connections; with not so similar dialects. Even in the plurality of territories, the desolation of certain places in Calabria is, however, the same. Here is the 'unitary' characteristic of the 'ndrangheta: not the unity of intent in the clans' operational capacity, not their organization – more often than not based on 'exceptions', 'adaptations' and territorial specificities – but the convergence and the isomorphic nature of their existential traits. The struggle for identity is similar; the same pride and the same willingness to form and sustain *something, anything.*

But how different might Platì seem from Filadelfia, a small town in the province of Vibo Valentia whose main clan, Anello, is an historical associate, in Switzerland, of the Mancuso in Limbadi and Nicotera.[60] The comparison between the *Piana* and Aspromonte reminds me of the comparison between Griffith and Mildura in Australia. In the former, the structures of the 'ndrangheta are power structures, with an emphasis on political and social interests. In the latter, the dynamism of activities in the territory, linked to mafia business, appears more profit-oriented, with the emphasis on drugs. But there is no clear-cut line between profit and power. Mafias need both, they must balance both. And across different Calabrian provinces, they have shown a certain uniformity in their behaviours as they imitate one another or adopt the winning 'brand' of the Reggio–Aspromonte-based 'ndrangheta clans.

When Luigi Mancuso was again arrested in December 2019 in Operation Rinascita-Scott, the prosecutors argued that it was clear to see how the clans that recognized Mancuso as their local leader and referee had happily adopted the orthodoxy of the 'ndrangheta from Polsi, the same rituals, the same *doti*, the same language. This might not just be isomorphism across organizations; it could also be a result of individuals, families, places choosing to mirror into one another more now than they did in the past, when a higher degree of physical separation characterized the various Calabrian provinces.[61]

The separation between the Tyrrhenian and Ionian coasts, the west and the east coasts of Calabria, has often felt like a cultural separation in addition to being a geographical one.[62]

Could it be that some people – including some 'ndranghetisti – are realizing that what unites them is greater than what divides them?

Especially abroad, there is no 'ndrangheta of the west and of the east, no 'ndrangheta of the city of Reggio or of Aspromonte. This is because there is no distinguished migration from the east of Calabria or the west, just a general one, from the region. The relief of meeting a co-regional, the sense of *belonging* this might bring, is not linked to the origin *within* the region, but simply to the origin *from* the region. Abroad, mafias exercise manipulation of cultural codes through a commonality that language and origin seem to make easier. This positive feedback among people from different towns, but still Calabrians abroad, might also, in turn, affect Calabria and mafia families back home by promoting and facilitating connections and opportunities among groups that, in Calabria, might not have necessarily 'met'.

In Nicotera Marina, just beyond the urban and rural hostility, the harshness and ugliness of Rosarno, San Ferdinando and Gioia Tauro, in between semi-destroyed houses and a sense of lethargy when the sun shines too bright, the sunsets over the sea are to die for.

On the other side, on the Ionian coast, over the famous 106 State Road, also known as the E90, *the sun sets on the wrong side, behind the mountain. It's on* the wrong side over the beautiful cliffs of Africo or the large white beaches of Brancaleone and Bianco up the road until the archaeological site of Locri.

The sun there does not set over the water, which for me has pretty much always been the case with sunsets; the sun hides; it sets somewhere else.

The Ionian side is also cursed as a land with an enormous potential but also unfinished projects, ugly buildings, lack of services, lack of care for nature and for the places around it. This is in sharp contrast with the diffuse kindness of people and the deliciousness of the products of the land and the immense and authentic beauty of nature there.

Many people around there seem to develop a schizophrenic love–hate relationship with the places where they live. On the one hand, they wouldn't want to ever leave that place, but on the other hand, they don't really seem to care how these places look. There is the same breathtaking sea and crystal water, with different forms of sunsets, but also the difficulty in moving from one place to the other, the lack of proper infrastructure, the piles of garbage no one ever seems to collect, the sense of anguish and decline in the wilderness that all this brings.

This is both the west and the east of Calabria, especially in its southern part. But the east is not *really* my Calabria, you see? Even if I learned to know it and love it.

Could it be that mafia men, from either side of the region, recognize each other more now? That they shake hands with clans they historically did not join forces with, all while understanding the value of a common, or at least more uniform, identity, modelled after the strongest brand of Aspromonte 'ndrangheta? Could this be a sign that the distance and separation across the plural Calabrie is eroding away? Even if infrastructures are still lagging and physical distances are not easy to overcome?

Could it be the case that – beyond the initiatives of men of the clans and the opportunities abroad that bring people of different areas to work together – a mirroring, isomorphic, effect is at play? And that, indeed, recognition of unity across Calabrian seas, mountains and provinces is not such an implausible thought as it once was?

The sun is *wrong* on the Ionian Sea, but the mountain in between – Aspromonte, which separates the *Piana* from the Locride – is the same. Even if it sets on the wrong side, it's still the same sun, as it is the same mountain.

★★★

To the sanctuary of the Madonna of the Mountain, the throat of Polsi in Aspromonte, you can arrive from different roads – from the *Piana* over Delianuova through Gambarie or along the Ionian route through San Luca. *The roads on both sides are hell. Aspromonte wraps you, eats you up, and spits you down. Rollercoasters, holes and ditches in the middle of the road, rocks rolling over from above on one side, open precipices on the other side. And Google Maps doesn't exist here.*

From Polsi up and down to Montalto, over to Gambarie and following the road to Melito di Porto Salvo, you can arrive at the end of Calabria.

Splitting in two the Tyrrhenian and the Ionian coasts, there is the same mountain, my Aspromonte.

The sun over Melito is not quite on the wrong side yet, it stays at the corner of your eyes, still over the sea, just about. In front of you, the Etna Volcano and Sicily; behind you, Aspromonte; on the east side, the 106 State Road with the misery of that part of Calabria that struggles to affirm its beauty; on the west side, the start of the A2 motorway and the fastest route to the *Piana* and Vibo Valentia. A few kilometres west of Melito, towards the Strait of Sicily, lies the city of Reggio Calabria.

To the bones, it has been sucked dry, Reggio Calabria city.

8

'Ndrangheta City and Spiderwebs

Kicking the ball

What do you do when you see spiders? Do you kill them straight away or do you capture them and take them outside?

In the frame of the sumptuous Marconi Club in Sydney, Lillo Foti and Vince Foti had dinner in April 2015 to celebrate the partnership between the Marconi Stallions and the Reggina Calcio, two football teams recognizing their connection to Reggio Calabria, Italy, and soccer pride. The two Fotis are not related. Vince is the president of the Marconi Club and a successful businessman in Sydney, owner of a firecracker industry. Lillo (Pasquale) has been the president of the Reggina Calcio in Reggio Calabria and is an entrepreneur in the fashion industry. Among Lillo Foti's merits is the promotion of the Reggina team to the Italian Premier League (Serie A) for the first time in the history of the club. Lillo Foti, reported the newspapers, spent over a week in Australia on that occasion, in April 2015. He spent time in negotiations and formal or informal meetings with entrepreneurs of Italian origin in Sydney, Melbourne, Canberra; some of them were interested in investing in the football club in Calabria and in formalizing some sort of stable contact with the region that, from Australia, is at times difficult to maintain.

Six Australian businessmen were interested in the deal promoted by Nick Scali – that Nick Scali of Scali furniture we have met in previous chapters, from San Martino of Taurianova, province of Reggio Calabria.

The partnership between Reggina Calcio and Marconi Stallions is the first step. Nick Scali adores Calabria and, at least until 2015, he said he used to go back a couple of times a year for work and personal reasons. His was a choice from the heart, he told the newspapers.[1] Despite not being one of Italy's best football clubs, Reggina Calcio has a strong following in Australia due to the large Calabrian diaspora. Scali thinks of this partnership between Reggio and Australia also to promote exchanges between the two clubs, the players, the support teams. This could be a way to provide financial stability as well as a possible direct pathway for Australian players into Italian football. It was a significant investment: he wanted to buy most of the shares that Lillo Foti was selling.[2] But in the end the investment did not go through.

The Reggina club went bankrupt. Politicians got involved, the whole city was outraged.

There is no 'ndrangheta to blame for this, or not directly, at least. Lillo Foti and his wife were convicted of extortionate practices against their employees in his luxury fashion business in 2018;[3] he had also previously been convicted of sport fraud as part of the Calciopoli scandals in Italian soccer in 2011.[4] But no 'ndrangheta charges. Even if a collaborator of justice, Roberto Moio, in 2013 claimed that Lillo Foti was close to the 'ndrangheta boss Pietro Labate.

Reggina Calcio was declared bankrupt in June 2016. In 2018, the Guardia di Finanza in Reggio Calabria seized liquid and solid assets worth €3.1 million, including 69 buildings and company shares of four companies, traced back to Lillo Foti, still CEO of the club, and to Giuseppe Ranieri, executive manager of the club at the time. It was part of investigations into fraudulent bankruptcy, fraud, false invoicing, tax evasion and other financial criminal activities that both men, together with others, were allegedly responsible for.[5]

No, there is no clear 'ndrangheta involvement here, just 'unethical' business, apparently. But in a city such as Reggio, things can get very messy. In a city such as Reggio, overlapping interests, across the legal and the illegal, are the norm.

In 2018, in Operation Martingala,[6] anti-mafia prosecutors in Reggio Calabria uncovered a network operating from Bianco – one of the villages on Road E90, Statale 106, across the Ionian coast. The network operated through a series of companies often involved in non-existent commercial operations to move money abroad, money that was later withdrawn in cash and brought back to Italy. Carousel fraud. These companies were, prima facie, working regularly, but the whole system of – apparently legal – payments was fraudulent. The system was used by many to commit various illicit financial operations.[7] Among the clients were mafia families from different Calabrian towns, including the Piromalli from Gioia Tauro, and various businessmen of Reggio city. Backing up the network in Bianco were individuals close to the Barbaros from Platì as well as the Nirta from San Luca and also entrepreneur Antonio Scimone. The so-called Scimone System involved several real estate and construction companies, able to get into local works and contracts; it also serviced various other businesses in the area and reached out to major clients for future joint ventures. Among these clients was Reggina Calcio before it went bankrupt.

It's 2016, the club is struggling; its vice president, son-in-law of the 'ndrangheta boss Labate in Reggio City, has just been arrested; Lillo Foti has given his notice. But Foti has capital abroad, so if there was a way into the business of the club through the system of companies held in Bianco, it could go through him, Foti, via another broker/entrepreneur, a friend of his, working in the energy sector in Reggio.[8] This was Scimone's plan. The first trial in February 2020 confirmed the investigations and acknowledged the lack of evidence to sustain any wrongdoing by Foti in relation to these allegations – the operation Scimone had in mind did not go through in the end.[9]

An image in my mind here.

The roof. The roof that I thought of in Griffith, NSW. A dome-like capsule, above it all. Only here it's pictured in my mind as a spiderweb.

A bit like the word *krysha* (from the Russian крыша/krysha), which means 'roof' but broadly refers to a network of individuals providing a range of services, mostly illicit and informal, from protection to patronage, from settlement of disputes to corruption.[10] Yes, there is a krysha that, to me, takes the form of a spiderweb around and above Reggio and in its immediate proximity. A collaborator to prosecutors, in the Sicilian mafia, famously said that 'a mafioso is a like a spider. It builds networks of friendships, relationships, obligations'.[11] But no, this is not quite what I mean. There is not only one spider to take out, here, to watch the network fall apart, as argued by others.[12] I argue, instead, that this spiderweb I see, above the city, on the roof, is the result of many spiders – not only mafiosi – and many spiderwebs interconnected.

In this web, politicians and businessmen, small firms and companies, all get caught or risk getting caught. And it's difficult to see who the spider is or where it is or if there is only one spider. Just ordinary stories of how power and money get handled in Reggio Calabria. A giant spiderweb, the result of several smaller webs mixing in a space that is big enough to be exploited by many but also too small to satisfy all the 'spiders'. A giant spiderweb, with several spiders in different corners; some are small and actively seeking to eat their prey; some are big and stay in a corner of the web just waiting for the prey to go to them willingly or unwillingly; some get caught up themselves; some are taken out eventually. And the prey can be anyone – businessmen, politicians, regular people.

What do you do when you see spiders? Do you kill them straight away or do you capture them and take them outside?

Triad and quadrumvirate

Over the *lungomare* of Reggio Calabria on a summer day, the eyes bleed because of the sun, the skin has goosebumps from the wind, the heart thumps for the view. The Falcomatà waterfront, commonly known as the 'most beautiful kilometre of Italy', is one of a kind. Sicily on one side, the strait of Messina with its deep blue water in the middle, and the concrete of Reggio on the other side; the end of the Italian peninsula. Sunsets over the area of the Athena Goddess – the monument in the middle of the waterfront – are a mix of burning sun and pink air over the blue sea. Walking up and down that strip of land, as the sun sets on a warm August night, the eyes cannot help but notice the luxury of some of the clubs and bars overlooking the strait on the waterfront. The lush life that some people in Reggio surely enjoy. Reggio is an elegant city, a bourgeois city.

> 'He was all like … with that refined hair; he used to go clubbing, making noise … and they had to go and fix his messes, he got into fights with people, at like 5 or 6 in the morning. He didn't have a good conduct. […] this is why they sent him to Milan, they sent him away not to kick his ass … it's not just because he has a role in the De Stefanos' businesses in Milan, but also because in Reggio he was a real troublemaker. He did not give a good image … his cousin Giovanni did not like that. He was always going around with kids, like 25–26-year-old kids who were partying, and they were not calm people, they did not have a reserved life, they were too glamourous. He was eye-catching too after all. […] He used to spend like ten thousand euros a night for champagne …'

Words about Giorgio De Stefano, born in 1981, recorded in Operation Malefix of 2020.[13] He is the son of the powerful boss Paolo De Stefano, who had an extramarital relationship with Giorgio's mother, Carmelina Sibio Condello. He manages, among other things, 'L'Oro di Milano', a franchise of VIP restaurants in Lombardia. Notwithstanding the criticisms and the fact that he was born out of an extramarital affair, he is still a De Stefano, which in Reggio means a lot. It is the reason why someone will be a leader, even when he does not properly behave as one.

> 'They told me you are doing fine in Milan … where did you go … did you go on holiday? […] You need to be careful, Giorgio … visibility, the less, the better … Reggio is damned, you see? You need to be careful; experience teaches us that for nothing they'll give us thirty years in jail … And yet, one cannot let go … if you are not present here, if you are not here with your figure, your name, your history …'[14]

A convicted 'ndrangheta member close to the De Stefano and Tegano clans in the Archi district of Reggio apparently warned Giorgio De Stefano about the need to be careful and to live up to the surname he carries.

Reggio is 'damned', but Reggio is the epicentre of power of four families and their allies, who, perhaps more than any other in Calabria, have been able to adapt, grow and become that *entrepreneurial* mafia that many talk about. Reggio is damned, but you cannot leave if you are a De Stefano.

De Stefano – Tegano – Condello – Libri. The quadrumvirate of the 'ndrangheta of Reggio Calabria. At times a *triad* – depending on decision-making capabilities: De Stefano, Tegano and Condello. Not merely a confederation of clans, but a super-association of the strongest: those who, after the mafia war, which caused incalculable bloodshed in the city between 1985 and 1991, came out of it to bring order to the whole province. This is what judicial history reports. Giuseppe De Stefano, holding the highest rank of the 'ndrangheta *doti*, the *Crimine*; Pasquale and Domenico Condello and Giovanni Tegano, as co-managers; Pasquale Libri, with the function of mediator. These four historical families, while still managing their affairs individually, share extortion and interests in public works and procurement as a confederation. Various other clans, organized in different *locali* and including names that are well known to the locals – Serraino, Borgetto–Caridi–Zindato–Rosmini, Labate, Crucitti, Logiudice, Ficara–Latella, Rugolino and others – still exercise power and intimidation in specific districts of the city, at times on their own, at times with the blessing of one of the four families. Four gigantic spiders.

Their equilibrium in their spiderweb is thin but solid; it is the result of a war that included many of the main 'ndrangheta families in the field: Condello and allies on one side; De Stefano, with Tegano and Libri, on the other. The De Stefano made their fortune with the trafficking of cigarettes from the Balkans, smuggled through the port city of Crotone, with the help of some mafia family there (the Vrenna clan in particular); indeed, the familiarity of the De Stefanos with the Ionian clans, east of Reggio, is notorious. Also clans from the Tyrrenhian coast, from the west, helped the De Stefanos. From outside Reggio, the Pelle, Nirta, Morabito and Pesce, among others, were on the De Stefano side in the mafia war, and the Piromalli, Ursino, Macrì and Commisso were on the Condello side.[15] The pax mafiosa followed the murder of a judge of the Supreme Court, Antonino Scopelliti; not much has changed since 1991.

Reggio-Centre: *De Stefano, Tegano, Libri.*
Reggio-South: *Latella–Ficara and Labate.*
Reggio-North: *Condello, Saraceno, Fontana.*

Among others. Each *'ndrina* is autonomous, but they all "elect" a mother *'ndrina* among the main four, with whom they consult on bigger issues and to share business.

The super-association was partially confirmed in a sentence for one of the trials of Operation Meta but curiously was not confirmed in the sentence for a *second* trial within Operation Meta, leaving it open to further interpretation.

Without rankings, without affiliation, without baptism, without *doti*. Especially for the new generations, the 'ndrangheta in the city has less and less ritualism; it has cocaine, wealth, business acumen and an already settled reputation. It seems.

Following the history, social and judicial, of the 'ndrangheta in Reggio city is not an easy task; the amount of knowledge – trials, sentences, facts – is overwhelming. However, an analytical mind trying to unpack the complexity of the urban scenario finds that in Reggio, more than anywhere else, the modernity of the 'ndrangheta, *because* – and not *in spite* – of its traditionalism, is what really rules relations.

It's no secret that the quadrumvirate recognizes the supremacy of the De Stefano clan for their historical role in the formation of the 'ndrangheta as well as for the charisma of some of its leaders. Already the trials of Operation Olimpia between 1999 and 2002 confirmed the hegemony of the De Stefano–Tegano group in the area of Archi, their headquarters, in Reggio Calabria, and in nearby territories.[16]

Archi. Buildings without identity stacked against a postcard picture of the mountains behind.

The old guard of the 'ndrangheta in Reggio lives with the memory of Paolo De Stefano, killed in 1985 during a mafia feud. His sons, Carmine and Giuseppe, carried on their father's legacy as they shared his charisma: they too could maintain equilibria and end dissent and turmoil. Carmine apparently received the old boss Antonio Nirta, from San Luca, who sought his support in ending the feud between the Nirta–Vottari in San Luca and Platì. Nirta wouldn't have done that – considering his high reputation in the 'ndrangheta – if De Stefano was not at a high enough level. Once you have the role of mediator in the 'ndrangheta, which echoes the role of the *Capocrimine*, both at the level of the *locale* and above, you are pretty much settled. The reputation, the role, the surname, they all mean one thing: *you matter*. And you'll deserve respect for the foreseeable future – and your family with you – notwithstanding who leads the family.

> 'In Reggio we have these friends, these "Christians" [slang word for "individuals"], in addition to having the "San Giovanni" as well. You know, the San Giovanni must be respected, at least the way we think of it, the way you think of it … if we have a headache, we go to them in Reggio and say "Compare, see, I have this problem, what is it to do?" And they tell you how.'

'San Giovanni' refers to situation of *'comparato'* (family partnership) between two or three people from two different families. The 'San Giovanni' are the De Stefano in this case, as this is a member of the Ficara clan talking, quoted in Operation Gambling.[17]

'The *Comparato* is fundamental in trials', says my friend Sara, in Reggio Calabria. And she knows about anti-mafia trials herself, being a prosecutor. 'It is considered like brotherhood, at times even more; it's family lineage, it's a warranty, a religious bond.'

The De Stefano and Tegano surnames in the 'ndrangheta indicate the clans that, more than any other in Reggio Calabria, have been involved in extortion, arms trafficking and infiltration – and control – of many of the entrepreneurial and commercial activities around the city. They embody the mafia method/model: their reputation is solid because it is ancient and rooted in violence – the feuds and the blood spilled in the name of the 'ndrangheta undersigned by De Stefano; the control over economic activities, public contracts and illicit commerce, especially in the districts of the city where they live, is widespread and unchallenged. They are not just 'historical' clans, they are also *real* mafia: they seem to believe they are the rulers of the territory, from home or from jail, thanks to the prestige of mythical figures of the past and to the clan's ability, decade after decade, to both intimidate and ingratiate themselves with the population, while adapting to the reactions of law enforcement. The quadrumvirate – with shared leadership and equal spirit – is the confirmation of such power.

The new adds itself to the old, it confirms the old, and it perpetuates it. Geometry in the spiderweb through which Reggio Calabria is extorted and proceeds are shared almost equally to satisfy the spiders' hunger and expectations, while avoiding conflict.

The net they cast is wider and wider, it crawls up to Rosarno, for synergy with the Pesce clan, and to Santa Eufemia and Sinopoli, for an alliance with the Alvaro. Reggio is their powerhouse, but their profits can dematerialize and move away.

★★★

Six in Malta, one in Austria, two in Romania, two in Spain: 11 companies abroad and 45 in Italy, across Campania, Calabria, Lombardia and others; plus 82 websites, national and international. All seized or subjected to preventive seizure. These were some of the results of Operation Gambling in July 2015.

A few fake companies that formally respected the rules for bets and gambling would conceal websites to access illicit gambling. It was a complex structure whereby the collection of bets on online betting sites would not happen through online transactions but through cash or cheques collected by the 'master', the owner of each betting shop. This would essentially allow sums to be collected locally (and subjected to Italian regulations on gambling) but then transferred abroad, compensating losses and wins and cutting away brokerage fees. The organization was apparently managed by Mario Gennaro and Domenico Lagrotteria, who were the official owners of the gambling circuits – their technical structures based in the 11 companies abroad; their administrative structures based in the 45 local betting shops in Italy. All of this across Europe and against regulations of gambling that require identification of players and not intermediaries. And all apparently avoiding taxes and laundering money.

Local business and global profits. The usual 'ndrangheta recipe. Where was the 'ndrangheta here, anyway?

The organization of this gambling set-up started in Reggio Calabria in the first place.

The organization, which was said to control companies in Austria, Spain and Romania and had its base in Malta, used to change its business address, but not its brain power. Decision-making remained in Reggio. On the one hand, members of the Reggio-based 'ndrangheta took part in the network. On the other hand, and more importantly, it appears that the name/surname of a 'ndrangheta clan (Tegano in this case) was used to persuade the various owners of the betting shops to buy the software, activate the accounts and generally to push for compliance – *that's the mafia method.*

Seen in this way, the 'ndrangheta appears almost residual in this case; it seems far away, detached, just an enabler. Much more important are the various individuals, like Mario Gennaro, who orchestrated the whole commercial network and implemented the system, in his case as owner of UNIQ Group Buchmacher Gmbh, officially based in Austria. He was, however, the de facto dominus of many other companies of the UNIQ group.

Gennaro had certainly gained prestige in his industry – online betting – starting in Reggio Calabria. The authorities called him a 'homo novus' of the 'ndrangheta, someone who could act as guarantor of the infiltration of the lucrative business of online gambling as well as maintain an apparent clean face while laundering money using the BET UNIQ brand.

Would it change anything to know that Mario Gennaro was originally from Archi – the district of the De Stefano and the Tegano – and that he was considered an associate of the Tegano?

'He used to steal motorbikes, Mariolino, as he didn't have the money to buy socks, he was always in debt.'

That's what a 'ndrangheta *pentito* says of him. Gennaro eventually turned witness for the prosecution and confessed to the gambling system and other crimes, including theft, robbery and money laundering. He confirmed that in 1989 he was admitted into the Tegano clan. He then made his fortune through online betting and became country manager of the Maltese company BET UNIQ – and its shadow director – enjoying an unjustifiable amount of cash as well. Once in that position Mario Gennaro offered his 'services' not just to the clan he belonged to, Tegano, but to the whole of the 'ndrangheta in Reggio, attracted by easy earnings and the possibility of laundering money abroad.

'In Operation Gambling', said Sara, 'you have a perfect overlap between the agent for the business franchising and the individual who promotes the 'ndrangheta brand on the same territory.'

Mariolino was 'pimped' from Archi, brought up by the Tegano, to become the manager and dominus of BET UNIQ. That could have been due to either a successful attempt by the 'ndrangheta to groom its children or simply the ability of a lower-level member to seize his own opportunity and climb the ladder.

Or it could be the spiderweb in action. *On the one hand, you are brought up in an environment that promotes the mafia method and distinguishes you because of the affiliation with a powerful surname – Tegano.* This clan, notwithstanding the many arrests and sentences, always keeps its military power and intimidation force in Reggio Calabria. *On the other hand, individual capability will still play a role, and an important one, as in any (deviant) agency.*

The web is spread out, it's large: there are spaces that certain spiders occupy, where they can decide how to move on the web. If you are good enough, you can knit your own portion of the web.

This is not the only case where the 'ndrangheta of the city dematerializes in online shops and financial ventures abroad. Operation Galassia in 2017 again involved online betting shops from Reggio Calabria to Malta, again revolving around the Tegano clan. Operation 'Ndrangheta Banking in 2014, with sentences confirmed in 2018, also involving the Condello clan together with the Pesce–Bellocco from the *Piana*, revealed a system of parallel credit offered by these clans – through financial brokers – to entrepreneurs in Calabria and Lombardia, with the final aim of acquiring their businesses when they struggled to pay the interest rates.

Perhaps these were all attempts to distract the authorities from Reggio, to be less exposed in Reggio, and to use newer ways to launder money and intimidate.

A lot of money is also taken from local resources in the city. Operations Raccordo and Sistema[18] in the mid-2010s demonstrated how the economic and financial interests of the De Stefano, Tegano, Libri and Condello clans were aided by professionals who could support entry, infiltration and management of various economic and financial ventures beyond 'traditional' mafia markets (i.e., extortion and drugs). The same is true for Operations Archi, Agathos, Padrino, Meta, Fata Morgana, Sistema Reggio – *just pick one*. There were many cases of infiltration and business-related ventures: in the waste disposal industry; food distribution companies; the instrumental financial leasing of companies; the concession and collection of credits through financial intermediaries; real estate investments; public–private partnerships (for example, the Multiservizi Spa, whose case brought the dissolution of Reggio Calabria municipality for mafia infiltration).[19] On one side, the clans strengthen their entrepreneurial efforts; on the other, their mafia behaviour remains solidly rooted in brutality and intimidation. As Santo Crucitti, *capo-locale* of the Crucitti clan and ally of the De Stefano–Tegano, said in conversation with a business partner:

'Sasà, I am telling you. Do not put me in the condition of hitting you … because if I lay my hands on you … don't make me talk this way … I don't want to speak this way. If you don't solve my problem, I am going to hurt you. Do you want me to spell it out Sasà? I will break your arms, ok? And not just you […] they will arrest me, but if they do, you'll also be in trouble. […] Ok listen, I'll go and talk to your brother […] if he cares for you, he will understand. […] When someone has a problem, here, there are the right people who intervene. If the problem is not solved then, I won't have a choice.'[20]

Threats, intimidation and violence remain the core of the mafia behaviour, notwithstanding the sophistication and development of economic and financial ventures.

'Formally he never had a job.' A witness for the prosecutors is talking about Giorgio De Stefano Jr.[21] 'It's stuck in my memory as there was a period when I was working, and I was doing all right, and I was collecting 500-euros notes, and I had different kinds in my safe. He had bunches of them … they never ended … and I asked him "Giorgio, where do you get those? Do you print them?" and he had loads. Even in Milan, once I saw him … stuck in my mind it is, that he always had notes of 500 euros in his pockets. Sure, you go out with cash, but 500 euros notes …?'

As always in the 'ndrangheta, the clan looks a lot more granite-like from the outside than they are. But if you have a solid and intricate spiderweb, your individual falls might hit you just a little bit less.

What do you do when you see spiders? Do you kill them straight away or do you capture them and take them outside?

Especially spiders who are indoors. And trapped.

Inside out

'The problem here is not the 'ndrangheta … if I speak the same language to everyone, they won't touch me.'

These words were spoken by the former director of the prison of Reggio Calabria ('San Pietro', aka Panzera), Maria Carmela Longo, arrested in August 2020 and accused of external participation in a mafia association,[22] then released from house arrest in September.[23] Her trial started in January 2022.[24] While this was a serious accusation, most of what emerged from the files submitted with the arrest warrant were acts that speak more about the nature of governance, order and legitimacy in the prison of Reggio than about the former director's conduct.

But let's go in order.

The Panzera prison is in the city centre, tucked behind the roads between the central station and the main general hospital. The usual view of a jail, high walls and electric fences, is enriched by a sequence of iron bars alongside the road that is called via del Carcere Nuovo, New Jail Street. As usual, a feeling of something, the prison, that for many is supposed to be detached from the rest of the city, and yet it is right in the middle of it. This is the metaphor of the Panzera: detached from the city, and yet still influencing it and influenced by it.

By the spiders inside.

'On the 31st of July 2015, on the day of my arrest, as soon as I arrived in the prison in Reggio, I asked to be placed in the same jail with Totò … He told me that they had decided, together with other inmates belonging to Reggio clans, that they would separate the prison in two sections, Area A1 and Area M. In A1 would go those from Reggio Calabria city; in the other the inmates from the Reggio Calabria province. I then decide to go to the area with the others from Reggio and they ask me to sign an application, thanks to the support of a superintendent, so that I could transfer the day after. I learned that others had also asked for transfer and their application was still pending; the favours of the superintendent were for Totò and the others from Reggio city.'[25]

This is the testimony of Mario Gennaro. *Remember Mariolino, who was stealing motorbikes because he didn't have money to buy socks and who made his fortune, and misfortune, in Austria and Malta with online betting?* Mario Gennaro was detained in the Panzera prison when he started to collaborate with the prosecutors.

In Area A1, in June 2017 – as ascertained by the checks of the prosecutors[26] – of 106 inmates, there were 38 from Reggio city, 54 from the province and 14 from elsewhere; in Area M, of 107 inmates, there were 23 from Reggio city, 72 from the province and 12 from elsewhere. *Is it therefore true what Gennaro and others said about the nudging that some 'excellent' prisoners manage to do for the allocation of inmates?*

Area A1 is known as Cariddi while area M is Scilla, Scilla and Cariddi being the two mythological creatures, the former in Sicily and the latter in Calabria. *Scilla, by the way, is one of the most beautiful places in Italy, half an hour north-west of Reggio Calabria, over the Tyrrhenian Sea facing Sicily, where you can eat the best sandwich with swordfish ever. But that's beyond the point. Where were we?*

'One night a nurse, I don't recall his name, but I can describe him […], calling me by name, gives me a necklace, telling me that it was from Demetrio Condello, with his greetings.'[27]

The welcome to the prison by one of the men of the Condello clan: a legitimacy call?
Information about the prison of Reggio gives back images of a place where relations tended to be, at the very least, informal. For example, the prosecution witness Giacomo Ubaldo Lauro gave picturesque descriptions

of life in the Reggio jail at the turn of the 1980s, quoted in the one of the verdicts for the trial Gotha.[28]

It was August of 1979, in the prison of Reggio Calabria, section Camerotti, cell number 6, ground floor. It was the day of San Domenico. Domenico Libri was detained for the trial 'against the sixties', and so was Paolo De Stefano and many from the Piana [including Peppe Piromalli and Pasquale Condello]. So Mico Libri was celebrating his name day, Domenico, and I remember it was August because we were all wearing jackets in that heat ... I even said let's get rid of this jacket! ... I remember the words of Paolo De Stefano, after we did some cocaine, after lunch, eating pastries and drinking champagne, they were full of dust, the jackets! Mico Libri was complaining, Paolo De Stefano said, 'What are you complaining about, first you want to be a criminal, then you complain!'

But this was a long time ago. Was it?

And yet it is common knowledge – say the investigators – that if you behave well in jail, without creating any issue and without collaborating with the authorities, this will be a badge of honour and a reason for 'promotion' within the clan.

You know there are hierarchies in jail, right? According to family alliances, and the ability to spend your time with people you want to spend your time with, to cement friendships. If you have someone who makes your bed for you every morning, or cleans after you, or if you decide when it is time to leave the dinner table, it is because you count – and when you leave, you'll leave your stuff to someone that you want to be your successor.

Sara says this in a matter–of–fact kind of voice.

In jail, *'ndranghetisti* give *doti*, baptize new and old recruits, create alliances, strategize. This is both cause and effect of the persistence of the myths of forefathers, the golden ages of the clans or the mafia wars. Not even prison can destroy those myths; actually, it contributes to perpetuate them. The possibility to communicate and meet in prison, from different clans and different extractions, is certainly something that benefits many organized crime groups.[29]

Prison does not cut off the associative bond of the clans; neither does it affect the clans substantially. It is a fundamental characteristic of mafias to survive any event that might involve single associates because it is the reputation as a group that counts the most. Inmates and their families receive support from the clan and replacements on the ground are negotiated.

Jails are places of aggregation, notwithstanding the politics of isolation and punitiveness that the Italian state provides for most mafia members (article 41-bis of the Penitentiary Code provides for a maximum surveillance prison regime for mafia crimes). And they are places where careers and strategies are decided; they are places of power negotiation for the clans.

> The problem here is not the 'ndrangheta ... if I speak the same language to everyone, they won't touch me.

This statement made over and over by the former director of the prison of Reggio Calabria has stirred indignation. *Was she denying the very existence of the mafia? Was this a confession of having made a pact with the 'ndranghetisti in prison? Was this a declaration of defeat, signifying that the jail was in the hands of the mafia and there was nothing more to say or do but accept that?*

I have learned recently in my research, as I have explored Italian stories and history, that there is a moral question when it comes to mafia members in prison. Some people wish for mafia members to be punished more harshly than others because mafias are the quintessential enemies of the Italian Republic, after all.

How could we accept that the Reggio prison is not under the full control of the authorities? How is it possible that the 'ndrangheta also infiltrates – still infiltrates – the prison? Shouldn't there be, precisely in the Reggio Calabria prison, with many 'ndrangheta inmates, particular attention – perhaps even more incapacitating containment measures – to reduce those risks?

But these questions would be short-sighted. They assume that it is solely for the strength and the strategy of the 'ndrangheta that the prison in Reggio Calabria might be somewhat compromised. This assumption would fall into the all-too-common trap of mistaking social and relational processes for individual and intentional actions, of mafia prisoners and authorities in this case. Not everything is strategic nor intentional, especially with a criminal association.

> The problem here is not the 'ndrangheta ... if I speak the same language to everyone, they won't touch me.

Perhaps this sentence is a reflection on the fact that in prison the language spoken must be the same, whether an inmate is sentenced for 'ndrangheta crimes or for something else. Perhaps. In prison, after all, everyone is the same. Prison life has its own rules.

Prison governance concerns both economic exchanges – *how do you get goods that the prisoner wants, legally or illegally, even inside the prison?* – and social exchanges – *who decides the rules of conduct and any sanctions?* The rules and organizations that govern prison life are always a negotiation between what prisoners want (sometimes illegal goods and benefits) and what the authorities can do within the regulations and manage to do with the allocated resources they have.[30] In a prison like that of Reggio Calabria, pre-prison criminal careers (and therefore also and primarily 'ndrangheta ones) are certainly known to inmates. As researchers recall,[31] when assigned to a prison in the community of origin or reference, it is common for prisoners to organize themselves hierarchically within the prison; pre-prison *reputation* facilitates the creation of social networks in prison as well. This makes things easier because you can talk to family more often, and you can perpetuate and echo your presence from inside to outside.

And the 'ndrangheta clans' ability to maintain order is structured; it is not just left to chance.

'Think about Covid; in Reggio there was no prison riot – those who rioted were mafiosi within less structured, less orderly mafia groups, but no, not here, that's interesting, isn't it?', noted Sara.

Based on reading the various declarations of 'ndrangheta men, it is obvious that friends and associates of various 'ndrangheta clans know each other inside and outside the prison; inside and out, mafia reputation becomes the reason for respect and for recognition of authority. When one gets out of prison, those contacts and that reputation will continue to count. In a system such as the prison system, which is indeed perceived by the average prisoner as an 'illegitimate patriarchy',[32] the power and charisma of some 'ndrangheta clans create order inside and outside the prison. They maintain order and manifest legitimacy, especially because they are close to the territory where their power was born in the first place; they are often from Reggio, after all.

When we talk about mafia, and therefore about a system of values that does not recognize state authority as the only authority to be respected (*when it does not completely deny it!*), one more step is necessary: for the order imposed by the justice system to be accepted, it is necessary to secure a different form of legitimacy in addition to the routine of prison. *In other words, the imposed prison order needs to be accompanied by an order that is wanted, accepted, respected even by the mafia. Why?* Because of the terms of governance. Mafia groups in prison have the means and skills to manage prison governance; they can, if they wish, manipulate order and routine, create diversions and, above all, resort to violence, not only inside but also outside prison, despite being in prison. The link with the territory of reference – especially in Reggio Calabria – is not broken just because someone is locked up within prison walls. The delegitimation of the state is constantly on the agenda – indeed, the inmates from 'ndrangheta clans were convicted precisely for their contempt for public order and authorities. We can expect that order, in a prison like Reggio Calabria, to hang by a thread and to be in constant need of renegotiation and reinforcement: such reinforcement is needed to maintain stability and the non-violent, non-conflictual status quo in everyday life.

The problem here is not the 'ndrangheta ... if I speak the same language to everyone, they won't touch me.

Everyone under the jail roof is supposedly the same, with the same basic rights and limitations, and even when some have more limitations than others, privileges must be earned for conduct within the prison, not for the roles and the reputation or the money one had outside, prior to prison life. The operation where the former director of the Reggio jail was charged for external participation in mafia affairs also refers, among other things, to improper conduct, mostly favours granted to certain inmates. Among these inmates were 'ndranghetisti, lawyers and former politicians. All together.

Giuseppe Scopelliti, for example, has been an inmate at Panzera jail. Former mayor of Reggio Calabria (2002–2010) and Governor of Calabria (2010–2014), Mr Scopelliti has been serving time (four years and seven months) since April 2018, when the court convicted him of falsifying public documents while he was mayor of Reggio.[33] The court noticed how, while he was mayor, Mr Scopelliti acted often 'in contempt of norms and basic juridical principles [...] which constitute clear symptoms of gross negligence and obvious deviance from his duties of public service'.

Sebastiano Vecchio, pentito and witness in the trial Gotha, told the court in March 2021 – I heard the recordings of his testimony – that when Scopelliti was mayor, decisions were made elsewhere because all the main politicians were close to one or more 'ndrangheta clans.

'Scopelliti represented the De Stefano ... Antonio Caridi was also very close to the Fontana, but also Tegano ... there were other mediators, other interlocutors, everything came from that system.'

Antonio Caridi, former counsellor in Reggio council with Mayor Scopelliti, was found innocent at trial in July 2021. In any case, if Mr Scopelliti did receive favours in prison, he would not have been the only one. Paolo Romeo is a former member of the Chamber of Deputies, a Mason and a lawyer in Reggio Calabria; he was convicted in 2004 of external participation in mafia affairs. Arrested again in 2016 during Operation Fata Morgana[34] and at the centre of Operation Mammasantissima,[35] also in 2016, he is one of the protagonists in one of the most important trials of the city of Reggio Calabria, Gotha.

Romeo was also serving time in the Panzera when he had to attend court in Reggio. Favours or not, indeed; in jail, the language spoken by the authorities should be the same for all, as the conditions of inmates are expected to be the same. It is the reputations of the inmates, however, that are not the same, and this is what creates discrepancies, not only the deviance from prison regulations for single favours. Another web, prison, above the spiderweb.

Paolo Romeo, incidentally, is a giant spider.

Romeo was described by Sebastiano Vecchio, during trial Gotha, as 'the God of both 'ndrangheta and politics'.[36] Vecchio, witness and *pentito*, former policeman, former politician and associate to the Serraino clan, was also Mason of the Grande Oriente d'Italia (GOI), and was then 'put to sleep' (as they say in Masonic jargon when a Mason stops being active) to serve 'ndrangheta interests, as he himself recounted in front of the judges in March 2021. 'I knew of Paolo Romeo ... for me, as a politician, meeting him was like ... meeting Ronaldo!'

What do you do when you see spiders? Do you kill them straight away or do you capture them and take them outside?

'La Reggio-bene'

It is a very warm day in Reggio Calabria. My friend Sara welcomes me in her office; she is wearing one of her flowery dresses, with her glasses on, half-serious and half-playful, the way she is. She has this unique ability of saying that one thing, in the middle of a half-serious, half-playful conversation, that just sets the record straight in between the thousands and thousands of pages of an arrest warrant or a trial sentence.

When you study the history of the 'ndrangheta, you learn about the mafia wars, the Reggio Quadrumvirate, the politics of the city's clans following the new arrangements of the pax mafiosa. *But can you really understand Reggio without feeling it, without being there?*

The 'ndrangheta in Reggio is somehow different. *What is it? Fewer drugs, more politics? More extortion, more laundering? More corruption, less intimidation? Or perhaps same crimes, more power?*

'You can call it the Invisibles, the reserved list, the Masso–Mafia, the Santa, whatever. It's always the same thing, an intricate web. It's the Reggio-bene, the Reggio power elite, mixed up with the 'ndrangheta.' Sara.

The mix of the city elites, the Reggio-bene, with families and members of clans of the classic 'ndrangheta factions, is a characteristic of the city, or of the mafia in the city, or of the elites of the city; one can choose from which angle to look at the spiderweb.

Of course, you cannot see the spiderweb when you go to Reggio. Reggio is – like most of Calabria – schizophrenic.

'You love it, don't you? Some corners of sheer beauty, and the waterfront over Sicily, but all together, it's just ugly.' That's how Sara would explain it. From Turin, in the North of Italy, she has been living and working in Reggio for almost ten years and she now belongs here. She often seems more Calabrian than I am.

'They are going to make a TV series about you!' I joke with her. And some producers wanted to make a TV series about her, because she is one of the few young women to do what she does – an anti-mafia prosecutor in Reggio Calabria.

She is right about Reggio. I have never spent time in the city on a continuous basis; it was way too close – just a couple of hours' drive – to my hometown when I was little and yet out of reach when I was in Aspromonte, even if it was in the same province. I used to go to Reggio with my father, mostly when he was working as spokesperson for the Governor of Calabria, and then much later as I started researching the 'ndrangheta, for interviews, meetings, data collection.

One thing about Reggio gets under your skin from the beginning. That feeling that only a few cities in Italy gave me: Palermo, Catania, Naples. The obvious wealth and elegance of the past mixed with the obvious neglect and despair of the present. The liberty-style buildings of the last century and the shining remake of the waterfront; the desolation of some of the suburban districts; the ugly chaos in some streets of the city centre between loads and loads of cement, sign of an era, not long ago, when construction was done without a plan, or an idea, or a licence. The main problem, whenever my father was taking us there, was the sense and direction of the roads – illogical, so my father said – and, of course, the parking – too many cars, too narrow roads, never enough parking. 'There are more cars than *cristiani*' (Christians, people), he always said.

Like many other cities, Reggio is slave to real estate speculation. As a child and a teenager walking down the wealthy streets of the centre, with its elegant shop windows and, at Christmas, red carpets over the paved road, I always felt the energy of Reggio; it was probably the sea – *I loved the idea of a regional capital city with the sea!* Or perhaps it was the liberty style and the warm colour of concrete – that yellowish white. Reggio is messy, striving to preserve its elegance and wealth and yet entangled in urban chaos. And its elite, pretty much always the same, in the spiderweb.

Is there an imaginary table suspended on the spiderweb? If there was, would it be a round table?

That table would be a strong piece of furniture, I imagine, probably built during the famous 'summit' of October 1969 in Serra Juncari, near Montalto. Whoever has been in Montalto, on the highest spot of Aspromonte, knows that there is no actual summit possible there – probably they met to eat together, for a '*mangiata*'. But anyway, Montalto is also where the air is fresh, in the heat of summer, on the way to Polsi. It is a secluded, symbolic place, hence the word 'summit' perhaps.

The story of that 'summit' and the imaginary *table* that was built then is the history of Reggio Calabria. Individuals like Paolo Romeo and Giorgio De Stefano Sr have sat at that table. *But let's step back a second, because history here is fundamental.*

'I spoke to Giorgio De Stefano, about the facts of Reggio and the pact of 1968, 1969 ... he said, "it was about time ... it was about time that we changed the institutions" and that we needed to support the far-right militia because the communists and the socialists were against the 'ndrangheta.'[37] It was the time of the 'Moti di Reggio', the riots of Reggio, which in 1970 did see the city in turmoil, armed by the far right, over the allocation of the regional capital city status; a time that essentially led to a new settlement of power in the underworld as much as in the upperworld.

The meeting in Montalto was a pivotal moment in the history of the 'ndrangheta in Reggio. It essentially shaped the Reggio-bene[38] into what we have known in the past decades. During the trials for Operation Olimpia,[39] which was, and still is, one of the biggest operations against the 'ndrangheta at the end of the 1990s, a collaborator, Albanese, declared, as quoted in the trial Gotha:[40]

After Montalto, within the 'ndrangheta there was a division between those who wanted to maintain the traditional principles of the criminal world, and a group that instead wanted a new structure for the organisation. It must be remembered that, in principle, the organisation was against the state, and affiliates were supposed to live for the 'sgarro', for illegal activities. People on this side were Don Antonio Macrì [we talked about him when we talked about Siderno, remember?], Zappia, president of the summit at the time, Don Mico Tripodo [later on in the war against De Stefano] and Giuseppe Nirta [historical boss of San Luca]. The opponents, so to say, were the De Stefano brothers, Domenico Libri, Santo Araniti, and some from the piana as well, Mommo Piromalli, Saro Mammoliti and Giuseppe Pesce [all from Gioia Tauro and Rosarno] and some from the Ionian side, Pepè Cataldo [from Locri], Turi Aquino [from the Siderno/Gioiosa Ionica clans], and Antonio Pelle [from San Luca].

'Hey dad, what is the *Santa*?' That was my question in my mid-teens, when finally taking an interest in the stuff he was writing, waving the yellow cover of his book, *La Santa Violenta*, in front of him.

'The evolution of the 'ndrangheta in Reggio', was his reply. Years later, in 2012, upon meeting one of the leading prosecutors of Operation Olimpia, Vincenzo Macrì, in his Reggio home, I would learn what that meant. He showed me a passage from Operation Olimpia, another declaration from a mafia witness. The same passage is today cited in the trial Gotha.[41]

The rules of the Santa were revolutionary [...] not just because the formalities and rituals were different from the traditional ones of the Crimine, but also because they were much closer to the Freemasons

[...] The Santa had as ultimate goal the creation of armed groups, in the whole territory of Reggio. These groups could have been used at any time by the heads of the Santa over the whole territory, to support initiatives that could shake the democratic order of the state. Of course, they were all linked to the far-right.

The men of the ancient Order of Freemasons and heroes of the Italian Risorgimento – Mazzini, Garibaldi and La Marmora – are the ones invoked in the ritual of the *Santa* – another trio, another triad. *People do love symbolic numbers here.*

The *Santisti* could get involved in any type of criminal activity – including those that the old 'ndrangheta did not apparently 'allow' (such as kidnappings or drug trade). They were also supposed to exploit contacts with institutions, differently from the past, when that was prohibited.

The more I study these phenomena, the more I run around the world looking for explanations, clues, challenges to my knowledge and understanding, the more I see in this passage, in that moment in history, in the creation of the *Santa*, the true pivotal moment – the moment when the 'ndrangheta became a higher power, intertwined with political and economic power more than before. *This is what explains it all.*

The *Santista* could be selected from among families of any social class – not necessarily from the 'honoured' families of the 'ndrangheta – but he was also supposed to be prepared to betray his family, betray the 'ndrangheta even, to save the *Santa*.

> Within the large box of the traditional 'ndrangheta, there was a group, the Santisti, more secretive: the Santista was unknown to anyone with an inferior ranking, but all Santisti knew all affiliates.'[42]

Did they jump? Did they do it? Was, is, the *Santa* even real, operational, as they had imagined it?

Fast-forward 40 years or so. The collaborator Fiume is talking during the trial Meta, in Reggio Calabria, in 2012:[43]

> The De Stefano, somehow, they have always been part of this. [...] Deviant acts, friendships, have always protected them. It's a superior level, whose origins are with Giorgio De Stefano, brother of Paolo. [...] Paolo De Stefano was an entrepreneurial boss already, far from the old-style capobastone ... and his sons were already within the Reggio-bene.

Fast-forward again a couple of years more. Cosimo Virgiglio is collaborating with the prosecutors – it is the time of Operation Mammasantissima, part of the trial Gotha. It is June 2016.[44]

I confirm that Lawyer Paolo Romeo was member of the Gran Loggia del Principe Alliata [...] all these subjects were 'whispered only', to guarantee their privacy [they were not openly affiliated]. I say it again, that their role is to smooth relationships, and make them invisible [...] between the mafia component and other components of the Masonic circle. In relation to Mr X, he acted on behalf of the De Stefano family [...] he's the interface between the family and the Masonic lodge to whom Paolo Romeo also belonged.

The *Santa*, the Invisibles, the superior level. And their 'reserved' people – those who were not affiliates but were nevertheless at their disposal, on call, for some high-ranking member of the 'ndrangheta or the *Santa*. With the *Santa*, in the 1970s, the 'ndrangheta creates a structure to talk to institutions – *did this evolve into becoming part of the institutions to the point that it is impossible to discern where one ends and the others start?*

'Above the capo crimine, I am aware of the existence of another ranking, a superior one, the Invisible' – among the declarations of another collaborator, Luigi Bonaventura, to the anti-mafia prosecutors of Turin in 2011.

Giuseppe Tuccio, former chief prosecutor of Palmi and president of a section of the Court of Cassation, Italian Supreme Court, died in Reggio Calabria in April 2019. He was a defendant in trial Gotha, charged with belonging to the Invisibles; he was also a friend of Paolo Romeo and was accused, while in Palmi, of facilitating the clans. The collaborator Virgiglio pointed to Tuccio as one of the 'whispered' ones, as he was a magistrate at the time of the events. His links with the deviant Masons on the one hand, and his institutional role on the other, allegedly led him to use his power to favour clans like the Piromalli in Gioia Tauro. According to Aldo Micciché – right-hand man of Antonio Piromalli – in Operation Cento Anni di Storia (One Hundred Years of History), the judge was linked to them 'by feet, hands and ass'.[45]

Bosses Pasquale Condello and Antonino Imerti also seemed to be referring to Giuseppe Tuccio while in jail and in conversation with their wives, when discussing the fact that the sister-in-law of Condello was pregnant while in a relationship with Luigi Tuccio (son of Giuseppe and city counsellor when Giuseppe Scopelliti was mayor). The judge was 'always a good person, in the trials, even when he was judging something, if he could, he would help'.[46] They also believed that they were procuring votes to support Luigi's political career.

When, in 2012, the town council of Reggio was dissolved for mafia association, Luigi Tuccio was among those considered unfit to be a candidate again by the Court of Appeal, for proximities to the clans, especially because of his relationship with the sister-in-law of Condello and based on rumours and accusations that he had accepted votes from the 'ndrangheta circles.

It could be genius if it wasn't devious.

'There is no proof of a (more) secret mafia association, that is an abstract. Evidence proves that there is an apical and occult faction of the 'ndrangheta'.

Appeal sentence for the Gotha trial in 2021.[47] *This faction, out of the* Santa, *was also called 'Cosa Nuova', New Thing.*

Think about it. To preserve the 'ndrangheta overall – in order not to lose power over crime – a detached association is created from the 'ndrangheta, a separate body – *a denser part of the spiderweb where only certain spiders go –* whose networks were similar, overlapping, but not fully the same as the ones of the higher ranks of the 'ndrangheta. An association that could *blast* the 'ndrangheta itself, if needed. Yes, the *Santisti*, or the Invisibles, or whatever one might call them, can betray the rest of the 'ndrangheta – *the exposed one –* if it's needed for the survival of their own association.

Self-preservation through a (potential) self-destruction button. *A mafia lifeboat.* Too bad it was based on democratic subversion and high-level criminality.

If the Santista is not a 'ndranghetista anymore, as he has to renounce to the 'ndrangheta to enter the Santa, are we still talking about one organization only? I wonder whether 'ndrangheta and *Santa* have grown as two separate organizations, two different identities notwithstanding the birth of the latter from the former. If so, confusing them might be indeed counter productive for analytical purposes.

Many in Reggio Calabria have tried to pierce the veil of the spiderweb. The invisible spiders in the Gotha trial are (deviant) Masons, lawyers, politicians. *One might ask where the hell is the 'ndrangheta in all this, and the answer is not a simple one.*

As it goes beyond Reggio.

Pantaleone Mancuso, convicted boss from Limbadi, in Operation Purgatorio in 2013, back in 2008 when he was intercepted, gave his take on the 'ndrangheta:[48]

'The 'ndrangheta doesn't exist anymore! It once was, in Limbadi, Nicotera, Rosarno, there used to be ... the 'ndrangheta. Now the 'ndrangheta is part of the masonry. Let's say [...] it's beneath the masonry, but they have the same rules, the same things [...] what remained now? Now there is the masonry and those four 'storti' [slang for stupid] who still believe in the 'ndrangheta [...] once the 'ndrangheta was for the wealthy ... then they left it to the poor, the farmers ... and they relied on the masonry ... the rules are the same! [...] because the real 'ndrangheta it's not what they say it is ... because the 'ndranghetista does not do what they say he does

[...] now they are all youngsters with no rules, all drugged up ... common delinquency! ... the 'ndranghetista didn't even want to do drugs! And he didn't want to fight ... if someone was a pimp, do you think he could be on the roll? Or someone who was beating his wife, or got always drunk? He wasn't even supposed to enter the bar, the 'ndranghetista, the 'mastro di giornata' [the right-hand man of the boss] was roaming the street and if he saw you entering the bar and drink, he would beat you up! [...] Still with the 'ndrangheta ... it's over! Let's be modern, stop with the old rules ... the world changes and things need to change! Today we call it masonry, tomorrow we'll call it p4, p6, p9 ...'[49]

Mancuso, from Vibo province, shows that the unity of the 'ndrangheta – the isomorphic nature and the convergence of clans from various provinces to the structures of Reggio Calabria – requires adaptability and forward-thinking.

Remember that this was over ten years ago. *And beware, we don't have to 'believe' him*; in his discourse there is nostalgia for an imagined or long-gone past and idolatry of a past that was better and more 'honourable'. Interestingly, a judgement on the activities and modus operandi of the 'ndrangheta, or what is left of it, is advanced by using what seems to be the ultimate metaphor for occult power: the Freemasons. *I'll say it again, we don't have to believe this, or him, but we need to take this narrative for what it is, realistic for what it means to him and those he spoke with.*

It's the narrative that, since I can remember, has populated any serious commentary of the 'ndrangheta, with explicit references and with examples always new and, at the same time, always old, and always primarily from the city of Reggio Calabria. The mafia bourgeoisie.

> Giorgio De Stefano [can be considered] as the promoter and organiser of the apical and occult faction of the 'ndrangheta. [...] The function of the so-called 'reserved ones' is to offer their knowledge and their professional and relational abilities to the organiser of the association, with awareness to offer a contribution to maintain this association as a whole.

Again, Gotha Appeal sentence, 2021.[50] These reserved individuals, politicians, professionals, the 'Reggio-bene', exist in a spiderweb of Masonic and 'ndrangheta making.

Occult

There is that famous aphorism by Tomasi di Lampedusa in his book *The Leopard*: 'everything changes so that everything can remain the same', which I cited before in this book. Reggio Calabria.

'There is the visible and the invisible. And no one knows about the invisible unless they are themselves invisible', a collaborator told the prosecutors almost ten years ago, during Operation Bellu Lavuru.[51] *This is getting witchy, isn't it?*

The 'ndrangheta – or rather the *Santa* – becomes the red bow that wraps it all up: human relations; business relations; power relations; cultural relations; even ethnic relations, when abroad. It cannot disappear from Reggio – there is still extortion, arson, intimidation, all traditional mafia crimes. But mafia almost fades into the background; something bigger is at play; the spiderweb has many powerful spiders, and it has turned into a spiders' *nest*.

What does this mean? It means that informality reigns. Within informality, particularism prospers. And within particularism , criminality thrives. If you push with your elbows to gain some way, you might get some advantage in political, public and business life in the city of Reggio. 'Ndrangheta clans get disrupted daily and *'ndranghetisti* are arrested for drugs and extortion all the time; however, there will still be a few who will share something a lot less dirty, a lot more elegant, a lot more elusive: political, professional, financial power.

The circle closes in – all the feelings of losing *it*, inability to understand *it*, choking because *it* feels everywhere and yet nowhere. *It* all boils down to the elusiveness of the different sources of power and of the various human relations involved. Even more, it points to the fine line between *obedience* – to the rituals, to the rules, to the boss, to the market, to the established status quo of power, to the recognized authority, to the lodge – and *revolt or revolution* – the constant effort to elude authoritative control, to rebel against the 'oppressive' state, to gain further ground on an ideal social and political ladder. Creating an occult, secretive, *sect* of power, which is *both revolutionary and obedient*, is the ultimate result and victory; this settles for sure the narrative of the 'most powerful Italian mafia'. As in the sentence in *The Leopard*: challenging the status quo to keep obedience in place.

Between obedience and revolution. Between subjugation and rebellion. Between tradition and innovation. Between brotherhood and collusion. And with different names. Of course, one needs to contextualize it all. The Freemasons, and their power, for example, have a whole independent history from the 'ndrangheta, and it is only in the deviant and secret lodges – and in Reggio Calabria – that the occult power welcoming the 'ndrangheta exists.

As a collaborator says in the Gotha appeal trial:

[T]he Santa, as a secret sect is to the 'ndrangheta what a covert lodge is to official masonic lodges. There are relationships between the Santisti and the covert masons, and often the two roles could be found in the same person. We also need to say that the 'ndrangheta member cannot be a mason, but this is only for the 'inferior' 'ndrangheta and for public masonic lodges. But as said, the Santa is a secret part of the 'ndrangheta, where the traditional 'ndrangheta rules are only valid until they are compatible with the values of the association; if these values can only be maintained with masons entering the structure or vice versa, there are no obstacles.[52]

Professor John Dickie, in his 2020 book *The Craft*, provides a critical account of the history of the Freemasons across the past centuries. He notes that 'nowhere, among the Western democracies, is hostility to Freemasonry more widespread than in Italy. Nowhere more than in Italy has Freemasonry been tainted with corruption. Now the conviction has taken root in Italy's poorest region [Calabria] that the Freemasons are in league with the mafia, that bastard branch of the fraternalist tradition.'[53]

On the one hand, there are deviant Masonic lodges in Calabria that facilitate, or take part in, the 'ndrangheta's business. *'Ndranghetisti* need politicians, lawyers, entrepreneurs to intimidate or to corrupt in order to reach their goals. The Masonic lodges act as 'chambers of compensation': they provide networks, brokerage, money, support – as noted in a damning parliamentary anti-mafia commission report in 2017.[54] There are plenty of 'niche' unauthorized, covert or irregular lodges. They act as 'dating agencies' matching *'ndranghetisti* to mediators from among the professional classes and can offer a route to the very top of the grey zone where the criminal underworld meets the upperworld of politics and business. [55] For example, take the so-called 'sleeping' Masons: those who were affiliated with a lodge, but after not paying their fees for a while – or because they have been sanctioned – have disappeared officially from the register; nevertheless, they still behave as Masons, can still offer advice, deviant or not, as Masons. Sebastiano Vecchio revealed in the Gotha trial that he himself had been asked to 'go to sleep' when he started acting, in his political role, in the name of the Serraino clan. This is in line with the declarations made earlier about the interdependence of structures of power in the city.

'The Pelle clan [from San Luca] were Masons too, part of the unofficial lodges in Messina. They had contacts with Senator Antonio Caridi', Vecchio said in March 2021 during the Gotha trial. Which meant they were *Santisti*.

> Every one of us, politicians … those who have contacts with the 'ndrangheta, know it and recognise it … normally … with Caridi and the others, we talked normally about the 'ndrangheta … for fame this is what you do … we all have our 'friends', and Masons, connections … alas, this is Reggio Calabria.

On the shores of Reggio and opposite to Messina, there are official Masonic lodges, and unofficial ones, that are effectively secret. They create and nourish contacts and networks outside the official Freemasonry and in a chamber of compensation that can benefit legal, deviant or criminal behaviour or mafia linkages.

'Yes, Giovanni Tegano is what we call a Mammasantissima.'

'An historical boss, then. A capo-locale then?'

'Yes, a capo-locale [...] We have a modern 'ndrangheta now, with the De Stefano, today.'

'Yes, since the '90s, it's changed, the 'ndrangheta is more modern, more political. Back in our days [...] it was very different, in the '80s, very different.'

'Now, I have to ask, what does it mean that the 'ndrangheta is more political?'

'More political, as in politics has brought money to Reggio Calabria [...] every period of election, people make money, as I did [...] they buy votes, yes, like I did sell votes.'

'Buy with money?'

'Sure, with money.'

'Which elections?'

'In 2007 or 2008 but before as well.'

'And did you participate as Roberto Moio or as affiliate to the Tegano clan?'

'As affiliate to the Tegano.'

'Is there a tariff?'

'Not really [...] I asked 30 thousand euros for 200 votes.'

'And De Stefano?'

'[...]'

'Peppe De Stefano ... he is fashionable, he likes clubs, dresses well ... he collects clean people from the Reggio-bene, [...] it's a 'ndrangheta ... a little bit, more, how can I say, lighter, a little more camouflaged in the city, without reunions, without ... I don't know how to explain it.'[56]

One of the most important collaborators of recent years, Roberto Moio, in the trial Meta in 2014 and in following investigations, including the trial Gotha, explains the convergence between the 'ndrangheta and the Masons in Reggio Calabria; the links with drugs, extortion, violence and all the rest we do know. Individuals like him, other *pentiti* like Villani, Virgiglio, Belnome and others, had confirmed the metamorphosis of the 'ndrangheta *from within.* They highlighted the lack of trust in the old structures – *already too exposed, already too well known by the authorities.* They undress the 'ndrangheta of its *old* rituals – *they do not suffice anymore* – and they dress it up with *new* rituals – the occult power of the Masons, the occult power of a 'superior level', invisible to all but those who are also invisible.

'The world of the clans, the Masons, police, secret services … we need a new name to keep them all together, as they are together', said Sebastiano Vecchio during the trial Gotha in March 2021.

The perfect closure of the circle. The most elusive of criminal organizations merges with the most elusive of occult power, the deviant Freemasons. This covers the city in a spiderweb, where anything is possible if you know the right people – spiders; prey might succumb when facing this never-ending revolving door that turns one source of power into another, financial into political, social into financial, political into social.

A bar in the centre of Reggio, a beautiful summer evening. Sicily smirking on the other side of the strait and Mount Etna fuming as usual, as if it could explode at any moment. I was drinking a Coke Zero, sitting on some stairs facing the waterfront and reading a book, waiting for my father. A young man, not much older than me at the time, barely 20 perhaps, walked by – he was on the phone and walked by, hurrying up. He was talking about some place, a club or a bar, too expensive but worth investing in, 'in the city centre, opposite the waterfront, it's a bargain'; he was reassuring whoever he was speaking to that it was going to be okay, it was going to work. 'There is something in it for all of us', he said. He put the phone away; hands in his pockets, he moved a bunch of banknotes from one pocket to another. And I was there thinking, wow, this guy in Reggio, look at him, already so successful and so young, acting like an adult trapped in the body of a teenager. On the Via Marina, the waterfront, I thought how strange things happen in Reggio, where you could be that young and that powerful.

It is very rare, in Reggio Calabria, to keep only one identity, only one hat, especially when you taste some 'power'.

Ionian coast

On 26 October 1969, in Serra Juncari, during the famous 'summit' in Montalto, in Aspromonte, the old boss Giuseppe Zappia is said to have declared:[57]

> Here there is no 'ndrangheta of Mico Tripodo, there is no 'ndrangheta of 'Ntoni Macrì, there is no 'ndrangheta of Peppe Nirta! We must be all united, who wants to stay stays, who wants to leave can leave.

On 8 May 1998, an intercepted conversation between a defendant in the trial Armonia and another man:[58]

> There are mandamenti for a reason, compare Leo, there are … so that you get the ranking in one place … the ranking on the Tyrrenian side, or the Ionian side or City Centre … we are all men in the same way, all in the Crimine, criminals … that's it.

Further south than the south of Reggio, the spiderweb does not disappear, quite the opposite. When you drive through Reggio and leave the strait behind you, following the line of the road Statale 106, waiting to turn and leave the sun behind, be ready to bathe in the colours and the perfumes of the Ionian coast. One of the best seas ever, without the chaos of the tourist frenzy. It's the kind of sea, that of Bova Marina, Condofuri, Bianco, Africo, Brancaleone – and all the other localities on the Statale 106 all the way up to the border with the province of Catanzaro – where you can park pretty much on the beach, the showers are free, the kiosk will sell you beer for €1.50 and – to my surprise – you can drink that beer right on the beach while watching the waves. The simplicity of this part of the world, and yet its richness, is overwhelming even for me, still. All these villages, one after the other, in sequence on the Statale 106, evocative in their own way, sharing so much more than the road at the sides of which they all developed.[59]

When you pass between the piles of garbage on the side of the road – a constant, and sad, image on the Ionian coast of Reggio province – and upon arriving in Melito di Porto Salvo, you are entering the Calabria Grecanica: a handful of villages that have preserved some of their Greek cultural heritage in the dialect they speak, the rituals of their festivals, the costumes and music of their traditions. It's a time capsule thrown into the rest of the real world. This is where the sun starts setting on the wrong side, to me, the more you drive up the Statale 106.

You pass by Pentedattilo, from Greek, 'the town of the five-finger rock', hit throughout history by fires, earthquakes and other natural disasters – an abandoned village inhabited by a couple of dozen people only. The beauty of the view from the car climbing up the road to Pentedattilo cannot be fully captured by the writing. One must see it, the old houses, almost all collapsed, glued onto the rock. Aspromonte behind, the valley below running towards the sea of Melito; the view from above, from the village of Pentedattilo, is breathtaking. And indeed, breathtaking views are common in Grecanic Calabria down there. Swallowed, as you are, by thousands of prickly pears. Not joking, thousands of them. I spent two weeks of a too-hot month of August writing parts of this book in Pentedattilo. That's also where I took the picture for the cover.

Bova, just 20 minutes ahead of Pentedattilo, past Melito and Condofuri, is another village up on a rock, with just over 400 inhabitants in the small town 1,000 metres above sea level. If you go there at sunset, the blood orange of the sky will embrace you along with the warm yellow of the streetlights; your eyes will get lost in the horizon; the rest of the world is far away. The cobbled stone roads; a strange old locomotive parked in the middle of one of the main squares as a tribute to all the people from Bova who worked for the railways. An old Greek language on the street signs. *You'd eat the listopitta there, a delicious something flat and fried, lost in the traditions of the days gone by.*

At sea level is Bova Marina, a separate municipality, bigger than Bova, easier to get to, another village on the Statale 106, with the most beautiful clear and transparent sea, the piles of rubbish at the side of the road and the sun setting on your right-hand side on the beach.

It doesn't look like any money could be stolen here. What was worth any money, the contracts for the road, or the rubbish collection that doesn't work, or even the beach kiosk, has already been taken, perhaps exploited or just lost. Bova is pulsating with people coming and going, villagers at the marina and tourists in the town above; many leave, few stay and those who stay live their life over the Statale 106, in between Reggio Calabria and the Ionian Sea.

Far, far away people can go from Bova.

Jan Kuciak and his fiancée, Martina Kusnirova, both 27, were found dead in their apartment on 21 February 2018 in Veľká Mača, Galanta District, in Slovakia, 65 kilometres from Bratislava. The shooting was almost immediately connected to Jan's investigations for the news website Aktuality.sk into tax fraud by Slovak businesses and into Slovak connections with the 'ndrangheta from Bova. The case was, and still is, particularly shocking for Slovakia, to the point of causing street protests, revolts and a political crisis that led to the resignation of Prime Minister Robert Fico three weeks after the murders. As the investigations progressed, it became clearer that the murder was not connected to mafias and that Kuciak's enemies were others.

The existence and functioning of a locale of 'ndrangheta in Bova has been the object of various anti-mafia operations including Reale, Bellu Lavuru 2 and Mandamento Ionico, among others. Within this *locale*, the Vadalà *'ndrina* historically has been present. Domenico Vadalà, aka Micu u Lupu (Micu the Wolf), is one of the historic names of the *locale* of Bova; he had important friendships within the 'ndrangheta that count, from San Luca to Reggio Calabria; in Bova, the Morabito clan is also particularly active. Aktuality.sk published Kuciak's last story and revealed the names of the Italian businessmen with ties to organized crime who have settled in eastern Slovakia, allegedly embezzling European Union funds for development. It appears that the Vadalà first arrived in Slovakia in the early 2000s; they grew a successful agricultural business that has yielded them over €13 million in EU farming subsidies. These businessmen also had connections to high-ranking state officials, such as a deputy and the secretary of the State Security Council of Slovakia, and a former model who became chief adviser to Prime Minister Robert Fico. These businessmen were Antonino Vadalà, his brothers Sebastiano and Bruno, and their cousin Pietro Catroppa. Catroppa's father was apparently the '*mastro di giornata*' – right-hand man – in the Vadalà *'ndrina* in Bova Marina. The Vadalà surname and the connections with the 'ndrangheta in Bova and in Reggio Calabria did the trick – they were arrested in the investigation for the murder of Kuciak and Kusnirova. But the arrest did not stick for lack of evidence and the 'ndrangheta lead was eventually considered the wrong one. The wrong one for the murder, but not for the other criminal activities, as Antonino Vadalà was arrested for cocaine trafficking and money laundering, then extradited to Italy, upon request of the anti-mafia prosecutors in Venezia. The connections to the 'ndrangheta from the Ionian town of Bova and Melito, and the Morabito clans as well, are for business: importing cocaine to Venezia through the 'ndrangheta brokers and networks, all with the money from Vadalà and his associates in Slovakia, including his father-in-law, Diego Rodà, who was indicated but never charged as one of the leaders of the Italian mafia groups in Slovakia.[60] Vadalà has companies, cash flows, land and warehouses in Slovakia; importing stuff is easy and could be justified with legal businesses.

Drugs, drugs and more drugs. And money. Is this then the core of 'ndrangheta mobility in Europe?[61] It is. In a case that made the headlines because of the links among drug traffickers, entrepreneurs and the political class of Slovakia, is it really important to give the label – to attach the 'ndrangheta label? *Would the case matter the same without that label? And more importantly, what does the 'ndrangheta label actually add?*

★★★

The smaller spiders and the bigger spiders, with a net that stretches from the city out over the sea.

Sitting on a bench overlooking the sea, with giant white block letters behind me spelling 'Bova Marina' with a heart in place of the 'o', to make it picture perfect, I wonder, as usual. *What remains of that family power here? Where is the money? Not here, as this place looks like it's about to collapse.* And what is the link, if any, between that power, drug trafficking and money laundering activities in Slovakia? *Is this what the 'ndrangheta really is then, and what the mobility is about?* The exploitation of an accrued power – power over territories, over commerce, political machines, judiciary immunity, power to maintain equilibria, to convert one form of power into another – to further criminal activities wherever there is an opportunity? *Is this how the spiderweb works?*

It is perhaps that accrued composite power – made up of the ability to convert one form of power into another – that allows the 'ndrangheta to go from a small Calabrian town all the way to Slovakia for business: what was territorial power, governance, in Bova, has turned into economic power, and from Bova, it takes off to other lands. This is the meaning of the label of the 'ndrangheta for a man like Antonino Vadalà. That is the added value, if any, of the label. His activities, his interests, they are all about drugs and money. With money, of course, comes the privilege of – maybe, eventually, one day – being welcomed into the spiderweb and accessing the revolving door.

My head aches.

(In)conclusive

Losing the 'ndrangheta again. The rituals are often gone, as are the 'official' affiliations – especially in Reggio. Those involved in drugs are not necessarily those interested in any type of governance power, aside from the power that money can give. Those who have money might not be able to turn money into power or to use that power anyway. Those who have power – a legacy of their violent or potentially violent reputation, or as a key player in politics and the local economy – might not be the ones interested in directly criminal activities. It seems that the allure of the criminal life, which the 'ndrangheta rituals have been, and still are, promoting, has been substituted by the allure of privileged chambers of power.

The 'invisible' 'reserved chamber' – the original *Santa* – was created to safeguard the 'ndrangheta through the mechanism of self-destruction, but it was also independent from the 'ndrangheta. A chamber that converts one form of power into another – political power becomes financial power; professional influence becomes political influence. And it does so not just within one family, but across many families of the 'ndrangheta and outside the 'ndrangheta, in the professional, business and political worlds. Sure, the mafia – the 'ndrangheta – is an organization, a social artefact. But does it have organizational *boundaries*, as argued by scholars studying mafias as organizations?[62]

This mixing up of powers is not something that is advocated for in modern societies; it is not usual, and it is not desirable. Modern societies, in fact, are supposedly based on the autonomy of different *partitions* of power to develop and maintain legitimate forms of authority.[63]

I wonder. It appears that the very existence of this 'chamber of compensation' or 'reserved chamber', especially in Reggio, defies the 'management' of power in modernity, inasmuch as it brings different spheres of influence back into the hands of a few who can circulate and recirculate power among themselves and their circles.

Is this also the way in which the 'ndrangheta/Santa structures remain pre-modern? Is this another way for the 'ndrangheta to maintain its archaic roots?

What does that mean?

The 'ndrangheta rituals promote a certain identity, and that identity – depending on people, families, locations, times – has served, across time, different individual and collective criminal needs. It has been an identity of resistance to domination, one of subversion of the status quo, one of conflict with society, one of money-making, one of social prestige, one of cultural engineering.

What happens if necessities mutate and 'ndrangheta traditions and rituals are not providing the same solace or refuge anymore? What happens is what normally happens to any dogmatic doctrine: it either changes or it dies.

While once considered as one dogmatic subculture – some have defined it as archaic, or barbaric, others just as 'traditional' – the 'ndrangheta has come to a split to save itself. And part of this split – its most hidden, secret, the *Santa*, the Invisibles – has developed this revolving door capacity – a chamber of compensation – that puts different spheres of power in the city into communication with one another.

In a fast-changing world, with generational changes, increased mobility, the online revolution and repression by the state, the 'ndrangheta is constantly adapting. Its dogmatic core might try to resist but it will necessarily change.

Too many 'ndranghete – plural – then? Split, diverse, some more prone to keep local power, some more invested in banking, some still fighting feuds, some managing their power from Toronto and not from Calabria anymore.

It would be too easy and obvious to simply say that the phenomenon is not what it once was.

If there are too many 'ndranghete, some with different names even, maybe there is none at all? Most of what we call mafia crime could also be (and often is) treated as drug trafficking, public procurement fraud, embezzlement, political corruption, bribery, money laundering. This also would be imprecise, for all the victims of mafia subjugation, for all the blood spilled, for all the things that don't work because of systemic corruption by organized crime in Italy and beyond. *This mafia is more than just the sum of its crimes.* And surely, as has been said many times in this book, there is unity in the 'ndrangheta, if anything for the isomorphic nature of the groups and their convergence of interests.

So what?

So both.

The 'ndrangheta is a train with many carriages and each carriage has its own capo-locale. Then there is the capo of the train, even if that is temporary. This would be a local train. Then there is a high-speed train, where not everyone can get on, only the bosses. Above them there are people who travel by plane and they remain unseen, unknown to the people on the trains.

This is the powerful metaphor by *pentito* Antonino Fiume as recalled in the 'Ndrangheta Stragista trial.[64]

★★★

Alberto is driving up to the Statale 106; we are headed to Mammola, to eat stockfish and visit the beautiful town of Gerace afterwards. Road signs to San Luca, Platì, Bovalino, Siderno, Locri.

The rituals have survived – here – in some of these villages – have they? Or they migrated into new formulas within Masonic traditions and circles of the city of Reggio. I think aloud.

Whichever way, the 'ndrangheta still means something here. Even if it is just an echo, it means something.

Why doesn't anyone collect this rubbish really? What prevents a good governance of waste disposal? Alberto interrupts.

Perhaps fighting against it is something we need to do anyway – whatever the 'ndrangheta has been or has become – as a reaction against decline, against injustice, against the ugliness of rubbish and against the reasons why no one collects the rubbish on the Statale 106 and it is allowed to pile up.

Sometimes we need an *identifiable enemy* – and the 'ndrangheta is identifiable in all the knowledge we have about its past, present and evolution. Some other times we need an *abstract enemy*, something that embodies everything that we don't like and everything that we don't want to condone. And the 'ndrangheta, with its fluidity, its games of hide-and-seek, its evaporation from time to time into nothingness, its retraction into the occult – can also be that.

Calabria is beautiful, you know? Like, really, unexpectedly beautiful. Alberto says.

I know.

Why don't more people know that? How can it remain a secret?

Because it's a difficult land, there are not enough good roads, good services, good business …

… and the rubbish by the Ionian coast.

Yes, the rubbish.

So many Calabrians have done so much abroad, away from here, why not here?

It's difficult, or so I thought when I left. There are deeply rooted problems, the 'ndrangheta's power in certain areas being one of them, but when it's not about the 'ndrangheta, it is something else: resistance to progress, an unscrupulous political class, the central government not investing enough and so on. I've heard this litany since I was born.

Crushed by too many things beyond its control, then, this beautiful land.

Or maybe exploited to keep control, if control is also over identity, somehow.

Is it time to go back?

It is time to go back.

Epilogue

Nonna, do you like my bubbles?
   Always with these bubbles! Be careful, don't spill the soap on the floor!
   I can almost see her, *bella mia*. I can still see how her face would contort when singing that song about the Madonna, full of *pietas*, full of pain and hope. She was a modest woman, my grandmother, never showing too much emotion. But her last time in Polsi, she remembered, she was singing, she was feeling it all deep down. She did cry. And every time since, this song gave her some tears.

> *A li pedi di la Madonna*
> *e 'nu bellu vitellu' nci sta:*
> *dudici stelli attornu attornu*
> *e la luna splendori 'nci fa.*
> *(RIT) E jeu no' mi movu di cca,*
> *se la grazia Maria no' mi fa:*
> *facitimmilla, Madonna mia,*
> *facitimmilla pe' carità!*
> *At the feet of the Madonna*
> *There is a beautiful calf*
> *Twelve stars around all around*
> *And the moon shines on it*
> *(CHORUS) And I won't move from here,*
> *If Maria doesn't give me grace*
> *Please do, Madonna Mia,*
> *Please do, have mercy.*

Alberto had parked the car just outside the church. The whole village seemed dormant as usual. A Saturday afternoon, 15 August. My birthday. Everything was slow, everything was warm. Everything was muffled, as usual, in Aspromonte, and in Platì, even more.
   Why am I spending my birthday in Platì of all places?
   I want to pay my respects to these people who will naturally be curious about me, about us, in the church. Everyone knows each other and they don't know us.

Alberto and I sit at the back of the church, not many people inside; some turn around to look who just came in, but the majority are deeply focused on their praying and their singing, they don't even notice.

> *A la vita di la Madonna*
> *e 'nu bellu curduni 'nci sta:*
> *dudici stelli attornu attornu*
> *e la luna splendori 'nci fa.*
> *At the waist of the Madonna*
> *There is a beautiful cordon*
> *Twelve stars around all around*
> *And the moon shines on it*

I hear mainly women's voices, with the usual, so familiar, tone of voice, the voice that chants this litany. I know it all. I am taken aback.

> *A li vrazza di la Madonna*
> *e 'nu bellu bambinu 'nci sta:*
> *dudici stelli attornu attornu*
> *e la luna splendori 'nci fa.*
> *In the arms of the Madonna*
> *There is a beautiful child*
> *Twelve stars around all around*
> *And the moon shines on him*

Something inside me just kicks as they chant. It's an emotion of euphoria mixed with pain. Nostalgia mixed with love. My heart tightens, my breath is short, I feel the usual knot in my throat. It's the familiar memory that accompanies me when I think of her, *bella mia*. It's a warm feeling.

> *A la testa di la Madonna*
> *e 'na bella curuna 'nci sta:*
> *dudici stelli attornu attornu*
> *e la luna splendori 'nci fa!*
> *On the head of the Madonna*
> *There is a beautiful crown*
> *Twelve stars around all around*
> *And the moon shines on it.*

I feel the tears. *Her* tears, through me. It has been years since I heard that song. I cry a bit.

At the bar, I am the only woman. The three or four men inside are chatting among themselves without looking at us. An old movie, perhaps *Il Sorpasso,* is projected, black and white, on a wall. We order two Brasilenas, brought to us by someone other than the bartender.

What is the Brasilena, you ask? The drink I yearn for when I am away, they only sell it in the provinces of Reggio and Catanzaro, in Calabria. A fizzy drink made with coffee; sounds simple, but it's delicious.

Why the hell am I here really?

The bartender – who might also be the owner of the bar – clearly wonders the same and starts asking questions when he finally gets to us.

'*A cu apparteni?*'

Who do you belong to?

I have heard this question so many times. And yet it's the first time I realize how *relational* it actually is. There is never only one answer to this question. *The answer adjusts to where you are and who you are talking to. You reply by giving the person some details about people he might know; you relate your answer to him or her.* It is about establishing ways to recognize one another.

In Platì, I am my grandparents' granddaughter. *I 'belong' to them.* It's they who had the closest relationship with this village, with this part of the mountain. *It's they who give me the 'justification', reason, to be here.*

It's my grandmother's brother who married a woman from here, I say, and they went to Australia, I believe. *Oh, so you are in that family*; he says my surname. Not really, I reply, but sure, that makes sense to him. And it's my grandfather's family who still lives in Santa Cristina, he knows some of my relatives there. I speak in dialect, even if it's rusty. He replies to Alberto instead; the man in a couple is the one you reply to around here. A strange triad of voices and interactions, indeed, as Alberto understands one out of five words at a time.

It's paid for.
What?
The Brasilenas, they are paid for.
Alberto blinks twice. *What? Aren't we paying?*
Why? I ask the bartender.
The bartender doesn't smile, doesn't smirk. Just cold-stone face, *it's paid for, don't worry.*

A sense of déjà vu and flashback to Little Anna trying to avoid the *caffè pagato*. I don't like this. *Why is it paid for?* For the relatives I disclosed? Because I am from the area, and I am speaking dialect? For my surname …? *Why?*

I am uncomfortable. I want to leave. We leave. *Thanks*, but he doesn't reply. Odd. He has already left from behind the counter, without even saying goodbye.

The other men do say goodbye, quite cheerfully, instead.

Could it be just sheer generosity?
Or is it some sort of control?

Is it recognition, perhaps?
Or is it a debt of gratitude for the future?
A statement of authority?
Or just a welcome to the village?

Look, we are nice people, just take this.
He didn't say it, but he might as well have said that.
The problem lies in the fact that I doubt the gesture.
The sternness of the mountain in his eyes.

Getting out of there feels quick and rushed. I want to go. We saw two or three motorbikes already around town circling us, going back and forth, looking at us. *Don't be paranoid.* Of course, they notice visitors. Or maybe, they are sentinels; they want to – have to – report back on who we are and where we go.

My mounting paranoia also comes from the answer to that question that I ask myself.

Why the hell am I here, really?

Because I have written about Platì and its links to Australia. Because I have read so much about the 'ndrangheta here. Because I want to see whether I can find a link here, to what I have seen in Griffith.

There is a monument to remember the 1951 flooding and the displacement of people, and the migration, also to Australia.

But truly, I want to *connect*. Deeply connect with this place. I want to unpack; I want to comprehend. I want to understand both condemnations and justifications. Those who fear and those who are feared. The violence and the mitigations. I want to embrace the complexity and I want to find a way to explain it by using difficult words, such as culture, responsibility, society, context.

Why?

Because I belong here.

It's so obvious.

A man on a huge motorbike approaches, speeding behind us on the road to exit Platì. It looks as if he wants to overtake us. He doesn't. He is tailing us. On a road where there is no one else, in both directions, that is odd. We arrive at the end of the road, almost ready to turn right on the Statale 106; he turns around and leaves.

Who is more fearful here?

We don't understand what's happening and whether there is anything to fear.

They, whoever *they* are, don't understand why we are here and whether we represent some sort of threat.

Aspromonte has always felt too big to exist, too big to be contained in this part of Calabria. I used to look at the map as a child and couldn't see it, it's not possible, *it's too big to actually be where they say it is*. There must be a portal or something, to another – larger – dimension.

Aspromonte has eyes everywhere, that's what Nonna used to say, that the mountain had eyes everywhere, so there's nothing to fear because you'll always be seen.

And on the road to Polsi, on the way to Platì, I still feel those eyes. I have learned these are eyes that could kill. But to me, the mountain is just beautiful, and I feel as I felt when I was a child, just protected – when trotting up to the big fountain to get water, or getting lost to pick up blackberries. Nothing to fear, not even the ominous echo, not even the wild animals, not even the cliffs and the deep ravines full of falling rocks.

★★★

From within, I have known this mountain. Looking at it, and looked at by it, while living the rest of my life.

My memories.

My grandmother bent over the *gibbiola* – the stone-made water basin where she used to do the laundry. Half of her life was spent bent over that basin, washing clothes. Little Anna sitting there, on the short rock wall, just chatting, keeping her company.

My grandfather coming back from farming every day and Little Anna running towards him to bring him clean shoes.

Walking on the main street of Santa Cristina, 20 or even 30 years later, and still wondering whether someone has finally bought that beautiful villa with the green shutters overlooking the main square.

And walking in front of the Crai grocery shop. Adult Anna wonders whether people here still call it the *Tabacchino*, as was always the case before, even if it didn't just sell tobacco. Still there, anyway, with the letters worn off by weather and time.

A lot of dust, a lot of blood somewhere around here, tears, and that insignificant yet universal pain; a lot of real or fake changes.

The routine of my mountain – which never looked as if it could ever change.

And I left.

My journeys.

So much I have not been able to write about. About Calabria, about the 'ndrangheta, about the travels, *theirs* and mine.

Chasing *it* around the world, chasing myself, in the process.

Calabria, its struggles, traditions, festivals, blood, drugs, food, sea, sunsets, stones, rocks, unfinished buildings, breathtaking beauty, garbage.

Aspromonte, its Madonnas, litanies, interrupted roads, tears, eyes, violence, hopes, remoteness, authenticity, throats, winding curves, rivers, rises, descents, guilt, responsibility, condemnations.

Australia, its misunderstood religion, drugs, migrants, identities, enclaves, ethics, lack of ethics, politics, economy.

North America, its opportunities, smirks, fake freedom, real freedom, cold winters, hot summers, success, failure.

Europe, its opportunities, profits, calculations, rationality, money, drugs.

And me, my questions, doubts, confusion, frustration, challenges, ideals, lack of ideals, normality, exceptions.

I still blow bubbles when in Aspromonte. To give lightness to places that often feel too heavy.

Between bubbles and poetry, there is complexity.

I am again, as always, reminded of my favourite excerpt in T.S. Eliot's *Four Quartets.*[1]

> *We shall not cease from exploration*
> *And the end of all our exploring*
> *Will be to arrive where we started*
> *And know the place for the first time.*
> *Through the unknown, remembered gate*
> *When the last of earth left to discover*
> *Is that which was the beginning;*
> *At the source of the longest river*
> *The voice of the hidden waterfall*
> *And the children in the apple-tree*
> *Not known, because not looked for*
> *But heard, half-heard, in the stillness*
> *Between two waves of the sea.*

This quote resounds, as a litany, inside me.

I had to start *here.*

I shall continue from *here.*

Notes

Chapter 1

[1] M. Kundera, *Testaments Betrayed* (New York: Harcourt, 1995), p. 128.

[2] A. Sergi, 'Three tales /two threats: prosecutors in Italy, England and the United States narrate national and transnational organised crime', in P.C. Van Duyne, M. Sheinost, G.A. Antonopoulos, J. Harvey and K. Von Lampe (eds) *Narrative on Organised Crime in Europe: Criminals, Corrupters & Policy* (Oisterwijk: Wolf Legal Publishers, 2016).

[3] M. Levi, *Reflections on Organised Crime: Patterns and Control* (Oxford: Blackwell, 1998), p. 336.

[4] C.H. Cooley, *Human Nature and Conduct* (New York: Scribners, 1922).

[5] T. Scheff, 'Goffman on emotions: the pride–shame system', *Symbolic Interaction*, 37(1) (2014): 108–121.

[6] J. Mead, P. Berger and T. Luckman *The Social Construction of Reality* (London: Penguin, 1967).

[7] F. Nietzsche, *Beyond Good and Evil*, chapter 4 (London: Penguin Classics, 2003 [1886]).

[8] T. Hirschi, *Causes of Delinquency* (Berkeley, CA: University of California Press, 1969).

[9] L. Holmes, *Terrorism, Organised Crime and Corruption: Networks and Linkages* (Cheltenham: Edward Elgar, 2007).

[10] D. Gambetta, *The Sicilian Mafia: The Business of Private Protection* (Cambridge, MA: Harvard University Press, 1993).

[11] L. Paoli, *Mafia Brotherhoods: Organized Crime, Italian Style* (Oxford: Oxford University Press, 2008).

[12] P. Arlacchi and M.H. Ryle, *Mafia Business: The Mafia Ethics and the Spirit of Capitalism* (Oxford: Oxford University Press, 1998); V. Scalia, 'From the octopus to the spider's web: the transformations of the Sicilian mafia under postfordism', *Trends in Organized Crime*, 13(4) (2010): 283–298.

[13] F. Calderoni, 'The structure of drug trafficking mafias: the 'ndrangheta and cocaine', *Crime, Law and Social Change*, 58(3) (2012): 321–349.

[14] R. Siebert, *Mafia Women: The Affirmation of a Female Pseudo-Subject. The Case of the 'Ndrangheta* (New York: Springer, 2007); O. Ingrascì, *Gender and Organised Crime in Italy: Women's Agency in Italian Mafias* (London: Bloomsbury, 2021).

[15] P. Pinotti, 'The economic costs of organized crime: evidence from Southern Italy' (Banca d'Italia, 2012); B. Çayli, 'Social networks of the Italian mafia: the strong and weak parts', *CEU Political Science Journal*, 3 (2010): 382–412; C. Superti, 'Addiopizzo: can a label defeat the Mafia?', *Journal of International Policy Solutions*, 11(4) (2009): 3–11.

[16] N. Dalla Chiesa, *La convergenza: Mafia e politica nella Seconda Repubblica* (Milan: Melampo, 2010); E.U. Savona, M. Riccardi and G. Berlusconi (eds), *Organised Crime in European Businesses* (London: Routledge, 2016).

17 S. Lupo Cose Nostre, 'Mafia siciliana e mafia americana', in P. Bevilacqua, A. De Clementi and E. Franzina (eds) *Storia di Emigrazione Italiana* (Milan: Donzelli, 2002); J.S. Albanese, 'The Italian–American mafia', in L. Paoli (ed.) *The Oxford Handbook of Organized Crime* (Oxford: Oxford University Press, 2014).

18 F. Varese, *Mafias on the Move: How Organized Crime Conquers New Territories* (Princeton, NJ: Princeton University Press, 2011); F. Allum, *The Invisible Camorra: Neapolitan Crime Families across Europe* (Ithaca, NY: Cornell University Press, 2016).

19 A. Sergi, 'What's in a name? Shifting identities of traditional organized crime in Canada in the transnational fight against the Calabrian 'Ndrangheta', *Canadian Journal of Criminology and Criminal Justice*, 60(4) (2018): 427–454.

20 A. Sergi, 'The evolution of the Australian 'ndrangheta: an historical perspective', *Australian & New Zealand Journal of Criminology*, 48(2) (2015): 155–174; A. Sergi, 'Polycephalous 'ndrangheta: crimes, behaviours and organisation of the Calabrian mafia in Australia', *Australian & New Zealand Journal of Criminology*, 51(1) (2019): 3–22; A. Sergi, 'The 'ndrangheta down under: constructing the Italian mafia in Australia', *European Review of Organised Crime*, 5(1) (2019): 60–84.

21 R. Sciarrone and L. Storti, 'The territorial expansion of mafia-type organized crime: the case of the Italian mafia in Germany', *Crime, Law and Social Change*, 61(1) (2014): 37–60.

22 C. Visconti, *'La mafia è dappertutto: Falso!'* (Bari: Laterza, 2016).

23 G.T. Di Lampedusa, *Il Gattopardo* (Milan: Feltrinelli, 1958), p. 51.

24 A. Sergi, *From Mafia to Organised Crime: A Comparative Analysis of Policing Models* (London: Palgrave Macmillan, 2017).

25 G. Dworkin, *Morality, Harm and the Law* (Boulder, CO: Westview Press, 1994).

26 Sergi, *From Mafia to Organised Crime*.

27 M.S. Moore, *Placing Blame: A Theory of Criminal Law* (Oxford: Oxford University Press, 1997); M. Cancio Meliá, 'The wrongfulness of crimes of unlawful association', *New Criminal Law Review*, 11 (2008): 563–585.

28 A. Sergi, 'Scilla', in A. Lynes, C. Kelly and J. Treadwell (eds), *Dark Destinations: A Criminological Analysis of Contemporary Tourism* (Bristol: Bristol University Press, 2023, forthcoming).

29 N. Whithorn, 'Translating the mafia: legal translation issues and strategies', *The Journal of Specialised Translation*, 22 (2014): 157–173; G. Calienda and G. Scotto Di Carlo, 'The importance of Italian Mafia "culturemes" and their translation in the harmonisation of EU Anti-Mafia Legislation', *International Journal of Language Studies*, 13(4) (2019): 105–124.

30 D. Katan, 'Translation as intercultural communication', in J. Munday (ed.) *The Routledge Companion to Translation Studies* (Abingdon: Routledge, 2009), p. 9.

31 A. Sergi, 'The Italian anti-mafia system between practice and symbolism: evaluating contemporary views on the Italian structure model against organized crime', *Policing: A Journal of Policy and Practice*, 10(3) (2016): 194–205.

32 Whithorn, 'Translating the mafia'.

33 J.L. Albini, *The American Mafia: Genesis of a Legend* (New York: Appleton-Century-Crofts, 1971).

34 N. Harney, *Eh Paesan! Being Italian in Toronto* (Toronto: University of Toronto Press, 1998).

35 Processo Aemilia [Trial Aemilia], https:// www.processoaemilia.com

36 L. Paoli, 'An underestimated criminal phenomenon: the Calabrian 'ndrangheta', *European Journal of Crime, Criminal Law and Criminal Justice* 3 (1994): 212–238.

37 'Locri ricorda Francesco Fortugno ucciso dalla 'ndrangheta 16 anni fa', Ilario Bali, *LaCNews*, 16 October 2021, https://www.lacnews24.it/cronaca/locri-ricorda-francesco-fortugno-ucciso-dalla--ndrangheta-sedici-anni-fa_144396/

[38] 'A mafia family feud spills over', Stephanie Holmes, *BBC News*, 16 August 2007, http://news.bbc.co.uk/2/hi/europe/6949274.stm

[39] Paoli, *Mafia Brotherhoods*.

[40] A. Sergi and P. Sergi, *La Santa 'Ndrangheta: Da Violenta a Contesa* (Cosenza: Luigi Pellegrini Editori, 2021).

[41] Tribunale di Reggio Calabria, Sezione GIP-GUP, Sentenza 1 March 2018, DDA, RG GIP-GUP 663/2017 RG NR 6859/2016, NE. 80196, p. 196.

[42] Tribunale di Reggio Calabria, Sezione GIP-GUP, Sentenza 1 March 2018, p. 203.

[43] E. Ciconte, *'Ndranghet* (Soveria Mannelli: Rubbettino, 2011).

[44] G. Sorgonà, 'Società e 'ndrangheta: Il caso Reggio Calabria', *Laboratoire italien*, 22 (2019), https://journals.openedition.org/laboratoireitalien/2989?lang=it

[45] M. Casaburi, *Borghesia mafiosa: La 'ndrangheta dalle origini ai giorni nostri* (Bari: Dedalo, 2010).

[46] A. Sergi and A. Lavorgna, *'Ndrangheta: The Global Dimensions of the Most Powerful Italian Mafia* (London: Palgrave Macmillan, 2016).

[47] DNA, 'Relazione annuale sulle attività svolte dal Procuratore nazionale e dalla Direzione nazionale antimafia e antiterrorismo nonché sulle dinamiche e strategie della criminalità organizzata di tipo mafioso nel periodo 1° luglio 2015 – 30 giugno 2016' (Rome: Direzione Nazionale Antimafia e Antiterrorismo, 2017), p. 7.

[48] DNA, 'Relazione annuale sulle attività svolte dal Procuratore nazionale e dalla Direzione nazionale antimafia e antiterrorismo, p. 3.

[49] Storia, 'Fermo di indiziato di delitto e sequestro preventivo in via d'urgenza, Procura della Repubblica presso il Tribunale di Reggio Calabria, DDA', 'Operation Cento Anni di Storia', No. 6268/06 RGNR DDA, p. 20.

[50] Operazione Minotauro, Tribunale di Torino sezione dei giudici per le indagini preliminari – Ordinanza di applicazione della misura cautelare della custodia in carcere, no. 6161/2007 RGNR DDA, p. 81.

[51] Operazione Maglio III, Tribunale di Genova, Sezione dei giudici per le indagini preliminari – Ordinanza applicativa di misura cautelare coercitiva, No. 2268/10/21 RGNR DDA + No. 4644/11 RG GIP, p. 60.

[52] M. Catino, *Mafia Organizations: The Visible Hand of Criminal Enterprises* (Cambridge: Cambridge University Press, 2019).

[53] As cited in Sergi and Sergi, *La Santa 'Ndrangheta*, p. 118.

[54] T.S. Eliot, from 'Little Gidding', *Four Quartets* (London: Faber and Faber, 2001), originally published 1943.

[55] T. DeGloma, 'Awakenings: autobiography, memory, and the social logic of personal discovery', *Sociological Forum*, 25(3) (2010): 519–540.

Chapter 2

[1] 'Migration Heritage Centre, 1948 Griffith Lady of Loreto Statue', Crown copyright 2008, - http://www.migrationheritage.nsw.gov.au/exhibition/objectsthroughtime/statue/index.html – Platì is spelled Plati in the original.

[2] R.K.C. Pesman, *A History of Italian Settlement in NSW* (Parramatta: NSW Heritage Office, 1998).

[3] 'Migration Heritage Centre, 1948 Griffith Lady of Loreto Statue', Crown copyright 2008, http://www.migrationheritage.nsw.gov.au/exhibition/objectsthroughtime/statue/index.html

[4] P. Sergi, 'Nel cuore Platì' dove l'Italia appare lontana', *La Repubblica*, 28 August 1994.

[5] E. Ciconte and V. Macrì, *Australian 'Ndrangheta* (Soveria Mannelli: Rubbettino, 2009).

6   J.S. MacDonald and L.D. MacDonald, 'Chain migration ethnic neighborhood formation and social networks', *Milbank Memorial Fund Quarterly* 42(1) (1964): 82–97.

7   Pochi and Minister for Immigration and Ethnic Affairs [1979] AATA 64 (24 May 1979).

8   Pochi and Minister for Immigration and Ethnic Affairs.

9   'Australian mafia don Tony Sergi dies without being charged over Don Mackay's death', Riley Stuart and Moyra Shields, 31 October 2017, *Australian Broadcasting News*, https://www.abc.net.au/news/2017-11-01/mafia-don-tony-sergi-dies-in-griffith/9106258

10 'Griffith Memorial 1916–2016', http://www.griffith2016.com.au/cp_themes/default/page.asp?p=DOC-QMV-64-58-30 [webpage inactive since 2022]

11 'Griffith farewells local hero Domenico Sergi by Rebecca Hopper', 6 October 2016, *The Area News*, https://www.areanews.com.au/story/4211070/doms-charitable-tradition-lives-on/

12 Sergi and Minister for Immigration and Ethnic Affairs [1979] AATA 51 (10 May 1979).

13 Sergi and Minister for Immigration and Ethnic Affairs [1979] AATA 51 (10 May 1979).

14 Sergi and Minister for Immigration and Ethnic Affairs [1979] AATA 51 (10 May 1979).

15 Barbaro and Minister for Immigration and Ethnic Affairs [1980] AATA 76 (17 December 1980).

16 Barbaro and Minister for Immigration and Ethnic Affairs [1980] AATA 76 (17 December 1980).

17 Sergi, 'Polycephalous 'ndrangheta'.

18 Report Mr Justice Williams, *Australian Royal Commission of Inquiry into Drugs*, 21 December 1979, from paragraph A344.

19 Barbaro and Minister for Immigration and Ethnic Affairs [1980] AATA 76 (17 December 1980).

20 R v Sergi [1999] NSWSC 728 (19 July 1999).

21 Ciconte, *'Ndrangheta*.

22 H. Hess, *Mafia & Mafiosi: Origin, Power and Myth* (Adelaide: Crawford House Publishing, 1998 [1973]), p. 153.

23 A. Sergi, 'Stumbling upon places and cultures: an involuntary ethnography in researching the Australian 'ndrangheta', *Journal of Criminology*, 54(4) (2021): 448–465.

24 F. Ricatti, *Italians in Australia* (London: Palgrave Macmillan, 2018).

25 J. Cornwall, *Fruits of Our Labour: The History of Griffith's Italian Community* (Griffith: NSW Migration Heritage Centre and Griffith City Council, 2007).

26 L. Baldassar and R. Pesman, *From Paesani to Global Italians: Veneto Migrants in Australia* (Crawley: University of Western Australia Press, 2005).

27 Sergi, 'Polycephalous 'ndrangheta'.

28 S. Bennett, 'Undesirable Italians: Prolegomena for a history of the Calabrian 'ndrangheta in Australia', *Modern Italy*, 21(1) (2016): 83–99; Ricatti, *Italians in Australia*.

29 N. McCubben, 'Living Cultural Diversity in Regional NSW,' Proceedings, 'Everyday Multiculturalism Conference', Centre for Research on Social Inclusion, Macquarie University, 2007; D. Phillips, *Community Profile: A Guide to the Community Welfare Needs in the Griffith Area* (Wade Shire Council, 1981).

30 S. Marino, 'Ethnic identity and race: the "double absence" and its legacy across generations among Australians of Southern Italian origin. Operationalizing institutional positionality', *Ethnic and Racial Studies*, 42(5) (2019): 707–725.

31 A. Vannucci, 'Imperfette Simbiosi. 'Protezione, Corruzione, Estorsione, tra Mafia e Politica', in M. Santoro (ed.) *Riconoscere le Mafie: Cosa sono, come funzionano, come si muovono* (Bologna: Il Mulino, 2015).

32 Sergi, 'The 'ndrangheta down under'.

33 Report Mr Justice Williams, *Australian Royal Commission of Inquiry into Drugs*, 21 December 1979, p. 154.

34 'Italy convicts local Mafia', Nick McKenzie, Richard Baker and Jo McKenna, 16 June 2012, *The Sydney Morning Herald*, https://www.smh.com.au/national/italy-convicts-local-mafia-20120615-20fok.html

35 'Italy convicts local Mafia'.

36 Medici v The Queen [2013] VSCA 111 (14 May 2013).

37 D. Marratt, *Undercover* (New York: HarperCollins, 2005).

38 J. Morton and S. Lobez, *Gangland Australia* (Melbourne: Victory Books, 2010).

39 National Archives of Australia (NAA), Camorra, Black Hand, Mafia, Mano Nero Society, Volume 1, p. 27.

40 Mildura Club Da Vinci, https://www.milduraclubdavinci.com.au/history

41 Extract from Hansard [ASSEMBLY – Wednesday, 20 June 2012] p4100a-4117a – Mr Paul Papalia; Mr Frank Alban; Ms Rita Saffioti; Dr Tony Buti; Mr Tom Stephens; Mr Mark McGowan; Dr Kim Hames; Mr Michael Sutherland; Mr Rob Johnson; Mr Ben Wyatt; Mr Peter Abetz; Mr David Templeman – World War II Internment Camps.

42 G. Rando, 'Italo-Australians during the Second World War: some perceptions of internment', *Italian Studies in Southern Africa*, 18(1) (2005): 20–51.

43 'Big support for briscola', Nicolette Barbas, 15 October 2019, *Harvey-Waroona Reporter*, https://www.harveyreporter.com.au/news/harvey-waroona-reporter/big-support-for-briscola-ng-b881346308z

Chapter 3

1 E. Ciconte, *Riti Criminali* (Soveria Mannelli: Rubbettino, 2015).

2 F. Carabellese and C. Zelano, 'Il fenomeno dei sequestri di persona in Italia', *Rassegna Italiana di Criminologia*, 1(3) (2007): 55–76.

3 F. Veltri, *Sequestri: La Trattative Stato-'Ndrangheta* (Reggio Calabria: Città del Sole Edizioni, 2019).

4 Ciconte, *'Ndrangheta*.

5 Tribunale di Locri, n° 100/95, Sentenza nei confronti di Barbaro Francesco + 49, 4 novembre 1995 (aka sentenza 'Aspromonte').

6 Commissione Parlamentare d'inchiesta sul Fenomeno della Mafia e delle Altre Associazioni Criminali Similari – *Relazione sui sequestri di persona a scopo di estorsione* (Relatore: sen. Pardini) – approvata dalla Commissione il 7 October 1998.

7 Sergi and Sergi, *La Santa 'Ndrangheta*.

8 This reconstruction, albeit not referring to any specific case, is representative of the majority of them. It is, in fact, the product of several stories of kidnapped victims, whose details often converge in what is said here – these details are taken from the news, from books by Sergi, Veltri and Ciconte, and from court files.

9 'Madonna della Montagna, il vescovo Oliva: "Polsi non va accostata alla 'ndrangheta"', Redazione, *Reggio Today*, 2 September 2019, https://www.reggiotoday.it/cronaca/polsi-vescovo-francesco-oliva-.html

10 San Luca, 'Don Pino Strangio si dimette da parroco dopo la condanna in Gotha', Redazione, LaCNews, 6 August 2021, https://www.lacnews24.it/cronaca/san-luca-don-pino-strangio-si-dimette-da-parroco-dopo-la-condanna-in-gotha_140800/

11 S. Cohen, *States of Denial: Knowing about Atrocities and Suffering* (Cambridge: Polity Press, 2001).

12 C. Lawther, *Truth, Denial and Transition: Northern Ireland and the Contested Past* (London: Routledge, 2018).

13 R. Terdiman, *Present Past: Modernity and the Memory Crisis* (Ithaca, NY: Cornell University Press, 1993).

14 A. Talia, *Statale 106: Viaggio sulle strade segrete della 'ndrangheta* (Rome: Minimum Fax, 2019).

15 C. Turner, *Violence, Law and the Impossibility of Transitional Justice* (London: Routledge, 2016).

16 S. Amerio and A. Sergi, 'Le nuove forme di intimidazione ambientale, Il Diritto Vivente', *Rivista Quadrimestrale di Magistratura Indipendente*, 2020, https://www.rivistaildirittovive nte.it/le-nuove-forme-di-intimidazione-ambientale.htm

17 A. Placanica, 'L'identità del meridionale', *Meridiana*, 32 (1998): 153–182; Mayo P. Gramsci, 'Gramsci, la questione meridionale e il Mediterraneo', in G. Schirru (ed.) *Gramsci, le culture e il mondo* (Rome: Viella, 2011), pp. 209–224; J. Schneider (ed.), *Italy's 'Southern Question': Orientalism in One Country* (London: Routledge, 1998).

18 G. Hirschberger, 'Collective trauma and the social construction of meaning', *Frontiers in Psychology*, 9(1441) (2018): 1–4.

19 Sergi and Sergi, *La Santa 'Ndrangheta*.

20 Casaburi, *Borghesia mafiosa*.

21 C. Barbieri and V. Mete, 'Kidnappings by the 'ndrangheta: characteristics, institutional countermeasures and turning points', *Modern Italy*, 26(4) (2021): 425–444.

22 Carabellese and Zelano, *Il fenomeno dei sequestri di persona*.

23 https://www.repubblica.it/online/fatti/stabi/stabi/stabi.html

24 Ordinanza di custodia cautelare in carcere – Procedimento Penale n. 73989/10 R.G.N.R., Tribunale di Milano – Ufficio GIP, 11 March 2014.

25 E. Ciconte, *Ndrangheta Padana* (Soveria Mannelli: Rubbettino, 2010); N. Dalla Chiesa and M. Panzarasa, *Buccinasco, la 'ndrangheta la nord* (Turin: Einaudi, 2012).

26 Stenografico – Audizione Camera dei Deputati, Allegato A – Seduta n. 406 del 17/9/1998: http://leg13.camera.it/_dati/leg13/lavori/stenografici/sed406/aurg04.htm

27 P. Arlacchi, *La Mafia Imprenditrice* (Bologna: Il Mulino, 1983).

28 S. Amerio and A. Sergi, 'Dov'è finita la violenza mafiosa? Profili giurisprudenziali sulle nuove forme di intimidazione ambientale', *Studi sulla questione criminale online* (2021), https://studiquestionecriminale.wordpress.com/2020/12/02/dove-finita-la-violenza-mafi osa-profili-giurisprudenziali-sulle-nuove-forme-di-intimidazione-ambientale/

29 Relazione Annuale Sulla 'Ndrangheta (Relatore: Francesco Forgione) Approvata dalla Commissione nella seduta del 19 February 2008, p. 57.

30 Lamerica is a slang word, spoken mostly in the last century, to mean L'America, the America – used by migrants and their families to indicate broadly the United States and Canada.

31 D. Gambetta, *The Sicilian Mafia: The Business of Private Protection* (Boston, MA: Harvard University Press, 1996).

32 A. Blok, *The Mafia of a Sicilian Village 1860–1960: A Study of Violent Peasant Entrepreneurs* (Oxford: Basil Blackwell, 1974).

33 A. Brown, N. Kouri and W. Hirst, 'Memory's malleability: its role in shaping collective memory and social identity', *Frontiers in Psychology*, 3(257) (2012): 1–3.

34 Sergi, *From Mafia to Organised Crime*.

Chapter 4

1 'From St Kilda To Kings Cross', by Paul Kelly, 1985, Australia, Copyright © – Mushroom Records Pty. Ltd.

2 'From St Kilda To Kings Cross'.

3 A. Dijana, 'Shifting grounds: identity politics and Sydney's ethnic clubs', in A. Brown and A. Leach (eds) *Proceedings of the Society of Architectural Historians* (Australia and New Zealand, Gold Coast, Qld: Sahanz, 2013), p. 158.

4 'Mafia cash-for-visa scandal', Nick McKenzie and Richard Baker, *The Sydney Morning Herald*, 23 February 2009, https://www.smh.com.au/national/mafia-cashforvisa-scandal-20090222-8eoz.html

5 Four Corners, Fairfax Media, 'The mafia in Australia, 2015', https://www.abc.net.au/4corners/the-mafia-in-australia-part-one-promo/6573130

6 Bracher v Club Marconi and 12 Ors [1999] NSWSC 1193 (8 December 1999).

7 Bracher v Club Marconi and 12 Ors [1999] NSWSC 1193 (8 December 1999).

8 Labbozzetta v Director of Liquor and Gaming [1999] NSWSC 96 (23 February 1999).

9 'Wog Bashing lives on, claim Eels', *News Australia*, 17 August 2009, https://www.news.com.au/news/wog-bashing-lives-on-claim-eels/news-story/356b61b98cf6b3b1622b2c1c61b05a22?sv=ec1d8bd05a8c0379feb9e73f59ecda68

10 'Talk about the pot calling the kettle black', Kate McClymont, *The Sydney Morning Herald*, 28 February 2009, https://www.smh.com.au/national/talk-about-the-pot-calling-the-kettle-black-20090227-8k8z.html

11 'Mafia deeply entrenched in Australia', Jo McKenna, *The Sydney Morning Herald*, 15 March 2010, https://www.smh.com.au/national/mafia-deeply-entrenched-in-australia-20100314-q67f.html

12 Tribunale Ordinario di Roma – Sezione dei Giudici per le Indagini Preliminari – Ufficio 27 – RGNR No. 1348/08þ1895/08þ10379/08 R.GIP – Decreto di Archiviazione.

13 Transcripts of Operation Credo, ICAC Public Hearing, No. E12/2107/0821PUB02924, 1 May 2014, https://www.icac.nsw.gov.au/docman/transcripts/credo-spicer/4349-01-05-2014-operation-credo-spicer-transcript-pp-02924-03011-from-10-04am-to-12-52pm/file

14 'Labor mayor dined with developers', Wendy Frew, *Bega District News*, 9 October 2008, https://www.bombalatimes.com.au/story/816341/labor-mayor-dined-with-developers/

15 'ICAC Operation Credo finds Obeid, Tripodi, Kelly engaged in corrupt conduct, by Louise Hall and Sarah Gerathy', *ABC News*, 3 August 2017, http://www.abc.net.au/news/2017-08-03/icac-credo-findings-corrupt-conduct-obeid-tripodi-kelly/8769534

16 'Media Alert: Public inquiry into alleged attempts by the former Hon Edward Obeid MLC to influence official functions over Circular Quay retail leases, and other matters, starts Monday, Independent Commission Against Corruption', 23 October 2013, https://web.archive.org/web/20131111000938/http://www.icac.nsw.gov.au/investigations/current-investigations/article/4428 – The Obeid scandal is an infamous case of corruption and abuse of political power for private gain in Australian history.

17 Inaugural speech, Mr Joe Tripodi MP (Public Health Amendment (Tobacco) Bill 1996). Parliament of New South Wales, 30 April 1996.

18 'Tripodi behind trouble at Calabria club, court told', Kate McKlymont, *The Sydney Morning Herald*, 4 October 2012, https://www.smh.com.au/national/nsw/tripodi-behind-trouble-at-calabria-club-court-told-20121003-26zsk.html

19 In the matter of Calabria Community Club Ltd [2013] NSWSC 998 (26 July 2013).

20 In the matter of Calabria Community Club Ltd [2013].

21 'The ex-con, the CEO and the dodgy invoice', Kate McClymont, *The Sydney Morning Herald*, 12 July 2021, https://www.smh.com.au/national/the-ex-con-the-ceo-and-the-dodgy-invoice-20210709-p588ef.html

22 'Pillar who put dark past behind him', Debra Jopson and Gerard Ryle, *The Sydney Morning Herald*, 30 August 2006, https://www.smh.com.au/national/pillar-who-put-dark-past-behind-him-20060830-gdoa7l.html

23 Corte di Cassazione, Sezioni Unite Penali, no. 36958, 11 October 2021.

24 Sergi and Sergi, *La Santa 'Ndrangheta*.

25 C. Young, *The Politics of Cultural Pluralism* (Madison: University of Wisconsin Press, 1976).

26   T. Waters, 'Towards a theory of ethnic identity and migration: the formation of ethnic enclaves by migrant Germans in Russia and North America', *International Migration Review*, 29(2) (1995): 515–544.

27   M. Granovetter, 'Economic action and social structure: the problem of embeddedness', *American Journal of Sociology*, 91(3) (1985): 481–510.

28   J. Krase and C. Lacerra, *Ethnicity and Machine Politics* (Lanham, MD: University Press of America, 1991).

29   R.K. Merton, *Social Theory and Social Structure* (Chicago, IL: Free Press, 1957).

30   J.W. Salaff, A. Greve, W. Siu-Lun and L. Xu Li Ping, 'Ethnic entrepreneurship, social networks, and the enclave', in B. Yeoh T. Chee Kiong and M. Walter Charney (eds) *Approaching Transnationalism: Transnational Societies, Multicultural Contacts, and Imaginings of Home* (Boston, MA: Kluwer Academic Publishers, 2003).

31   'From St Kilda to Kings Cross'.

32   'Lygon Street Meltdown', by Melbourne Ska Orchestra, 2013 Copyright ©ABC Music.

33   'Lygon Street Meltdown'.

34   'Lygon Street Meltdown'.

35   Sergi, 'The 'ndrangheta down under'.

36   National Archives of Australia (NAA) Bundle Series Number A6980, Control Symbol S250529, Barcode: 7116944 – Allegations of Mafia Activities – Victoria Markets – p. 54 onwards.

37   National Archives, A6980.

38   National Archives, A6980.

39   National Archives, A6980.

40   Sergi, 'The evolution of the Australian 'ndrangheta'.

41   National Archives of Australia (NAA) Bundle Series Number A6980, Control Symbol S250529, Barcode: 7116944 – Allegations of Mafia Activities – Victoria Markets – p. 37.

42   Operation Cerberus – Intelligence concerning XXX (Informant name) – Italian Criminal Organisation, Debriefing of Informer XXX (1989) – Confidential.

43   Operazione Siderno Group – Tribunale di Locri, Sentence 6 April 1996 + Corte d'Appello di Reggio Calabria Sentence 24 July 1998.

44   Operation Cerberus, Debriefing of Informer XXX (1989).

45   Processo a carico di Rocco Schirripa per l'omicidio del Procuratore della Repubblica di Torino Bruno Caccia – udienze in 2017, https://www.radioradicale.it/soggetti/184 964/domenico-agresta

46   'Mafia on the move: How the 'ndrangheta came to Australia', Connie Agius, 1 October 2017, https://www.abc.net.au/radionational/programs/backgroundbriefing/mafia-on-the-move-how-the-ndrangheta-came-to-australia/8995964

47   Prosecutor Pennisi interviews Annunziatino Romeo, 16 May 1996, Appendix no. 523 to Operation Mandamento Ionico, Proc. Pen. 1095/2010 R.G.N.R. D.D.A., Procura della Repubblica presso Tribunale di Reggio Calabria.

48   'Blitz contro la 'ndrangheta: tra i 13 arrestati Antonio e Rocco Barbaro, di Stefano Zanette, Il Giorno (Pavia)', 10 January 2022, https://www.ilgiorno.it/pavia/cronaca/blitz-contro-la-ndrangheta-tra-i-13-arrestati-antonio-e-rocco-barbaro-1.7232594

49   'Tribunale di Milano, Sezione GIP, Ordinanza di applicazione di misure cautelari personali, RGNR 38565/19; RGGIP23084/19', p. 78.

50   A. Sergi, ''Ndrangheta dynasties: a conceptual and operational framework for the cross-border policing of the Calabrian mafia', *Policing: A Journal of Policy and Practice*, 15(2) (2021): 1522–1536.

[51] J. Kansikas and M. Nemilentsev, 'Understanding family dynasty: nurturing the corporate identity across generations', *International Journal of Business Science and Applied Management*, 5(3) (2010): 1–21.

[52] J. Tokarczyk, E. Hansen, M. Green and J. Down, 'A resource-based view and market orientation theory examination of the role of "familiness" in family business success', *Family Business Review*, 20(1) (2007): 17–31.

[53] H.E. Aldrich and J.E. Cliff, 'The pervasive effects of family on entrepreneurship: toward a family embeddedness perspective', *Journal of Business Venturing*, 18 (2003): 573–596.

[54] P.D. Olson, V.S. Zuiker, S.M. Danes, K. Stafford, R.K.Z. Heck and K.A. Duncan, 'The impact of family and the business on family business sustainability', *Journal of Business Venturing*, 18 (2003): 639–666; T.G. Habbershon, M.L. Williams and I. MacMillan, 'Familiness: a unified systems theory of family business performance', *Journal of Business Venturing*, 18(4) (2003): 451–465.

[55] D.T. Jaffe and S.H. Lane, 'Sustaining a family dynasty: key issues facing complex multigenerational business- and investment-owning families', *Family Business Review*, 17(1) (2004): 81–98.

[56] See background in Madafferi v The Queen [2021] VSCA 1 (15 January 2021).

[57] Karam v The Queen [2015] VSCA 50 (31 March 2015); DPP v Agresta [2014] VCC 2328 (11 September 2014); DPP v Karam and Ors [2013] VSC 133 (30 April 2013).

[58] DPP v Karam and Ors [2013] VSC 133 (30 April 2013).

[59] For a summary see Operation Mandamento Ionico, Proc. Pen. 1095/2010 RGNR. D.D.A., Procura della Repubblica presso Tribunale di Reggio Calabria.

[60] Note no. 01333/Criminalpol 5 November 1984.

[61] Administrative Appeals Tribunal General Division, VG 752 of 1997, Melbourne Registry, Francesco Madafferi Applicant and Department of Immigration and Multicultural Affairs Respondent – Statement of Wayne Bastin, 12 May 1998.

[62] Administrative Appeals Tribunal General Division, VG 752 of 1997.

[63] 'Joseph Acquaro killing: Pizza boss Tony Madafferi 'prime suspect' in murder hit', Michael Bachelard and Mark Russell, *The Age*, 16 March 2016, https://www.theage.com.au/national/victoria/tony-madafferi-alleged-mafia-don-fails-to-suppress-information-about-alleged-plot-to-kill-joseph-acquaro-20160316-gnktya.html

[64] Final Report of the Royal Commission into the Management of Police Informants, aka 'Lawyer X' (https://www.rcmpi.vic.gov.au) November 2020 – available at https://content.rcmpi.vic.gov.au/sites/default/files/2020-12/0214_RC_Final%20Report_06_Full%20Report_0_0.pdf

[65] R v Crupi [2019] VSC 810 (11 December 2019).

[66] 'Man to stand trial for murder of underworld lawyer Joseph Acquaro', *9News*, 14 November 2019, https://www.9news.com.au/national/joseph-acquaro-man-to-stand-trial-for-victorian-lawyer-murder-news-melbourne/4c2d3fe3-6175-45ff-a436-866779c0f4df

[67] 'Tony Madafferi behind $200,000 bounty on Melbourne lawyer Joseph Acquaro, police told court', Dan Oakes, *ABC News*, 17 March 2016, https://www.abc.net.au/news/2016-03-17/tony-madafferi-behind-bounty-on-melbourne-lawyer-police-say/7254264

[68] Madafferi v The Queen [2021] VSCA 1 (15 January 2021).

[69] Final Report 'Lawyer X'.

[70] Madafferi v The Queen [2021] VSCA 1 (15 January 2021).

[71] Madafferi v The Queen [2021] VSCA 1 (15 January 2021).

[72] R v Crupi [2019] VSC 810 (11 December 2019).

73 'Mafia figure Frank Madafferi to be deported after two decades of trying by immigration', Chris Vadelago, *The Age*, 23 July 2021, https://www.theage.com.au/national/victoria/mafia-figure-frank-madafferi-to-be-deported-after-two-decades-of-trying-by-immigration-20210723-p58cdk.html

74 'Mafia figure Frank Madafferi to be deported after two decades of trying by immigration', *The Age*.

75 'Drug trafficker Francesco Madafferi denied bail on appeal case', Cameron Houston, *The Age*, 2 December 2021, https://www.theage.com.au/national/victoria/drug-trafficker-francesco-madafferi-denied-bail-on-appeal-case-20211202-p59e4c.html

76 'The Mafia, the mountains and the art of holding your tongue', Nick MacKenzie, *The Age*, 8 August 2017, https://www.theage.com.au/national/victoria/the-mafia-the-mountains-and-the-art-of-holding-your-tongue-20170807-gxr15s.html

77 Francesco Madafferi Applicant and Department of Immigration and Multicultural Affairs Respondent – Statement of Wayne Bastin, 12 May 1998.

78 'Mr Antonio (Tony) Madafferi', *The Age*, 2 May 2016, https://www.theage.com.au/national/victoria/mr-antonio-tony-madafferi-20160502-gok6l2.html

79 'Matthew and Madafferi: Opposition Leader Matthew Guy dined with alleged mobster', Nick McKenzie, Richard Baker and Richard Willingham, *The Age*, 7 August 2017, https://www.theage.com.au/national/victoria/matthew-and-madafferi-opposition-leader-matthew-guy-dined-with-alleged-mobster-20170807-gxqsoc.html

80 Matthew and Madafferi: Opposition Leader Matthew Guy dined with alleged mobster, *The Age*.

81 'Apology to Mr Tony De Domenico', *The Age*, 15 May 2020, https://www.theage.com.au/national/victoria/apology-to-mr-tony-de-domenico-20200515-p54tfq.html

82 A. Cordova (n.d.) ''Il Voto di Mafia', *Il Sasso nello Stagno* (1): 7–12.

83 Talia, *Statale 106*.

84 'Court told revenge behind alleged death plot by Francesco Madafferi', *The Sydney Morning Herald*, 23 April 2009, https://www.heraldsun.com.au/news/a-matter-of-revenge/news-story/bae2904060ed4c6c13e135741ef4676c?sv=7424b4dec26e6ad2aabcc15212615ab8

85 Fairfax Media/Four Corners, 'The Mafia in Australia', min. 07 onwards

86 Madafferi v The Queen [2021] VSCA 1 (15 January 2021).

87 Tribunale di Reggio Calabria, Sezione GIP-GUP, Ordinanza di Applicazione di Misure Cautelari, n.408/19 RGNR DDA, n. 2863 RGIP DDA, n. 33/19 ROCC DDA., Op.Eyfhemos.

88 Op. Eyfhemos., p. 1954.

89 Op. Eyfhemos., p. 453, RIT 1603/17 DDA Transcript of the conversation no. 237, session 355 at 12:05 hour of the 04.11.2018, Cosimo Cannizzaro speaking.

90 Op. Eyfhemos., p. 1949, RIT 1603/17 DDA – Transcript of conversation no. 255, session 355, intercepted at 11:54hr on 04.11.2018, Cosimo Cannizzaro speaking.

91 'Two Australians named in Italian court as alleged leaders of the mafia' Nick McKenzie, Chris Vedelago and Gabriella Coslovich, *The Sydney Morning Herald*, 26 February 2020, https://www.smh.com.au/national/two-australians-named-in-italian-court-as-alleged-leaders-of-the-mafia-20200226-p544nw.html

92 Sergi, 'Polycephalous 'ndrangheta'.

93 'Police alleged Madafferi ordered Brighton hit on underworld money man', Chris Vadelago, *The Age*, 15 August 2020, https://www.theage.com.au/national/victoria/police-alleged-madafferi-ordered-brighton-hit-on-underworld-money-man-20200814-p55ly0.html

94 'Two Australians named in Italian court as alleged leaders of the mafia', Nick McKenzie, Chris Vedelago and Gabriella Coslovich, *The Sydney Morning Herald*, 26 February 2020,

https://www.smh.com.au/national/two-australians-named-in-italian-court-as-alleged-leaders-of-the-mafia-20200226-p544nw.html

Chapter 5

1. 'Australia's Peter Lehmann wines sold to Casella, maker of Yellow Tail', Harvet Steiman, *Wine Spectator*, 12 November 2014, https://www.winespectator.com/articles/australias-peter-lehmann-wines-sold-to-casella-maker-of-yellow-tail-50841

2. 'Blackmailer of Casellas sent to jail', Kate McClymont, *Fairfield City Champion*, 25 November 2010, https://www.fairfieldchampion.com.au/story/905836/blackmailer-of-casellas-sent-to-jail/

3. 'Yellow Tail wines brother charged over his alleged involvement in a big drug syndicate', Nick Ralston, *Financial Review*, 13 November 2014, https://www.afr.com/life-and-luxury/food-and-wine/yellow-tail-wines-brother-charged-over-his-alleged-involvement-in-a-big-drug-syndicate-20141113-11lla2

4. Casella v R [2019] NSWCCA 201 (29 August 2019).

5. Fato v R [2017] NSWCCA 190 (11 August 2017).

6. DPP (NSW) v Saverio Ciampa & Pasquale Sergi – 2014/275197.H55889356 & 2014/278237-H56708265, 3 November 2015.

7. Bronze Wing International Pty Ltd v SafeWork NSW [2017] NSWCA 41 (9 March 2017).

8. 'The councillor, the drug boss and the Liberal Party's pot of gold', Kate McClymont, *The Sydney Morning Herald*, 6 July 2020, https://www.smh.com.au/national/nsw/the-councillor-the-drug-boss-and-the-liberal-party-s-pot-of-gold-20200619-p554b8.html

9. John Casella v Fairfax Media Publications Pty Ltd & Ors [2011] NSWSC 1256 (27 October 2011).

10. R v Perre [2019] SASCFC 100 (14 August 2019).

11. Inquest taken on behalf of our Sovereign Lady the Queen at Adelaide in the State of South Australia, on the 6th–30th days of April, 3rd–7th days of May, 31st day of May–18th day of June, 28th–30th days of June, 1st–29th days of July, 10th–13th days of August, and 17th day of September, 1999, before Wayne Cromwell Chivell, a Coroner for the said State, concerning the death of Geoffrey Leigh Bowen (aka 'The Bowen Inquest').

12. The Bowen Inquest.

13. The Bowen Inquest.

14. The Bowen Inquest.

15. 'Domenic Perre pleads not guilty to murder, attempted murder over 1994 NCA bombing', Meagan Dillon, *ABC News*, 17 February 2020, https://www.abc.net.au/news/2020-02-17/domenic-perre-enters-not-guilty-plea-over-nca-bombing-murder/11970926

16. Supreme Court of South Australia, Criminal Jurisdiction; SCCRM 57 of 2020; Queen v Domenic Perre – Prosecution Opening Address, 8 October 2020, pp. 10–11.

17. R v Perre [2019] SASCFC 100 (14 August 2019).

18. See Police v Perre, Remarks on Penalty of Magistrate Chin, 7 April 2017; Perre v Police [2007] SASC 347.

19. 'NCA bombing accused Domenic Perre jailed for cannabis trafficking and firearm offence', Natarsha Kallios, *ABC News*, 22 September 2020, https://www.abc.net.au/news/2020-09-22/nca-bombing-accused-domenic-perre-jailed-for-drug-trafficking/12688892

20. 'NCA bombing suspect's son charged after drug raid', *The Advertiser*, 10 March 2017, https://www.adelaidenow.com.au/subscribe/news/1/?sourceCode=AAWEB_WRE170_a_GGL&dest=https%3A%2F%2Fwww.adelaidenow.com.au%2Fnews%2Flaw-order%2Fnca-bombing-suspects-son-anthong-perre-admits-guilt-over-drug-raid-charges%2Fnews-story%2Fd2066b1ac1a81df57d62359f74fa8350&memtype=anonymous&mode=premium&v21=dynamic-warm-test-score&V21spcbehaviour=append

21 'SA lawyer in hot water after alleged breach of suspension', Tony Zhang, *Lawyers Weekly*, 10 May 2020, https://www.lawyersweekly.com.au/biglaw/28252-sa-lawyer-in-hot-water-after-alleged-breach-of-suspension

22 Inquiry into the Conviction of David Harold Eastman for the Murder of Colin Stanley Winchester – Report of Board of Inquiry Submitted to the Registrar of the Supreme Court of the Australian Capital Territory pursuant to section 428 of the Crimes Act 1900 (ACT) (aka 'Eastman Inquiry') 2014.

23 D. Hamer, 'The Eastman case: implications for an Australian Criminal Cases Review Commission', *Flinders Law Journal*, 17(2) (2016): 433–450.

24 R v Eastman (No 40) [2018] ACTSC 174 (14 June 2018).

25 Exhibit 243 Eastman Inquiry.

26 Exhibit 243 Eastman Inquiry – Operation Peat (1989): 'Suspicion of Calabrian Organised Crime Involvement the Murder of Assistant Commissioner Colin Stanley Winchester'.

27 Exhibit 243 Eastman Inquiry.

28 'Bowen Inquest', p. 48.

29 Supreme Court of Northern Territory, Queen v Antonio Perre, Domenic Romeo, Vincenzo Rocco, Francesco Perre, Antonio Spagnolo, Bruno Musitano, Domenic Vottari, Stavros Smyrneos and Robert John Helps, Sentence, SCC Nos 122 and 140–147, 1993.

30 Exhibit 243 Eastman Inquiry – Operation Peat evidence.

31 Ciconte and Macri, *Australian 'ndrangheta*.

32 Ciconte, *Riti Criminali*.

33 Sergi, 'Polycephalous 'ndrangheta'.

34 Operation Cerberus – Intelligence concerning XXX (Informant name) – Italian Criminal Organisation, Debriefing of Informer XXX (1989) – Confidential.

35 Updated View of Cerberus – A Joint-Agency Overview of Italo-Australian Organised Crime 2000–2002 – Project Conducted by a Joint-Agency Team of analysts from Cerberus Task Force agencies, facilitated by the NCA/ACC, March 2003.

36 Updated View of Cerberus.

37 Updated View of Cerberus.

38 Sergi, 'The 'ndrangheta down under'.

39 D. Brown, 'Italian transnational criminal networks before 1945: a way forward towards better perspectives', *Altreitalie*, 53(2017): 5–28.

40 'A tale of two Pasquale Barbaros - both shot dead', John Silvester, *The Sydney Morning Herald*, 15 November 2016, https://www.smh.com.au/national/a-tale-of-two-pasquale-barbaros--both-shot-dead-20161115-gsq0v8.html

41 R v Sultani; R v Munshizada; R v Baines; R v Danishyar [2021] NSWSC 1654 (17 December 2021).

42 Updated View of Cerberus.

43 Gambetta, *The Sicilian Mafia*.

44 Catino, *Mafia Organizations*.

45 R. Sciarrone, 'Il capitale sociale della mafia: Relazioni esterne e controllo del territorio', *Quaderni di sociologia*, 18 (1998): 51–72.

46 'Queensland police scale back strawberry probe to one full-time detective', Mark Solomons, *The Sydney Morning Herald*, 15 October 2018, https://www.smh.com.au/business/consumer-affairs/queensland-police-scale-back-strawberry-probe-to-one-full-time-detective-20181015-p509ti.html

47 'Charges dropped against Qld woman accused of putting needles into strawberries', Blake Antrobus, *News.com.au*, 14 July 2021, https://www.news.com.au/lifestyle/food/food-warnings/charges-dropped-against-qld-woman-accused-of-putting-needles-into-strawberries/news-story/6a66c9640dc3ab7b5b0b6913cc9b14c4

48 'The family at the centre of new twist in strawberry case', John Silvester, *The Sydney Morning Herald*, 22 September 2018, https://www.smh.com.au/national/new-twist-in-strawberry-case-20180919-p504rq.html

49 'Italian Prosecutors ask for 15 years' imprisonment for Maltese-Australian in 500kg cocaine haul', *Malta Independent*, 25 October 2011, https://www.independent.com.mt/articles/2011-10-25/news/italian-prosecutors-ask-for-15-years-imprisonment-for-maltese-australian-in-500kg-cocaine-haul-300731/

50 Procura della Repubblica presso Tribunale di Reggio Calabria – Direzione Distrettuale Antimafia – Proc. Pen. N. 6268/06 R.G.N.R. DDA Fermo Di Indiziati Di Delitto E Sequestro Preventivo In Via D'urgenza – Operazione 'Centro Anni di Storia', p. 20.

51 'Accused mafia boss "hid in Perth"', Gabrielle Knowles and Grace Millimaci, *PerthNow*, 23 June 2017, https://www.perthnow.com.au/news/wa/accused-mafia-boss-hid-in-perth-ng-32b5186fe730966cbaced88135992ebb

52 Domenico Nirta; Antonio Giorgi; Stefano Pelle v R; R v Stefano Pelle; Antonio Giorgi; Domenico Nirta; Giovanni Mammoliti; Filippo Pizzata; Domenico Condemi [1983] FCA 330; (1983) 79 FLR 190 (7 December 1983).

53 Due to the confidential nature of the narration of some events that I received, this reconstruction is based on the merging of two different characters and their personal vicissitudes mixed with some other events that relate to other individuals. While based on real events, therefore, this narration cannot be ascribed to any single person and must be considered a work of fiction.

54 'Coordinated crackdown on 'Ndrangheta mafia in Europe', Europol Press Release, 5 December 2018, updated 1 January 2019, https://www.europol.europa.eu/newsroom/news/coordinated-crackdown-ndrangheta-mafia-in-europe

55 Sergi, 'The 'ndrangheta down under'.

56 J.E. Douglas, A.W. Burgess, A.G. Burgess and R.K. Ressler, *Crime Classification Manual: A Standard System for Investigating and Classifying Violent Crime* (New York: Simon and Schuster, 1992).

57 P. Thompson and P. Findlay, 'Changing the people: social engineering in the contemporary workplace', in L. Ray and A. Sayer, *Culture and Economy after the Cultural Turn* (London: SAGE Publications, (1999), pp. 162–188; G. Kunda, *Engineering Culture: Control and Commitment in a High-Tech Corporation* (Philadelphia, PA: Temple University Press, 2009).

58 A. Sergi, 'A qualitative reading of the ecological (dis) organisation of criminal associations. The case of the 'Famiglia Basilischi'in Italy', *Trends in Organized Crime*, 19(2) (2016): 149–174.

59 S. Marino, *Intergenerational Ethnic Identity Construction and Transmission among Italian-Australians: Absence, Ambivalence and Revival* (Cham: Palgrave Macmillan, 2020).

60 S. Perera, *Australia and the Insular Imagination: Beaches, Borders, Boats, and Bodies* (Cham: Springer, 2009).

61 '2011 Census QuickStats - All people - usual residents - Stirling (WA) Code SSC50740 (SSC)', http://www.censusdata.abs.gov.au/census_services/getproduct/census/2011/quickstat/SSC50740

62 Proc. Pen. NR. RG ORD/DDA 3655/11 GIP-GUP 3655/11 NR NG 1389/08 Sentenza N.106/12 Tribunale di Reggio Calabria Sezione Gip – Gup Sentenza resa nell' Operazione 'Crimine' Capolista: Agnelli Giovanni + 126, Third Volume, p. 2265.

63 'Shocked former Stirling mayor Tony Vallelonga denies mafia connection', Nicole Cox, Lucy Carne in London, Corey Stephenson, *PerthNow*, 9 March 2011, https://www.perthnow.com.au/news/nsw/shocked-former-stirling-mayor-tony-vallelonga-denies-mafia-connection-ng-4d8903cdbb5f0eee79e82dbdb7b6d6fa

[64] 'The inside story of Operation Ironside – and the Adelaide olive merchant named by the FBI as a key player in a global conspiracy', Nigel Hunt, *The Advertiser*, 11 June 2021, https://thewest.com.au/news/crime/the-inside-story-of-operation-ironside-and-the-adelaide-olive-merchant-named-by-the-fbi-as-a-key-player-in-a-global-conspiracy-c-3084956

Chapter 6

[1] Direzione Investigativa Antimafia (DIA) – Centro Operativo Reggio Calabria IV–VII Sezione – Cat.125/RC/H4 di prot.753- Reggio Calabria, 20 October 1992 – Associazione per delinquere di stampo mafioso aka 'Siderno Group', Indagini + Allegati.

[2] Proc. Pen. NR. RG ORD/DDA 3655/11 GIP-GUP 3655/11 NR NG 1389/08 Sentenza anno 12 No. 106 Tribunale di Reggio Calabria Sezione Gip – Gup Sentenza resa nell' Operazione 'Crimine': Agnelli Giovanni + 126, Volume III, p. 2265.

[3] Proc Pen. NR. RG ORD/DDA 3655/11 GIP-GUP 3655/11 NR NG 1389/08 Sentenza anno 12 No. 106 Tribunale di Reggio Calabria Sezione Gip – Gup Sentenza resa nell' Operazione 'Crimine': Agnelli Giovanni + 126, Volume III, p. 2265.

[4] 'Census Profile, 2016 Census – Vaughan, Woodbridge [Federal electoral district], Ontario and Ontario [Province]', https://www12.statcan.gc.ca/census-recensement/2016/dp-pd/prof/details/page.cfm?Lang=E&Geo1=FED&Code1=35111&Geo2=PR&Code2=35&SearchText=Vaughan--Woodbridge&SearchType=Begins&SearchPR=01&B1=All&GeoLevel=PR&GeoCode=35111&TABID=1&type=0

[5] Proc. Pen. N. 7498/2010 RGNR Dda, Procura della Repubblica presso il Tribunale Ordinario di Reggio Calabria, Direzione Distrettuale Antimafia, Decreto Di Fermo Del Pubblico Ministero, Aquino + 48.

[6] Drug Enforcement Administration (DEA), 'The resurgence of the Siderno organized crime group in New York City', Intelligence Report [heroin] (1993), p. 1.

[7] DEA, 'The resurgence of the Siderno organized crime group', p. 5.

[8] A. Sergi and L. Storti, 'Survive or perish? Organised crime in the Port of Montreal and the Port of New York/New Jersey', *International Journal of Law, Crime and Justice*, 63 (2020): 100424; Sergi, *From mafia to rganized crime*.

[9] DIA – 'Siderno Group'.

[10] DIA – 'Siderno Group', pp. 3–4.

[11] S. Lupo, *History of the Mafia* (New York: Columbia University Press, 2009).

[12] DEA, 'The resurgence of the Siderno organized crime group', p. 6.

[13] DEA, 'The resurgence of the Siderno organized crime group'.

[14] DIA – 'Siderno Group'.

[15] S.A. Cohen and S. Gössling, 'A darker side of hypermobility', *Environment and Planning*, 47 (2015): 1661–1679.

[16] A. Sergi and A. Rizzuti, 'Mafiaround-Europe. A Report for the CRIME (Countering Regional Mafi Expansion), 2021', https://www.essex.ac.uk/research-projects/countering-regional-italian-mafia-expansion

[17] Proc. Pen. No. 2960/2019 DDA – Procura della Repubblica Presso il Tribunale di Reggio Calabria Direzione Distrettuale Antimafia – Decreto di Fermo di indiziato di delitto, 'Operation Canadian Connection', p. 192.

[18] 'Operation Canadian Connection', pp. 340 and 183.

19 'Canadian 'ndrangheta connection', Sette assoluzioni, *Corriere della Calabria*, 5 March 2021, https://www.corrieredellacalabria.it/2021/05/03/canadian-ndrangheta-connection-sette-assoluzioni/. 'Processo Canadian, in appello cade l'associazione mafiosa per tutti gli imputati', Ilario Bali, *LaCNews*, 10 May 2022, https://www.lacnews24.it/cronaca/processo-canadian-in-appello-cade-l-associazione-mafiosa-per-tutti-gli-imputati_154305/

20 'Questura di Reggio Calabria - Operazione Canadian Connection 2', August 2019, https://questure.poliziadistato.it/ReggioCalabria/articolo/9145d4d4972c0837771328023

21 'Operation Canadian Connection'.

22 'Charges stayed in one of Ontario's largest Mob busts after alleged illegal conduct by investigators', Dexter McMillan, Joseph Loiero, John Lancaster, Ivan Angelovski, *CBC News*, 24 February 2021, https://www.cbc.ca/news/canada/toronto/sindacato-charges-stayed-mob-york-police-1.5925133

23 D. Ralph and L.A. Staeheli, 'Home and migration: mobilities, belongings and identities', *Geography Compass*, 5(7) (2011): 517–530.

24 S. Lucas and B. Purkayastha, '"Where is home?" Here and there: transnational experiences of home among Canadian migrants in the United States', *GeoJournal*, 68(2–3) (2007): 243–251.

25 M. Marcheva, 'The networked diaspora: Bulgarian migrants on Facebook', *M/C Journal*, 14(2) 2010, http://journal.media-culture.org.au/index.php/mcjournal/article/view/323

26 A. Sergi, *'Ndrangheta Dynasties*.

27 Proc. Pen. No. 2960/2019 DDA – Procura della Repubblica Presso il Tribunale di Reggio Calabria Direzione Distrettuale Antimafia – Decreto di Fermo di indiziato di delitto.

28 R. v. Ursino and Dracea, 2019 ONSC 1171.

29 A. Sergi, *The Border & the Mafia: Narratives of Italian-American Mafias in Ontario and the Niagara Region* (forthcoming).

30 Proc. Pen. NR. RG ORD/DDA 3655/11 GIP-GUP 3655/11 NR NG 1389/08 Sentenza anno 12 No. 106 Tribunale di Reggio Calabria Sezione Gip – Gup Sentenza resa nell' Operazione 'Crimine'- Agnelli Giovanni +126.

31 P.J. DiMaggio and W.W. Powell, 'The iron cage revisited: institutional isomorphism and collective rationality in organizational fields', *American Sociological Review*, (1983): 147–160.

32 A. Sergi, *The Border & The Mafia*.

33 'Operation Canadian Connection'.

34 'Twenty-four defendants with ties to powerful italian organized crime syndicate known as the 'ndrangheta arrested in coordinated U.S.-Italian takedown', Department of Justice, U.S. Attorney's Office, Eastern District of New York, Press Release, 11 February 2014, https://archives.fbi.gov/archives/newyork/press-releases/2014/twenty-four-defendants-with-ties-to-powerful-italian-organized-crime-syndicate-known-as-the-ndrangheta-arrested-in-coordinated-u.s.-italian-takedown

35 Sergi and Lavorgna, *'Ndrangheta*; Operation New Bridge, No. 3273/12 R.G.N.R. DDA, Tribunale di Reggio Calabria.

36 'IRONSIDE: Alleged Australian drug boss and syndicate nabbed after 160kg cocaine import in Melbourne', *AFP* Press Release, 20 June 2021, https://www.afp.gov.au/news-media/media-releases/ironside-alleged-australian-drug-boss-and-syndicate-nabbed-after-160kg

37 'Drug pair jailed by Adelaide judge', *ABC News*, 29 November 2007, https://www.abc.net.au/news/2007-11-29/drug-pair-jailed-by-adelaide-judge/972536

38 DiMaggio and Powell, 'The iron cage revisited', p. 148.

39 A. Sergi, *The Border & The Mafia*.

40 Sergi, 'What's in a name?'

41 'Operation Canadian Connection', pp.184–185.

42 'Dead man walking: Mobster Pat Musitano has been shot and killed. What happens now?', Dan Taekema, *CBC News*, 12 July 2020, https://www.cbc.ca/news/canada/hamilton/musitano-death-mafia-mob-1.5646395

43 'Murdered mob boss Pat Musitano symbolized Ontario's Mafia with his gangster chic — and the mayhem that shadowed him', Adrian Humphreys, *National Post*, 12 July 2020, https://nationalpost.com/news/canada/murdered-mob-boss-pat-musitano-symbolized-ontarios-mafia-with-his-gangster-chic-and-the-mayhem-that-shadowed-him

44 S. Schneider, *Iced: The Story of Organized Crime in Canada* (New York: Wiley & Sons, 2009).

45 His brother was Ontario's pre-eminent Mafia boss, but long-suffering Frank Papalia was still his keeper. 'Frank was [Johnny Pop's] buffer. He would screen people for him. He'd protect Johnny. If you wanted to talk to Johnny you'd go see Frank', Adrian Humphreys, *National Post*, 18 April 2014, updated 25 January 2015, https://nationalpost.com/news/canada/his-brother-was-ontarios-pre-eminent-mafia-boss-but-long-suffering-frank-papalia-was-still-his-keeper

46 D. Puccio-Den, 'Mafiacraft: how to do things with silence', *Journal of Ethnographic Theory*, 9(3) (2019): 599–618; M. Santoro, 'Mafiacraft, witchcraft, statecraft, or the politics of mafia knowledge and the knowledge of mafia politics', *Journal of Ethnographic Theory*, 9(3) (2019): 631–637.

47 A. Humphreys, *The Enforcer: Johnny Pops Papalia, A Life and Death in the Mafia* (Toronto: HarperCollins, 1999).

48 A. Sergi, *The Border & the Mafia.*

49 'Members and associates of Gambino and Bonanno organized crime families arrested in coordinated U.S.-Canadian takedown', Department of Justice, U.S. Attorney's Office, Eastern District of New York, Press Release, 9 November 2017, https://www.justice.gov/usao-edny/pr/members-and-associates-gambino-and-bonanno-organized-crime-families-arrested

50 R. v. Violi, 2018 ONSC 3738.

51 ' "Congratulations": Undercover agent inducted into Mafia in secret ceremony captured on video by police', Adrian Humphreys, *National Post*, 9 November 2017, https://nationalpost.com/news/canada/congratulations-undercover-agent-inducted-into-mafia-in-secret-ceremony-in-canada-captured-on-video-by-police

52 DIA – Siderno Group, p. 116

53 A. Sergi, *The Border & the Mafia.*

54 Project Otremens, Italian Mafia Criminal Organization, Agent Debrief Report Summary Excerpts.

55 'HUNTER: What does release of reputed mob boss Violi mean?', Brad Hunter, *Toronto Sun*, 17 November 2021, https://torontosun.com/news/world/hunter-what-does-release-of-reputed-mob-boss-violi-mean

56 Project Otremens.

57 Project Otremens, p. 15.

58 'Operation Canadian Connection', p. 182.

59 Project Otremens, p. 1.

60 'Suzanne', by Leonard Cohen, Copyright © 1967 Sony Music Entertainment (Canada) Inc.

61 P. Edwards and A. Nicaso, *Business or Blood: Mafia Boss Vito Rizzuto's Last War* (Toronto: Random House of Canada, 2015); A. Nicaso and L. Lamothe, *Project Omertà and the Fall of the Mafia's Royal Family* (Toronto: HarperCollins, 2001); L. Lamothe and A. Humphreys, *The Sixth Family: The Collapse of the New York Mafia and the Rise of Vito Rizzuto* (Toronto: John Wiley & Sons, 2008).

62 Sergi, 'What's in a name?'

63 Report of the Commission of Inquiry on the Awarding and Management of Public Contracts in the Construction Industry Schemes, Causes, Consequences and Recommendations, aka 'Charbonneau Commission', Volume 3, p. 45.

64 Gambetta, *The Sicilian Mafia*; Paoli, *Mafia Brotherhoods*; A. Pizzorno, 'Lo scambio occulto', *Stato e mercato*, 34(1) (1992): 3–34.

65 D. Gambetta and P. Reuter, 'Conspiracy among the many: the mafia in legitimate industries', in *The Economic Dimensions of Crime* (London: Palgrave Macmillan, 1995), pp. 99–120.

66 'Cathedrals', by Jump Little Children, copyright ℗ 1998 EZ Chief/Jump Two, LLC.

67 'Cathedrals'.

Chapter 7

1 Sentenza 'Porto' proc. n. 290/98 R.G.T. – Sicari Giuseppe + 27.

2 Sentenza Porto, p. 124.

3 Procura della Repubblica presso Tribunale Ordinario di Reggio Calabria, DDA, no. 3023/2011 RGNR, Fermo di Indiziato di Delitto, Operazione 'Puerto Liberado', p. 135.

4 Operazione 'Puerto Liberado'.

5 A. Sergi, 'Policing the port, watching the city: manifestations of organised crime in the port of Genoa', *Policing and Society: An International Journal of Research and Policy*, 31(6) (2021): 639–655.

6 Relazione Annuale Direzione Nazionale Antimafia e Antiterrorismo, July 2019.

7 Direzione Investigativa Antimafia, Relazione Semestrale, 2019, II semestre, https://direzioneinvestigativaantimafia.interno.gov.it/semestrali/sem/2019/2sem2019.pdf

8 Procura della Repubblica presso Tribunale di Reggio Calabria – DDA – Fermo di Indiziato di Delitto – Proc. Pen. n. 206/2017 RGNR DDA, Operation 'Provvidenza', p. 1756.

9 Tribunale di Reggio Calabria, Ufficio del GIP, Ordinanza di applicazione di misura cautelare, RGRN DDA n.736/2019, OCC n. 36/2020 – Operation Geolja.

10 Tribunale di Reggio Calabria, Sezione GIP-GUP, Ordinanza di applicazione di misura cautelare, RGRN DDA 5183/2919+ 24/21, Operation Nuova Narcos Europea.

11 Operation 'Cento Anni di Storia', p. 12.

12 Operation 'Cento Anni di Storia', p. 836.

13 'Strage sulla spiaggia in mezzo ai bagnanti', Pantaleone Sergi, *La Repubblica*, 9 August 1990, https://ricerca.repubblica.it/repubblica/archivio/repubblica/1990/08/09/strage-sulla-spiaggia-in-mezzo-ai-bagnanti.html.

14 Proc. Pen. N. 3798/15 RGNR DDA – N. 1261/16 RGIP DDA – N. 122/16 ROCC – Tribunale di Reggio Calabria – Sezione dei giudici per le indagini preliminari – Ordinanza Applicazione Misura Cautelare, Operazione 'Ndrangheta Stragista'.

15 Operazione 'Ndrangheta Stragista', cfr. verbale del 4.6.2014, faldone 3 sottofascicolo 11, p. 265.

16 Operazione 'Ndrangheta Stragista', cfr. verbale del 21.1.2014, faldone 3 sottofascicolo 1, p. 265.

17 The P2 Masonic lodge headed by Licio Gelli.

18 Proc. n. 1120/2017 R.G.N.R. DDA Procura della Repubblica presso Tribunale di Reggio Calabria – DDA – Richiesta per L'applicazione di Misure Cautelari Personali – artt. 272 e segg. c.p.p. – Richiesta di Sequestro Preventivo per Equivalente – 322 ter c.p., 104 d.lv.271/89 – 'Operazione Waterfront'.

19 Operazione Waterfront, p. 56.

20 E. Banfield, *The Moral Basis of a Backward Society* (Glencoe, IL: Free Press, 1958).

21 Banfield, *The Moral Basis of a Backward Society*, p. 8.

22 M. Huysseune, 'Theory travelling through time and space: the reception of the concept of amoral familism', *International Journal of Politics Culture and Society*, 33 (2020): 365–388; E. Ferragina, 'The never-ending debate about the moral basis of a backward society: Banfield and "amoral familism"', *JASO-online*, 1(2) (2009): 141–160.

23 A. Pizzorno, 'Amoral familism and historical marginality', *International Review of Community Development*, 15 (1966): 55–56.

24 R. Catanzaro, 'Struttura sociale, sistema politico e azione collettiva nel mezzogiorno', *Stato e Mercato*, 8 (1983): 271–315.

25 S. Meier, L. Piercec, A. Vaccaro and B. La Cara, 'Trust and in-group favoritism in a culture of crime', *Journal of Economic Behavior & Organization*, 132 (2016): 78–92.

26 D. Gambetta, 'Mafia: the price of distrust', in D. Gambetta (ed.) *Trust: Making and Breaking Cooperative Relations* (Oxford: Blackwell, 1988), pp. 158–175.

27 Procura della Repubblica presso Tribunale di Reggio Calabria – DDA – N.1348/01 RGNR, 'Operation Arca'.

28 Procura Della Repubblica Presso Tribunale di Reggio Calabria – DDA – N. 4302/06 RGNR, 'Operation All Inside', p. 120.

29 Procura della Repubblica presso il Tribunale Ordinario di Reggio Calabria – DDA – N. 9762/2011 RGNR – 'Operation All Clean 2'.

30 'Operation All Inside', p. 531.

31 A. Perry, *The Good Mothers: The True Story of the Women Who Took on the World's Most Powerful Mafia* (London: HarperCollins, 2018).

32 Operazione All Clean 2 – v. annotazione di servizio CC Tenenza Rosarno del 19 maggio 2011.

33 Procura della Repubblica presso il Tribunale di Reggio Calabria - Direzione Distrettuale Antimafia, Nr. 891/12 R.G.N.R.-D.D.A, p. 41, 'Operation Tramonto'.

34 *Sgarro* is an insult, an affront; it is a typical mafia 'offence' of medium gravity.

35 *Infame* means someone who has betrayed, who cannot be trusted; *infamita* is a mafia offence, of serious gravity.

36 'The mystery of Maria Concetta Cacciola', Connie Agius, *ABC Radio*, 3 December 2016, https://www.abc.net.au/correspondents/content/2016/s4586494.htm; 'The Italian mafia and violence against women', Connie Agius, *Open Democracy*, 3 December 2016, https://www.opendemocracy.net/en/5050/italian-mafia-and-violence-against-women/.

37 See also 'Italian mafia and violence against women'.

38 'Operazione Costa Pulita', *Polizia di Stato*, Press Release, 20 April 2016, https://www.poliziadistato.it/articolo/operazione--costa-pulita-1

39 'La "strana" morte di Santa Buccafusca e il sospiro di sollievo dei clan', Giuseppe Baglivo, *LaC News*, 30 July 2020, https://www.lacnews24.it/cronaca/morte-santa-buccafusca-sollievo-clan_121561/

40 L. Skurnick, *Pretty Bitches: On Being Called Crazy, Angry, Bossy, Frumpy, Feisty, and All the Other Words That Are Used to Undermine Women* (London: Hachette, 2020); M.R. Decker, C.N. Holliday, Z. Hameeduddin, R. Shah, J. Miller, J. Dantzler and L. Goodmark, 'You do not think of me as a human being: race and gender inequities intersect to discourage police reporting of violence against women', *Journal of Urban Health*, 96(5) (2018): 772–783.

41 B. Cayli, 'Performance matters more than masculinity: violence, gender dynamics and mafia women', *Aggression and Violent Behavior*, 29 (July–August 2016): 36–42.

42 O. Ingrascì, *Gender and Organized Crime in Italy: Women's Agency in Italian Mafias* (London: Bloomsbury, 2021).

43 'Calabria, ucciso a colpi di pistola in spiaggia a Nicotera', *La Repubblica*, 12 August 2018, – https://www.repubblica.it/cronaca/2018/08/12/news/calabria_ucciso_a_colpi_di_pistola_in_un_campeggio-203971897/

[44] Song written by Giovanni Falduto, a local artist in Limbadi, as a folk song – translated it would be 'Limbadi Beach. (x4) the high street above, the one below, and you'll never get bored!' The song is not protected by Copyright.

[45] Procura della Repubblica presso il Tribunale di Catanzaro – Direzione Distrettuale Antimafia P.P. N. 2239 /14 R.G.N.R./MOD. 21/D.D.A. – 'Operation Rinascita-Scott', p. 597.

[46] Law decree no. 164 of 1991, then inserted in articles 143–146 of law decree no. 267 of 2000.

[47] 'Manette al boss: fu il primo degli eletti nel suo comune', Pantaleone Sergi, 30 August 1985, https://ricerca.repubblica.it/repubblica/archivio/repubblica/1985/08/30/mane tte-al-boss-fu-il-primo-degli.html

[48] 'Operation Rinascita-Scott', p. 597.

[49] This narration is the product of the mix of two different individual stories, to avoid qualifications and recognition.

[50] G. Sykes and D. Matza, 'Techniques of neutralization: a theory of delinquency', *American Sociological Review*, 22 (1957): 664–670; D. Matza, *Delinquency and Drift* (New York: Wiley, 1964).

[51] 'Operation Rinascita-Scott'.

[52] Communal Archive, Limbadi, Passport Office and Register.

[53] N. Harney, 'Building Italian regional identity in Toronto: using space to make culture material', *Anthropologica*, 44(1) (2002): 43–54.

[54] Tribunale di Reggio Calabria – Giudici per le Indagini Preliminari – Ordinanza di Applicazione di Misure Cautelari Personali N. 5398/2016 RGNR DDA. N. 2480/17 RGIP. DDA. N. 29/2019 R. O.C.C. – 'Operation Magma'.

[55] Operation Magma, p. 231.

[56] To do/have the '*faccia lavata*' (washed, clean face) is a way of saying that one did the correct thing, even just as a formality.

[57] 'Operation Magma', p. 242.

[58] A. Sergi and A. Rizzuti, 'Mafiaround–Report. A Report for Project CRIME, Countering Regional Italian Mafia Expansion', 2021, https://www.essex.ac.uk/research-projects/cou ntering-regional-italian-mafia-expansion

[59] 'Operation Magma', pp. 234–236.

[60] Procura della Repubblica – Presso il Tribunale di Catanzaro – Direzione Distrettuale Antimafia – Decreto di Fermo di indiziato di delitto N.7198/15 RGNR – 'Operation Imponimento'.

[61] C. Carlino, *La Calabria, le Calabrie, i Calabresi* (Catanzaro: Progetto, 2003)

[62] G. Anania, D. Cersosimo and D. Costanzo, 'Le Calabrie contemporanee: Un'analisi delle caratteristiche dei sistemi economico-produttivi sub-regionali', in G. Anania (ed.) *Scelte pubbliche, strategie private e sviluppo economico in Calabria: Conoscere per decidere* (Soveria Mannelli: Rubbettino, 2001); F. Cordova, *Il fascismo nel Mezzogiorno: le Calabrie* (Soveria Mannelli: Rubbettino Editore, 2003).

Chapter 8

[1] 'Reggina, Nick Scali: "questa trattativa è chiusa, ma per il futuro resta aperta una porticina…"', Peppe Caridi, *StrettoWeb*, 25 June 2015, http://www.strettoweb.com/ 2015/06/reggina-nick-scali-intervista/293418/

[2] 'Australian consortium involving Nick Scali in talks to buy Reggina Calcio', Dominic Bossi, *The Sydney Morning Herald*, 22 April 2015, https://www.smh.com.au/sport/soccer/australian-consortium-involving-nick-scali-in-talks-to-buy-reggina-calcio-20150422-1mr0vs.html

3   'Reggio Calabria, Lillo Foti e moglie condannati dal Tribunale per "estorsione" dopo la denuncia di una dipendente dei negozi di abbigliamento', by Ilaria Calabrò, *StrettoWeb*, 7 July 2018, http://www.strettoweb.com/2018/07/reggio-calabria-lillo-foti/725073/

4   A. Testa and A. Sergi, *Corruption, Mafia Power and Italian Soccer* (London: Routledge, 2018).

5   'Reggina Calcio Spa. Contestata la bancarotta fraudolenta, scatta il sequestro per Foti e Ranieri', *CN24*, 14 December 2018, http://www.cn24tv.it/news/183991/reggina-calcio-spa-contestata-la-bancarotta-fraudolenta-scatta-il-sequestro-per-foti-e-ranieri.html

6   Proc. Pen. no. 54/14 RGNR DDA of Reggio Calabria, 'Operation Martingola'.

7   Relazione Semestrale Direzione Investigativa Antimafia, first semester 2018, https://direzioneinvestigativaantimafia.interno.gov.it/semestrali/sem/2018/1sem2018.pdf

8   ' "Vello d'oro-Martingala": le mire del gruppo Scimone sulla Reggina Calcio di Lillo Foti', Claudio Cordova, *Il Dispaccio*, 21 February 2018, http://ildispaccio.it/reggio-calabria/170583-vello-d-oro-martingala-le-mire-del-gruppo-scimone-sulla-reggina-calcio-di-lillo-foti

9   'Riciclaggio, condannati gli imputati dell'operazione Martingala', Fabio Papalia, *Corriere della Calabria*, 26 February 2020, https://www.corrieredellacalabria.it/2020/02/26/riciclaggio-condannati-gli-imputati-delloperazione-martingala/

10 'Krysha (Russia, Ukraine, Belarus)', Yulia Zabyelina and Anna Buzhor, *Global Informality Project*, https://www.in-formality.com/wiki/index.php?title=Krysha_(Russia,_Ukraine,_Belarus)

11 P. Arlacchi, La mafia imprenditrice: l'etica mafiosa e lo spirito del capitalismo (Bologna: il Mulino, 1983), p. 27.

12 R. Sciarrone, 'Mafia e potere: processi di legittimazione e costruzione del consenso', *Stato e Mercato*, 78(3) (2006): 369–401.

13 Tribunale di Reggio Calabria, Giudice per le Indagini Preliminari, N. 4902/19 RGNR DDA N. 4005/19 RGIP, Ordinanza di Custodia Cautelare N. 12/20, 'Operation Malefix', p. 466.

14 'Operation Malefix', p. 276.

15 Sentence Tribunale di Reggio Calabria, Giudice per l'Udienza Preliminare, n. 80/2018 – 1 March 2018, proc. 6859/16 RGNR, 'Trial Gotha' [Araniti Antonino + 37].

16 Proc. Pen. no. 46/93 RGNR DDA, Corte d'Assise Reggio Calabria, sentence of 19 January 1999 and 8 May 2002.

17 Tribunale di Reggio Calabria – Sezione del Giudice per le Indagini Preliminari Proc. N. 7497/2014 RGNR – DDA Proc. N. 1690/2015 RGGIP N. 26/20115 Ordinanza di applicazione di misura cautelare, 'Operation Gambling', p. 106.

18 Proc. n. 4614/06 R. G. N. R. – D. D. A. Proc. n. 3470/07 R. G. G.I.P. N. 41/2012 R. Ordinanza di Custodia Cautelare – Tribunale di Reggio Calabria – Sezione GIP/GUP – 'Operation Raccordo-Sistema'.

19 Sergi, *The Evolution of the Australian 'ndrangheta*.

20 'Operation Raccordo-Sistema', pp. 78–79.

21 'Operation Malefix', p. 467.

22 Corte di Cassazione n.33748, 20 September 2005.

23 'Accusata di avere favorito i boss, scarcerata ex direttrice del carcere di Reggio Calabria', *LaC News24*, 23 September 2020, https://www.lacnews24.it/cronaca/favori-boss-torna-libera-ex-direttrice-carcere-reggio-calabria_124044/

24 'Il carcere di Reggio Calabria in mano ai clan, a processo l'ex direttrice di Alessia Candito', *La Repubblica*, 26 January 2022, https://www.repubblica.it/cronaca/2022/01/26/news/il_carcere_di_reggio_calabria_in_mano_ai_clan_a_processo_l_ex_direttrice-335359312/

25 Proc. Pen. No. 638/2016 RGNR DDA, Proc. N. 117/2017 RG GIP DDA; no. 30/ 2020 Ordinanza su richiesta di Applicazione di Misure Cautelari, Tribunale di Reggio Calabria, Sezione GIP-GUP, p. 31. 'Operation Gambling'.

26 'Operation Gambling', p. 35.

27 'Operation Gambling', p. 32.

28 Trial Gotha, p. 222.

29 D. Skarbek, *The Social Order of the Underworld: How Prison Gangs Govern the American Penal System* (Oxford: Oxford University Press, 2014).

30 D. Skarbek, *The Puzzle of Prison Order: Why Life Behind Bars Varies Around the World* (Oxford: Oxford University Press, 2020).

31 Skarbek, *The Social Order of the Underworld*.

32 T. Mathiesen, *Defences of the Weak: A Sociological Study of a Norwegian Correctional Institution* (London: Tavistock, 1965), p. 100.

33 Procura della Repubblica di Reggio Calabria Proc. Pen. n. 1576/2011 DDA.

34 Procura della Repubblica di Reggio Calabria Ordinanza di custodia cautelare, n. 43/ 2016 R. O. C. C DDA, 'Operation Fata Morgana'.

35 Tribunale di Reggio Calabria – Sezione GIP-GUP – Proc. n. 9339/2009 RGNR DDA Proc. n. N. 5448/2010 R.G.I.P.; N. 50/2015 OCC. Ordinanza su Richiesta di Custodia Cautelare in Carcere – 'Operation Mammasantissima'.

36 "Ndrangheta, al processo Gotha Seby Vecchio il pentito dai mille volti', Alessia Candito, *La Repubblica*, 17 March 2021, https://www.repubblica.it/cronaca/2021/03/17/news/ ndrangheta_al_processo_gotha_seby_vecchio_il_pentito_dai_mille_volti-292700807/

37 'Operation Mammasantissima', Declarations of the collaborator Ubaldo Lauro, p. 207.

38 'Reggio-bene' is a common way to indicate the higher social classes of the city including businessmen, politicians, professionals and others who might have access to elite spaces and networks.

39 Corte d'Assise di Reggio Calabria, N.104/95 R. G. N. R. DDA N. 85/96 R.G. G.I.P. DDA N. 15/98 R G ASSISE N. 3/2001 R.G. Sentenza, including P.P. N. 42/97 R. G. N. R. DDA N. 40/98 R.G. GIP DDA N. 10/98 R.G. ASSISE – 'Processo Olimpia'.

40 Trial Gotha, p. 237.

41 Trial Gotha, p. 237.

42 'Operation Mammasantissima', p. 180.

43 Verbale d'udienza 11.7.2012, n.1118/11 (Condello Pasquale + 17). Allegato nr. 397, 'Trial Meta'.

44 Tribunale di Reggio Calabria Sezione GIP-GUP, Sentenza Data Dispositivo 1.03.2018 (Araniti Antonino + 37), RGNR 663/2017+ 6859/2016, Ruolo Ord/DDA Sentenza No.80/2018 – 'Gotha, Abbreviato', p. 359.

45 Proc. Pen no. 6268/06 RGNR. DDA, cited in 'Trial GOTHA', p. 402.

46 N.29 informativa R.O.S. Carabinieri – Reparto Anticrimine Reggio Cal. n.21/13–37 prot.2013 14.03.2015, relativa a conversazione del 16.9.2010 – Decreto n. 3820/08 RGNR DDA e n. 2546/09 RIT DDA, relativo alle comunicazioni/conversazioni tra presenti tra Imerti Antonino ed i suoi familiari all'interno della sala colloqui della Casa Circondariale di Voghera, in 'GOTHA Abbreviato', p. 409.

47 Corte d'Appello di Reggio Calabria, No. 27/2021, sentenza del 1 January 2021, depositata in cancelleria il 25 October 2021, p. 235, 'Trial Gotha Appeal'.

48 Fermo di indiziato di delitto n. 1878/07 RGNR DDA – allegato progr. 10416 e segg., decr. 139/11 Reg. Int., proc. 196 pen. 3800/09 RGNR Procura della Repubblica di Catanzaro, 'Operation Purgatorio'.

49 This is a reference to the (in)famous Masonic Lodge P2 (Propaganda 2) headed, in his latter period, by Licio Gelli. P2 and Gelli were expelled by the Lodge of the Grand Orient

of Italy in 1976, but the lodge ran illegally until 1981 and was famous for its reach into political and economic circles in Italy.

50 Gotha Appeal sentence, pp. 236–237.

51 Ordinanza di Custodia Cautelare n. 1481/09 RGNR DDA, n. 2562/09 RG GIP DDA e n. 33/11 ROCC, Altomonte Giuseppe + 37, emessa il 30.12.11 dal GIP presso il Tribunale di Reggio Calabria, nell'ambito dell'operazione convenzionalmente denominata 'Bellu Lavuru'.

52 Gotha Appeal sentence, pp. 258–259.

53 J. Dickie, *The Craft: How the Freemasons Made the Modern World* (London: Hodder and Stoughton, 2020), p. 775 [ebook].

54 Commissione Parlamentare d'Inchiesta sul fenomeno delle mafie a sulle altre associazioni criminali, anche straniere. Proposta di relazione sulle infiltrazioni di Cosa Nostra e 'ndrangheta nella massoneria in Sicilia e in Calabria (relatore Rosy Bindi), 21 December 2017.

55 Dickie, *The Craft*, p. 787 [ebook].

56 Extract from the conversation between the Public Prosecutor and Roberto Moio. Sentenza n. 712/2014 Tribunale in composizione Collegiale di Reggio Calabria 02.05.2014, relativa a proc. pen n. 7734/10 R.G.N.R. DD.A., 'Processo Meta0; sub-faldone n.42, Sottofascicolo n.22).

57 Sentenza Tribunale di Locri del 2 ottobre 1970, pag. 27, cd. Operazione Montalto, in Sentenza del Tribunale di Reggio Calabria del 26 ottobre 2002, processo c.d. Armonia, faldone 59.

58 Informativa Patriarca dei Carabinieri, con riferimento al processo Armonia.

59 Talia, *Statale 106.*

60 https://www.occrp.org/en/unfinishedlives/the-cocaine-cowboys

61 A. Sergi and A. Rizzuti, *Mafiaround Europe. A Report for the Project CRIME* (Countering Regional Italian Mafia Expansion), https://www.essex.ac.uk/research-projects/counter ing-regional-italian-mafia-expansion

62 M. Catino, *Mafia Organizations. The Visible Hand of Criminal Enterprises* (Cambridge: Cambridge University Press, 2019), p. 17.

63 M. Weber, *Economy and Society: An Outline of Interpretive Sociology* (San Francisco: University of California Press, 1978).

64 'Operation 'Ndrangheta Stragista', p. 601.

Epilogue

1 Eliot, from 'Little Gidding'.

Index

Printed in the USA
CPSIA information can be obtained
at www.ICGtesting.com
JSHW011541190224
57673JS00012B/300